Fueling Development

Fueling Development

How Black Radical Trade Unionism
Transformed Trinidad and Tobago

Zophia Edwards

Duke University Press   *Durham and London*   2025

© 2025 DUKE UNIVERSITY PRESS. All rights reserved
Project Editor: Ihsan Taylor
Cover designed by A. Mattson Gallagher
Typeset in Garamond Premier Pro and Futura Std
by Westchester Publishing Services

Library of Congress Cataloging-in-Publication Data
Names: Edwards, Zophia, author.
Title: Fueling development : how Black radical trade
unionism transformed Trinidad and Tobago /
Zophia Edwards.
Description: Durham : Duke University Press, 2025. |
Includes bibliographical references and index.
Identifiers: LCCN 2025004862 (print)
LCCN 2025004863 (ebook)
ISBN 9781478029052 (hardcover)
ISBN 9781478032458 (paperback)
ISBN 9781478061243 (ebook)
Subjects: LCSH: Labor unions—Trinidad and Tobago—
History. | Labor movement—Trinidad and Tobago—
History. | Labor disputes—Trinidad and Tobago—History. |
Trinidad and Tobago—Race relations.
Classification: LCC HD6595.7 .E393 2025 (print) |
LCC HD6595.7 (ebook)
LC record available at https://lccn.loc.gov/2025004862
LC ebook record available at https://lccn.loc
.gov/2025004863

Cover art: Illustration by Shawn Peters.

For Mummy, John, and Adira

Contents

Abbreviations

ALCOA	Aluminum Company of America
ATSEFWTU	All Trinidad Sugar Estates and Factory Workers' Trade Union
ASCRIA	African Society for Cultural Relations with Independent Africa
BEW&CHRP	British Empire Workers and Citizens Home Rule Party
BGLU	British Guiana Labour Union
BP	British Petroleum
CLC	Caribbean Labour Congress
CPTU	Council of Progressive Trade Unions
DLP	Democratic Labour Party
EIDL	East Indian Destitute League
EINA	East Indian National Association
EINC	East Indian National Congress
FWTU	Federated Workers' Trade Union
IMF	International Monetary Fund
ISA	Industrial Stabilization Act
JLP	Jamaica Labour Party
MPCA	ManPower Citizens' Association

NJAC	National Joint Action Committee
NTUC	National Trades Union Congress
NUFHBAW	National Union of Foods, Hotels, Beverages, and Allied Workers
NWCSA	Negro Welfare Cultural and Social Association
OWTU	Oilfield Workers' Trade Union
PAC	Political Affairs Committee
PDP	People's Democratic Party
PNC	People's National Congress
PNM	People's National Movement
PNP	People's National Party
PPP	People's Progressive Party
SOE	state-owned enterprise
TCL	Trinidad Citizens League
TIWU	Transport and Industrial Workers' Union
TLP	Trinidad Labour Party
TTTUC	Trinidad and Tobago Trades Union Congress
TWA	Trinidad Workingmen's Association
UNIA	Universal Negro Improvement Association
WFP	Workers and Farmers Party
WFTU	World Federation of Trade Unions
WMA	Workingmen's Association

ARCHIVAL ABBREVIATIONS

GOTT	Government of Trinidad and Tobago
LL	Labour Leader

NATT   National Archives of Trinidad and Tobago

POSG   Port of Spain Gazette

TG   Trinidad Guardian

TNA   The National Archives (UK)

TP   The People

Acknowledgments

It took a village to produce this book. It represents the accumulation, engage-ment, bungling, and rejection of so many ideas, musings, discussions, and de-bates over several years from many people and communities across multiple continents. I owe my greatest intellectual development to Julian Go, who gen-erously devoted so much of his time and energy to nurturing my ideas, helping me to hone them, and ensuring that I stayed on task. His patience, motivation, humor, and support through the writing blocks and moments of self-doubt and his assurance that the academic enterprise can indeed be worthwhile no doubt helped steer this manuscript to completion.

My special thanks to the other people who helped cultivate the arguments in this book when they were merely seeds in early research, including Susan Eckstein, John Gerring, Sigrun Olafsdottir, and John Stone. My academic peers have walked with me and this project over the years, watching it grow, providing feedback, and keeping me sane—Adrienne Lemon, Ricarda Ham-mer, Kristin Plys, Meghan Tinsley, Patricia Ward, Jake Watson, and Alexandre Sasha White. Words cannot express how lucky I was to be part of this commu-nity of graduate students who insisted on creating more hospitable intellectual spaces and doing the work we wanted to do.

I am tremendously grateful to Michael Burawoy, Paget Henry, Brinsley Sa-maroo, and Beverly Silver, who, along with Julian Go, read and workshopped the entire manuscript, providing invaluable feedback and suggestions that helped me strengthen and streamline these ideas. I cannot thank Beverly enough; in the few short years I have been at Johns Hopkins University, she has provided a wealth of guidance and support for this project. The Arrighi Center for Global Studies at Johns Hopkins University also hosted a workshop and seminar discussion for this book manuscript. Many thanks to the graduate students, postdocs, faculty, and mentors for their brilliant and thoughtful comments: Samantha Agarwal, Joel Andreas, Rishi Awatramani, Alonso Burgos Cisneros, Ryan Calder, Aabid Firdausi, Jo Giardini, Maria Haro Sly, Keely Kriho, Michael Levien, Minkah Makalani, Leana Mason, Mateus Mendonça, Corey Payne, Sandy Peeples, Baran Sahinli, Robbie Shilliam, Ben Taylor, Kaori Taylor, Christy Thornton, Hailey Tomlinson, Nima Tootkaboni, Inés Valdez, and other participants. I am also especially thankful for Horace Campbell, Michael O. West, Mario Nisbett, José Itzigsohn, and Michael Goldfield, who generously shared their time, feedback, and advice to help me further refine my arguments and sharpen my interventions.

I am also indebted to numerous people in Trinidad and Tobago who eagerly gave of their time to share their knowledge, experiences, and insights as trade unionists and movement organizers—David Abdullah, Alva Allen, Gerry Kangalee, and Gregory Rousseau. The research for this book was also facilitated by some amazing archivists, librarians, and personnel at various institutions in the United Kingdom and especially in Trinidad and Tobago, including Janelle Duke, Narine Goolabsingh, and the staff at the National Archives; the team at the Oilfield Workers' Trade Union (OWTU) library and the Alma Jordan Library at the University of the West Indies, Trinidad; and administrators at various libraries in different government ministries.

Writing in groups provided the accountability, intellectual stimulation, and social enrichment I needed to push this manuscript to completion. Thanks to the Black Women's Writing Collective, the Postcolonial Sociology Works in Progress Group, the Hopkins Write on Site group, and the Providence Writing Group, which included helpful feedback from Kara Cebulko and Cedric De Leon. I give special thanks to Orly Clergé and Trina Vithayathil, who have been steady supporters, intellectually and personally, throughout the development of this manuscript. They read more versions of this work than we can remember. I am forever grateful for the friendship, advice, and comradeship of these sister-scholars. And still others provided feedback on portions of the work, including the wonderful graduate students and faculty at the Comparative Research Workshop at Yale University and the Theory and Research in Comparative Social Analysis Seminar at the University of California, Los Angeles; the sociology departments at the University of California, Berkeley, Case Western University, the University of Tennessee, Knoxville, and the Center for the Study of Race and Ethnicity in America at Brown University. Research for this project—from inception to final manuscript—was supported by the many institutions I traversed over the years, including the Graduate School of Arts and Sciences and Department of Sociology at Boston University, Providence College, and Johns Hopkins University.

I strive to embed my academic work in the political struggles of ordinary people, which requires unlearning and learning, reasoning, and organizing outside of the walls of the academy. Thank you to the people and communities who link social theory to the political urgencies of the masses, for whom the personal is the political, and whose embrace and dedication to liberation nourish, enliven, and sustain. They include bredrins and sistrens like Jason Jackson, Jenna Marshall, and Keston Perry and our co-creation—the Caribbean Political Economy Group—my steadfast crew in the Global Pan African Movement, North America, and the remarkable community that is the Walter Rodney Foundation.

I was incredibly fortunate to have a fierce and loving community of some truly phenomenal comrades, mentors, and friends at a rather oppressive institution where most of the ideas in this book were developed: Kendra Brewster, Ana Cláudia Dos Santos São Bernardo, Rahsaan Mahadeo, Jessica Mulligan, Anthony Rodriguez, Monica Simal, Ashley Smith-Purviance, and Trina Vithayathil. I especially thank Julia Jordan-Zachery, whose generosity, mentorship, and support were critical not only to my professional survival but to co-creating spaces of thriving. Dozens of other friends, colleagues, and mentors provided nourishing spaces, conversations, and/or collaborations over the years—Rina Agarwala, Onwubiko Agozino, David Austin, Emily Barman, Vilna Bashi, Ruha Benjamin, Gurminder Bhambra, Nicole Burrowes, Andy Clarno, Sam Cohn, Nathan Connelly, Selwyn Cudjoe, Claire Decoteau, Karl Doyle, Talia Esnard, Deidre Flowers, Fatma Müge Göçek, Kiri Gurd, Peter Hudson, Ho-fung Hung, Larry Jackson, Ryan Jobson, Tamanisha John, Jessica Marie Johnson, Nati Kamau-Nataki, Angela Lewis, Matthew Quest, katrina quisumbing king, Patsy Lewis, Zine Magubane, Brandon Martinez, Brian Meeks, Ali Meghji, Charlotte O'Kelly, Tina Park, Rhoda Reddock, Michael Rodríguez-Muñiz, Tyehimba Salandy, Keisha Samlal, Stuart Schrader, Ẹniọlá Ànúolúwapọ̀ Ṣóyẹmí, Lester Spence, Alissa Trotz, Hilbourne Watson, Vesla Weaver, and my new colleagues in the sociology department at Johns Hopkins University. I am also extremely grateful for the friends who provided much-needed encouragement and respite during smooth and rough times: Keisha Baptiste, Melissa Blackman, Becky Borlan, Rosa Cabrera, Samyra Cox, Carleen De Souza, Fran Oduekun, Shannon Gopaul, Laurie-Ann Jackson, Sacha Lewis, Anne Murray, Jess Pius-Nwagwu, Tracey-Ann Rullow, Chrystal St. Cyr, Terry-Anne Suer, Colleen Stuart, Christina Toro, Ruth Toulson, Jake Williams, and Dichelle Wilson.

My sincerest gratitude to Elizabeth Ault, editor at Duke University Press, for the enthusiasm, care, and diligence with which she carried this project through the peer review and publishing process. I am also thankful for the careful reading, constructive critique, and useful suggestions by the anonymous reviewers. The manuscript also benefited significantly from the developmental editing and copyediting skills of Tamara Nopper and Aurora Chang. And it was a real pleasure working with Benjamin Kossak, Ihsan Taylor, and the editorial team at the press, who so smoothly turned computer files into book product.

My family is my foundation. My eternal love and appreciation go out to my parents, brothers, in-laws, cousins, aunties, uncles, and those I call "aunty" and "uncle." They were my biggest supporters and my fiercest critics and were there to embrace me whenever my fugitive spirit craved something other than. I cannot imagine how I would have completed this manuscript without the love and support of my husband, John Lyneis. I am exceptionally fortunate to have a partner who listened, helped, pushed, and cheered me on throughout this endeavor. I thank my daughter, Adira, for wisdom that surpasses her years on earth; with her, I experience a kind of joy that is truly unmatched. And my dear mother, Joslyn—the bearer of the biggest laugh, the warmest hug, the sharpest mind, the knowledge and spirit of generations of hardworking and caring women. She insisted, despite my protestations, on reading every chapter of this book and providing detailed suggestions for revisions. I am so thankful for her steadfast encouragement. I come from a lineage of rural African peasant farmers and self-employed artisans and Indian sugar estate workers and cane farmers. Their blood, sweat, tears, and laughs are in these pages. I am eternally grateful to all my ancestors, whose stories, inspiration, and guidance made this book possible.

Introduction

I have been working here since 1919. We, women, have been working here for the government all this time. . . . We have been breaking stone blasted from the drilling and making it
into metal. The government started to pay us 38 cents per cubic yard. It was brought down
to 30 cents, and now . . . 28 cents. . . . The Harbor scheme people came and took over. . . . This
week, they came and told us they want no breakers . . . [they] told us we must quit by
tomorrow. We feel it is hurtful. We have nowhere else to work and nobody to depend on.
—A laboring woman in the then British Caribbean colony of Trinidad and Tobago, 1935

This woman's statements reflect the general sense of vulnerability, exploitation,
and frustration felt by the predominantly African and Indian working people
in the British colony of Trinidad and Tobago in the first decades of the twentieth century.[1] Economic and social conditions in the colony were dreadful.
While workers generated significant wealth for their employers from the agricultural plantations and oil extraction and did backbreaking public works for

the colonial government, they themselves struggled to live. Wages were so low that many could not afford adequate food and basic necessities.[2] Sanitation, access to health and social services, schools, and public utilities like domestic water supplies were scant. Malnutrition and deficiency diseases were widespread among the general population, and many suffered and died from preventable illnesses such as hookworms.[3] State violence, racist laws, and other government policies kept the laboring masses in a position of subjugation. Like in so many other European colonies across the world, the general conditions of life for the masses in Trinidad and Tobago were deplorable.

However, by the early 1980s, Trinidad and Tobago had quietly emerged as one of the most remarkable, and improbable, cases of relatively high redistributive and democratic development in the formerly colonized world. Life expectancy, access to education, and the standard of living had dramatically increased. Trinidad and Tobago now stands among the countries in the world with the highest levels of human development.[4] The adult literacy rate reached approximately 98 percent in 2000, including a 97 percent rate for women, and maternal and infant mortality rates are among the lowest in the Global South, indicating that education and social services are available to a wide proportion of the population.[5] There is a low prevalence of malnourishment and diseases that are preventable by inoculation and public health services.[6] Relatively high average per capita incomes also indicate a decent standard of living, and the country now ranks among the high-income economies of the world, according to the World Bank.[7] Furthermore, the multiracial population of Indigenous First Peoples, Africans, and Indians and the descendants of those who came from Europe, South America, the Middle East, and China enjoy relatively high political and civil liberties and a stable parliamentary democracy.[8] Indeed, by the early 1980s, Trinidad and Tobago, which won its independence from British colonial rule in 1962, had come a long way from the economic, social, and political conditions of the colonial era.

This book explores how, over the course of the twentieth century, Trinidad and Tobago was able to achieve such significant gains in economic and social development. Understanding Trinidad and Tobago's impressive performance is crucial for tackling long-standing questions in development theory and has paramount practical implications for contemporary societies—what forces drive improvements in human living conditions and well-being, and how? According to contemporary theories on the determinants of development, Trinidad and Tobago did not have the ingredients necessary for such broad-based enhancements in average incomes and social welfare. In fact, it had all the makings for long-term economic and social malaise. Its colonial history of plantation slavery and other forms of labor exploitation and weak institution building, its "petro-statehood" or economic dependence on oil and gas extraction, and its racial diversity should have produced a corrupt, clientelistic state that was incapable of directing and implementing development policies, managing the resource wealth, promoting the equitable distribution of public goods, and maintaining political stability.[9] Yet, despite these theoretically unfavorable conditions, Trinidad and Tobago exhibits noteworthy developmental achievements.

I argue that the key to explaining this outcome in Trinidad and Tobago is the presence of a militant mass labor movement, which I call *liberation unionism*. This form of working-class unionism was rooted in Black radical struggles for liberation from racialized and gendered superexploitation, imperialism, colonial domination, and white supremacy. With its Pan-African and diasporic orientation, liberation unionism challenged these interconnected oppressive systems. This Black worker–led movement was multiracial and inclusive of women. The resulting unity strengthened the movement in terms of its numbers and encouraged welfare gains to be distributed across the entire population.

Liberation unionism emerged in the colonial period in Trinidad and Tobago and, having taken advantage of a geopolitical context that favored worker demands, forced the colonial state to enact institutional reforms that increased the state's capacity to redistribute the oil wealth, improve the welfare of the masses, and enhance democratic rights and civil liberties. This agency from below persisted into the early postindependence period and pushed the newly independent state to further increase its capacity to manage the oil wealth and improve the quality of life for the masses, leading to long-term robust redistributive and democratic development.

This book argues that liberation unionism was the critical force for enhancing equitable development in Trinidad and Tobago, in the way it moved the state apparatus to better meet the needs of the masses. From W. E. B. Du Bois and Karl Marx to a range of contemporary scholars across the social sciences, the potential of workers' collective action to make a decisive difference in the course of history has long preoccupied our thinking about the relationship between capitalism and human well-being. This focus on the agency of ordinary people constitutes the foundation on which this book builds.

A Case for Trinidad and Tobago in Contemporary Development Theories

Trinidad and Tobago might not appear as a case of interest in academic literature on development or in the discourse of international development agencies, but its development performance is far from trivial. Table I.1 shows how measures of economic and social development in Trinidad and Tobago, such as life expectancy, literacy, and maternal mortality rates, have improved over time. In addition, Trinidad and Tobago performs quite well compared to other widely praised cases of equity-enhancing development, such as Kerala, India, and other commonly studied cases in development literature (see table A.1 in appendix).

How Trinidad and Tobago came to achieve these levels of equitable development is a puzzle for those well versed in the dominant theories of development. It is well established in the development literature that, within capitalism, it is not the invisible hand of the unfettered market that improves human well-being but, rather, those states with the *capacity* for planning and coordinating the massive tasks involved in increasing national income and a redistributive agenda, which includes welfare provision, social insurance, land reforms, and other policies to enhance equity and economic security.[10] In the state-centered, Weberian-inspired scholarship on rationalization and bureaucracies, state capacity that is conducive to this kind of development encompasses three main dimensions. The first is that the state must have relative autonomy from the capitalist class, which allows it to formulate and implement collective national development goals that do not maximize profit for either economic elites or political officeholders. Second, there must be a state bureaucracy characterized by an efficient organizational structure and staffed by qualified, experienced personnel, transforming individual rational-instrumental orientations into shared aims and commitments. Such a bureaucratic machinery also enables the state to coordinate a multitude of actors and complex tasks on a large scale, such as providing collective social goods like education, transportation, roads, health services, and sanitation throughout its territory. Third, dense ties between the state and the vast array of communities in the society are required for development, as these enable the state to access information about people's needs and to harness the skills and expertise of the populace in the creation and execution of development programs and policies. By contrast, states with a weaker capacity for development are characterized by patrimonial ties, self-interested personnel, a lack of coordination between government agencies, and apparatuses that repress the masses. These states tend to be ineffective in formulating people-centered policies and often exacerbate inequality and underdevelopment.

The perplexing thing about Trinidad and Tobago is that, according to the conventional development theories, the country had the key conditions that should have produced a weak state capacity and, therefore, low levels of development: European colonizers, oil dependence, and racial diversity. The

TABLE I.I. Economic and Social Indicators over Time, Trinidad and Tobago

Year	1962	1983	2019
GDP per capita (constant 2015 US$)	4,835	8,105	17,401
Human Development Index	–	0.656 (1990)	0.813
Literacy rate, adult total (% of people ages 15 and above)	–	95 (1980)	98 (2000)
Life expectancy at birth, total (years)	63	68	74
Mortality rate, infant (per 1,000 live births)	53	31	15
Mortality rate, under 5 (per 1,000 live births)	64	36	17
Maternal mortality (deaths per 100,000 live births)	–	74 (2000)	26
Political rights	2 (1972)	1	2
Civil liberties	3 (1972)	2	2
Population (millions)	0.9	1.2	1.4

Sources: Freedom House, *Freedom in the World 2024* (indices of political rights and civil liberties are on a seven-point scale ranging from 1 [least democratic] to 7 [most democratic]); United Nations Economic Commission for Latin America and the Caribbean, CEPALSTAT: Statistical Databases and Publications, 2024; UNDP, Human Development Index dataset, 2024; World Bank, World Development Indicators, 2024.

historical-institutional scholarship on the developmental legacies of European colonizers argues that in territories with low European settlement and/or where colonizers ruled through collaboration with Indigenous elites such as kings and chiefs, there was an ineffective transfer of Western economic, political, and cultural institutions. Here, despotic states that lacked the bureaucratic and legal-administrative structures based on formal rules derived from European law emerged, that is, states that lacked the capacity for achieving long-run postcolonial development.[11]

The resource-curse perspective, in turn, posits that resource dependence, especially on oil, tends to inhibit rather than enhance economic and social development and to weaken democracy and political stability.[12] The "rents," or external income from taxes and royalties on natural resource production, free these states from having to tax the local population to generate income and, therefore, from accountability to their citizenry. Consequently, these revenues tend to weaken state capacity for development in these "rentier states," or "petro-states" in the case of oil, by fostering corruption, clientelism, excessive distribution, economic mismanagement, and the building up of authoritarian and repressive capacities.[13] Except for the few that "escaped" the resource curse, owing, supposedly, to private ownership in the resource sector, oil dependence tends to hamper development.[14]

Finally, according to the diversity-development thesis, described as "one of the most powerful hypotheses in political economy," countries with greater racial and/or ethnic heterogeneity tend to have slower economic growth, more political instability, and less public goods provision than ethnically "homogeneous" countries.[15] Some trace this outcome to competition between ethnic groups for state power and the distribution of resources along racial and/or ethnic lines, often leading to ethnic violence and civil war.[16]

According to all these accounts, the odds were stacked against Trinidad and Tobago. The resident European population was small, and white capital and colonial administrators established extractive institutions of plantation slavery (for sugar, coffee, cacao) based on African labor, Indian indentureship, and natural resource exploitation.[17] The colonial state was authoritarian, nepotistic, understaffed, and underresourced.[18] With respect to oil dependence, Trinidad and Tobago's economy and state are heavily reliant on oil and gas revenues and have not been immune to the "Dutch disease" and the vagaries of international oil prices.[19] Still, Trinidad and Tobago has a Human Development Index comparable to and in some cases surpassing those of other countries that are widely acclaimed to have escaped the resource curse; moreover, it has maintained democratic governance since its independence from colonial rule.[20] Finally, Trinidad and Tobago has a multiracial population, but the country is not stuck in perpetual poverty, calamity, and interracial violence or war. Trinidad and Tobago challenges existing predictions about its development path and complicates dominant accounts about the factors and processes that stimulate or inhibit development.

Trinidad and Tobago's experience illustrates that there is more to the story than only European colonizers *or* natural resource economic dependence *or* ethnic heterogeneity. We are missing possible alternative actors and causal pathways to institutional development. This book shows that at the intersection of colonialism, oil production, and racial and/or ethnic projects, there are the masses of ordinary people, whose agency should never be underestimated. *Fueling Development* provides an account of Trinidad and Tobago's development that exposes the critical but heretofore underemphasized role of racialized colonized working people.

Labor, Race, States, and Development: A Black Radical and Institutional Approach

Labor studies provide a useful entry point into understanding how workers influence development. A core finding in labor studies is that worker agency shapes state policy, state institutions, and the state's orientation toward capitalist development. Consistent with this scholarship, this book argues that working people were the decisive force spurring institutional changes within the Trinidad and Tobago state that resulted in its impressive development outcomes.

Labor studies tend to focus on class, which, defined in Marx's terms, refers to relations of exploitation where the capitalist class (owners of capital) extract surplus value from the laboring class (those who must sell their ability to work). Through analyses of class structure and class struggles, these works show the key role organized labor played in bringing about universal suffrage, decolonization, and democracy; the emergence and expansion of the welfare state and welfare benefits; and stronger institutions of governance, including transparency and effective bureaucracy.[21] The character of working-class movements matters for the different models of capitalist development.[22] For example, the unified mobilization of workers and peasants can produce social-democratic states and robust equitable development, as was the case in Kerala, India.[23] Conversely, labor mobilization that is beset by divisions along racial, gender, and ideological lines, as Ray Kiely sees in Trinidad and Tobago, can result in uneven development, which he defines in terms of levels of industrialization.[24] Also, in the absence of militant trade unions and class-based organizing, rapid industrialization and economic growth may occur, as was the case with the East Asian "miracles."[25] However, such transformations were predicated on authoritarian rule and extreme forms of labor repression, which negatively impact human well-being.[26] Like this labor-centered scholarship, this book also recognizes social class to be an important driver of conflict and a collective identity around which people mobilize, producing a more equitable distribution of power and resources.

Class is not, however, the only source of grievance and basis for mobilization.[27] Labor studies may acknowledge other forms of hierarchy and antagonism, such as race and gender, but nevertheless it tends to stress class as the primary axis of inequality and conflict in capitalism. For a "class in itself" to become a "class for itself," in Marx's terms, and "realize its historic role" as collective actors shaping the course of history, this research tends to search for and even prescribe the elevation of class consciousness over and above other concerns. However, for people living at the intersection of different oppressive hierarchical systems, including class, race, and gender, their experiences, subjectivities, and manifest struggles can and do span several dimensions simultaneously.[28] The analytic challenge is to examine how these different cleavages intertwine as sources of conflict, mobilizing identity, and collective action. The form and motive of working people's agency in Trinidad and Tobago cannot be understood through class interest and mobilization alone, as it also involved collective action based on racial interests, as well as the simultaneous weight and political opportunities of imperialism and colonial domination. This book develops an overarching framework with which to holistically and systematically make sense of how different axes of inequality and subjectivity, such as race and class, are related and imbricated with imperialism and colonialism; how they shape movements; and, in turn, how they impact development.

To meet this challenge, this book draws on the literature on race and capitalism from the Black radical tradition to ground its analysis of development in Trinidad and Tobago. The Black radical tradition is broadly defined as the distinct political and intellectual struggles of global Africans against the global history of chattel slavery and racism, imperialism, and capitalism. It is vast and comprises many different ideas, practices, discourses, and strands of political thought, including various forms of Black nationalisms, socialisms, Pan-Africanisms, Marxist feminisms, and more.[29] Within these traditions of Black radicalism, I draw primarily on those who had varying levels of engagement with and critical appreciation for Marxism. Some were Pan-African Marxist intellectuals, such as C. L. R. James, Kwame Nkrumah, and Walter Rodney, who theorized the political economy of race and racism, colonialism, and capitalism through a dialectical and materialist approach to history. Pan-African Marxist feminists, such as Claudia Jones, urged attention to the compounded effects of gendered oppression and the indispensability of Black working women to liberation struggles. I also draw on others, like W. E. B. Du Bois and Frantz Fanon, who over the course of their lifetimes increasingly engaged with Marxism, and those who shifted away, such as George Padmore. And still others, such as Oliver Cromwell Cox, who rejected the Marxist label and distanced himself from Pan-Africanism, yet nevertheless laid the intellectual foundations for academic research on the racial order of capital accumulation. Together, these thinkers constitute a Black radical approach to the study of political economy—one that has been historically marginalized across multiple academic disciplines.[30] At its core, this Black radical literature on race and capitalism advances an integrated account of how capitalist imperialism subjugates the racialized masses and also sets the conditions for their self-directed liberation. The research and debates among these thinkers have generated powerful analytic tools for understanding the development experience of Trinidad and Tobago.

Analyzing development using a Black radical analytic approach challenges us to attend to the racial and colonial architecture of global capitalism, not as a side issue or marginal concern, but rather as a central feature of the world-scale organization of wealth accumulation and the production of poverty. For these thinkers, capitalist classes and imperial states seek to maximize profits not by homogenizing labor, as Marx and Friedrich Engels had theorized, but rather by producing social difference, particularly the modern idea of race. As capitalism developed, Europeans invented white supremacist ideology and race to justify the incorporation of labor and lands into a global regime of accumulation by genocide, expropriation, dispossession, racial slavery and various forms of labor superexploitation, and colonial domination.[31] As Oliver Cox explained, "It would be next to impossible for, say, the British in East Africa to conceive of the masses as normal human beings and yet maintain their exploitative designs toward them."[32] This social construction of race alongside hierarchical center-periphery extractive relations has real developmental consequences. The capitalist imperial countries amass wealth, which becomes the basis of world power, industry, technological expansion, and so on by creating impoverishment, human suffering, and dependency in peripheralized regions. Thus, a deep historical analysis of how the people, land, and resources in Trinidad and Tobago were incorporated into the global economic system, and how people were racialized in the mode of production, is crucial for understanding its developmental constraints and possibilities.

What later came to be called dependency theory and world-systems analysis reiterates that the development of individual countries is conditioned by their structural position in the international division of labor in the world capitalist system.[33] The "Caribbean dependency thought" of the New World Group, a radical intellectual movement in the anglophone Caribbean in the 1960s, maintained that the plantation economy based on slavery structured capitalist (under)development of the region well beyond emancipation through the persistent dependence on foreign multinationals, cheap raw material exports, and foreign loans, which reduced economic autonomy and produced economic instability.[34] These literatures have tended to emphasize economic structural dependence, leading many within them to call for more attention to race in an analytic manner.[35] In *Fueling Development*, I analyze race as part of many dynamic forces shaping Trinidad and Tobago's development experience.

Many terms have emerged to capture the racial, colonial, and imperial underpinnings of capital accumulation and underdevelopment. They include *racial capitalism*, *racial and colonial capitalism*, *racist capitalism*, *racialized capitalism*, and *race and capitalism*.[36] Du Bois speaks of a world divided by a "global color line." Others, like C. L. R. James, bring race and colonialism into the class analysis without adding a descriptor to the term *capitalism*. These labels are not entirely interchangeable, as there are notable differences in how scholars theorize the timing of the emergence of race and racism, their precise roles in capitalism, and their necessity or contingency to capitalism.[37] This book uses Walter Rodney's terminology—the "white capitalist system."[38] Although Rodney never explicitly defined the term, he used it in a way that is a useful anchor for this text. Located in the Pan-African Marxist tradition, Rodney views the invention of race and white supremacist ideology as specifically tied to the emergence of capitalism. The adjective *white* forces analytic attention to a global system dominated economically, politically, militarily, and culturally by white capital and capitalist imperialism, and to white supremacy as an ideological basis for racialized labor exploitation.[39] This term encapsulates those conditions that oppress the masses and stunt the development of peripheralized regions.

Once we accept the postulate that racialization, labor exploitation, and colonial domination are conjoined dynamics shaping capitalist development, we must then "stretch" the Marxist analysis, according to Fanon, to include in our theoretical frameworks how race, class, and colonialism shape social and economic divisions, the state, and the politics of development within countries.[40] The distribution of power, economic resources, rights, and privileges runs not just along racial or class lines but along complex hierarchies of race-class intersections that vary among countries and over time. Comparative racial and ethnic studies have documented cross-national variations in racial classifications and social mobility of racialized groups.[41] At the same time, class position also reciprocally reinforces racialization and racialized identity. Fanon captured this complexity in the famous quote: "You are rich because you are white, you are white because you are rich."[42] Thus, the various cleavages, identities, and interests that stem from different configurations of race *and* class in the social hierarchy shape the content of the struggle over material resources and political power and the balance of power between groups.

Thus, *Fueling Development* attends to how economic and political conflicts and their outcomes are shaped by both racial fissures within a class and class chasms within a racialized group. Black radical thinkers have long established that shared class conditions, among workers, for example, may not inevitably generate class action because of investments in socially constructed racial identities, racism, and colorism, thereby constraining the collective power of workers to obtain greater socioeconomic gains, democratize the state, and transform society.[43] Within the middle class as well, color and/or ethnic-based rivalries can cause and/or exacerbate conflicts, which weaken their class coherence and shape cross-class alliances.[44] Likewise, intraracial class antagonisms, such as between the Black working class and the Black middle class, also shape politics, state building, and development. Black political and economic elites were created and cultivated by capitalist imperialism and colonial states to serve imperial interests and became dependent on the state apparatus for their own reproduction. Additionally, having internalized white supremacist colonial education, they tended to be preoccupied with mimicking and attaining equal status with white elites. Consequently, rather than struggling together with Black workers and peasants for socialism and self-determination of post-colonial states, the Black middle class, Black radical thinkers observe, has historically co-opted radical movements, facilitated neocolonial exploitation, politicized race to serve their own interests, prevented democracy, and conserved the capitalist social order, all of which have prevented improvements in conditions of life for the masses.[45] Thus, neither the shared experience of racial domination nor a common class condition necessarily produces shared economic and/or political outlooks. This is why race cannot be reduced to class and vice versa. Both must be analyzed in their concrete historical situation to understand political struggles, states, and development.

Thus far, we have discussed how *Fueling Development* draws on Black radical theories to understand the various oppressions that constitute the white capitalist system and prevent human development. The dialectical thinking in this tradition also pushes us to expose how those very conditions of subjugation simultaneously invigorate agency from below and spur social change. "Below," for these intellectuals, is not the white industrial working class in the imperial core. This group tends to be more reformist than revolutionary. It cherishes the economic and democratic concessions obtained from capital and bourgeois nation-states, who in turn obtained that wealth through imperial exploits, as well as what Du Bois called the "public and psychological wage" of whiteness, that is, the status, privileges, and social deference they receive simply from being racialized as white.[46] Below this white working class in the core are the "inferior darker folk" who, in accordance with the racial doctrines of modernity, are denied equality with whites.[47] These are the "real exploited and exploitable proletariat of the system," as they are precluded from similar wages, welfare, or protections for white workers.[48] These conditions of racialized exploitation and colonial oppression contain within them the potential for the racialized colonized working people—the real agents of history—in certain conducive historical situations to develop a critical consciousness and spring into radical collective action.

As C. L. R. James asserts, "Economic development on the grand scale is first of all people," and the "only way of changing the structure of the economy and setting it on to new paths is by mobilizing the mass against all who will stand in the way."[49] From Haiti to Kenya, South Africa, the United States, and beyond, such mobilization has profoundly impacted the global economy and the trajectories of individual countries therein, including ending slavery, expanding democracy or intensifying authoritarianism, and triggering global shifts in the movement of white capital and the organization/regimes of capital accumulation.[50] The complexities of race and class do not affect only the unity of the movement. The subjectivities and lived experiences that develop out of the destructive dialectic of the white capitalist system embody not only material concerns but also racial ones. As Rodney put it, to understand the masses in action, "the question of the inter-relation between race and class consciousness is of the utmost importance."[51] The triple oppressive forces of race, class, and gender, and the role of Black working women in liberation movements, also cannot be ignored.[52] Because of their location at the nexus of these compounding structures, Black working women have historically advanced an agenda that addresses not only formal productive activities but also the devalued reproductive labor of caring, sexual violence, and family and social reproduction generally. As such, following the Black radical political economic tradition, I analyze Black struggles against the white capitalist system. In *Fueling Development*, I center the visions, strategies, and actions of racialized subordinate classes in their quest for liberation and investigate the outcomes of mass action.

In explaining Trinidad and Tobago's economic and social development, I corroborate the Black radicals' view on how racial and colonial domination impedes development, but I also more explicitly develop the other side of the dialectic that these thinkers advanced but theorized less, which is *how* the agency of working people can improve their economic and social conditions. These thinkers maintained that better conditions for the masses could only be realized through the agency of Black working people, but they were not conceptualizing that "development" as the pursuit of Western economic, political, and cultural formations. They rejected this liberal and normative framing of development. These "advancements," after all, are derived from intensive and widespread racist and gender-motivated violence, exploitation, degradation, inequality, and political repression, all of which are occluded in the hegemonic European conceptualization of development and progress.[53] The only true development for working people is a global, anticapitalist, antiracist, feminist, anti-imperial, and anticolonial socialist order.[54] For most of these thinkers, only worker- and peasant-controlled property, production, and socialist state apparatus grounded in the principle of egalitarian distribution will satisfy the wants and needs of all members of the society—housing, health, public schools, and general welfare—and uphold all human freedom and dignity. Du Bois for example, asserted that the success of a multiracial social democracy required a military-backed "dictatorship of the proletariat."[55] C. L. R. James rejected representative government and advocated for direct democracy comprising popular councils and worker self-management.[56] Anything short of this is reformist, not revolutionary, and reforms are insufficient, or, more aptly, an obstacle to true mass liberation.

The Trinidad and Tobago state is not a socialist one, and the workers do not own or control the means of production. The country may now register as a high-income economy, but with its reliance on exports, access to foreign markets, and foreign capital, it has not broken the chains of structural dependency. It has not leapfrogged out of the economic position and resource-exporter role into which it was placed during British colonial domination. In this sense, Black radical thinkers would not call Trinidad and Tobago a developmental success. Similarly, the New World Group might have interpreted the shifts in the standard of living for Trinidad and Tobago's working people as "continuity with change" or "adjustment without transformation."[57]

This book does not dispute the persistence of Trinidad and Tobago's structural dependency in the global white capitalist system. However, the unintended by-product of emphasizing structural stasis is the constriction of the intellectual space for understanding the agents and activities responsible for the instances, whether fleeting or lasting, of positive change. In the late 1960s, development scholars began to recognize that development was more dynamic, and outcomes, whether defined as industrialization, average income, social well-being, or all of the above, varied considerably among states outside of the core.[58] Others noted the many contradictions of developmental "success," where states like Trinidad and Tobago might remain in the same relative position in the global hierarchy of wealth and power but nevertheless undergo major social and economic transformations.[59] Material conditions and human welfare *have* improved remarkably in Trinidad and Tobago, so how do we account for this shift? This book argues that the mobilization of working people within the constraints of the white capitalist system, while falling short of socialist revolution, still had important enduring successes, through the way it forced changes in the state apparatus.

Also following this group of Black radical intellectuals, this book draws on a range of archival sources, government documents, and databases, and employs a historical and dialectical materialist analysis that aims to trace how the past informs the present. Using their narrative strategy, which is also common in North American comparative-historical research methods, I attend to the temporal order, event sequences, conjunctures, and contingencies.[60] Also consistent with Black radical thinkers' analytic approaches, I aim to overcome what recent scholars have called *methodological nationalism* and attend to the interrelations among actors, events, and processes across time and space that shape outcomes in Trinidad and Tobago.[61] My methodology is described in detail in the appendix. The next section lays out the details of the book's argument regarding Trinidad and Tobago's worker movements, state structure, and development.

The Argument: Liberation Unionism, State Capacity, and Development

I trace Trinidad and Tobago's development over the course of the twentieth century to the mobilization of a specific form of working-class unionism, which I call *liberation unionism*. Liberation unionism in Trinidad and Tobago had three main defining features: (1) it was internationalist, meaning imbued with the Pan-African anticolonial, anti-imperial, diasporic connections primarily of Garveyism and later Black Power; (2) it united workers across racial and sectoral lines and was also inclusive of women; and (3) it advocated for economic, political, and social transformations. Liberation unionism emerged during the interwar years, erupting in 1919 and 1937, under crucial contextual factors that workers took advantage of, namely, a wider geopolitical context where the British Empire viewed the colony of Trinidad and Tobago as its only secure source of oil. While not eliminating the underlying exploitative racial and economic structures, these movements forced the colonial state to enact institutional reforms that increased state capacity for development. Liberation unionism triggered the construction of a welfare-enhancing state apparatus, which enabled the Trinidad and Tobago state to achieve remarkable gains in such gargantuan tasks as lowering infant mortality, increasing life expectancy, expanding access to education, and generally raising living standards and well-being.

This form of unionism differed from the far more insular "business unionism," in which unions struggle to improve the working conditions of their members, narrowly defined.[62] Other forms of unionism, such as political unionism, social justice unionism, and social movement unionism, adopt a broader scope, where workers not only fight for better wages and working conditions but also make political claims for human rights, democratization, and/or the needs of the larger community.[63] Liberation unionism, as defined in this book, encompasses all these demands but has its basis in a phenomenology of racialized and colonized subjectivity. It is a distinctive form of worker organizing that is deeply rooted in independent Black struggles for freedom and self-determination. The designation *liberation* is not meant to imply that other traditions and forms of unionism do not also seek some kind of liberation from exploitation and oppression. The Communist Party–affiliated social movement unionism in India, South Africa, Hawai'i, the United States, and across Latin America and the *sindicalismo de liberación* in late 1960s Argentina, as it was called by labor organizer Raimondo Ongaro, all at one point or another contained or embodied expressions of anti-imperial working-class socialism.[64] The term *liberation* is also not meant to suggest that totally breaking free from the white capitalist system was achieved. The conflict-compromise relationship between capital and labor constrains what labor unions and movements can accomplish.[65] The *liberation* in *liberation unionism* denotes the distinctive Black radical political philosophies, strategies, and expressions of *Black liberation* that orient and give meaning to the workers' self-directed collective action.

The next chapter (chapter 1) lays out the conditions favoring the emergence of liberation unionism in Trinidad and Tobago. I explore the social structure, the lived experiences and interests of the three main actors involved in institutional development—workers, colonial state officials, and private capital—and the history of resource and labor extraction in colonial Trinidad and Tobago prior to the first colony-wide worker mobilization in 1919. I also highlight the lack of institutions for addressing these conflicts and promoting equitable human development. Chapters 2 and 3 chronicle the events and institutional changes following the 1919 and 1937 worker mobilizations, respectively.

Despite being the most cohesive and prominent political force during the colonial period, the working people did not win control of the state apparatus during formal decolonization. Chapter 4 presents how liberation unionism was severely weakened, although not eliminated, during this period. I argue that labor's failure to win state control was consequential for development in the long run. It enabled militant unions to remain organizationally independent of political parties and the state and to retain their radicalism, whereas foreign intervention and party and political incorporation of labor in so many other former colonies resulted in longer-lasting depoliticization of worker movements. This relative autonomy of labor led to open confrontation just after independence between labor, on one side, and the state and private capital, on the other, over the unfulfilled dreams for economic and social justice and transformation.

Liberation unionism survived and resurged in the postindependence period, crucially between independence in 1962 and the first oil boom of 1973. It paralleled and innovated on the Black radical activity of the colonial era, and the timing was crucial for shaping how the state invested the massive oil windfalls. As shown in chapter 5, this postindependence liberation unionism reinforced the path-dependent process of institution building and forced the newly independent state to further increase its capacity, leading to long-term robust development.

Across chapters 2 to 5, I demonstrate how liberation unionism shaped long-term development by pushing the despotic state to institutionalize greater legal-administrative capacity to devise and implement development policies and provide public goods. I show how the movement forced the colonial and post-colonial states to loosen entanglements with white foreign and local economic elites, thereby carving out some autonomous space for state action that was more oriented toward the masses. Through liberation unionism, working people also enhanced the coherence and meritocracy of the state as they compelled the state to provide developmental goods to the African and Indian masses across the country. Finally, I show how worker mobilization in the colonial and independence period propelled the Trinidad and Tobago state toward democracy and the expansion of political rights and civil liberties, and encouraged greater transparency and accountability of the state to the public. The institutional features of increased autonomy from the dominant class, enhanced bureaucratization, and greater embeddedness with the masses helped promote economic and social development in Trinidad and Tobago.

Chapter 6 compares the findings from the in-depth case study of Trinidad and Tobago with an abbreviated study of Guyana over the same time period to sharpen the concept of liberation unionism and demonstrate how it might be used to understand development in other contexts. Guyana is another former British colony in the Caribbean region where workers had significant structural power on account of the geostrategic importance of their natural resources—bauxite—to British imperial efforts. Guyana's history of plantation slavery with a multiracial African and Indian worker base closely resembles Trinidad and Tobago's, and liberation unionism did emerge there during the interwar years. However, Guyana ended up with comparably less equitable development outcomes.

The Guyana case reinforces the argument that geopolitical contexts shape the extent to which liberation unionism stimulates reformist welfare-enhancing state building. Unlike Trinidad and Tobago's workers, who were unsuccessful at the polls during decolonization, in Guyana a radical Marxist political party representing working people won state power and began constructing a socialist state. But to the British and United States, such a state threatened their interests and the existing global order. These imperial powers repressed liberation unionism and the socialist party, reversed democracy, and ensured that the Guyanese state, upon constitutional independence, was in the hands of leaders who professed alignment with imperial interests. As such, state building after constitutional independence proceeded in ways that impeded democratic and redistributive development. This comparison shows that liberation unionism is not unique to Trinidad and Tobago per se, but that its exclusion from state power spared the state and masses from imperial interventions and generated concessions that positively affected development.

In arguing that liberation unionism had developmental impacts, I am not saying that this process was smooth and uncontested or resulted in a steady march toward mass upliftment. I am also not asserting that working people should eschew revolution and aspire only to concessions, thereby leaving the overall white capitalist system intact. My argument is simply that the agency of working people matters, and I show empirically how their self-directed struggles led to changes that improved their everyday lives. State-building processes are path dependent.[66] Once the colonizers invaded and constructed institutions in a particular way, these institutions became very difficult, if not nearly impossible, to change as entrenched interests favored and defended the status quo. Worker mobilization threatened the legitimacy and dominance of the white elites and the colonial and independent regimes. Gains were uneven and at times were rolled back as the white ruling elites retaliated with the repressive capacity of the state and novel methods of labor exploitation, resource extraction, and accumulation.

Still, I show how after the first set of institutional changes stimulated by liberation unionism in 1919–20, subsequent mobilizations tended to reinforce those previously established patterns of relations between the state and the working people. During formal decolonization, state reforms did not involve dismantling the existing structure and creating something different. Instead, movement-driven reforms increased the size of the state and its capacity, and further enhanced public participation, resulting in the consolidation of an institutionally robust democratic and redistributive development.

My analysis of Trinidad and Tobago covers the full sweep of the twentieth century, with a specific focus on the period from 1919, when the first instantiation of liberation unionism erupted, to 1983, when the global neoliberal current of the 1980s pulled in the Trinidad and Tobago state. In the concluding chapter, I review the argument about Trinidad and Tobago's development story, which I trace to worker struggle and its long-lasting institutional impacts. My framework helps make sense of trends in the mid-1980s and thereafter, which are more dispiriting as global economic restructuring has increased labor precarity, the state has embraced certain elements of neoliberalism, unions have been severely weakened, and the indicators of social dislocation, most notably crime, have skyrocketed. In *Fueling Development*, one theme is clear: when labor strikes, capital strikes back. The conclusion situates these contemporary conditions in the *longue durée* of state-capital and state-society relations and in the global context of the ever-evolving white capitalist system. Liberation unionism suffered challenges after World War II, but it reemerged in the 1960s. Thus, the neoliberal turn is a downside for worker organizing, but this is one part of a longer struggle, and the fate of worker movements is not given. *Fueling Development* is a story of hope, tragedy, and ongoing struggle with liberation unionism at the heart of it. I end by discussing the implications of this book's findings for other countries and for the future of human development.

1

Proletarianization, Race Making, and Capital Accumulation, 1498–1914

To comprehend how liberation unionism emerged in 1919, we have to understand the economic, political, geopolitical, and racial circumstances that shaped working people's lives from colonial annexation in the late fifteenth century to the early twentieth century. Christopher Columbus's arrival in Kairi (the Indigenous name for Trinidad; the neighboring island, Urupaina, was later renamed Tobago) in 1498, followed by the British annexation of Trinidad from Spain in 1797, initiated violent changes that eventually led to liberation unionism. Tobago, after centuries of being passed between French, Dutch, and British control, was taken by the British for a final time in 1814 and administratively united with Trinidad in 1888. Europeans never established large permanent settlements in these colonies due to the harsh climate, the absence of precious metals, and strong Indigenous resistance.[1] As with many other Caribbean territories, Europeans forcibly incorporated the islands into the white capitalist system through dispossession of the Indigenous peoples' land and the successive importation of differentially racialized and gendered labor for agricultural and natural resource production.[2]

I follow C. L. R. James's *Black Jacobins*, Walter Rodney's *History of the Guyanese Working People*, and W. E. B. Du Bois's *Black Reconstruction in America* to examine the conditions, lived experiences, and subjectivities of racialized working people in Trinidad and Tobago from the bottom up, through the eyes of the people who suffered under the engine of economic "progress." The analysis documents how social connections of not just class but also race and colonial subjecthood became central to people's dispositions, ideologies, and collective actions.[3] This chapter lays the groundwork for understanding the emergence of liberation unionism, the state responses to that worker mobilization, and the developmental consequences of this form of collective action.

The term *race*, in most sociological works, refers to socially constructed differentiations based on perceived phenotypical features and/or cultural traits. There have been lively debates over whether *race*, meaning phenotype or ancestry, and *ethnicity*, meaning shared culture, are analytically distinct categories.[4] Vilna Bashi notes that the difficulty in disentangling the two terms stems from the fact that all ethnic groups are racialized.[5] As such, *ethno-racial* has become the preferred terminology to capture how people can simultaneously be a racial object and identify with one or more ethnicities. In line with the socially constructed perceptions of the period discussed in this book, I primarily use the term *race*. The major groups in colonial Trinidad and Tobago were regarded by the colonizers, and came to regard themselves, as races.[6] The special contexts where ethnic differences within racial groups became salient are explained when they arise in the analysis.[7] Among the historical evidence presented, two explicitly derogatory terms come up in the text—*nigga* and *coolie*—the latter a Tamil word that originally indicated a type of laborer. They were used to degrade and dehumanize Africans and Indians, respectively. Because this remains the case today in contemporary Trinidad and Tobago, I do not reproduce these words uncritically.[8] It is my hope that this book will elevate how African and Indian workers defined themselves in their own words and their actions.

A united interracial movement seems unlikely because of the colonizers' effective divide-and-exploit strategies. The white plantation-owning and business elite assigned the world's people to different economic activities, separating them into "kinds" that were supposedly suitable for certain types of work: Indigenous and African labor in cacao production, African and later Indian labor on sugar plantations, and predominantly African labor in the oil sector. As predicted in much of the social scientific literature, colonial racialization, the sowing of conflicts over differences in land ownership, wages, and taxes between workers, and worker investments in racial identity prevented workers from uniting across these socially constructed divisions in the period prior to World War I.[9] Despite differences, these working people shared similar lived experiences: racialized and gendered exploitation by a small, ethnically diverse white elite; repression by the colonial state; and dependency of the colony's economy on production for white capital and empire. These common sources of oppression and exploitation became the foundation for a formidable workers' movement—liberation unionism—which ultimately contributed to development.

This chapter supports arguments in the US and European sociological literature regarding the structural and political conditions shaping working-class formation. It confirms that changes in the organization of production impact the size and strength of the working class; that state repression in favor of the dominant class can both stimulate and deter collective action; and that dependency, export-oriented economies, and economic downturns act as catalysts for worker mobilization.[10] Additionally, as historians have demonstrated, labor in and from the colonies was instrumental in building empires.[11] This chapter emphasizes how empire, in turn, shaped labor, revealing how the interlocking forces of colonialism and racialization were deeply intertwined in processes of proletarianization in Trinidad and Tobago.

The Racialized Workers

Amerindian Land and Labor

Consistent with Indigenous peoples' experiences across the New World, the Spanish drive to accumulate wealth in Trinidad through agricultural production, beginning in the late sixteenth century, involved expropriating the lands of the local Indigenous people—known locally as Caribs or Amerindians— and forcing them to labor in encomiendas consisting of mostly tobacco and cacao plantations, public works projects, and mission villages under the guise of protection and Catholic conversion.[12] The Spanish justified dispossessing Amerindians by perpetuating ever-shifting racial tropes of civilized/uncivilized, Christian/heathen, and mission/nonmission. They developed the category "Indio" to distinguish between those considered allies and political enemies, as well as between free laborers (Indios) and those who could be enslaved and sold to Hispaniola. Moreover, Indios were entitled to inalienable land and exempt from paying taxes, yet they remained legally bound to missions.[13] Cacao cultivation based on Indigenous labor grew in prominence, but, overall, Spanish efforts to develop plantations were largely limited by droughts, famine, crop diseases, and a drastically reduced Indigenous population due to brutal labor conditions, murder, food shortages, and European diseases.[14]

Amerindians experienced intensified dispossession and erasure under British domination from 1797. To obtain the land needed to transform Trinidad into a major sugar-producing colony the likes of older colonies, such as Jamaica and Barbados, the British deployed colonial extinction narratives that claimed the "indolent harmless race" of Trinidad's Amerindians was (becoming) extinct.[15] The developing racial ideology also emphasized Indigenous racial purity and reclassified the many people of Indigenous-Spanish descent, many of whom self-identified as Indigenous, as not pure or real Indios. This racialization justified ignoring land treaties and selling mission properties and valuable cacao-growing lands.[16] Having lost the legally enshrined access to land and work that came with being categorized as Indio, many fell into abject poverty, some relocated into the forests and hills, and others moved to South America.[17]

Many others became peasant farmers alongside *cocoa payoles*, the local name for people of Indigenous-Spanish-African descent. Most *cocoa payoles* migrated to Trinidad from Venezuela in the late eighteenth to early twentieth century. As the name reflects, they were central to the Trinidad cacao industry's expansion from the 1840s on and the boom between 1866 and 1920 when British demand for chocolate increased.[18] Some of these peasant farmers purchased Crown land to cultivate cacao and then sold the plots to white landowners when the trees began to bear. Others worked on contract to cultivate plots owned by white landed elites. Over time, this group came to see themselves, and were seen, as "mixed" or a kind of "modified" African.[19] Overall, the development of the cacao industry and the history of racialization of Indigenous people justified land dispossession and their confinement to the cacao sector.

African Workers

African and African-descended labor in Trinidad and Tobago was the result of enslavement, migration, and racialization. Several terms have been used to describe people perceived to possess an "African" phenotype and ancestry, including *African, West Indian, Black, Negro*, and, after independence, *Afro-Creole* and *Afro-Trinidadian/Trinbagonian*.[20] Following conventions in most contemporary scholarship on race in Trinidad and Tobago, I use the terms *African* and *Black* interchangeably throughout the text.[21] Later in the book, I highlight the special circumstances where workers attempted to expand the meaning of *Black*. The brutality of slavery, dehumanization, depraved living conditions, and severed ties both regionally and between Africa and the New World molded the collective memory and struggle in what later became liberation unionism.

Diverse in ethnicity and geographic origin, Black working people in Trinidad and Tobago were brought together by the European transatlantic trade of enslaved Africans. Torn from their families, communities, and lands, their yearning for homeland, autonomy, and freedom became the basis for their unification, global outlook, and collective struggle. In 1776 the Spanish intensified efforts to stimulate production and accumulation in Trinidad through a new immigration policy—the Cédula de Población (population decree, revised in 1783)—which allowed immigration by Catholics from states friendly to Spain. Incentives included land grants to white men and free Black or "colored" immigrants (who received half of what was allotted to white men), with larger provisions if bringing enslaved people, and political privileges and job opportunities within the colonial state after five years of residence. This generous offer attracted French Catholic plantation owners from Cayenne (French Guiana), Dominica, Grenada, Guadeloupe, Martinique, St. Lucia, St. Vincent, and even Tobago.[22] These terms were especially attractive to French plantation owners who were fleeing the Haitian Revolution, which started in 1791, and seeking to rebuild their wealth and reestablish their status elsewhere. Between the 1783 Cedula and British conquest in 1797, the enslaved population increased from 310 to 10,009; the number of free people increased from 421 to 6,527; and the French grew to outnumber the Spanish by twenty to one, dominating the Spanish colonial institutions.[23]

The population of enslaved Africans from the continent and neighboring islands further increased under British domination. At the time the British annexed Trinidad, there was still an abundance of uncultivated land (about 870,400 acres) that could be transformed into large-scale sugar plantations but not enough enslaved laborers in relation to that land.[24] The enslaved population, brought mostly from other Caribbean islands and Africa, doubled in Trinidad's first decade as a British colony, going from 10,009 in 1797 to 20,761 in 1806.[25] More people might have been brought directly from Africa, but British colonization of Trinidad coincided with a peaking abolitionist movement and a new stance by British capitalists and parliamentarians that slavery was no longer essential to capital accumulation. These currents profoundly impacted the acquisition and recruitment of labor to the colony. After the formal abolition of the European trade in African people in 1807, a vibrant illicit inter-Caribbean trade developed. Plantation owners, with the full support of the local colonial authorities, brought in enslaved men and women from other colonies, such as Barbados, Dominica, and Grenada.[26] The diasporic character of the African population persisted long after slavery ended, eventually shaping the emergence of liberation unionism.

Enslaved Africans were the primary source of labor generating superprofits for Europeans who owned sugar, coffee, cacao, and cotton plantations. In 1813, 47.5 percent of enslaved people were assigned to field labor, 18.8 percent were domestics, 8.8 percent were skilled tradespeople, and the rest were dispersed in a variety of transportation and service work and fishing.[27] A significant proportion (almost 25 percent) of enslaved men and women worked not on plantations but in the urban area of Port of Spain.[28] While initially more men were brought in than women, shortly before emancipation, there were 104.4 enslaved men for every 100 enslaved women.[29] This urban trend, coupled with violent displacement from various parts of Africa and forced interisland Caribbean relocation, shaped the formation of the Black working class in Trinidad and Tobago.

Enslaved Africans performed backbreaking labor in the blistering heat, battling exhaustion and fatigue. They were subjected to excessive workloads and work hours and given inadequate food and clothing. They were housed in crude huts and barracks called *nigger yards*, which were long rectangular wooden buildings with galvanized roofs that were subdivided into single rooms using partitions. Overcrowding, shared cesspits, lack of privacy, and squalor degraded working people, leaving them highly susceptible to various diseases. Enslaved adults, their children, and in particular infants suffered exorbitantly high rates of malnutrition, disease, and mortality.[30] Common and often fatal maladies included fevers, dysentery, hookworm, yaws, leprosy, diphtheria, whooping cough, ulcerated sores, and neonatal tetanus.[31]

The superexploitation of Black women created the structural conditions for them to be at the forefront of resistance movements. In the institution of slavery across the New World, and in Trinidad and Tobago too, Europeans required enslaved African women to toil and produce as much as the men, while simultaneously harnessing their reproductive labor to care for white families, as well as their reproductive capacities to produce more humans and thereby increase property and capital.[32] This burden of domestic and care work and sexual abuse continued to fall on women after emancipation.[33] Enslaved children were also superexploited as toiling on the estates began at age four.[34] The whole system of plantation production and white supremacy was underpinned by systematic physical violence and the production of suffering, including imprisonment, fines, and an array of punishments such as flogging and torture, the most heinous of which was meted out to enslaved African women.[35]

These diverse Africans were unified not just by enslavement but also by the white supremacist racial ideologies underpinning the superexploitation of their labor. Europeans justified their turn to and treatment of Africans by constructing notions of the latter's inherent biological inferiority to all other races.[36] For example, US-born William Hardin Burnley, the largest plantation owner in Trinidad, asserted that Africans were, in his words, "things far short of human," who were lazy by nature and for whom enslavement and violent punishment was the only corrective.[37] According to Burnley, "the cultivation of the export-able produce of the West Indies can only be carried on advantageously by the people of the African or other southern races," meaning "the negroes [are] in every point of view preferable," the only alternative being people from the Azores, Canaries, and Cape Verde, "who probably have all of them some African blood in their veins."[38] The enslaved African plantation workers therefore did not share the partially free, partially bonded status of Indigenous people.

Abolition ushered in new unfree labor regimes intended to maintain Black workers' dependence on the plantation, the smooth accumulation of capital, and white racial dominance. The plantocracy instituted an apprenticeship system, which deferred full emancipation of adults for six years and required the formerly enslaved to work on estates in exchange for food, clothing, and housing, not wages. Furthermore, the plantocracy charged exorbitant prices for land to prevent Black landownership. Burnley expressed it explicitly: "The chief object of putting a price upon the land is to prevent any laborer from ever hoping or expecting to become a proprietor, which is not by nature or by education qualified to undertake successfully the cultivation of land on his own account."[39] In addition to hoarding land, the plantocracy also implemented other repressive employment practices and labor laws, such as refusing to pay wages; eliminating allowances; passing trespassing and vagrancy laws, enforced with heavy fines and imprisonment, to restrict movement within and across colonies; and continuing corporal punishment (flogging) as a central pillar of the colonial "justice" system.[40] According to geographer Bonham Richardson, "Slave emancipation in the British Caribbean represented perhaps less a sharp break with the past than it did a continuity of oppression."[41]

In this postemancipation context, four main occupational types emerged among formerly enslaved labor. First, a small number remained exclusively tied to the estates. The majority, however, moved off the plantations, squatting on abandoned estates or Crown lands due to high land prices, and established villages close to existing plantations and around the major towns. Among these, a second group earned enough from peasant farming in cacao production and later cane farming to free themselves from wage labor.[42] The third and largest group were those who cultivated small plots of land for provisions, fruits, and vegetables, rearing a few animals, such as cows, chickens, goats, and pigs, while continuing to work on the sugar estates in a seasonal capacity, thereby blurring the lines between wage earner and peasant. These two groups' self-sufficiency in agricultural and food production outside of the white-owned plantation structure gave them a small measure of independence that vexed the plantocracy. The fourth group abandoned agriculture altogether, joining the ranks of the colony's already notable urban Black population. They worked in trades—many enslaved Africans had been skilled artisans—and as domestics, porters, urban laborers, and petty traders.[43]

With the rise of oil production, many African-descended workers became primarily wage earners in this sector, forming a cornerstone of liberation unionism. With the first oil well drilled in 1865 and the first appreciable output for export in 1910, according to one British official, "the credit for one of the first successful oil wells in the world might fairly be claimed by Trinidad."[44] The oil sector drew on internal labor from agriculture as well as external labor from other British Caribbean colonies, as it provided a higher-paid employment alternative to laboring on a plantation. In addition to "unskilled" manual labor, other jobs in the oil sector included rig labor for drilling and production, rig builders, chauffeurs, firefighters, masons, molders, painters, other artisans, trades helpers, general laborers, pump operators, and pipe fitters.[45] Formal records list average number of persons employed per day in the sector at 1,194 men and 15 women in early 1914, which increased to 6,430 men and 71 women in 1930.[46] Employment in agriculture, by contrast, was about 40,000, according to the *Report of the West India Sugar Commission 1929–30* (Olivier Commission).[47] The specialized technological and foreign-owned enclave character of the industry produced an oil proletariat of significant consequence for the colony's development trajectory.

The oil fields were inhumane. While oil production and refining are capital intensive, they are most labor intensive during the initial phase of exploration, drilling, and construction of infrastructure, such as roads, pipelines, ports, and camps.[48] The reserves were located in the dense, remote forested areas of southern Trinidad. Often barefoot and without hard hats, working men and women in the early phases moved heavy equipment into the forests and wild bush, felled trees with axes, and dug and moved tons of soil with forks and shovels to construct well sites and miles of roadways. Between the dangers of nature (such as malaria, yellow fever, and venomous snakes) and the dangers of the technology (explosions, fires, accidents), the oil industry took many workers' lives.[49] Bigger towns were far away, roads were impassable, and there was no public transport. Rum shops became recreation centers for workers.[50] Oil towns that sprang up near the oil fields, such as Fyzabad, had "a reputation for seediness and tough public order policing; its poor housing and lack of amenities [were] inversely matched by the large numbers of unemployed laborers, prostitutes and street hawkers."[51] Under these living and working conditions, oil towns, agricultural estates, and urban areas became ripe for worker agitation.

Finally, the inter-Caribbean character of the Black working class in Trinidad and Tobago extended well beyond emancipation, as significant numbers of African-descended immigrant workers continued to stream into Trinidad. Laboring classes left other British colonies such as Jamaica and Barbados in the late 1870s to 1918 due to a number of forces, including intensified poverty linked to declines in the sugar industry, land privatization and dispossession, and a series of natural disasters. These workers were drawn to places that seemed to offer new opportunities and a stable livelihood, like Panama, Cuba, the United States, the United Kingdom, and Trinidad.[52] Trinidad's greater land availability and higher wages were particularly attractive, and with more oil sector and public works jobs, its economy was also less dependent on sugar than were other British Caribbean colonies.[53] Consequently, Trinidad and Tobago lost a comparably smaller proportion of its residents compared to other British Caribbean colonies in this period and instead was a destination for intra-Caribbean migration.[54]

Furthermore, Trinidad and Tobago's plantation owners hired foreign workers in a deliberate attempt to undercut local worker wages, create cleavages in the labor force, and prevent worker unity against employers. According to official numbers, which most certainly are an underestimation, approximately 10,278 immigrants from other British Caribbean colonies came to Trinidad and Tobago between 1839 and 1849, and up to 65,000 between 1871 and 1911.[55] To the plantocracy's dismay, the majority of Black Caribbean immigrants did not remain on the sugar estates for long; many became cane farmers, and the majority moved to the major cities, Port of Spain and San Fernando, and larger towns, working alongside and merging with the African locals in skilled crafts, the public sector, other urban occupations, and the oil industry.[56] The ongoing displacement and domination of people marked as Black long after emancipation created the conditions and shaped the subjectivities that fueled later mobilization.

Indian Workers

Indians, or the population who migrated from India and their descendants, comprised the second-largest group of racialized working people in colonial Trinidad and Tobago.[57] The plantocracy brought them explicitly to undercut Black labor and maximize profits after emancipation. As they did so, they imagined similarities and distinctions between Indians and Africans that served their own interests.

Insufficient labor for expanding sugar production and the refusal to employ and pay decent wages to the newly freed Black workers precipitated the plantocracy's turn to new sources of labor to superexploit.[58] That labor recruitment went hand in hand with the invention, flexing, and molding of racial categories to organize the colonial division of labor and justify their labor-extractive interests. Initially, European plantation owners maintained that Africans were the only people suitable for plantation work, but the supply of Black workers from other British Caribbean colonies was insufficient for the labor needs, and attempts to recruit free Black laborers from the United States and Canada failed.[59] The plantocracy and colonial state officials even considered bringing Africans from Sierra Leone.[60] Such was the dogged determination to continue superexploiting global Africans in the postemancipation period.

Chinese, Portuguese, and some other European laborers were also recruited.[61] But to Burnley, European immigrants were not suitable for plantation labor and should instead serve as superintendents because of their "superiority over the African race."[62] Similarly, the plantocracy came to see Chinese workers as an unsuitable replacement for Black labor, because, according to one official, "They are not habituated to it, nor will they take to it in the same way, nor can we force them by the same methods."[63] The "industrious" Chinese men and women, colonizers hoped, would form families and be "a free race of cultivators," cut cane, attend mills, and work as mechanics, and politically, they would form a "racial barrier" between the white and the African populations.[64] Regardless, these efforts were all largely unsuccessful because of several factors: too few numbers were recruited, many did not survive the treacherous journey and cruel plantation conditions, immigration costs were high, and there were negative optics associated with seeming to retain the enslavement of Africans in an era of liberalism.[65]

India became the most viable solution to the plantocracy's labor needs, and the first Indians arrived in Trinidad and Tobago in 1845. India was a British colony with a vast pool of labor, and transit costs were lower than from China. In 1844 the British government drew up plans for a system of Indian indentureship. As Eric Williams noted, the British invented new racial alibis to justify trafficking labor from far across the seas and keeping people in subhuman, semiservitude conditions to generate profits for the sugar industry.[66] On the one hand, they vilified Indians using the same terms they deployed for Africans and Amerindians—"liars, filthy in their habits, lazy."[67] At the same time, they also emphasized socially constructed differences that served the interests of capital. Burnley's racialization of Indians for plantation labor is encapsulated in his description of them: "a docile and intelligent class of laborers . . . to whom the climate would present no drawbacks and whose very prejudices of caste would keep them from combining with the slaves, who, so long as slavery should exist, would be always more or less disposed to revolt."[68] Thus, in addition to framing Indians as physically fit for sugar production, plantation owners like Burnley had hoped that investments in caste differentiation would perhaps overlap onto race and prevent Indians and Africans from coming together to overthrow the plantation complex. These Indians rebooted the sugar sector and inspired larger investments in the industry.

As enslaved Africans had experienced, the New World plantation system began to flatten ethnic and linguistic—as well as caste—differences among Indians. From 1845 to 1917, approximately 143,939 Indians were brought to Trinidad.[69] The vast majority came from the United Provinces, many within Oudh, and Bengal (including Bihar), Madras, and a few from Orissa, Chota-Nagpur, North Bengal, Assam, and other areas.[70] Of those brought between 1876 and 1917, 85.9 percent were Hindus, 14 percent were Muslims, and 0.1 percent were Christians. Of the Hindus, 40.5 percent were of "low caste," 31.5 percent "agricultural castes," 7.6 percent "artisan castes," and 16.8 percent "Brahman castes."[71] The majority of Indians spoke Hindi, but other languages included Bhojpuri and Urdu, as well as Tamil, Telugu, and Malayalam.[72] A Bhojpuri Creole evolved over time and became the lingua franca among the Indians in the late nineteenth and early twentieth century, and standard Hindi was used in religious services.[73]

While specific caste identities may have been retained or reconstituted in different ways, the caste system as it existed in India could never be fully transplanted. Caste in India was a hierarchical system of social relationships that was highly localized in the village context, linked to economic interdependence, occupational specialization, and an ontological continuum of relative purity and pollution.[74] On the sugar plantations of the Caribbean, Indian laborers from all over India were brought together as "coolies," regardless of their caste background, and their economic and social relationships were managed by white colonizers.[75] Plantation owners deliberately undermined caste hierarchies by handpicking lower-caste individuals as overseers of groups of higher-caste workers.[76] In addition, significantly more men than women were brought in, which eroded caste endogamy and contributed to high rates of violence against Indian women, including murder over alleged infidelity.[77] Brahmans retained a leading religious role as pandits but offered services that were previously reserved for their own to all, regardless of caste background.[78] As sociologist Narayana Jayaram makes clear, even though caste survived as a "socio-cultural idiom" of ideal ranking, as a "structural principle," caste "has no relevance to the structure of the wider society in Trinidad, and it has been dissolved as a functional socioeconomic form."[79] The plantation system transformed prior social relations.

In addition to importing Indian indentured workers to undercut African free labor on the sugar estates, the economic elite and colonial state created tensions between the two groups through a range of policies and practices. Indian indentureship was state subsidized through public funds generated by taxes on emancipated African workers. These funds financed the transportation of Indian laborers to Trinidad and back to India, the Office of Protector of Immigrants, medical services for indentured workers, and the repressive state apparatus for labor control.[80] In other words, African workers were paying to compete with Indian workers for their livelihoods. In addition, spatial segregation prevented the two groups from interacting. Africans were concentrated in urban areas and around the oil fields, and most Indians were confined to the sugar estates and rural Indian villages. Further, mutual cultural ignorance between Africans and Indians also caused tensions. Africans adopted the colonial attitude of favoring Christianity over Hinduism and Islam, for example, and Indians detested unions between Indian women and African men given the low numbers of the former in the colony.[81] These colonial divide et impera policies and prejudices contributed to antagonisms between the two groups.

Still, there is little evidence of direct conflict between Indians and Africans in the pre–World War I colonial period. According to Bridget Brereton, "There was no serious competition for jobs; estates continued to employ Creoles for factory work and for better-paid field tasks, and jobs here became more available when cultivation expanded between the 1850s and 1870s."[82] There were some cases of clashes between individuals and small groups of Africans and Indians, but given the long time span, they were infrequent and did not turn into large-scale violence.[83]

Despite the differential racialization of African and Indian colonial toilers, the colonial state and white elite assigned them a similar structural position in the economy, which served as the common material and experiential basis for the later emergence of liberation unionism. This workforce was brought together under the brutality of various unfree labor regimes, racialized and gendered oppression, and resource extraction. One governor lumped the Africans and Indians together as hopelessly doomed to labor: "They are not, neither Africans nor Coolies, fit to be placed in a position which the labourers of civilized countries may at once occupy. They must be treated like children—and wayward ones, too—the former, from the utterly savage state in which they arrive; the latter, from their habits and religion."[84] Thus, colonial officials and economic elites intended for both groups to occupy a similar role in the economy and a similar location in the social hierarchy. Those shared experiences set the conditions for the worker mobilization to challenge these interlocking oppressions.

Africans and Indians faced similar harsh working and living conditions. Whether rented or provided by employers, in the rural agricultural estates, oil

FIGURE 1.1. Barracks at Waterloo Estate, Trinidad, 1930s. *Source:* Copies of photographs supplied to the Trinidad Disturbances Commission, 1938–1939, UK National Archives, CO 950/826.

fields, and urban areas, the primary accommodations for working people were the dreadful barracks (see figure 1.1).[85] In fact, Indians moved into some of the same estate barracks that had housed enslaved Africans, suffered in similar unsanitary conditions, and were afflicted by the very same diseases and preventable deaths.[86] Indian women were also paid less than men and faced greater sexual violence along with gendered superexploitation.[87] Indian children also labored, doing tasks such as weeding, loading carts, leading oxen, carrying heavy objects, applying fertilizer, gathering cacao, picking coconuts, and performing domestic work and other dangerous and/or menial tasks. Well into World War I, children as young as seven years old were working as many as twelve hours a day, for pittances, and were denied a formal education.[88] Furthermore, even though employers could not legally flog or torture indentured workers, as they had done to enslaved Africans, coercion and racist violence remained integral to the postemancipation plantation system and wider social control. Estate managers and police routinely beat and whipped Indian workers. Imprisonment, fines, flogging, and other punishments were used as methods of labor control for both Indian and African workers.[89]

In addition, although Africans and Indians were mostly geographically segregated, there were some areas of interaction. Up through the war years, most of the Indian population lived on or close to estates and in rural villages and settlements. Fewer than one in four returned to India upon the abolition of indentured immigration in 1917, per their entitlement under the terms of the contract.[90] In lieu of return passage home, many Indians accepted plots of Crown lands near the estates from the colonial state, while others bought Crown land. Many of them became peasant proprietors and joined Africans in cane farming, with a smaller number in cacao.[91] By 1902 the number of Indian cane farmers approximately equaled the number of Africans, and by 1906 Indians exceeded Africans. African and Indian cane farmers experienced similar challenges, such as unfair prices for their canes. As such, they sometimes came together to voice their grievances against the sugar factories and management.[92] In addition, a few postindentured Indians became hucksters and shopkeepers, and a very small subset moved into urban areas. The shared conditions and racial subordination would serve as a common basis for a united movement of working people.

The Middle-Class Medley

While the vast majority of the laboring class was African and Indian up through the early 1900s, of equal importance is the notable social differentiation that emerged within the larger "nonwhite" population, especially after emancipation. By the turn of the twentieth century, the middle class was a medley of lighter-skinned "mixed" people, some Europeans, Chinese, Africans, and Indians. As future chapters show, apart from a handful of individual radicals who threw themselves into the worker movement, the middle strata tended toward conservatism and would not become a consequential political force until after World War II.

Like in so many multiracial societies, people intermixed and had children across racialized groupings. Of the various "mixed" persons in colonial Trinidad and Tobago, only the "coloreds" (people with any degree of both Black and white ancestry), specifically the free coloreds, had political salience as a group during the early years of British colonization. The free coloreds already outnumbered whites by 1765, and the 1783 Spanish Cedula attracted so many that by the 1830s Trinidad had the largest population of free coloreds in the English-speaking Caribbean.[93] Many acquired land, and some held enslaved people and established small estates in cacao, coffee, and provisions.[94] Still, they were not considered white. Their presence haunted the French and British colonizers with nightmares of the Haitian Revolution, aggravated no less by the fact that they were mostly republicans.[95] Under British domination, they were stripped of many of the rights and privileges they had enjoyed under Spanish law and faced a range of discriminations, such as subjection to a special curfew and tax on dances and public entertainments.[96] As we shall see in the next section, the British decision to institute Crown Colony rule was driven by the desire to prevent this group from voting. Further, many of them lost their estates in the 1840s and 1880s as larger plantation owners and companies amalgamated and consolidated smaller estates. They largely ended up alongside the slowly emerging Black middle class in the postemancipation period in white-collar jobs as teachers, journalists, lawyers, doctors, civil servants, and clerks.[97]

The middle class also included a group of whites who were mostly English or Scottish European-born and Creole, as well as some Irish and Italians who worked as overseers on estates, shop assistants, teachers, journalists, noncommissioned police officers, and artisans, as well as in printeries.[98] Portuguese and Chinese estate laborers, having been freed from their terms of indenture earlier than Indians, took up economic activities such as shopkeeping and other types of small-scale entrepreneurship.[99] Due to their association with estate labor, the European landed and business elite did not accept the Portuguese as white, but rather as a category distinct from European creoles and from the Africans and Indians.[100] In the late nineteenth and early twentieth centuries, Syrian and Lebanese groups also migrated to Trinidad and became small traders and shopkeepers.

Educated Black and mixed people formed the most sizable portion of the expanding middle class after emancipation, later joined by an emergent Indian middle class. Despite limited educational opportunities and facilities, the newly freed Black laborers placed greater emphasis on their children receiving schooling to keep them away from plantation labor. A Western/colonial education was essential to their rise in status. Without capital or political influence, it was the only thing distinguishing them from the masses. They became teachers, civil servants, clerks, and journalists, eventually moving into law and medicine.[101] For Indians, education and conversion on Christian missions was a path to becoming a Western-educated professional.[102] Furthermore, some Indians who had become landowners accumulated wealth by subletting their land and becoming creditors to Indian cane farmers.

The racist colonial structure of the territory stunted the desired upward mobility of these African and Indian middle-class colonial subjects in terms of income, employment (particularly in the civil service), and self-realization. As such, they deeply understood the plight of the racialized working class from which they came, and there were some individuals among them who expressed racial pride.[103] However, as Amílcar Cabral, C. L. R. James, Frantz Fanon, and Walter Rodney note, the local national and petty bourgeoisie in the colonies internalized and aspired to European ideals, in material terms and in status.[104] Likewise, in Trinidad and Tobago, they displayed their command of British culture with pride; emulated European racist and colorist values, norms, and practices; and ridiculed their darker-skinned, non-Christian, and poorer counterparts.[105] According to James, up until the 1940s, this middle class had been "quiet as mice," only organizing themselves occasionally "[to be] admitted to the ruling circle of expatriates and local whites."[106] Other than agitating for entry into and promotions within the civil service and constitutional reform in the 1880s and 1890s, this class largely set itself apart from working people.

The White Elite and the Colonial State Machinery

Beyond shared material conditions and lived experiences, the formation of the racialized working class in Trinidad and Tobago was also shaped by certain characteristics of the "white" or "European" elite themselves, the structure and ownership of the main industries, and a repressive colonial state built to deny the humanity of those deemed nonwhite.

The White Elite

The ruling class in colonial Trinidad and Tobago comprised Europeans and European-descended "white creoles." People of European descent always remained less than 10 percent of the total population between 1838 and 1950. By 1960 they represented only 1.9 percent of the population.[107] Even though they were numerically small, they were not a homogeneous group. The white elite consisted of three main segments. The first was the white creoles who were born in Trinidad and descended from mostly French but also Spanish, Irish, German, and some English "old families." The second was the British (mostly English and Scottish), who were primarily merchants and dominated the islands' import-export trade in goods and African people during slavery. Some were also plantation owners. The third group were British colonial administrators.[108] These ethno-national, religious, and linguistic differences—creoles versus expatriates, Spanish versus French versus English, Catholic versus Protestant—often became points of contention within this group. During British colonial domination, the French-British rivalry was the most pronounced of the rifts.[109] The French Creoles, a particularly close-knit, exclusive white ethnic segment of the population, resented the British officials, whom they perceived as displacing them from their aristocratic social superiority. They fought intensely over the introduction of British culture and institutions, such as the form of colonial rule, the constitution, religious schools, and English-language education.[110] According to Brereton, these antagonisms eased by the 1870s.[111] Still, the animosities never disappeared entirely, which, as we shall see, had significant consequences for how the colonial state responded to working-class mobilization.

The white population enjoyed a standard of living and social status above that of the racialized African and Indian masses, and they routinely referred to themselves as the "better class."[112] The spectacular plantation mansions of the white plantocracy, with well-manicured lawns, stood in obscene contrast to the working peoples' overcrowded and unsanitary barracks. Likewise, white foreign managers and staff received better company housing, services, and benefits than did the masses, like mosquito-proof bungalow accommodations replete with a domestic worker who would cook and clean. Recreational facilities, such as staff clubs and golf courses, were reserved for the white employees.[113] In Trinidad's oil sector, the drilling crews who came mainly from the United States and Canada received lavish salaries, which allowed them to order caviar and whiskey at the cost of eighty-four cents a bottle (almost two days' pay for a local laborer).[114] Managerial positions in the oil fields were dominated by white South Africans, whose racist practices stirred much ire among the oil workers.[115] The companies started training local Black workers as technicians in the 1920s, but the racism and salary gaps drove many of them (and many low-wage laborers) to Venezuela, where they were treated comparatively better as expatriates.[116] The racist organization of social and professional life in the oil fields, plantations, rural areas, and cities mapped onto great visible extremes of white wealth and African and Indian poverty.

The British Colonial State

The British colonial state, like the Spanish one before it, organized the colony to serve its own capitalist and imperial interests. The prewar colonial state was understaffed and underresourced, and lacked both the will and the capacity to enhance the welfare of the masses. Moreover, the colonial state's "rule of colonial difference" largely excluded nonwhite colonial subjects from the state administration.[117] Its structure, orientation, and policies created the conditions that facilitated expropriation and exploitation for capital accumulation and the general degradation of working people.

The European plantocracy and merchant class effectively controlled the prewar colonial state. The Spanish cabildo, or town council, was the earliest iteration of colonial administrative machinery. For about two hundred years after its establishment in 1592, just a handful of Spanish families, and later mostly French landowners, occupied cabildo positions. It was solely an advisory body; it could not make laws. Successive governors turned a blind eye to European abuses, as they were under constant threat of being overthrown for failing to please the ruling class.[118]

In 1831, more than thirty years after the British had seized the colony, they instituted a highly centralized and despotic form of domination that was sui generis—a Crown Colony. The retention of the cabildo and Spanish law (of which the British were largely ignorant) while simultaneously introducing new English-occupied courts created confusion and increased despotism.[119] Despite agitation by the plantocracy for internal self-government modeled on other British Caribbean colonies like Jamaica and Barbados with elected assemblies (based on limited franchise) with lawmaking powers, the British imperial government and colonial administrators adamantly refused. When the British arrived in Trinidad, they encountered a Spanish colony administered by Spanish laws with French landowners who dominated the economy and also largely occupied and controlled the state and cultural institutions, so much so that French Creole was the lingua franca. Furthermore, the free-colored population outnumbered whites.[120] Worse, in the eyes of the British, they owned property—both land and enslaved people—and they enjoyed relatively more legal and social privileges under Spanish law than in other British Caribbean colonies.[121] The perceived threat the free-colored population posed to the racialized economic order was captured in the words of the first British governor of Trinidad, Thomas Picton, who described the territory as "a country composed of such combustible material."[122] Thus, the British established Crown Colony domination in the territory to ensure imperial control relative to the non-British white colonial elites and, primarily, to deny the vote to otherwise qualified property-owning free coloreds.[123]

Under the Crown Colony system, the Crown ruled the colony through the secretary of state, who created and sent legislation for the colony from London directly to the governor; any locally generated legislation required the approval of the Colonial Office. The colony had a legislature and an Executive Council, but like the cabildo, these were advisory bodies that had no lawmaking powers.[124] The Crown Colony system was a novelty in British colonial administration but no less authoritarian in its relationship to the masses compared to other forms of colonial domination.

While, in theory, the Crown Colony system would enable colonial state autonomy from French and Spanish landed and business elites, in practice, the latter continued to wield power in the local councils, which, for the colonial toilers, meant a continuation of repression. Like the Spanish governors before them, British governors rarely went against the wishes of the local landed and business elite, because these unofficial council members could make their lives difficult, such as by voting to reduce the governor's salary or by appealing to the imperial government to intervene in their favor. Further, while the French and Spanish elite fiercely resisted the British Crown Colony system, they aligned with the British on the need for racialized labor exploitation, the superiority of white men, and white control of all economic, political, and social institutions. Many British colonial administrators owned land, managed estates, and held shares in commercial ventures. British officials on the councils showed considerable deference to plantation owners and merchants on the councils related to self-enriching taxes, duties, and expenditure on and relief to private industry.[125] Corruption, such as patronage and the sale of offices, permeated the institution.[126] Burnley, for example, who had amassed his initial wealth by using his position as *depositario* (officer for the administration of estates and minors) in the Spanish colonial state to plunder the widows and orphans fund, remained on the Legislative Council of the British colonial state.[127]

All of this, along with the repressive labor laws and the punishments—fines, incarceration, "preemptory imprisonment," whipping of juveniles and adults, and detentions for criminalized acts that offended employers—was rightly understood by workers as a state–elite collaboration to keep them in bondage.[128] Thus, even though ethno-national differences certainly shaped interpersonal relations among these whites, as a ruling class, they formed what Brereton describes as "a single power bloc."[129] Over time, this state–elite entanglement would continue to draw workers together into a unified front to challenge employers and the colonial state.

Furthermore, owing to its small size, limited infrastructural reach, and racially exclusive bureaucracy, the colonial state had neither the will nor the capacity to provide proper housing and basic health and social services to the masses. In 1840 the British abolished the cabildo and later replaced it with a mayor and town councils (later called borough councils) for Port of Spain and San Fernando. But just like the cabildo, these councils had neither the budget nor the personnel needed to perform their duties, such as collection of license fees and taxes on land and buildings, water and electricity distribution, sanitation, public works and drainage, cemetery maintenance, and other services.[130] In 1847 the colonial administration divided and subdivided the colony into divisions, counties, districts, and wards, and the governor appointed wardens with such duties as collecting taxes, arranging road repairs, enforcing sanitation regulations, maintaining public schools and paying teachers, and so on. However, these wardens were mostly members of the landed elite and largely uninterested and ineffective in their responsibilities.[131] As such, this small, underfunded state was mostly restricted to urban centers.

The colonial state did not assume any responsibility for providing proper housing for working people. The Indian and African colonial toilers either rented or got barrack housing from their employers as part of their contracts.

Despite numerous investigations and recommendations for a comprehensive government land settlement policy to alleviate these living conditions, land policy was the purview of the Legislative Council, which saw no need to improve housing and sanitation for working people.[132]

The British government and colonial state slowly developed a public education system funded by taxes after abolition in 1849, but access remained very limited and geared to colonial interests. A dual education system emerged with government schools and Christian denominational schools, both of which received government funding.[133] By 1914–15 there were 277 elementary schools, of which 54 were government primary schools, and 4 secondary schools, with most of them concentrated in urban areas.[134] Furthermore, since many African and Indian children were wage-earning workers, if they did enter primary school, they often left before completion. The proselytizing element in Christian schools also repelled many Indians.[135]

Health and welfare services were rudimentary. While the white elite could receive medical treatment in their homes or in the metropole, the Legislative Council resisted increasing health expenditure to provide better services to the masses.[136] In the years after emancipation, the colonial state constructed two hospitals (one in each of the major cities), an asylum to treat leprosy, a mental illness facility, and a small clinic for indentured workers. With the urban bias, ill people in rural areas had to trek long distances to access the hospitals or suffer in their homes. State-provided social security was virtually nonexistent, and welfare services were left to churches, charities, and philanthropists.[137] Up to 1916, the few that existed were largely available only to Port of Spain residents.[138] In sum, the colonial state provided very little to alleviate the strain of everyday life for working people.

British hostility to political representation increased local resistance to Crown Colony domination. Competitive examinations for the civil service were introduced in 1867, opening a path to middle-class status for educated Africans. However, as the number of Black entrants to the civil service increased, white civil servants organized to abolish the exam in favor of the governor's absolute discretion in appointments.[139] In addition, in 1898 British officials abolished the only avenues available to the African middle class to participate in elections and in public service—the town or borough council—and replaced it with an entirely governor-appointed board of commissioners.[140] While the civil service and town council largely affected Black and "colored" professionals, who made up a small group compared to working people, these actions nevertheless aroused the generalized discontent of the masses with British racism and authoritarianism.

Dependency and Peripheralization

The economic and social strains on working people were conditioned by Trinidad and Tobago's colonial status and dependent integration into the white capitalist system, which persisted long after the preeminence of slavery-based capital accumulation.[141] Periods of expansion and recession in the colony followed the metropolitan business cycles and hinged on the fortunes of the export products in European markets. These, in turn, affected the everyday lives of workers in Trinidad and Tobago.

Workers' lives and livelihoods were tightly bound to the international prices for Trinidad and Tobago's commodity exports. Sugar prices dropped in 1852 when the British imperial government abandoned its policy of exclusion and preferential duties, which had protected products from colonies, and again in the 1880s and 1890s due to competition from European beet sugar.[142] Furthermore, multiple cycles of depressions in Europe (1873–79, 1882–86, 1890–96, 1901–2) decreased demand for the colony's exports. In response, plantation owners cut production costs as much as possible to maintain profits, which included wage cuts and task increases.[143] They also modernized factory technologies, so much so that Trinidad and Guyana became widely recognized as technologically progressive.[144] The nature of work also changed as plantation and factory owners turned to cane farmers to externalize the risks of growing cane and further cut costs. With all these changes, laborers in sugar suffered underemployment and seasonal employment, low wages, higher workloads, late wage payments, and increased hardships.[145]

Restructuring also included the abandonment and amalgamation of smaller estates, which increased the concentration of British capital in sugar. As Howard Kimeldorf, Moon-Kie Jung, and others have argued, intense capital concentration enhances employers' capacity for self-organization and labor repression.[146] Throughout Trinidad's fifty-five years of plantation slavery (1783 to 1838), agriculture was based on small estates operated by a small number of enslaved Africans, in contrast to the advanced plantation complexes with dense populations like in Jamaica and Barbados. In addition, Trinidad and Tobago's agriculture was somewhat more diversified than the monocrop plantation economies of other Caribbean territories. Sugar plantations were the majority, but there were also substantial numbers of cacao, coffee, and cotton estates.[147]

Low sugar prices in the 1880s and 1890s squeezed smaller resident French creole sugar estate owners out of the sector, and giant British corporations and individual British proprietors took over. In 1871, out of 129 estates, 43 were owned by British companies and individuals residing in the United Kingdom, 43 by British or English creole residents, and 40 by French creoles. By 1895, out of 59 estates, 34 were owned by British interests, 20 by resident English, and only 3 by French creoles.[148] Moving into the twentieth century, the somewhat diversified European ownership in sugar had become decidedly British. Furthermore, the number of sugar plantations went from 206 in 1838, to 52 in 1896, to 32 (owned by ten companies) in 1936.[149] The consolidation of estates led to an increasing concentration of nonresident British capital in the local sugar industry. Decision-making became more centralized in the metropole and was driven by profit rates on a global rather than local scale. French plantation owners shifted from sugar to cacao, and with the boom in cacao prices between 1866 and 1920, fueled by increased British demand for chocolate, they prospered.[150] Trinidad became one of the world's three leading cacao exporters, alongside Venezuela and Ecuador, in the latter part of the nineteenth century.[151]

The development of the Trinbagonian oil sector was also driven not by the colony's needs but by the demand for fuel for the British Royal Navy. Navies were crucial to imperial expansion and economic dominance, including Britain's defeat of Napoleonic France in 1815 and its emergence as a global imperial hegemon. The British Admiralty sought to adapt, innovate, and expand its naval capabilities to maintain its position in the global capitalist system, particularly in response to the rise of rival powers in the late nineteenth century (Germany, the United States, France, Russia, and Japan).[152] In 1910 the British turned from coal, the main fuel for the British Admiralty between 1870 and World War I, to oil due to its higher calorific value and ease in refueling. Oil enabled smaller boiler rooms on ships, increased vessels' speed, and improved battle efficiency.[153]

A major challenge for the British was the minuscule oil supplies within the empire. All British Empire sources produced only 1.3 percent of the total world oil production in 1901, the most significant of which was in Burma.[154] Outside of Burma, most admiralty oil before 1910 was obtained from the United States.[155] As the global imperial oil-fueled naval race escalated, British fears about maintaining naval supremacy and its global hegemonic position intensified.[156] Despite its oil supply problem, when the German navy began using oil as an auxiliary to coal in 1910, Winston Churchill announced that same year that Britain would transition to solely oil-powered vessels. In a letter to Admiral Sir John Fisher, First Sea Lord from 1904 to 1910, Churchill wrote, "You have got to find the oil: to show how it can be stored cheaply: how it can be purchased regularly and cheaply; and with absolute certainty in war."[157]

Churchill's 1910 declaration made Trinidad and Tobago a focal point for British oil interests. It came just five years after the first appreciable oil output was extracted in Trinidad and Tobago. By 1914–15 ten foreign oil companies were recorded as actively operating in Trinidad.[158] The most significant of them in terms of production were Trinidad Leaseholds Limited (a subsidiary of a South African firm), United British Oilfields of Trinidad (a subsidiary of Shell), and Trinidad Central Oilfields. The colonial state charged no taxes in the form of export duties, and government royalty rates were a mere 10 percent on Crown lands (and 0 percent on privately owned land), plus there was the potential for even more reduced rates. One report noted that royalties in Burma and Assam were approximately double the Trinidad rates and that overall "there is no doubt about the leniency of the royalty rates hitherto demanded."[159] Likewise, one leading petroleum journal reported that oil investment in Trinidad was not "hindered by harsh obligations and burdensome royalties."[160] As Black radical thinkers and world-systems and dependency scholars have theorized and demonstrated, such concentration of ownership in foreign hands, combined with low taxation and royalties, facilitates the remission of profits abroad and the underdevelopment of colonies.

Crude oil extraction increased rapidly from the first 125,112 barrels in 1910–11 to crossing a million—1,050,112 barrels—in 1914–15.[161] The first refinery was built in 1912, and refined oil production also expanded as leases required a refinery for at least 50 percent of their crude output within two years, going from 11.6 percent of crude output in 1916 (107,822 barrels) to 89.14 percent in 1927 (4,796,223 barrels).[162] According to Trinbagonian writer Gérard Besson, "Trinidad became for all intents and purposes, a gas station in the South Atlantic."[163] Trinidad and Tobago became a strategic raw material supplier to the imperial center, meaning it provided a product that the British deemed essential to military and industrial requirements. Strategic materials are often nonrenewable, noncultivatable, and found in limited supply within the metropole's borders.[164] The importance of these products was also a source of worker power in these strategic dependencies, due to their potential to cut capitalists' profits and weaken empires.[165] In sum, the concentrated foreign capital and production for export and imperial interests were, for workers, sources of both economic woes and bargaining power.

Thus, by World War I, a complex multiracial milieu had been formed in Trinidad and Tobago. As table 1.1 shows, Africans and Indians comprised most of the population. Like their counterparts in other parts of the British Empire, racialized working people made every effort to carve out their own autonomous space of existence and thriving. "Everyday resistance," in the words of James Scott, was ubiquitous, including deliberate delays, false compliance, desertion of the plantations, theft, arson, various forms of sabotage, complaints against employers before magistrates, and occupation of Crown lands.[166] Larger-scale demonstrations were also visible, such as the Prison (1849), Belmanna (1876), Canboulay (1881), Hosay (1884), and Water (1903) protests.[167] The masses' audacity and capacity to organize and demand the end of subjugation consistently stunned the plantocracy and the British colonial state. However, these mobilizations often focused on specific issues, confined to particular locales, and were swiftly repressed by the colonial state.

Racial ideology legitimated the sorting of people into different kinds of work, justified different rates of exploitation, and prevented working people from uniting to mobilize. Several organizations emerged around the special disadvantages each racialized group faced. By far the most dominant institution serving the welfare of ordinary people before emancipation was community-led Friendly Societies. These were mutual aid and benefits organizations that raised funds for medical attendance, medicines, elderly health care, burials, maternity benefits, and yearly bonuses, and cultivated community ties at the local level.[168] Other organizations emerged to address the specific concerns of racialized groups. The East Indian National Association and the East Indian National Congress were established in 1897 and 1909, respectively, by the emergent Indian middle class to advocate for the end of Indian immigration and indentureship, the amelioration of conditions for the Indian population, and the retention and recognition of Indians' civil rights, for example, Hindu and Muslim marriages.[169] Indeed, toward the end of the nineteenth century, vibrant organizations were emerging to address the conditions and welfare of laboring people.

The first iteration of a labor organization was the Workingmen's Association (WMA), formed in 1894 in Port of Spain as a political pressure group to stir up public support for the borough council in a dispute over funding from the colonial government. The president, Sydney de Bourg, had been born in Grenada and was an ex–school principal, commissioner, and small cacao estate owner (through marriage to the owner—a Black woman). He devoted himself to rectifying, in his words, the "gross denials of justice particularly where the interests of the poor members of my race are in conflict with the rich and wealthy fair skin."[170] The organization attracted mainly skilled African workers, such as masons, carpenters, railway workers, and so on. By 1897 the WMA had about fifty members doing "skilled" and manual work, but the organization remained small and generally inactive for about a decade. The WMA was revived in 1906 in response to the colonial government's decision to form a nominated rather than an elected town board. That year, the members renamed the WMA as the Trinidad Workingmen's Association (TWA) and organized for political

TABLE I.I. Population of Trinidad and Tobago, 1911 and 1921

Country of birth	1911		1921	
	N	%	N	%
Trinidad (not of Indian descent)	140,708	42.18	159,236	43.50
British West Indies	51,874	15.55	50,705	13.86
Africa, China, Venezuela, etc.	8,673	2.60	8,803	2.40
Trinidad (of Indian descent)	59,535	17.85	84,066	22.97
India	50,585	15.16	37,341	10.20
Total Indian population	110,120	33.00	121,407	33.18
(by birth and descent)				
UK and colonies	1,428	0.43	2,372	0.65
Total population	333,552	100	365,913	100

Source: Ramesar, "Impact of Indian Immigrants," 7.
Note: The total population of Tobago was 20,749 (6.22 percent of the total population) in 1911 and 23,390 (6.40 percent) in 1921.

reforms, improved wages and working conditions for laborers, public health concerns, lower food prices and taxes for the working poor, and an end to indentured immigration. To the almost exclusively African members of the TWA, indentureship was a system of state-subsidized semislavery that drove down African workers' wages and increased poverty and unemployment.[171] This organization, small and fledgling up through World War I, would go on to become the dominant working-class organization in the colony during the interwar years and would have significant impacts on the colonial state and development.

Over time, a vibrant racial and class consciousness developed among African and Indian working people. Concentrated in the oil belt, on the sugar estates, and in urban areas, workers developed the ideologies, networks, and mobilization strategies to challenge capital and the state. These areas became hubs of strikes, protests, and labor uprisings that forced the state toward democracy and redistribution.

Conclusion

This chapter examined the formation of the racialized working class in the colonial period up to World War I, highlighting that the colonial state had neither the interest nor the capacity to provide welfare to the masses. It was not designed for this purpose. One mechanism for maintaining control in a context of labor repression and poor remuneration was the deliberate creation and fomentation of racial divisions. Capital, the imperial state, and the colonial state, embedded in the larger global ideological framework of white supremacy, constructed and deployed categories of Indio, African, West Indian, and Indian to justify their interests in capital accumulation in agriculture and oil. The Europeans conceived these categories specifically to turn one group against the other. As Moon-Kie Jung notes, the discourses and practices of both class and race "produce, institutionalize, justify, naturalize, contest, subvert, and otherwise relate to economic inequalities. . . . This overlap in relation to material inequalities allows class claims and practices to conjoin seamlessly with racial ones, and vice versa."[172] In the crucible of racialized working-class formation, workers began to consolidate life around these emerging racial identities. However, as Walter Rodney notes, the emphasis on racial identity can and does coexist with powerful upsurges of class consciousness.[173] The next two chapters focus on how these racialized groups in Trinidad and Tobago, unlike in many parts of the world, successfully overcame these divisions to create a united multiracial labor movement and how that movement pressured the state to develop the capability to provide broad social welfare.

2

The 1919 Uprising and the Emergence
of Liberation Unionism

It takes a very jaundiced eye to read a people's history as a record of undiluted compliance and docility.
—WALTER RODNEY, *A History of the Guyanese Working People, 1881–1905* (1981)

"Heave, heave," the dockworkers chanted as they surrounded the business premises of one shipping agent on the wharf where a strikebreaker had scampered in to hide.[1] It was December 1, 1919, and the dockworkers in Trinidad and Tobago had had enough. Since November 15, 1919, they had been on strike. Through the Trinidad Workingmen's Association (TWA), they had submitted a written list of demands to the principal shipping companies, which included a wage increase from two dollars a day to three dollars, a reduction of their work shift from nine hours to eight, and forty-eight cents per hour for overtime, with the amount to be doubled on Sundays and public holidays.[2] The shipping firms refused to recognize the TWA as the bargaining agent of the workers and rejected calls to negotiate, which prompted eight hundred stevedores to go on strike. For two weeks, employers and the colonial government rejected the workers' collective bargaining efforts and steadfastly refused to engage with the TWA.[3] The firms initially enlisted Venezuelans residing in the city and laborers from outer districts as strikebreakers and continued operations, despite workers' attempts to dissuade the replacement workers.[4]

On the morning of December 1, the dockworkers' frustrations with their employers and the colonial state erupted. They entered the wharf, forced the strikebreakers to leave the premises, confronted shipping agents at their office entrances, and marched through the streets of Port of Spain.[5] C. L. R. James, a teacher in the city at the time, reported that the dockworkers "patrolled the town, made business close down, and were at one time, in charge of the city."[6] One shop owner failed to comply with the crowd's order to close their premises, so the protesters broke the doors down.[7] The governor, frantic to contain the strike, dispatched constables to the wharf to arrest those who were preventing the strikebreakers from working. However, by the afternoon strikes had spread throughout the colony—to the oil fields, agricultural estates, the public sector, domestic work, and even the informal sector—lasting into January 1920. The strike wave was so forceful that the governor had to call for external force to crush it, ultimately provided by the warship HMS *Calcutta*.[8] For the first time in Trinidad and Tobago, there was a sustained and organized colony-wide general strike, and it catalyzed major reforms toward a more democratic and redistributive state.

Labor mobilization in Trinidad and Tobago in the interwar years was part of a broader global trend. The outbreak of World War I in 1914 resulted in immeasurable loss of life, extensive human suffering, and colossal physical destruction around the world. These conditions also intensified social upheaval. Indeed, what Beverly Silver describes as "the most striking feature" of her time series analysis of labor unrest over the twentieth century "is the strong interrelationship between waves of labor unrest and world wars."[9] In particular, 1919 to 1920 stand out as peak years of worker mobilization. From Mumbai to Boston, Canada to Chile to Argentina, Australia, China, Hawai'i, Italy, Sierra Leone, Senegal, the United States, and more, strikes in transport, steel, public works, textiles, and a variety of other industries enveloped the globe.[10] As the analysis in chapter 1 shows, the structure of capitalist development and patterns of proletarianization and racialization in Trinidad and Tobago provided the conditions for the formation of a racialized working class. But this level of analysis did not address how workers thought or acted consciously or collectively under those conditions.[11] In this chapter I show how the organization of social life, production, and workers' experiences linked to the foreign-dominated export-oriented economy, outlined in chapter 1, produced a specific kind of labor unionism—liberation unionism—in Trinidad and Tobago, one that effected development through its impacts on state structures.

The liberation unionism that the workers constructed differs from other forms of unionism previously described in labor studies. Business unionism refers to narrow workplace struggles for better wages and working conditions.[12] Political unionism is oriented toward alliances with political parties and incorporates demands for political participation and political reforms.[13] Social movement and social justice unionism expands these demands even further and links up with community organizations to advance improved conditions for the working class as a whole.[14] Liberation unionism, as it emerged in Trinidad and Tobago in the early twentieth century, was motivated by the lived experiences of the racialized colonized working people and rooted in historic Black freedom struggles; led by Black workers, it was an effort to mobilize workers and other constituencies for collective action to upend the interrelated oppressive structures and ideologies of racialized and gendered economic exploitation, colonialism, and imperialism that constitute capitalism and to promote the radical reconstitution of society and the global order.

Concretely, liberation unionism in Trinidad and Tobago exhibited three main characteristics: (1) it was inclusive along different sectoral and racial lines, as well as across gender lines; (2) it was internationalist, meaning rooted in Pan-African ideologies, organizational infrastructure, and Black diasporic struggle against imperial and colonial domination; and (3) it sought economic, political, and social transformation. Workers viewed their power to withdraw labor and collectively bargain as a primary tool in the struggle for Black liberation, and since the emancipation of all racialized toilers around the world was understood to be intimately bound to Black liberation, liberation unionism was the means to liberation for all.

Given the absence and illegality of unions in the colony, there are few grounds to expect that workers would have organized themselves into labor organizations. African workers could have turned to the Friendly Societies that were thriving in the late nineteenth and early twentieth centuries to make their demands on the colonial state. Indian workers could have organized through their cultural organizations. Instead, they turned to unionism. How did working people come to recognize unions as the primary organizational vehicle for representing the interests they believed they shared? How did they express their grievances and make their claims to employers and the colonial state? To what extent were they successful in achieving their demands, and why? These are all questions that motivate this chapter.

The precise meaning of *liberation* in liberation unionism reflects a terrain of contestation within the movement. As many scholars have noted, multiple Black liberation ideologies exist, such as integrationism, socialism, Black feminism, and Black nationalism, the latter in itself comprising Black separatism and Pan-Africanism.[15] As political scientist Michael Dawson notes, "Taking to arms versus using 'legitimate' politics, protesting versus voting, and looking towards socialism versus capitalism have all been seriously considered as viable options by many blacks throughout the centuries-long quest for black freedom, justice, and self-determination."[16] The heterogeneity of positions on the "right" vision of and road to Black freedom has both enlivened and divided Black worker movements around the world, and Trinidad and Tobago is no exception. The concept of liberation unionism advanced here does not aim to flatten these variations. This book recognizes this diversity, and the way these visions and strategies sometimes compete and sometimes overlap, while aiming to pinpoint how the precise expressions of liberation unionism may shift depending on the context.

As a concept, liberation unionism is bound by specific parameters. Following George Fredrickson's study of the ideologies of Black protests in his text *Black Liberation*, I do not refer to resistance by enslaved workers or colonized people against the original imposition of European imperial hegemony, or to military resistance. Although working people obviously carried forward knowledges, tools, and strategies of resistance that were developed and refined in the crucible of plantation slavery and indentureship in the colonial context, liberation unionism refers to the specific kinds of organizing developed when workers had some formal right to make their grievances known. After the enslaved won legal freedom, their new status came with some formal recognition, minimal entitlement, and standing, however infinitesimal, and was the basis on which more worker demands were made. In addition, the term *liberation* as an adjective to describe unionism might evoke reference to liberation theology. There are obvious ontological and political corollaries between the two. In addition, religious leaders, institutions, and symbolism certainly played a role in fostering the emergence of liberation unionism, especially in the absence of formal legal unions. However, working people were the vanguard and constituency in liberation unionism, and they specifically sought to build labor organizations as a vehicle for social change.

In this chapter I also discuss ruling-class efforts to suppress liberation unionism in the interwar years. The white economic and colonial administrators had entrenched interests in preserving the more-than-hundred-year-old system of extracting superprofits from racialized labor in plantation production and resource extraction and felt a sense of racial superiority over them. The liberation unionism movement challenged the hierarchical and oppressive social order, punctured the profits of the white plantation-merchant and foreign capitalist class, destabilized the colonial state, and had the potential to undercut and weaken the British imperial system. As such, they sought to crush liberation unionism and the uprisings that threatened their material interests and their relative social position.

However, certain political openings facilitated the growth and expansion of liberation unionism and the winning of concessions. The repressive capacity of the state was not commensurate with the force of the worker movement. Ethnic fractionalization within the white colonial population weakened the unity of the ruling class on the question of repression. Perhaps most important, Trinidad and Tobago occupied a position of strategic importance to the British Empire during the war and interwar years as an oil supplier to the British navy. I show how despite the attempts of the white economic elite and colonial state to destroy the movement, the coalescence of these factors compelled the ruling elite to negotiate with the workers and concede to several of their demands. Consequently, in the decade following the 1919 general strike, the colonial state underwent its first-ever wave of institutional reforms geared toward enhancing relative state autonomy from the white economic elites, increasing state bureaucratization and reach, and opening political participation to a greater portion of the population.

I begin this chapter with the conditions leading up to the general strike of 1919. I pinpoint the features of liberation unionism that contributed to its success in forcing the colonial state to undergo the institutional changes needed to promote more equitable development. I also discuss how workers further developed and fostered liberation unionism through the 1920s and early 1930s. My overall argument is that the emergence and consolidation of this form of unionism in the interwar years, with its specific characteristics and orientations, had a lasting impact on the long-term development outcome in Trinidad and Tobago.

Prelude to the 1919 General Strike

The working class's conditions during World War I (1914–18) embodied the contradictions of capitalism that create the potential for worker mobilization and collective action. The economy prospered during the war, in terms of production, exports, and revenue. As table 2.1 shows, the value of total exports increased from £4,201,341 in 1914 to £5,149,579 in 1918; the amount that was locally produced increased by about 43 percent.[17] According to one colonial annual report, the trade conditions were "fairly prosperous," owing to the "high prices ruling for the principal products of the colony, viz., cacao, coconuts, copra, rice, maize and sugar and its by-products, molasses and rum."[18] From 1914 to 1918, colonial government revenue rose by about 25 percent, and surpluses of assets over liabilities were recorded in 1917 (£124,821) and 1918 (£173,263).[19] With respect to oil, imperial demand for fuel oil for the Royal Navy increased during the war. By 1918 twelve oil companies were operating in the colony.[20] The number of oil wells drilled jumped from 239 in 1914–15 to 410 in 1918, and oil production tripled over the same period.[21] By 1918 Trinidad had become the second-largest annual oil producer in South America after Peru.[22] The Trinidad colonial state received £18,314 for operations on Crown lands in 1918.[23]

However, as private capital and the state reveled in increasing wealth, the standard of living of the masses declined. Inflation skyrocketed. By 1919 the cost of living index was 126 percent higher in Port of Spain than before the war, 167 percent higher in San Fernando, 140 percent higher in rural districts, and 171 percent higher in Tobago.[24] A 1918 report states, "While trade generally was fairly satisfactory, the year was a difficult one for the large majority of the population, and particularly for the laboring classes."[25] Due to "the high level of prices of both imported goods and locally grown foodstuffs," the report continued, "and as there was little corresponding increase in wages, the high cost of living was severely felt."[26] In 1919 even the governor admitted that "the poorer classes" were "experiencing great hardships in maintaining themselves and their families."[27] Deprivation was widespread among the working people.

The economic pressure of the war years was further exacerbated by unemployment and the unabated racialized repression meted out by the capital-state alliance. Soldiers who had volunteered to fight for the British in the war faced not only racism and degradation abroad during their service but also ridicule and economic exclusion when they returned home, and they were not given the remuneration and benefits promised to them by the British.[28] Further, Indian indentured immigration ended in 1917, largely due to strong opposition in India, but also locally, and to transportation difficulties stemming from the war.[29] As had happened to newly emancipated Africans some years earlier, the plantocracy and colonial state devised new repressive methods of keeping Indians tied to and dependent on the plantation. The 1918 Habitual Idlers' Ordinance, which imposed punishments such as imprisonment with or without compulsory labor on a person deemed able to work but who "habitually abstains from

TABLE 2.1. Major Exports, 1914–1936

	1914	1918	1936
Total number of oil wells	239	410	2,416
Petroleum exports (gallons)	12,153,784	40,856,298	434,182,775
Petroleum exports (£)	64,735	400,610	3,314,716
Sugar exports (tons)	48,088	35,104	142,671
Sugar exports (£)	591,193	811,068	1,276,579
Cocoa exports (lbs)	63,447,876	58,638,562	28,339,136
Cocoa exports (£)	1,469,893	1,547,085	487,578
Total value of exports (£)	4,201,341	5,149,579	6,236,362
Total value of locally produced exports (£)	2,484,576	3,559,201	5,609,390
Revenue (£)	934,524	1,172,700	2,616,732

Sources: Great Britain Colonial Office, *Trinidad and Tobago Annual General Report for the Year 1918*, 11, 14, 15, 19, TNA, CO 295/522; Colony of Trinidad and Tobago, *Mines Department: Report of the Inspector Mines for the Year 1915–15*, 4; Colony of Trinidad and Tobago, *Mines: Administration Report of the Inspector of Mines for 1918*, 2; Colony of Trinidad and Tobago, *Mines: Administration Report of the Inspector of Mines and Petroleum Technologist for the Year 1936*, 3; Great Britain Colonial Office, *Trinidad and Tobago Report on the Blue Book for 1914–15*, 10, 14, TNA, CO 295/499/44; Colony of Trinidad and Tobago, *Trinidad and Tobago Blue Book 1936*, 47, 391, 623; Mercer, Collins, and Harding, *Colonial Office List for 1920*, 407; Harding and Gent, *Dominions Office and Colonial Office List for 1938*, 481.
Note: Conversion after 1934 at BWI $1 = 50 pence.

work," was designed to prevent Indians from moving into the cities to find nonagricultural work.[30] These conditions heightened the climate of agitation.

Economic despair and grievances are an important determinant of worker mobilization, but as social movement theorists emphasize, material interests do not automatically generate collective action. Aggrieved groups must "fashion shared understandings of the world . . . that [help] legitimate and motivate collective action."[31] Further, collective action requires an organizational infrastructure that can facilitate mobilization. In the years immediately preceding the 1919–20 labor uprising, workers were increasingly organizing, but they achieved limited success. In February 1917 the mostly African oil and asphalt workers went on strike for several days after two British oil companies denied their request for wage increases.[32] In early 1919 several petitions and spontaneous strikes emerged in separate sectors, including among railway and dockworkers, workers at the Waterworks and Sewage Department of the Port of Spain Borough Council, civil servants, and workers at a rice mill and local match factory.[33] In these cases, repression by both the government and the companies was swift and brutal. In response to the oil and asphalt strike, the colonial state deployed ex-soldiers from the British West Indies Regiment and arrested and sentenced strike leaders. The oil companies threatened to fire the workers and evict those who lived in company barracks, all of which forced workers back to work.[34] Worker discontent was brewing, but at this time it lacked coordination and planning.

While workers seemed to be losing the struggle for a better quality of life, there was at least one major success. The Trinidad Workingmen's Association (TWA), as mentioned in chapter 1, originally formed in 1894 as a political pressure group to advocate for working-class interests and self-determination, had heretofore been a fledgling organization.[35] For the duration of World War I, the organization was embroiled in internal strife. A conservative faction led by Alfred Richards (then president) saw the TWA as a political organization and focused largely (albeit sluggishly) on nonconfrontational campaigns for political reform for a more representative government. Conversely, a radical wing led by John Sydney de Bourg pushed for labor unionism, greater militancy from the rank and file, and the use of strike action to improve the standard of living.[36] For years, the organization functioned as two groups conducting their own affairs under the same umbrella, with the radical group attracting more and more support due to its focus on workers' immediate needs.

By the 1917 TWA elections, rank-and-file support enabled the radicals to win control of the TWA executive, ushering in dockworkers David Headley and James Brathwaite to the presidency and the position of secretary, respectively. Under this new leadership, the TWA passed unanimous resolutions in March 1919 to make representations on behalf of any group of workers and to accept applications from groups of workers seeking membership.[37] In effect, the organization decided to actively support workers on strike. To rectify the lack of organization of the 1917 asphalt workers' strike, in May 1919 the TWA established a branch in La Brea, a small town in the colony's oil belt, and immediately started organizing. That same month, the TWA represented workers in negotiations with the asphalt company and successfully secured a 33.3 percent wage increase, a one-hour reduction in the length of the working day, a 150 percent increase in overtime rates, and a commitment from the company to improve housing conditions and provide plots of land for vegetable gardens.[38] This win was crucial for demonstrating to the working people the benefits of the TWA and trade unionism. From March to November 1919, the TWA concentrated on organizing waterfront workers and other laborers in Port of Spain, leading to the effervescence of the worker mobilization that I call *liberation unionism*. The following pages describe the distinct features of the liberation unionism that emerged in 1919 and its development over the 1920s and early 1930s.

The Anatomy of Liberation Unionism

The characteristics of liberation unionism made it not only a force to be reckoned with but a movement that pushed the colonial state toward a developmental agenda: it was united across sectoral lines and racial divisions and involved racialized women workers; it was internationalist in terms of its Pan-African character; and the demands went beyond narrowly defined union-member issues and advocated for economic, political, and social transformation in the colony of Trinidad and Tobago.

Inclusiveness

DIFFERENT SECTORS. In liberation unionism, workers were united across economic sectors. The 1919–20 strikes involved the workers in the most economically important sectors in the colony—docks, oil, and sugar. Consistent with theories of worker power, these workers held significant structural power stemming from their essential roles in the "commanding heights" of the economy and in tightly integrated production and trade processes.[39] The dockworkers' strike in November and December, which involved male stevedores and female coal carriers, placed a severe strain on the island's import/export trade and interrupted coal supplies to the colony's railways and the fueling of steamships. Oil and asphalt workers at multiple companies went on strike, disrupting production for British interests.[40] In the agricultural sector, the unrest involved laborers on sugar and cacao estates across Trinidad and Tobago.[41] According to the *Trinidad Guardian* newspaper, these sugar workers' strikes gave the "authorities grave cause for alarm."[42] These estates were not concentrated in particular areas but rather spanned the northern, southern, and central regions of Trinidad and Tobago. Thus, the movement was truly a colony-wide uprising that threatened to cripple the major economic sectors, thereby grabbing the attention of the economic elite and the colonial state.

Government workers also participated in the 1919–20 movement. Within days of the stevedores' strike, people working for the city council, the Public Works Department, and the Water and Sewerage Department in both Trinidad and Tobago went on strike and submitted claims for higher wages, bonuses, and/or adjustments of working hours through the TWA.[43] These laborers included waste sorters, cart carriers, night and day sweepers, fitters, and penmen.[44] Lower-ranking civil servants also pressed for a war bonus.[45] As an employer itself, the colonial state was compelled to respond.

The general strike also empowered working people in the informal sector, which contributed to the disruption in the whole colony. For example, the mostly Indian charcoal vendors refused to sell at the established low government fixed price, and some even inflated their prices, thereby interrupting the city's charcoal supply.[46] Striking Indian laborers also prevented the city from receiving fodder provisions for the early markets by blocking Indian grass cutters from transporting and delivering grass on their donkey carts.[47] The extensiveness of the movement made it impossible to ignore and difficult to crush.

This multisectoral feature of the 1919 uprising became institutionalized in the TWA throughout the 1920s. According to most historians of the period, the TWA engineered the strikes involving dockworkers in Port of Spain and asphalt workers in La Brea, but it is less clear that the organization directly organized workers in other areas.[48] Workers outside of these two locations mostly organized themselves and flocked to the TWA after they had already gone on strike. The TWA attracted such a wide range of workers due to its grassroots organizing strategies, evidence of victories, and a broad definition of worker that encompassed everyone from "'professional men' to the ordinary casual laborer."[49] Membership in the TWA boomed as workers from various sectors submitted applications to join.[50] Kelvin Singh notes that by 1925 the TWA had seventeen occupational sections: "waterfront workers, porters, shipwrights, ironworkers, transport workers, domestic servants, clerical workers, clerks [sic], printers, tailors, seamstresses, workers in gold and silver, agricultural laborers, general laborers, railway workers and casual workers ... [and] a separate women's section."[51] The TWA's membership went from two hundred in 1909 to ten thousand in 1919, just ten years later.[52] By the early 1930s, membership stood at seventy thousand, according to one estimate.[53] The number of branches increased rapidly from thirteen in 1924 to fifty-four in 1928 and covered both urban and remote rural areas.[54] Between 1919 and the early 1930s, the TWA was the only trade union (though not yet legally allowed) in the colony. It united and represented workers in a range of industries and dominated the political landscape.

The 1919 general strike relied on and empowered people at the community level. In fact, in working-class areas during this time, the workplace-community distinction was not as pronounced as it is today. As Robin Kelley notes, what contemporary "social movement unionism" scholarship might characterize as a recent phenomenon or "new" feature of postindependence newly industrializing countries appears in earlier periods of labor organizing.[55] The success of many strikes in the United States in the late nineteenth century, for instance, often depended on the fact that communities—that is, families, friends, and sympathetic organizations—were also mobilized and sided with the strikers and supported the unions. Similarly, in Trinidad and Tobago in the early twentieth century, workers and unions took up workplace issues *and* fought for improved conditions in working-class and poor communities (the specific demands are discussed later in this chapter). The TWA coordinated campaigns with several Friendly Societies and literary/debate clubs on labor-related issues, such as the petition for the repeal of the 1918 Habitual Idlers' Ordinance, which was signed by about two thousand persons, including Miriam Lord (a seamstress), James Smart (a baker in Port of Spain), and the entire membership of the TWA.[56] Such collaborations persisted well into the 1930s.[57] In 1919 organizers gave speeches in public squares, through which they garnered the sympathies of the unemployed.[58] Other general community members also joined in support of the workers and made demands of their own around the high prices of goods and services. For example, a group of theatergoers demanded a reduction in the price of admission to watch motion pictures in a theater in San Fernando.[59] In sum, workers in the private and public sectors; independent, self-employed workers; and community members were united in the movement and coalesced as one in the TWA.

MULTIRACIAL UNITY. The liberation unionism that was birthed in the 1919–20 movement was also multiracial. As chapter 1 showed, economic sectors were racially differentiated. The multisectoral mobilization was therefore also multiracial as the mostly African workers in the ports, urban areas, and oil sector struck alongside the predominantly Indian sugar workers. But to imply that the movement was multiracial only because racially differentiated sectors struck simultaneously would be inaccurate and overlook the agency of workers in forging racial unity. Moon-Kie Jung defines interracialism as "the ideology and practice of forming political community across extant racial boundaries" and argues that it does not require de-emphasizing racial identity.[60] The TWA, both at its inception and throughout its time as the dominant working-class organization, was well known as having mostly Black membership and leadership. Still, the union engaged in interracialism and institutionalized Indians in leadership positions, which helped facilitate the expansion of Indian membership in the TWA.

The TWA's organizers, particularly the Indian ones who were also active in cultural organizations, such as the East Indian National Congress (EINC) and East Indian National Association (EINA), played a key role in drawing Indian workers into the union. Many studies have shown that the working class's capacity to achieve its objectives is linked to alliances with other classes or organizations, such as the peasantry, petty bourgeoisie, and community organizations. As Amílcar Cabral and other Black radicals predicted, the majority of petty bourgeois Indian leaders who comprised the leadership of the

EINA and EINC did not engage in "class suicide" and thrust themselves into identification with the working class and service to the liberation struggle.[61] Instead, they issued a declaration advising the Indian laborers to return to work.[62] However, most Indian workers disregarded these leaders and flocked to the predominantly Black TWA, which embraced them.[63]

Only a couple of EINA and EINC leaders stand out as exceptions whose commitment to advancing the worker movement and efforts to help the TWA further attract Indian workers were indispensable for building a multiracial movement. One was Hindu proprietor C. B. Mathura (formerly Chandra Bahadoor, he changed his name to Charles Bliss and went simply by C. B.). He had been vice president of the East Indian Destitute League (EIDL), founder of the Young Indian Party in 1921, editor of the *East Indian Weekly* newspaper, and secretary of the EINC in 1922 and 1930; he was also an energetic TWA member and vice president of the Port of Spain clerks section.[64] Another was Adrian Cola Rienzi (formerly Krishna Deonarine). Rienzi's involvement in labor politics began in 1921 when he was sixteen years old, and in 1925 he was elected president of the San Fernando TWA branch. He also served on the executive of the EINA and proposed the formation of an East Indian National Party and Young Socialist League.[65] Throughout the 1920s and 1930s, Mathura and Rienzi presided over mass meetings, including on sugar estates, in attempts to recruit Indian workers to the TWA.[66] For these organizers, the development of a shared Indian identity did not conflict with building working-class consciousness. They played crucial roles in building the interracial and multisectoral character of liberation unionism.

A third notable figure was Mohammed Orfy, a Muslim merchant and president of the EIDL. Orfy wrote articles in *Argos*, a leading radical newspaper at the time that was closely affiliated with the TWA, about the brutal system of indentureship and the need to repatriate Indians.[67] There is also evidence of Orfy collaborating with organizer George F. Samuels in Tobago.[68] These Indian organizers, through their work and their leadership roles in both Indian-centered organizations and the TWA, served to bridge Indian and African workers and expand the union.

The organization even welcomed one radical white activist into its fold. Arthur A. Cipriani, the son of a white Corsican planter, joined the organization in August 1919 and served on the Management and Executive Committees in 1921. Widely considered to be a champion of working-class people, Cipriani was elected TWA president in 1923, a role he held until his death in 1945.[69]

Beyond the Indian interlocutors, African workers in the TWA also explicitly and intentionally attempted to recruit workers across other ethnic and geographic boundaries. For instance, the striking stevedores encouraged the Venezuelan strikebreakers to become members of the TWA, even going so far as to pay the membership fees for them to join.[70] They also chartered motorcars to travel to where shipping companies were recruiting these men to try to induce them not to engage in strikebreaking.[71] In sum, racial divisions were not insurmountable, as many labor scholars tend to assume. Workers toiled to build solidarities and increase union membership across industrial and occupational sectors as well as racial lines.

WOMEN. Liberation unionism in Trinidad and Tobago was also inclusive of women workers, which was crucial to the movement's success. Black working-class women, in particular, and children were central to the movement. The scholarship on the centrality and leadership of Black women workers in liberation movements across the world is well established.[72] As work by historian Rhoda Reddock demonstrates, this pattern is also found in Trinidad and Tobago. Black women workers enabled liberation unionism to grow in size and militancy, to take seriously the specific issues affecting African and Indian working women and children, and to deepen the ties between the union and communities.

From the outset, women were on the front lines of the 1919 movement and the formation of liberation unionism. The women coal carriers on the wharf, of both African and Indian descent, were among the earliest to go on strike in December 1919, demanding a pay increase from eighty cents a day to one dollar and expressing their intent to join the TWA.[73] Several witness reports described the presence and active involvement of women and children as strikers and protesters.[74] In the crowds of union members and supporters, the *Trinidad Guardian* newspaper reported, "Not a few of them [were] womenfolk."[75] One report on the Tobago Public Works Department strike noted that "the men were armed with sticks, women were included and were the greatest agitators and opponents of peace."[76] Women were also among those who were wounded by the police who fired into the crowd at that strike, including two domestic workers—twenty-two-year-old May McKenzie and seventeen-year-old Albertha Critchlow.[77] Among the thirteen persons arrested in this strike, five were women.[78] One police officer testified about women's involvement in the sugar estate strikes as follows: "On my way [to Perseverance Estate] I met Theophilus Bute and many other people, about one thousand strong, some of them had sticks in their hands. It was a rather excited crowd. . . . I saw some women standing. Rhoda Ottley was one of them. . . . On the way to the station, I heard a woman saying: 'Mr. Hart must dead to-day,' and a man said: 'I am going for a stick.'"[79] Women's active involvement in the strikes undoubtedly enlarged the size and militance of the movement.

Beyond strike participation, women's involvement in the TWA also broadened the scope of struggle and increased multisectoral unity. Pan-African Marxist feminists such as Claudia Jones highlight how Black women face "triple exploitation" or "triple oppression"—racialized, gendered, and class-based superexploitation—on account of their structural location in a global capitalist system constituted by white supremacy, patriarchy, state terror, imperialism, colonialism, and fascism.[80] Into the early twentieth century, Black women remained concentrated in domestic work, exploited at the expense of their own families, abused and degraded, and ignored by even the most progressive labor organizations, namely, the Communist Party (US).[81] The TWA, however, had an early commitment to domestic workers. According to Reddock, "The [TWA's] very broad concept of 'worker' facilitated the large-scale mobilization and organization of women including domestic servants, petty trades, housewives and the self-employed."[82] These women advanced both general working-class concerns, such as wages and retrenchment, and issues affecting women specifically, such as the need for more humane conditions for imprisoned women.[83] Albertha Husbands, for instance, was the head of the TWA Domestics Section and organized cooks and household workers. In the 1919 disturbances, she was accused of advocating that domestic workers poison their employers and was threatened with deportation to her home of Barbados.[84] Regardless of the truth of the matter, the colonial state's reaction illustrates the white population's great fear of domestic worker mobilization, which is another reason women in the TWA were crucial to liberation unionism's success.

As the union developed in the 1920s, women were central to expanding the TWA to all corners of the colony, thereby linking the union with communities. They organized, led, and ran women's sections in the capital city and throughout the colony.[85] These sections engaged in fundraising and social work and organized events for union and nonunion members alike, such as Labor Day and Emancipation Day celebrations.[86] A juvenile section, founded in 1935 by Randolph Mitchell of the St. James Section, was led by Miss W. Phipps and held regular concerts and dance performances that were open to the general public.[87] Without the involvement of these working women, the 1919 unrest and liberation unionism would not have been as expansive in numbers or as broad based in its demands.

The inclusive, united nature of the unionism in Trinidad and Tobago, which successfully embraced workers from different economic sectors, racialized groups, men, women, and children, led to a formidable colony-wide movement. In the aftermath of the agreement between shipping companies and the stevedores, the TWA secretary addressed the large crowd of workers and their supporters, numbering some two thousand people, and urged them to stick together and show their unity to the public. The crowd chanted and cheered in response: "We will, we are."[88] This unity was expanded throughout the 1920s and early 1930s, and the TWA reigned in the hearts and minds of working people as the sole organization representing their interests. With so many workers directly involved, and sympathizers spread throughout the colony, it was difficult for the colonial state and economic elite to ignore the workers' demands.

Internationalism

Sympathy, support, experience, aid: these are but a few of the resources to be gained from connections with allies outside of one's geographic borders that can bolster working-class capacity, according to Black radical thinkers as well as other labor scholars.[89] From India to South Africa to Hawai'i and many other parts of the colonized world, communism served as a powerful mobilizing ideology, and communist organizations provided operational structures and created transnational linkages that furnished local worker struggles with technical expertise, financial resources, and other forms of support.[90] In Trinidad and Tobago, communist periodicals circulated in the colony, and some individual labor organizers connected with Black Bolshevism and the Communist International (Comintern). But even as authors such as Margaret Stevens have highlighted how critical local radicals were to the global development of Communism between the World Wars, they also acknowledge that Comintern never achieved a substantive organizational presence or ideological embeddedness among working people in the colony.[91] Further, the Comintern later reneged on its support for Black liberation in the 1930s, leading prominent Pan-African Marxist revolutionaries such as George Padmore to break with the organization.[92] The conservative TWA leaders in the pre-1914 period bore a close affinity to the British Labour Party, but that party generally ignored the smaller nonsettler colonies and confined its role to serving as a conduit to bring working-class concerns from the colonies to the House of Commons for discussion.[93] Pan-Africanism, particularly Marcus Garvey's Pan-African project, was by far the most significant transnational political formation that shaped liberation unionism's emergence in 1919 and subsequent propagation in the interwar years. It served as the main mobilizing discourse, organizational infrastructure for resource circulation, and source of organizing expertise for liberation unionism in Trinidad and Tobago, along with additional diasporic circuits of Black resistance.

MARCUS GARVEY'S PAN-AFRICANISM. Pan-Africanism generally involves ideas, organizations, and movements concerned with the economic, political, social, and cultural emancipation of global Africans and is underpinned by the belief that global Africans have a shared history, purpose, and destiny and should unite for their collective advancement.[94] Among the various streams of Pan-Africanism that emerged in the early twentieth century, such as the New Negro movement (more commonly called the Harlem Renaissance) and W. E. B. Du Bois's Pan-African Congresses, Marcus Garvey's movement most profoundly shaped African workers' and labor organizers' visions and discourse of liberation in Trinidad and Tobago. Garveyism inspired race consciousness and, in a creative and pragmatic manner, was the discourse through which race consciousness was linked up with class consciousness. Further, its anti-imperial and anticolonial elements facilitated multiracial movement building.

Born in Jamaica in 1887, Marcus Garvey led what was arguably the largest international organized mass movement of global Africans in the twentieth century.[95] Through his organization, the Universal Negro Improvement Association (UNIA), headquartered in Harlem and with branches and divisions around the world, Garvey spread ideas of Black racial pride, unity, self-determination, anticolonialism and anti-imperialism, and the liberation of all global Africans. In Garvey's heyday (from 1919 until his imprisonment in 1925), his Black nationalist ideas took hold among the local population, including TWA members.[96] C. L. R. James, who played cricket regularly with some of the 1919 strike leaders, noted that he was "positive that they were Garveyites."[97] Seafarers and returning soldiers brought in Garvey's *Negro World* publication despite the colonial state's ban, and it was read aloud in TWA meetings.[98] Members of the UNIA, such as C. Leo Langton, traveled to Trinidad and Tobago in August 1919 and gave lectures, which were well attended.[99]

Through Garveyism and Pan-Africanism more broadly, workers mobilized around a shared identification with the racial struggles of oppressed Black people around the world. Huge crowds of the urban Black working population came out to listen to the lectures of Pan-Africanists like Felix Eugene Michael Hercules (who was born in Venezuela, grew up in Trinidad, and moved to England).[100] Hercules rejected some of Garvey's major tenets, but he shared a desire to promote international Black racial solidarity and Black economic and political advancement. The *Argos* periodical welcomed him as a "son of the soil" who "was imbued with love for his race and the desire to do something to better its condition."[101] Hercules's speech in Trinidad in September 1919 highlighted the white racial violence against Black people in London, Liverpool, Cardiff, and South Africa; he said, "There was no single quarter of the globe and no flag under which people of African descent received FairPlay [*sic*] and that measure of justice to which they were entitled."[102] To overcome this, he argued, "Peoples of African origin, regardless of pigment, should acquire racial consciousness. . . . [T]hey should get to know each other and act in sympathy and unison. . . . [T]hey should strive to acquire a measure of economic independence, by which alone they would be able to fight their present disabilities."[103] Garveyism and the Pan-African spirit served as a discourse for enlivening Black racial consciousness.

Workers saw no incommensurability between Garvey's race-first position and collective action in their class interests. Garvey himself did not advocate for Black worker unionization, since he believed that if Black and white worker wages were equal, employers would no longer favor hiring Black labor.[104] However, the relationship between Garveyism and trade unionism took many different forms in the places where they interacted.[105] In Trinidad and Tobago, TWA leaders were not doctrinaires. Cipriani, for example, was a close friend of Garvey and invited him to give public speeches in Trinidad, even though he disagreed with some of Garvey's specific goals, such as "Back to Africa."[106] Echoing Adam Ewing's analysis, I find that TWA leaders worked class-based grievances into the framework of redemption from racial subjugation. Labor organizers modified and molded Garveyism to "articulate" race and class in this historical conjuncture, in Stuart Hall's sense.[107] They deployed Garvey's discourse of Black race consciousness, Black racial uplift, and freedom from imperialism, intertwining this with class aspirations and the importance of unionism. In the words of one organizer, James (Jim) Barratt, through Garveyism they sought "to awaken the consciousness of the black man, that he is a man like any other man. But then we go further than that. It want [*sic*] something more than that. To be proud to be a black man is not all, but I want real freedom, as a human being. . . . So as a class I must be treated within the society, my own society as a human being as anybody else."[108] Such bindings of racial and class consciousness are exemplified in the following speech at a TWA meeting in October 1919 by Secretary James Brathwaite: "You are a powerful race and our power was proved in the gigantic struggle for British liberty. You can see in His Honor Justice Russell's writing the Negro as a hero which prove [*sic*] to you the capabilities and tenacity of the negro and what he can do. You don't think it is a shame for the intelligent negro to remain sleeping and waiting for amelioration? No, we must fight. If we can die for the white man against his German brother we can die better for ourselves."[109] Through the fusion of Garveyism and unionism, labor leaders deployed a practical, rather than orthodox, approach to building the movement such that the vigor of race consciousness did not preclude the development of class consciousness.

The TWA and working people also saw no incompatibility between enhancing Black racial solidarity and building multiracial unity with Indian workers. This paradox has received little scholarly investigation. Historian Jerome Teelucksingh, one of the few scholars who have attempted to explain it, argues, "The particularism of its [Garvey's] race ideology and its Pan-African appeal obviously precluded the interest and participation of East Indians," later noting that it contributed to "the polarization of Africans and East Indians in the colony."[110] Yet, empirically, Indian workers joined the TWA, and the organization welcomed them. Teelucksingh argues that they joined, not because they identified with Garveyism, but because they found the TWA expedient to achieving their class interests.

While this is certainly the case, two more compelling reasons drove the coexistence of multiracial unity and Black racial pride within the TWA. First, Indian representation in the leadership and the important work of Indian and other TWA organizers were crucial to drawing Indian workers into the union. Second, the anti-imperialism and anticolonialism of Garvey's movement may have resonated with the Indian population, a factor that Teelucksingh also acknowledges. The UNIA and Garvey himself, while emphasizing the Black cause, also promoted international solidarity and alliances with activists and movements against Western imperialism in China, Egypt, India, Ireland, and elsewhere.[111] One leading Garveyite, Samuel Haynes, wrote specifically about African and Asian unity, pointing to a brewing "possibility of a cultural and spiritual cohesion between the two, out of which may be born a common brotherhood looking towards a unification of efforts in checking the ambitions of white men."[112] Garvey's own speeches urged Black people, "If you keep organized, as the Hindus are organizing, as the Indians are organizing, . . . these heretofore oppressed groups will shake the foundations of the world."[113] Labor organizers in Trinidad and Tobago emphasized this unity against imperialism. For example, the *Labour Leader* printed an article about Garvey's plan to meet with Mahatma Gandhi.[114] Thus, similar to Hawaiian unionism in the 1940s, workers did not suppress their racial identity in favor of class consciousness in order to build a movement across racial lines.[115] Through an emphasis on the anti-imperial and anticolonial strivings of Garveyism, African and Indian TWA labor organizers reduced any perceived incommensurability between the Black-centered orientation of Garveyism and Indian membership in the TWA. Garveyism, as expressed in liberation unionism and the TWA, was concerned *primarily but not only* with the liberation of people racialized as Black, thereby facilitating the assembling of multiracial solidarities.

Liberation unionism in Trinidad and Tobago was embedded in and benefited from the networks, infrastructure, and resources of Garvey's international UNIA organization. As historian Tony Martin has shown, a number of TWA leaders also held top positions in the UNIA.[116] For example, John Sydney de Bourg was a prominent figure in the UNIA in New York. Two TWA secretaries—James Brathwaite and William Howard Bishop—also served at different times as presidents of the UNIA branch in Port of Spain.[117] Bishop was also editor of the *Labour Leader* in the 1920s—the TWA's first newspaper, launched in 1922—through which he intentionally and actively disseminated Garvey's philosophy.[118] According to Ewing, "during the strike TWA meetings often became de facto UNIA rallies."[119] Not only was this cadre instrumental in the production, spread, and circulation of Garvey-infused unionism, but their knowledge of and expertise in international political organizing in hostile repressive environments was crucial to the construction of the movement. In terms of infrastructural support, throughout the 1920s, the TWA meetings were held in the same building that served as the UNIA's de facto Trinidad headquarters and in UNIA-owned properties.[120] The concrete organizational linkages between the TWA and Garvey's UNIA served as a source of both mobilizing discourse and "mobilizing structure" for liberation unionism, generating, organizing, and coordinating the level of collective action needed to confront white capital and the colonial state.[121]

DIASPORIC CONSTITUTION. Liberation unionism also had an internationalist character through its very Pan-African constitution. Immigrants to Trinidad and Tobago from other British Caribbean colonies, as described in chapter 1, and locals who had experiences with racism and radicalism abroad formed a core cadre of organizers who were instrumental in helping enlarge liberation unionism and foment its unity. According to Ron Ramdin, "it was well-known that most of the activists in the TWA were immigrants from the neighboring West Indian Islands," and many of them had held key leadership positions in the organization.[122] For instance, James Brathwaite (TWA secretary, 1918–21), Albertha Husbands (head of the Domestics Section), and Bruce McConney were all from Barbados; Elma Francois (public events speaker) was from St. Vincent; John Sydney de Bourg (president, 1896; secretary, 1913–18) was from Grenada; and William Howard Bishop (secretary, 1921–30) and Brutus Ironclad were from Guyana.[123] Mohammed Orfy of the EIDL was reportedly born in Kent, England, to South Asian parents and arrived in Trinidad in 1914 from Guyana.[124]

These revolutionary immigrants tended to be well traveled and had lived in and had actively been contesting the laws of multiple other colonies and/or European countries before arriving in Trinidad and Tobago. For instance, Rev. E. Seiler Salmon, who was deported for his suspected involvement in the 1919 unrest, was a native of Jamaica and had reportedly resided in Tobago and Costa Rica before moving to Port of Spain. The acting British consul in Costa Rica reported that Rev. Salmon repeatedly conducted marriages of West Indians in a manner contrary to the prevailing marriage laws there. Further, according to the consul, "not only did he try to incite laborers to strike, but racial prejudice was his special teaching."[125] He was denied an Anglican parish because, according to colonial officials, he was "causing mischief" and intended to "stir up racial prejudice."[126] The diasporic leadership and mobilization of immigrant workers was an outstanding feature of the 1919–20 uprising and liberation unionism of the interwar years.

Many locally born labor organizers also had international connections and experiences that were central to the emergence and sustenance of liberation unionism. The returned British West Indies Regiment soldiers were subjected to racism and exposed to Garveyism through contacts with other West Indian soldiers abroad, and they brought these ideas back home.[127] Likewise, TWA leader Rienzi, while pursuing legal studies in the United Kingdom from 1930 to 1934, became a member and regular speaker with several anti-imperial and anticolonial organizations there, such as the League Against Imperialism, the Indian Freedom League, and the Indian National Congress.[128] He contributed immensely to these organizations abroad and also returned home with enhanced organizing skills and professional credentials as a lawyer, which he put to use to represent workers.

Local union leaders also forged bonds with unions abroad. For instance, David Headley, the president of the TWA in 1919, also served as a delegate to the British Guiana Labor Union in Georgetown. Headley reportedly said he intended to plant TWA tenets in every corner of Trinidad and Tobago and, when the workers were thoroughly organized, to affiliate with the workers' union in Demerara, Guyana, and fifteen other West Indian colonies. Such a consolidation of labor, he argued, would build solidarity among workers across the region and frustrate the colonial government's strategy of sourcing strikebreakers from neighboring British colonies.[129] Thus, the diasporic constitution of the working people was a critical element enabling the activation of the TWA in the interwar years, and the unity of the movement enhanced its success both in numbers and in the distribution of gains.

Economic, Political, and Social Transformation

While liberation unionism mostly comprised Garveyites, a few of the organizers were communists, such as Elma Francois, Vivian Henry, and Adrian Cola Rienzi, and still others, like Cipriani, were social democrats. Given this medley of leftists, each with slightly different and sometimes incompatible visions, it might have been challenging to generate an agreed-on set of demands in pursuit of the shared goal of liberation from the shackles of the white capitalist system. The tendency to avoid orthodox ideological positions facilitated the formulation of a set of practical demands, which, in effect, was a broad-based developmental agenda. As in social movement unionism, workers centered issues of wages and working conditions but did not confine the struggle to these topics. Table 2.2 is an illustrative list of these multifaceted demands. Workers framed economic independence, political empowerment, social justice, and self-determination as inseparable from overturning colonial, imperial, and racial structures and ideologies.

In terms of workplace-specific issues and colonial economic and labor policy, workers and the TWA pushed for an eight-hour workday, the passing of workers' compensation legislation, and a range of demands around refashioning the economy away from oppressive labor policies and practices. These included abolishing child labor, repealing legislation permitting forced labor, and pushing for the creation of new laws and institutions to allow trade unions and collective bargaining.[130] The TWA also pushed the colonial state to alter its relationship to capital and the economy. For instance, it advocated for redistribution of oil wealth from foreign companies to the masses through taxation policies.[131] The union also demanded the construction of state agencies to address unemployment, even taking the lead by establishing a labor bureau in the capital city with several branches throughout the colony to help its members find employment.[132] Workers also wanted an agricultural credit bank to serve small farmers (including cane farmers, small proprietors, wage earners, and unemployed people).[133] These demands presented a different economic vision from what had heretofore existed in the colony.

With regard to political rights and civil freedoms, workers wanted to wrest control of the colony's institutions from the British and local white elite. The TWA advocated for constitutional reform for adult franchise, self-government, "purely elective" rather than nominated boards for local government, and a representative Legislative Council. The union also pressed for a federated British West Indies.[134] Through their demand for competitive examinations for the civil service, workers in the TWA also sought to eliminate racism and nepotism within the colonial state and to push the institution to become more meritocratic.[135] The movement fought for the rights of people to determine their own laws and development path.

The workers and the TWA also pursued social investments and social protections. These included a noncontributory old-age pension, a health insurance

TABLE 2.2. Worker Demands During the Interwar Years, 1919–1939

Economic	Political	Social
• Wage increases • Abolishment of payment in liquor instead of wages • Eight-hour workday • Wage parity between non-white and white workers • Workers' compensation legislation • Abolition of child labor exploitation • Trade union legislation • Repeal of the Sedition and Habitual Idlers Ordinances • An agricultural credit bank for small farmers • Redistribution of oil wealth from oil companies to the masses through increased taxation • State control of industries unable to increase wages • Land reform	• Seats for women on city councils • Competitive examinations for the civil service • Entirely elective rather than nominated boards for local government • A representative legislative council • Home rule/internal self-government • A federation of British Caribbean territories • Adult suffrage	• Better roads, transport, housing, and sanitation • A health insurance scheme • Access to mental health care for women • Compulsory education for children • Greater access to postprimary education • Pensions • Legislation allowing divorce • Legislation to end racial discrimination in the workplace • Prison reforms—abolition of dark cells and solitary confinement, abolition of childbirth in prison • Poor relief • Dole for unemployed workers and relief from taxes and bills • Auctioneer's Ordinance • Moneylending Ordinance • Public recreational facilities • Annual commemoration of Emancipation Day

scheme, greater gender equity through seats for more women on the city council, mental health care for women, and compulsory education.[136] Workers also wanted more affordable housing, improvements in roads and sanitation in their communities, and the decentralization of some state functions (that is, more community offices for, e.g., registration of births and deaths).[137] The TWA also campaigned for the public celebration of Emancipation Day to commemorate the end of slavery.[138] Working people did not partition the workplace from the plight of the community writ large in the struggle for self-determination and a dignified standard of living. As such, they pushed a broad-based set of economic, political, and social demands for transforming life in the colony of Trinidad and Tobago.

Toward the end of World War I, the global and local conditions were ripe for working-class mobilization. The agency of racialized colonized working people in engendering liberation unionism out of these conditions, with its unified, Pan-African, and transformative orientation, reflected creativity and resourcefulness in overcoming the divide-and-rule strategies of the colonial oppressors.

Repression

The white plantocracy, the foreign merchant and industrial class, and the colonial state thoroughly resisted liberation unionism. They despised the notion of Black self-determination. One member of the white elite class described the labor leaders as "all imbued with the idea that there must be a Black world controlled and governed by the people of their own race."[139] Colonial administrators and economic elites alike construed Black race consciousness as "racial feeling" against whites, and the business elites and plantocracy in particular claimed the Black masses planned to eliminate the whites.[140] So audacious was the idea of Black autonomy that, at first, the local white elite and colonial officials denied and downplayed that it could even exist in the colony. They blamed the strikes on "agitators from elsewhere" and "acute racial feelings stirred up by returned soldiers," nothing that a few deportations and the banning of Black radical newspapers could not solve.[141] The idea that there was widespread discontent among the masses and that workers had the intelligence and capacity to organize had until then been inconceivable for the white economic and political elite. As C. L. R. James wrote in *The Black Jacobins*, "The slaves had revolted because they wanted to be free. But no ruling class ever admits such things."[142] Once the workers made their demands ineluctable, the white elites deployed several strategies to crush the 1919–20 unrest and liberation unionism and retain control of the colony's institutions: the continued racialization of workers to prevent multiracial worker consolidation, refusal to negotiate, and police repression.

First, the white elite relied on their time-tested strategy of deploying racial ideologies to divide and rule. Capital and colonial states the world over have used racism and offered symbolic and material concessions to sections of the working class to weaken and contain insurgent multiethnic working-class unity and restore the smoothness of capital accumulation.[143] White settlers and business elites had hoped their engineering of politically opposed "races" might forestall a unified movement: "In the years gone by the large East Indian indentured population, numbering many thousands and largely under the control of their respective plantation owners, managers and overseers, was looked upon as a substantial safe-guard against trouble with the negroes and vice versa. With the abolition of immigration such a counterpoise has ceased to exist and the 'creole coolie' will either remain an interested spectator or join the mob."[144] The 1919 uprising answered this question as the Indian laborers joined forces with the African workers.

However, neither colonial officers nor employers offered substantive concessions to either Indian or African workers to the extent of reconfiguring the race-class hierarchical order. Instead, the colonial administration offered small allowances, such as appointing a committee to help returned soldiers find employment and distributing small land grants to encourage cultivation.[145] The acting governor foolishly anticipated that this would demobilize the movement: "The men are, I think, appreciating efforts made by the Authority on their behalf, and I am pleased to be able to report that the racial feeling appears to be less acute than it was some weeks ago."[146] Without noteworthy concessions to either segment of the racialized working class, such small appeasements did not suffice, and the divide-and-rule strategy broke down.

Second, employers and the colonial state resisted negotiating with workers, hoping that strikebreakers and repression would force them back to work. As chapter 1 showed, capital in sugar and oil was highly concentrated in just a few companies. At the docks, twelve steamers dominated the import/export trade, and among them, just three shipping agents controlled most of the business.[147] According to Jung, the higher the concentration of capital, the less willing employers are to compromise with labor and the greater their opposition to unionization and negotiation.[148] One shipping company representative said the TWA "had no authority from the men to make such representations."[149] Walking in lockstep with the companies, the governor also ignored TWA appeals to meet, saying the TWA had "no authority to represent the stevedores."[150] After two weeks of pressure, when the governor finally agreed to meet with the stevedores, he reiterated reluctance to intervene in industrial disputes other than to restore order or protect strikebreakers.[151] Thus, employers and the colonial state were initially united in their resistance to worker demands and collective bargaining through the TWA.

Third, state capacity and propensity for repression is one of the main factors shaping the ability of groups to mobilize and attain their demands. It can quell attempts at collective action due to the high risk involved for mobilizing actors.[152] During the 1919 unrest, the white economic elite unequivocally advocated not just any repression but violent force specifically meted out by white troops. The local police force, which was largely confined to the capital city, comprised Black noncommissioned "officers and men" and a few senior white officers. There was also an auxiliary force of white yeomanry and mounted infantry, but their numbers were very small. Both the white economic elite and the colonial state doubted whether the Black constabulary "could be relied on in a racial riot."[153] Of their lack of confidence in Black officers, the local white elites wrote, "That any one in a position of responsibility is ignorant or fatuous enough to rely on protection on our first line of defense in the shape of our black constabulary, we decline to believe. To place our wives and children in such a position would be criminal."[154] Given their distrust of Black officers, as early as July 1919, at the earliest signs of organized worker discontent, the white business elite called on the empire to provide "a body of white regular troops" for protection and to enlist "the services of every white man available" in the colony.[155] The Chamber of Commerce passed a resolution stating that "the authorities here have displayed a manifest, if not acknowledged incapacity to deal with the situation; Be it resolved that this Chamber pledged itself to seek the intervention of the highest authority should that become necessary in order to secure the re-establishment of law and order and the protection of inhabitants of the colony from similar violence and danger in the future."[156] In alignment with the white plantocracy and business elites, the colonial state did indeed repress liberation unionism. A white overseer had already killed one Lal Beharrysingh, who was persuading laborers at one estate to strike.[157] Police killed one Nathaniel Williams and wounded multiple people in a reckless open fire on protesters.[158] In addition to the constabulary, the colonial state hired motorcars and dispatched returned white soldiers of the Merchants' and Planters' Contingent (volunteers comprising the sons of the white elite who had enlisted to join British forces in the war) to crush the strikes on estates and in the districts.[159] The governor also called for white troops to be brought into Trinidad from Jamaica to shore up the repressive forces, and ultimately the warship HMS *Calcutta* intervened after the strikes took a colony-wide turn.[160]

The colonial state also rounded up and punished the masses. By early December 1919, the police had arrested and charged ninety-nine persons with "riotous behavior," assault, and other offenses during the strikes, of which eighty-two were found guilty of assaults and unlawful acts.[161] The TWA's James Brathwaite and Bruce McConney were among those who were fined and sentenced to imprisonment and hard labor.[162] In addition, the colonial state enacted new legislation to destroy the militancy of liberation unionism and restore order for capital accumulation. In 1920 alone, the colonial state passed several repressive ordinances: the Seditious Ordinance criminalized any act, speech, or production and circulation of publications deemed critical or contemptuous of the British Empire and its colonial auxiliaries, such as the *Negro World*, *Argos*, *Clarion*, and *Crisis*; the Firearms Amendment Ordinance restricted access to firearms; and the Strikes and Lockouts Ordinance sought to delay strikes.[163] Deportation was a primary tool of the colonial state to repress liberation unionism. After the 1919 strikes, numerous labor leaders and strikers were deported to neighboring British Caribbean colonies, such as John Sydney de Bourg (Grenada) and Bruce McConney (Barbados).[164] The ruling elite resisted worker efforts to realize a new social order.

Repression with Relative Restraint

Liberation unionism was also made possible by factors operating outside of the mobilizing workers. C. L. R. James, for instance, found that a combination of local and international forces helped create favorable occasions and/or settings for certain levels of mobilization, strategies, and the ultimate success of the Haitian Revolution.[165] Social movement scholars call these contextual factors "political opportunities."[166] Three such openings shaped the emergence and impact of liberation unionism in the colony—the limited repressive capacity of the colonial state, the lack of unity between the local white economic elite and British colonial state administrators, and the strategic position of Trinidad and Tobago within the British Empire.

Inadequate Repressive Capacity

The repressive capacity of the Trinidad and Tobago colonial state was simply no match for the force of the movement, thereby opening political space for collective action and movement success. In 1918 there were 730 mostly Black noncommissioned officers for a population of 381,309, meaning 1 constable to every 522 persons. The force was actually stronger in 1905, when the ratio was 1 to 452, and even then, numerous reports expressed concerns about the size of the police force and cited the need for more officers, but the colonial state failed to address the issue.[167] Several months before the December uprising, the inspector general of the constabulary wrote that while he was confident about the various measures in place to manage the protests, "The only anxiety I have is the strength of the force."[168] When the stevedores struck, the colony's Executive Council worried that the size of the local police force was "inadequate to maintain order."[169] As the unrest persisted, the governor reported that the Colonel on duty expressed "that unless an attempt were made to bring about a settlement he would be unable to control the situation with the forces at his disposal."[170]

Beyond its insufficient size, the colonial state's repressive capacity relative to the worker mobilization was weakened by the constabulary's poor working conditions, low wages, and lack of resources and training. According to one report, the constabulary hospital accommodations did "not conform in comfort nor amenities with modern practice," were overcrowded with patients, and were unsanitary.[171] The virtually all-white Trinidad Light Infantry Volunteers lacked proper musketry and training manuals, and social amenities in the training facilities were in a "moribund state," which officials noted negatively affected recruitment and morale.[172] The governor acknowledged that "the great difficulty to be contended with is the lack of real enthusiasm" among the Light Infantry Volunteers, "who, while willing enough to turn out on the occasion of public ceremonies, are less prepared to give up part of their leisure to the more important matter of serious training."[173] The all-white Trinidad Light Horse troops were drawn from overseers and managers of various sugar and cacao estates. They worked only part-time. As one investigator put it, "It is not reasonable to expect a man whose livelihood depends on business or some profession to give that attention to detail and be always available, as is necessary if any force is to be a success."[174] Moreover, they had to provide their own horses.[175]

Ad hoc solutions to repressing the 1919 strikes created dangerous precedents. These included outsourcing violence to white vigilantes and establishing a semimilitary special constabulary. The latter "earned so much hostile comment from a large section of the public that it had to be abandoned"; not only was the public generally suspicious of this force, but it lacked training.[176] Overall, the police force was incommensurate with the force of liberation unionism, which shaped the success of the movement and its expansion into the 1920s and 1930s.

State-Elite Conflict

Although united by investments in profit making and white supremacy, disunity between the British colonial state and the local white, mostly French creole, population produced yet another important political opening shaping the movement's strength and the state's response. As mentioned in chapter 2, the resident French creole community resented a British-occupied state and the ascendancy of the Anglosphere. British state officials were aggrieved about French resistance to their authority. These tensions sparked disagreements during the uprising that prevented the congealing of a coherent unified tyrannical force against the movement.

As chapter 1 established, British colonial officials viewed the local white creoles, especially the French, as a parochial and self-interested lot. In 1919 colonial state officials initially felt that the white residents were overreacting, calling them "extreme and pessimistic," and disagreed with their call for sustained repression by white internal and external forces.[177] Given the prevalence of liberation unionism throughout the colony, colonial officials feared that some tools of containment might further aggravate worker discontent. For example, regarding local elites wanting a largely white force to preemptively rain down violence on the Black population, the inspector general of the constabulary advocated some restraint: "To attempt to arm every white man, and arrange concentration camps for women, to mount guards at the various places mentioned at this juncture would in my humble opinion be a fatal mistake . . . [because of] the difficulty of drawing the dividing line between whites and blacks, and also of the offense it would give to the hundreds of decent and law abiding persons who happen to be colored or black."[178] In other words, he feared such action would push the mixed and African middle class to join liberation unionism and further enlarge the movement.

Colonial officials resisted early pleas from local whites for external white troops. For example, the same officer in August 1919 wrote, "If the white people in the Colony would only cease cackling and spreading and enlarging on the wild rumors that are going around, the situation would soon clear. I am absolutely against taking any of the extreme measures as suggested by Mr. Huggins [of the Chamber of Commerce]. . . . I do not consider a body of white troops necessary here. If the unrest continues and should spread throughout the West Indies then perhaps such a course may become necessary. All I recommend is the stationing in these waters of one or two Cruisers."[179] The governor expressed similar hesitations: "I do not, however, think that sufficient reason has been shown for the establishment of a garrison of white troops in the Colony."[180] Even at the height of the uprising, the colonial state approved of short-term interventions by external white repressive forces to contain the strikes and protests but thought it was unwise to permanently station white troops in the colony.

These disagreements persisted long after the uprising was contained, allowing for the survival of liberation unionism into the 1920s and 1930s. While the colonial state deported many strike leaders, it disagreed with the local elites who wanted to expand the already frivolous justifications for deportations to include the promotion of "racial hatred," fearing that it would backfire and re-ignite worker agitation. The solicitor general warned, "I think great care should be taken in making deportations of British subjects . . . [as it can] do a lot of harm and very likely provoke disorders." He continued to argue that "racial hatred" is not just cause for deportation: "I am afraid if all negroes in Trinidad who from time to time in conversation with their friends express hatred of the white man are to be deported . . . the population will be seriously depleted."[181] In other words, whereas local whites were motivated to use whatever measures possible to eliminate any threat to the status quo, colonial officials recognized the limitations of using racial concerns as a pretext for deportation given the prevalence of race consciousness in the population.

Colonial administrators also expressed awareness that, as part of the Crown Colony system, they were ultimately answerable to the imperial government. Whereas before the uprising they may have wanted to assert their authority over white creole capital but were unable to, worker mobilization afforded them the policy space to act independently of local capital. They could rely on the fact that all colonial policies required approval from the imperial government, which, as the next section shows, had its own interests that were neither motivated by benevolence to workers nor entirely aligned with the interests of the white landed and business elites in the colony. This came through in the discussion of linking racial antipathy to whites with deportation and sedition. According to one colonial official, "There seems to be a tendency to treat industrial offenses as seditious to a degree that would be difficult to justify in Parliament."[182] Thus, state-elite discord afforded some space for liberation unionism to emerge and thrive.

Strategic Position as Oil Supplier for the Empire

According to Oliver Cromwell Cox, "The two world wars . . . have given backward countries invaluable opportunities to extricate themselves from the capitalist system."[183] A third factor that opened political space in Trinidad and Tobago for worker mobilization and the ultimate concessions and institutional changes they were able to attain was the colony's strategic position within the British Empire during the wars. World War I came at a time when Britain was the preeminent global imperial power: The empire extended over eleven million square miles and dominated over fifty-five million people.[184] The navy was crucial to British supremacy.

Capitalist imperialist interests in the colony's oil deposits shaped the British response to the Trinbagonian rebellion. In World War I, it was clear that Britain was dependent on the United States for wartime oil. In 1917 the navy consumed 3,310,000 tons of oil fuel, from the following sources: United States, 2,367,000 tons (71.5 percent); Mexico, 251,000 tons (8 percent); Trinidad, 69,000 tons (2 percent); Persia (Iran), 332,000 tons (10 percent); Borneo, 41,000 tons (1 percent); and imperial home production (Scottish shale, which was expensive to extract), 250,000 tons (7.5 percent).[185] The United States, therefore, not only had the potential to defeat Britain in war but could also prevent Britain from defeating other imperial powers. Thus, the British imperial state was especially concerned about price raising by the two major international oil monopolies—Standard Oil (US) and Shell (Dutch).[186] Britain needed a plentiful and stable supply of oil from a territory over which it exercised or could exercise control. Trinidad and Tobago was Britain's only oil source with colonial status and was the nearest to the metropole.[187] Plus, oil exploration promised more extractable deposits.[188] The Trinbagonian oil industry, the requisite refineries, and the ports were specifically to supply oil fuel of a certain specification to the admiralty. Thus, although Trinidad and Tobago's oil production was negligible in terms of global output levels, the colony was of utmost strategic value to British imperial interests.

Consequently, the British were not convinced that the white plantocracy and business elite's vigorous campaign for more white troops and for a permanent British naval station to repress labor was the correct course of action to restore lasting peace in the colony. In a time of war, for this empire clinging tooth and nail to its position in the global hierarchy of states, imperial policy saw concession as the more expedient method of securing regular oil supplies. In 1919 the secretary of state for the colonies instructed the governor to increase wages to avert strikes. He wrote, "In the event of it becoming necessary to intervene further in strikes or labor troubles you should use your influence in favor of increases of laborers wages up to a level at least sufficient to admit of pre-war standard of living. . . . such increases should be given without waiting for serious agitation."[189] He went on to instruct the governor to inform employers that this would be the colonial state's course.

The force of liberation unionism threatened British imperial military interests, which compelled the colonial administration to concede to several worker demands. At the structural level, colonial states might enjoy a significant amount of independence from their imperial states.[190] Still, they are in a subordinate position with respect to the state in the metropole, as colonial administrators must ultimately follow directions from the imperial state or face reproach or termination.[191] In fact, implementing orders from the metropole was the entire purpose of the Crown Colony administrative structure. While the governors of Trinidad and Tobago hardly exercised independence from the plantocracy and business elite, the confluence of liberation unionism and the imperial need for oil forced the colonial governor to follow the tenor in the metropole and act more independently of capital in the colony.

Trinbagonian workers were fully aware of their structural power in the British imperial system. As Walter Rodney asserted, the wealth that capitalist empires appropriate from the exploited regions of the world is for them both a source of strength and a potential weakness: "The peasants and workers of the dependencies are awakening to a realization that it is possible to cut the tentacles which imperialism has extended to their countries."[192] Workers in the colony noted the effects of stolen oil wealth on laboring people. According to one submission in the *Labour Leader* under the name "The Subaltern":

> The whole outlook is extremely serious.... We have seen crises in the smaller colonies.... Trinidad, however, is in a different position from that of her smaller sisters, and but for the fact of her vast resources, would have been already in the throes of penury and bankruptcy.... We have heard some of the greatest men [of] all times refer to the influence that the stomach has on the mind ... [to quote a local truism] "It is all very well and good for full-belly to tell hungry-belly to keep heart." ... [T]he cocoa estates have been giving only three and four days a week, public works have been shortened, and oil fields have discharged hundreds of their employees at short notice. The laborer is being steadily deprived of what is his inherent right—the right to live.... [W]e are determined to go to the limit in an effort to save our peasantry and the laboring man of the island of Trinidad and Tobago.[193]

The centrality of Trinidad oil to the British Empire, state-elite conflicts, and inadequate internal repressive forces all provided openings that the working people exploited to foster liberation unionism and press their demands.

State Capacity Building

Frederick Douglass, in his 1857 speech commemorating West Indian emancipation, noted, "Power concedes nothing without a demand."[194] The 1919 general strike forced employers and the colonial state to respond to working people and set the colony on a path to relative economic and social development. Liberation unionism did not produce the mass return to Africa that Garvey preached, an independent Black republic like Haiti, or a socialist state. The institutional changes that unfolded reflected some elements of social democratic corporatism, namely, a class compromise where employers and unions come together, mediated by government, to create mutually beneficial policy and manage capitalist growth.[195] However, under authoritarian colonial domination, what emerged could hardly be accurately labeled a social democratic corporatist state. As Patrick Heller notes, class compromise "can only be democratically organized," or the lack of legitimate procedures and representational negotiation will produce opportunistic behavior.[196]

While liberation unionism was met with repression, it nevertheless stimulated sweeping changes within the colonial state and capacity building to address the needs of the masses: relative state autonomy from foreign and local capital was enhanced; bureaucratic strength and infrastructural reach increased to provide public goods; and the boundaries of political participation expanded, per the workers' demands. With all these changes, the TWA remained organizationally separate from the state while simultaneously having one foot in the state apparatus through the labor representatives in the legislature. As such, the TWA was able to advance its policy goals, while at the same time retaining its independence.

State Autonomy

Liberation unionism pushed the state to carve out a more autonomous space for itself to better serve the welfare needs of the masses, which required new bodies and structures. After finally recognizing the TWA, the governor and the inspector general of the colony, G. H. May, oversaw the creation of a conciliation board to fulfill the newly adopted role of mediator between racialized labor and white capital. On considering the TWA's proposal for how to structure this body, the governor ultimately agreed to a board of two stevedore representatives, two shipping company representatives, two independent appointees of the governor, and a chairperson to be elected by those six members, either from among them or from outside.[197] The arbitration board met on December 2, 1919, and a stevedore-shipping company settlement was signed on December 3. Similarly, the colonial state established new committees to study and make recommendations about the general conditions of working people, such as the Wages Committee.

The governor came to view the new bodies and committees as essential to public policy and encouraged the white plantocracy and business elite to accept that the new relationship between the colonial state and private capital would thenceforth necessarily involve labor. His appeals to the shipping companies to convene with the TWA on the conciliation board exemplify the shift in state orientation:

I was aware that they had up to then taken up a firm attitude on the question of meeting the strike leaders, and I recognized they would be unwilling to change their views, but it was necessary to face facts; the situation was such that some small incident might lead to loss of life and destruction of property. If they would consent to serve, they were at liberty to say that they did so yielding to pressure from me, and I had represented to them that it was desirable on grounds of public policy that they should meet the strike leaders with a view to endeavoring to come to an agreement.[198]

Likewise, the colonial administration expended much energy persuading the Chamber of Commerce to agree on and pass a resolution supporting the creation of this government-appointed Wages Committee and the inclusion of TWA representatives on the body.[199] According to the governor, the TWA was too influential an organization to be ignored. He warned:

Although the employers might succeed at first in resisting the claims of the workers to secure recognition of their chosen representatives, experience showed that the workers in the end were almost always successful in forcing employers to yield to that demand . . . it was almost certain that they [local labor leaders] would continue to agitate until the Workingmen's Association was recognized by the employers. I suggested that it would be wise of them to recognize the Workingmen's Association now, instead of delaying until they were compelled to do so by strikes and agitation. The Workingmen's Association had now great influence among the working classes.[200]

Out of fear of the TWA and a desire to maintain industrial peace in the colony, the governor encouraged the chamber to concede and went on to appoint two TWA officials to the committee.[201] These were major steps toward improving the laboring class's living standards.

More evidence of the enhancement of colonial state autonomy because of liberation unionism included the elimination of a number of labor-repressive laws that favored the white economic elite. This included the repeal of the 1918 Habitual Idlers' Ordinance in 1926 and the outlawing of child labor in 1927.[202] The colonial state also passed new ordinances in labor's interest, such as the Labour Bureau Ordinance (1919), which allowed for the establishment of a labor bureau; the Truck Ordinance (1920), which prohibited the payment of wages in forms other than money; a Profiteering Ordinance (1919) to set protections and price controls on goods determined to be in common public use; the Workmen's Compensation Ordinance (1926), which allowed for the creation of a Workmen's Compensation Court, with a commissioner who would adjudicate the cases; and the Trade Union Ordinance (1933), permitting the formation and registration of unions (albeit with severe restrictions).[203] In response to the demand for increased taxation of oil companies, in 1926 the government commissioned Sir Thomas Holland to investigate. Newly elected labor representatives in the legislature introduced labor's demands in the form of bills and resolutions and pushed for them to be adopted, monitored, and enforced.

Despite these major achievements for workers, the gains were not always evenly distributed. For example, regarding the Workmen's Compensation Bill, workers had succeeded in defining "Member of a Family" broadly to include stepparents, stepchildren, half siblings, and children with unmarried parents, in alignment with the variations in working-class family formations.[204] However, then TWA President Cipriani agreed to exclude domestic and agricultural workers from the Workmen's Compensation Bill, the very occupations with large proportions of women, under the assumption that it would not have passed otherwise. Cipriani and other TWA leaders pushed to amend the ordinance after it successfully passed, but the fact remained that the women who made the movement had to wait.[205] Therefore, the gains were at times uneven, and structural problems persisted, but the reforms were nevertheless sweeping.

Bureaucratic Expansion and Infrastructural Reach

The aforementioned legislation required significant expansion in the state structure in order to effectively implement these new state functions. The state needed to construct a Workmen's Compensation Court, for example, with an organizational structure and procedural rules to adjudicate worker claims. The TWA submitted proposals for what forms those new bureaucratic arms would take, which often served as the starting point for designing those institutions. The design process itself involved negotiations among the state's, labor's, and capital's competing visions, and the outcomes often did not match exactly what any of these parties wanted. For instance, the court ultimately consisted of a single commissioner, even though the TWA wanted an arbitration board consisting of a chief commissioner and two assistant commissioners. The colonial state also imposed a fee of two shillings on all applicants, which would have deterred the already underpaid workers. As such, labor kept advocating for their initial proposal even after the legislation had passed in April 1926. Still, labor's ability to prompt institution building and assert their proposals in the design process was a momentous achievement. As early as December 1926, workers had begun taking companies to court and winning awards.[206] Workers also recognized the need for comprehensive occupational safety and improved working conditions, and labor representatives on the Legislative Council urged the government to appoint independent engineers and qualified personnel to create systems for promoting and monitoring workplace safety. The worker movement promoted bureaucratic state expansion to address the plight of working people.

Worker demands not only enlarged the state but also changed its composition. The colonial state initially resisted the TWA's call to introduce meritocratic requirements for entry into the civil service, thereby maintaining nepotistic, racist, and patron-client methods of recruitment and promotion.[207] However, under pressure to reform these practices, competitive examinations were finally introduced in 1935, and an independent Civil Service Selection Committee was established.[208]

Reforms stemming from liberation unionism also increased the infrastructural power of the state to expand and improve access to education, health services, and social welfare. In the 1920s the colonial state diverted more revenues to address these needs. Funding also came from the Colonial Development and Welfare Act, first passed in British Parliament in 1929 to administer grants to the colonies for education, health services, housing, land settlements, and labor departments.

With respect to education, the number of primary schools increased only by one, from 293 in 1918 to 294 in 1936, but the ability of students to access an education increased markedly as the number of pupils in these schools went from 45,501 to 72,119 over those years. In addition, the number of secondary schools more than doubled in the same period (from four to nine).[209] The colonial state also established five intermediate schools in the first half of the 1920s, which made secondary education more accessible and affordable for the lower middle class.[210] Teachers formed a Trinidad and Tobago Teachers' Union in 1919 and advocated for better pay, pensions, and job security; they also sought to participate in education policy, eventually succeeding in getting a teacher representative on the board of education in 1932.[211] Liberation unionism also stimulated increased state capacity to provide health care and services. After the 1919 uprising, the government added nine more government medical officers, bringing the total to thirty-nine in 1933.[212] Mortality rates for infants under one year old hovered at an average of 154 per thousand live births (1906–10) and 152 per thousand live births (1916–20) for the first two decades of the twentieth century.[213] With greater attention to maternal and infant health, the rate was reduced to 97 in 1936.[214] In addition to the two general hospitals, seven district hospitals, and several health offices dispersed throughout the colony, the colonial state added specialized facilities: a mental health hospital and a leprosarium.[215] Better health outcomes were also made possible by state investments in public health measures in the 1920s and 1930s.

Expansion of Political Participation

The worker movement of 1919–20 also prompted constitutional reform and the expansion of the franchise, albeit to a limited extent. After the uprising, the British Colonial Office conceded and allowed for seven members of the Legislative Council to be elected under a franchise with gender, age, literacy, income, and property restrictions. Only men over twenty-one years of age who were literate in English and had a minimum property value of $12,000 in local currency from which an annual income of at least $960 was earned, or an annual income of at least $1,920, could run for elections. The franchise applied only to men aged twenty-one years or older and women thirty years or older who were literate in English and possessed significant property and income (minimum annual salary of $300). Under such high requirements, only 6 percent of the total population of Trinidad and Tobago registered to vote for a small number of representatives in the first-ever elections in 1925, after 128 years of British colonial control.[216] The TWA had proposed income qualifications for voters of $20 per month, or an annual rent payment of $96, and an income of $100 per month or capital of $2,400 as qualification for membership in the legislature.[217] The expansion of the franchise was celebrated, but its limited nature contributed to a second uprising.

In the first election in 1925 with this expanded franchise, workers campaigned for and successfully elected their first representative to the Legislative Council—Arthur A. Cipriani—who served from 1925 to 1937. Cipriani was joined by three other labor representatives, F. E. M. Hosein, Sarran Teelucksingh, and Timothy Roodal, who all served from 1928 to 1932 (Roodal and Cipriani continued until 1937). Once on the Legislative Council, these representatives pushed for the aforementioned reforms in favor of working people. By design, the new council retained the powers of the governor, the power of the colonial state, and the overrepresentation of the local white elite. The unofficial seats were increased from eleven to thirteen (seven elected and six nominated), and the official members were increased from ten to twelve.[218] Still, labor was, for the first time, represented in the dominant governing body of the colony.

Liberation unionism also opened the way for women to hold public office. In the wave of postuprising progressive reforms, Cipriani presented a motion for women to hold office in the Port of Spain City Council in 1924. After much public debate and two failures to pass, the motion successfully passed in 1930 and became law in 1935. San Fernando Borough Council followed suit a year later. In 1936, Audrey Jeffers, a Black middle-class woman, Pan-Africanist, and social worker, became the first women elected to the Port of Spain City Council.[219] Jeffers was not a TWA member, and her record of activism and advocacy was much more middle class in orientation, revolving around educational opportunities for girls and Black middle-class women's entry into salaried employment. Still, the 1919 labor uprising, Cipriani's role in legislative reform, and his political support for Jeffers was crucial to removing the legal and institutional barriers that excluded women from holding public office in the colony.

As expansive as this institution building was, the colonial state nevertheless maneuvered its way out of addressing certain demands, a process Trina Vithayathil has called "bureaucratic deflection."[220] In this case, colonial state officials deliberately sought to divorce the economic factors from race and forestall deep structural change. At the start of the 1919 unrest, for example, the governor said he believed that "racial feeling" and "racial propaganda" were "the main cause" of the uprising and also admitted that "the present labor unrest is not without its economic causes."[221] Another colonial official noted, "It is of course very difficult in a place like Trinidad to separate racial and industrial issues, as they are in fact mixed up."[222] Yet despite these acknowledgments, separating race and class was a colonial tool that allowed capital and the state to make some concessions while preserving the overall racial architecture of global capitalism. For example, one official concluded, "The causes of the riot seem to be fairly clear; the economic side of the matter is being looked into and there is not much purpose in further ventilation of the racial side of the matter."[223] The governor echoed this sentiment: "The causes of the general state of unrest are partly racial and partly economic. The racial question is not suitable for inquiry by a commission; and the difficulties of the economic situation will, I hope, be eased by the work of the [Wages] Committee."[224] The colonial administrators were therefore fully aware of the complex race-class dynamics of the white capitalist system and knew that workers had mobilized to challenge this order. However, to address the fact that labor superexploitation and racial subordination were inextricably linked would be tantamount to overturning the basis of capital accumulation.

To deal with the "racial question," colonial officials symbolically included African and Indian representation on governing bodies. For example, in constructing the Wages Committee, the governor stated, "As the racial aspect of the present unrest had to be taken into consideration in selecting the members of the [Wages] Committee . . . of the twenty-four members thirteen are

Europeans, nine are colored and two are East Indians."[225] This symbolic inclusion aimed at placating worker militance, restoring the ideal conditions for continued capital accumulation, and retaining white dominance. Still, African and Indian labor representation in the state was inconceivable to whites prior to the uprising. For the first time in the colony, the colonial state began to carve out some relative autonomy from the white economic elite, and racialized working people had a voice in the colonial state through these newly created bodies and state structures.

Conclusion

Working people in colonial Trinidad and Tobago constructed liberation unionism in 1919 and nurtured this form of organizing through the interwar years. Labor's open confrontation with employers and the colonial state drove the latter to increase its capacity for more equitable development—to enhance its autonomy from the white economic elite; to create, expand, and staff structures that could deliver public goods, including education and improved public health and sanitation; and to widen political participation beyond the white propertied class. Labor representatives in the state bureaucracy—on elected bodies, committees, and boards—pushed the colonial state to build the structures needed to implement these new development priorities. The resulting new configuration of state-society relations and enhanced state capacity laid the basis for long-term improvements in social and economic development in Trinidad and Tobago.

The main features of liberation unionism were oriented toward unity, internationalism, and transformation, and workers' organizing strategies and visions of freedom were rooted in Black liberation philosophies and organizational forms. Workers centered the discourse of race from Pan-Africanism, especially Garvey's Pan-African project, and attached to it class consciousness and unionism. That Black consciousness within liberation unionism did not produce racially exclusive or racist unionism. Black workers deliberately sought to enlist other workers who were not racialized as Black into the movement. But that interracialism did not involve color-blind strategies of mobilization. Labor organizers endeavored to build unity without any group having to de-emphasize or relinquish their racial identity and cultural expressions *and* without ever losing sight of the struggle against anti-Black racial subjugation. The anti-imperial and anticolonial resistance of Pan-Africanism not only facilitated this bridge building between African and Indian workers in the colony but also tied in the local workers' plight with racialized colonial toilers elsewhere in the global periphery. Such institutional and ideological openness also shaped the broad demands of the movement for more than higher wages and better working conditions and for a reorganization of the society.

Some of the elements of liberation unionism may have been present in specific locales and at particular historical junctures in other contexts. For example, Local 65 in New York from the 1930s to the 1950s was a racially and gender-inclusive union led by Jewish workers, many of whom affiliated with the Communist Party and saw worker organizing as a way to change the social, economic, and political order.[226] Similarly, the 1870s and 1880s working-men's campaigns of the US Knights of Labor, the Industrial Workers of the World (US) in the 1910s to 1920s, worker organizing in multiple industries across the US South during the 1930s and 1940s, the Congress of Industrial Organizations (US) from the mid-1930s to 1950s, and the International Long-shoremen's and Warehousemen's Union in Hawai'i in the 1940s and 1950s all developed strategies of generating interracialism, scholars assert, under the umbrella of Communist Party organization and ideology.[227] Organizers took the discourse of class and incorporated race to build multiracial unions. The distinguishing feature of liberation unionism was its embeddedness in Black political organizations and traditions, where racial emancipation was the anchor to which class grievances were tied.

In this chapter I also discuss how the white business elite and the colonial state responded to worker agency and which contextual factors facilitated the relative success of the movement—a police force that was incommensurate with the movement, state-elite frictions, and imperial oil interests. Some may argue that these political opportunities were the more decisive factors shaping the movement's success. As I have shown, the colonial state and the white economic elite demonstrated no prior inclination to ameliorate the conditions of workers. More than that, they resisted negotiating with people whom they deemed inferior, and they sought to suppress workers' radical ideas and activities. Had it not been for the consolidation of liberation unionism as a social force, employer concessions and the construction of state structures to address the needs of the masses may not have occurred on the scale that they did. There is no indication that the state would have reformed itself during the interwar years if the movement had not forced it to do so.

These waves of institutional change stimulated by worker mobilization were hard-fought and achieved tangible wins along many dimensions. Still, the white capitalist system was obviously not dismantled, and racialized and gendered labor exploitation remained intact. Furthermore, the colonial state and private capital were also innovative. They wasted no time replacing the overturned methods of labor exploitation with new ones, thereby reproducing the prevailing oppressive systems. They passed the new 1920 Sedition Ordinance, for instance, to repress working-class organizing and expression that threatened the colonial order under the banner of "libel" and "seditious" acts and publications. As such, the fight was not over. The confluence of factors that sparked the mass uprising in 1919–20 would rear its head again in the 1930s.

Regardless, 1919 was remarkable. Worker strikes all around the world shook the foundations on which capital accumulation rested. Liberation unionism emerged in this conjuncture in Trinidad and Tobago, and its persistence through the 1920s and early 1930s under the aegis of the TWA established a pattern of state-society relations characterized by worker mobilization, repression, and concession, which laid important foundations for future worker organizing and development-promoting state institutions. Despite challenges to the movement, from without and from within, liberation unionism would continue to profoundly shape the development path of Trinidad and Tobago.

3

The 1937 General Strike and the
Deepening of Liberation Unionism

Many a day persons haven't a meal
They too decent to beg, too honest to steal
They went looking for work mostly everywhere
But saw signboard marked "No hands wanted here"
The Government should work the wastelands and hills
Build houses, factories and mills
Reduce taxation and then we would be
Really emancipated from slavery.
—GROWLING TIGER, "Workers Appeal" (1936 calypso)

At 5:30 a.m. on the morning of June 19, 1937, in accordance with a prearranged signal among the oil workers to commence a sit-down strike, two oil wells owned by Apex Company were set ablaze. The governor met with the managers of seven oil companies and sent police into San Fernando and the oil belt to suppress the workers and arrest Tubal Uriah "Buzz" Butler. Butler was a Grenadian who had moved to the Trinidad oil fields to work as a pipe fitter and who, by then, reigned as the undisputed megastar organizer of the Trinbagonian working people. Throughout the day the police threatened and beat the working men and women and their supporters to break up the gatherings. Around 6:00 p.m. that day, while Butler was addressing a crowd of about two hundred people at his regular open-air meeting spot in Fyzabad, Corporal Charlie King (a Black police officer) came forward to arrest him. Butler asked the crowd if he should go with the police. They cried no. As Butler turned to escape through the crowd, the workers turned to the police officers. Butler would remain on the run for about three months, until he eventually surrendered to authorities in September 1937. During that time the movement that erupted was another open confrontation between the working class, on one hand, and white capital and the colonial state, on the other. With women at the helm, King was beaten and burned to death, and other police officers were injured in the fray. As nightfall approached, reinforcements consisting of forty armed constables tried to clear the crowd and retrieve King's body. The workers and their supporters stoned and fired at the officers, killing one white officer, Sub-Inspector W. S. Bradburn, and forcing the rest of the police to retreat until more officers arrived. That night, the governor sent a telegram to Bermuda to request external reinforcements.[1]

Starting the following day, on a scale even larger than in 1919, workers of different races and sectors, the unemployed, and people in communities across Trinidad and Tobago brought the colonial state and capital to their knees in six tumultuous weeks of revolt (see figure 3.1). It seemed that nobody could pacify the movement. Newspapers reported that workers were going from estate to estate, plant to plant, encouraging, and in some cases intimidating, other workers to stop working.[2] The leaders of the Trinidad Labour Party (TLP), formerly the Trinidad Workingmen's Association (TWA), called for an end to the striking, to no avail.[3] Butler, who had initially envisioned a sit-down strike, wrote to fellow labor organizer Adrian Cola Rienzi two weeks into the unrest while still in hiding, saying, "I find myself in the perhaps unhappy position of not being able to call off the strike which has caused so much hurt to the colony and its inhabitants as a whole. The workers, I am told, are in the main prepared to put up a 'last-ditch' fight to secure at least a general all-round increase in their wages as a prerequisite to going back to work."[4] The whole situation had exceeded the labor leaders. This time, it took two warships, HMS *Ajax* and *Exeter*, to subdue the movement. By the time the uprising was contained, the police had killed seventeen civilians and injured sixty-six, and the crowds had killed two police officers and injured nine in the police and volunteer forces.[5]

There may be a temptation to view the 1937 uprising through the lens of the popular adage "History repeats itself." After all, the state reforms stemming from the 1919 uprising went a long way toward ameliorating the hardships workers faced, but the white capitalist system that generated deprivation was not dismantled. The stock market crash of 1929, followed by the Great Depression,

FIGURE 3.1. Workers on strike, southern Trinidad, June 1937. *Source: Trinidad Guardian,* June 27, 1937.

hurt companies, but they adjusted to forestall losses, such as by laying off employees.[6] Throughout the 1930s the colonial state recorded a "very satisfactory" financial position as surplus funds increased significantly, and the balance of trade and public debt favored the colony.[7] White capital continued to accumulate considerable profits. The most dominant oil company in the colony, Trinidad Leaseholds, paid 25 percent dividends in 1935–36.[8] New oil deposit finds and the drilling of deeper oil wells promised ever more riches for foreign operatives.[9] In addition, exports of sugar, asphalt, copra, coffee, bitters, molasses, and grapefruit also showed impressive increases (see table 2.1), news of which was reported in local papers.[10] Overall, Trinidad and Tobago's resources continued to spawn impressive amounts of wealth for capital.

Working people, however, were suffering. Workers' wage gains from the 1919 negotiations were offset by rapidly rising costs for necessary products like foodstuffs, household items, and housing.[11] In addition, many of the 1919-stimulated reforms proceeded at a frustratingly slow pace. Despite presentations in the legislature in 1920 and 1935 about the importance of maintaining a cost-of-living index, up to 1937 the government still had not enacted one.[12] The colonial state also still had not implemented a minimum-wage statute, despite several official reports recommending that and a 1935 Labor (Minimum Wage) Ordinance and board tasked with setting the rates.[13] Oil workers reported on companies' use of so-called employment records called *red books* and *discharge tickets* as a way of circulating information about and denying employment to alleged troublemakers.[14] They spoke of virulent racism in the workplace, especially on the part of white South African managers.[15] These parallels with the conditions that produced the 1919 uprising evoke a sense that history was repeating itself, peaking with the 1937 colony-wide labor unrest.

Black radicals, from Pan-African Marxists to Black nationalists, understood the flaws of treating history as events and not processes. Kwame Ture, for example, noted, "History does not repeat itself; it cannot. Nothing can . . . everything changes, all the time."[16] The local reforms stemming from the 1919 unrest, in addition to the changes in the global political and economic environments, shifted the terrain on which labor was organizing in the late 1920s and 1930s. This chapter tracks liberation unionism during the latter part of the interwar years, exploring how the TWA lost its preeminent position as the sole representative of the working class as new organizations and new leaders and unions developed. The analysis is attentive to the new conflicts that emerged within the movement and to the ways in which they were overcome.

Remarkably, workers managed to deepen liberation unionism throughout the 1930s and retain those crucial characteristics and orientations that enabled this form of organizing to have the impacts on the state that it had in 1919 and the 1920s. It remained united and internationalist, and continued to push a transformational agenda. The white economic elites and the colonial state relied on their usual tool kit to suppress this movement. However, repression again was relatively more restrained than it otherwise might have been, particularly because the colony's oil was even more important to the British imperial war effort in the 1930s than it had been in 1919. After the 1937 uprising, liberation unionism again forced a second wave of concessions to worker demands and institutional reforms that further enhanced the state's capacity for development.

Crisis in the TWA

The TWA had blossomed after the 1919 uprising, but several points of contention emerged among the leaders and between the leaders and the rank-and-file membership in the late 1920s. Constitutional reform and expansion of the franchise in response to the 1919–20 uprising moved racialized workers' struggles from the streets to the seats. Labor leaders, such as Arthur A. Cipriani, increasingly sought to advance worker interests through their representation on the Legislative Council rather than through direct action, and the gradual and procedural nature of government reform began to frustrate African and Indian workers. In addition, Cipriani, already a Fabian socialist who favored and maintained communications with the British Labour Party, became increasingly conservative. By the late 1920s and early 1930s, Cipriani's TWA started exhibiting what Robert Michels called the "iron law of oligarchy," where power becomes concentrated in a small group of leaders who tend toward conservatism as their concern for organizational survival outweighs their members' interests.[17] Historian Adam Ewing describes the 1920s as a period when unions retreated in order to survive the repressive postrebellion environment.[18] But more than this, Cipriani's stance diverged from his rank and file's on several issues, including his antidivorce position on the TWA-supported 1926 Divorce Bill permitting divorce in cases of infidelity; his inability to deal with criticisms; his physical assault of a fellow TWA member for daring to defy him; his lack of support for strike action; and his decision in response to the 1932 Trade Union Ordinance to change the TWA into the Trinidad Labour Party (TLP) in 1934, choosing to sacrifice the ability to strike (in accordance with the legislation) so that the organization could pursue political objectives.[19]

Workers started organizing outside of the TWA/TLP structures. Several strikes emerged in the mid-1930s. In 1934 some fifteen thousand Indian men and women workers on several sugar estates protested against rising unemployment, excessive work tasks, low wages and delayed payments, and other economic hardships.[20] In 1935, in three separate events, government workers in the Public Works Department went on strike, about three thousand people held a demonstration against unemployment, and a hundred Apex oil workers organized a hunger march protesting low wages, excessive fines, arbitrary wage reductions, and blacklisting of workers who were critical of company management.[21] Cipriani did not support these strikes and publicly admonished the oil workers for the hunger march. Butler, then a TWA/TLP member, stood up and called Cipriani "loud-mouthed, but cold-footed."[22] In another venue, Elma François called him "Britain's best policeman in the colonies," and the crowd sang a chorus: "We will hang Cipriani on the sour apple tree / When the red revolution comes."[23] Workers rejected the increasingly conservative TWA/TLP leaders.

These conflicts fractured the TWA/TLP, and former members formed new rival working-class organizations. In 1934 Elma François, James (Jim) Headley, and Jim Barratt launched the National Unemployed Movement, later renamed the Negro Welfare Cultural and Social Association (NWCSA)—an anti-imperial Marxist-Leninist feminist working-class organization where most members were women, who focused on organizing both workers and the unemployed.[24] Rienzi, Butler, and John Rojas established a pressure group called the Trinidad Citizens League (TCL) in 1935. Butler subsequently parted ways with the TCL in 1936 and created his own organization—the British Empire Workers and Citizens Home Rule Party (BEW&CHRP; hereafter called the Butler Party). The membership of these alternatives to the TWA/TLP expanded rapidly, and the Butler Party ultimately became the TWA/TLP's main rival organization. By the mid-1930s, the TWA/TLP had lost its preeminent position as the voice of the working class.

Liberation Unionism Rejiggered and Retained

The 1930s segmentation of the TWA into several working-class organizations could have undermined working-class unity. The differences in personality and ideology were notable. Butler was an individualist, fiery, religious messianic force who was truly the beloved "Chief Servant," as he called himself, of the suffering classes. The NWCSA, conversely, believed in careful collective planning and secular organizing and understood they could not match Butler's charisma and popularity with the masses.[25] Leaders also disagreed on what Trinidad and Tobago's relationship should be to the British. The NWCSA and TCL pressed for a complete and total break with the imperial oppressor and the creation of an entirely new society free of exploitation. Conversely, Butler vacillated between the severing of all ties with the British and a more reform-oriented position of home rule or internal self-government where British rights would be extended to the population in Trinidad and Tobago, as some argue that he believed in the "essential goodness" of the British government and often referred to himself as a "Black Britisher."[26] These leaders struggled not to contradict each other in public fora and managed to maintain a united front.[27] According to Bukka Rennie, on the issue of ideology, the Butler Party and the NWCSA identified and bracketed their differences, forging a common political platform around their points of convergence.[28] These radical labor organizations maintained close ties. The Butler Party remained closely connected with the TCL and NWCSA.[29] The radical labor leaders spoke regularly on each other's platforms and attended each other's events.[30] Table 2.2 in chapter 2 illustrates their list of demands, some of which had remained unfulfilled after the 1919 wave of reforms.

The Pan-African character of liberation unionism continued to serve as a unifying force and ideological basis for rallying the masses throughout the 1930s. From apartheid in South Africa to worker conditions in Jamaica and British Guiana, every example of capitalist imperialism, colonial domination, and racialized labor exploitation was used to mobilize Black consciousness, Pan-African solidarity, and multiracial African-Indian unity in the colony.[31]

Perhaps the most prominent issue that enlivened the racial and anti-imperial consciousness of racialized workers in the colony was the Italian invasion of Ethiopia. Ethiopia held great symbolic significance in Marcus Garvey's movement as the only African territory to remain independent during European colonization of the continent. In fact, Garvey's Universal Negro Improvement Association anthem was "Ethiopia, Thou Land of Our Fathers." Garvey may have lost influence after the US government arrested him on trumped-up mail fraud charges in 1922 and subsequently deported him to Jamaica. Further, Garvey incensed and lost many of his supporters when he publicly admonished Haile Selassie for his handling of Ethiopia's resistance.[32] This, plus his open condemnation of the 1937 general strike—he claimed that communists in London incited Trinbagonian workers for their own ends—sealed the fate of Garvey, the man, as a waning icon for local workers.[33] Yet Garveyism—the ideology and networks that his organization established in the struggle for Pan-African unity—as well as Black autonomy, liberation, and repatriation continued to influence the strategies of African labor organizers in the colony. Thus, when the news reached Trinidad and Tobago that fascist dictator Benito Mussolini had sent Italian troops to conquer and colonize Ethiopia in 1934, local organizers sprang into action.

Virtually every major labor leader was involved in organizing around Ethiopia. Together, they wrote letters and articles, held mass meetings to educate the public, called for boycotts of Italian companies and products, and fundraised to send aid to Ethiopia.[34] The headlines of *The People* read "Negroes Awake" and "Members of the Black Race Show Your Sympathy with Abyssinia."[35] The NWCSA played a leading role in rallying support for the cause.[36] A resolution unanimously passed by an NWCSA meeting of "over 500 [N]negroes and other sympathetic people" in July 1935 began with "We, the Negro people of the Island of Trinidad, protest against the sending of troops to the Abyssinian border."[37] Even colonial officials noted how Italian imperial aggression stimulated Black racial consciousness: "Racial feeling generally was very strong, and was stirred up by the constant stream of news in the press about Abyssinia and by news from America (There was close communication between the negroes and Harlem, and American wireless also played a prominent part)."[38] This colonial administrator's observations also reflect how Black racial solidarity was being constructed and transported through Pan-African networks.

Labor leaders also continued to build racial consciousness alongside class consciousness. "Trinidad Negro Workers Arise!" was a rallying cry. Organizers stressed that the racial kinship that bound Black workers in Trinidad to Ethiopians was the basis for racial solidarity in the liberation struggle. In the Butler Party's membership drive, pamphlets read, "My dear Fellow-Workers & Citizens:— Greetings! This is an invitation. . . . Already hundreds of loyal liberty-loving Britons in whose veins flow generations of incomparably Ancient Ethiopian Warrior blood have accepted the Fascist-Imperialist-Capitalist challenge to war and have sworn to fight under black leadership . . . for 'Black Shirt' and Capitalist-Imperialist defeat and extermination."[39] Butler and others linked the ideology of Pan-Africanism, with its emphasis on Black connectedness as racialized subjects of white capitalist system, with class interests to birth a discourse that mobilized Black toilers in the colony.

As multiracial movement building proceeded in the 1920s, this Black race consciousness aroused by the Italian invasion did not repel Indian workers. On the contrary, organizers spotlighted this and other evidence of imperial and colonial domination to build class consciousness across racial divides. In a public meeting in 1935 called "A New Movement for Afro-Indian Unity," twenty years before Bandung, prominent labor organizers of African descent, such as Ralph Mentor, and Hindus and Muslims of South Asian descent, such as Rienzi (labor leader), J. H. Dube (Hindu, president of the local Arya Samaj, an Indian Hindu reform movement), and Gool Mohamed (imam of a mosque), came together to give speeches in English and Urdu about the need to be united for Ethiopian freedom.[40] Rienzi, when interviewed by *The People* about the motivation for the event, is quoted as saying that he "hoped that the campaign waged in Trinidad against Italian aggression would unite Afro-West Indians and East Indians. The issues of their unity would result in the independence of Africa and India. . . . When they met to protest against Italian Imperialism they protested against all kinds of Imperialistic exploitation and pressure."[41] To radical labor leaders like Rienzi, Ethiopia exemplified the experience of all racialized colonized toilers and was a way to build Afro-Indian interracial solidarity.

Organizers emphasized shared historical experiences of imperial violence to build the movement, fundraise, and recruit more members and supporters. For example, Hugo Mentor (editor of *The People*) urged, "One and all must help Ethiopia. . . . I should like to embrace the opportunity of reminding our Moslem friends of the great historic association between Ethiopians and the land of Mohammed's right hand man, Bilal, an unmixed Negro . . . remember the butchery of the Mohammedan members of my race (Berbers, Hausas, and Arab Negroids) in Tripoli when the Italians conquered it from the Turks; to recall Kafur, one of the greatest black Mohammedan rulers of Egypt. . . . We, Trinidad Africans and our fellow Indians, must play our part."[42] The anti-imperial spirit of Pan-Africanism unleashed by events in Ethiopia became a way to unify African and Indian workers in the colony.

Trade unionists also centered British colonial domination as a primary target through the Italian invasion of Ethiopia. Butler, for instance, in a public speech bellowed, "The present British Government is not a working Government. England today is spat upon for her Criminal actions and dirty slackness in assisting Mussolini in conquering Abyssinia. The British Government is the worst Government in the Empire. . . . we are going to fight and fight like hell against the white men . . . who are oppressors of this colony[.] [W]e demand tonight that we are going to stand up and fight like hell against Colonel Hickling and most of these white English men[.] [W]e are prepared to shed blood."[43] Ethiopia was just one of many points on which interracial solidarity was constructed. Organizers used other cases of imperial atrocities to link workers across race and fuse global dynamics with local problems. For example, Elma François, when placed on trial for "sedition" in the 1937 uprising and asked to describe her public speeches, explained, "The subject of my address was 'World Imperialism and the Colonial Toilers.' . . . In dealing with my subject, I dealt with world conditions linking them up with local conditions; I dealt with land reservations in the Kenya Colony. . . . I dealt with Nigeria. I dealt with the natives there protesting against increased taxation. . . . I discussed Germany and Russia also. . . . I spoke about the Negro and East-Indian workers who sleep under the Town Hall and in the Square through poverty. I wanted their conditions to be bettered."[44] When asked in the trial to define "World Imperialism and Colonialism" she explained that it was the relationship between the ruling classes of the world and the exploited workers of the colonies.[45] Highlighted shared histories of oppression facilitated the galvanizing of both racial and class consciousness.

Such organizing was successful in that the 1937 uprising retained the multisectoral and multiracial character of the 1919 mobilization. African and Indian workers from all the major oil companies and in agriculture (sugar and cacao) were striking together in the streets.[46] Waterfront workers in Port of Spain and San Fernando ceased work, which held up cargo ships and left sugar that was to be loaded for export on the docks of the harbor.[47] Public sector laborers for the Public Works Department and Trinidad Government Railway, city street cleaners, and lightermen all went on strike, leaving streets unswept, littered, and rancid in smell.[48] Whatever little manufacturing existed in the colony was also affected. For example, hundreds of workers at a new paper factory and at Trinidad Clay Products walked out.[49] In transportation and food services, bus drivers, conductors, and bakers joined the strike wave.[50] Reports noted solidarity or "sympathetic strikes" by estate workers in Tobago to support workers elsewhere.[51]

When the striking broke out in 1937, Elma François of the NWCSA traveled to the southern areas to gather information and returned to the northern towns to organize support for the strikers and "to demonstrate in a tangible way their sympathies for the oil workers."[52] At the NWCSA solidarity marches, placards read "Sympathy with the Strike" and "Not bayonet and blood, but more pay."[53] The NWCSA fundraised to pay for the legal defense of workers who were arrested, to source and spread information that was essential to the struggle, and to impede police efforts to find Butler.[54] Strategies for fundraising and movement building centered on creating a collective consciousness: "The general cause had to be related to each individual situation, since the middle-class, the intellectuals, the industrial workers, the agricultural workers and peasants all had particular struggles that were in some way connected to the whole, therefore it was made clear to all and sundry that it was in their interests to donate money [to sustain the movement]."[55] As such, labor organizers explicitly strategized how to mobilize separate industrial sectors and middle-class sympathizers to form a united multisectoral, multiracial movement, which effectively ground the colonial economy to a halt.

Having now abandoned the TWA/TLP, workers formed new unions by industrial sector to negotiate with employers, and they still collaborated across them. In 1937 oil workers formed the Oilfield Workers' Trade Union (OWTU) when Butler went into hiding. The OWTU founders and leaders included plumbers, motor mechanics, drivers and transporters, pipe fitters, well attendants, and boiler cleaners.[56] Rienzi organized sugar workers into the All Trinidad Sugar Estates and Factory Workers' Trade Union (ATSEFWTU). Oil sector workers were also instrumental in the formation of the Federated Workers' Trade Union (FWTU) for railway and construction workers.[57] The labor movement became de facto unified again in 1937, when Rienzi, head of the sugar union, was voted in as president of the African-dominated oil union, making him head of the two most important trade unions and industrial sectors in the colony. Furthermore, his involvement in the FWTU resulted in an OWTU-ATSEFWTU-FWTU alliance that united workers in the colony's two principal industries (oil and sugar) with workers in the transportation and public sectors, also uniting the two major racial groups. Rienzi also provided legal assistance to Butler and other strikers who were arrested.[58]

Besides these three leading unions, other unions registered in 1937 included the Seamen and Waterfront Workers Trade Union, the Amalgamated Building and Woodworkers Union, and the Public Works Workers Trade Union.[59] Even though workers formed separate unions by industry and the leaders held different ideological positions, active collaboration across union, sectoral, and racial lines enhanced the strength of liberation unionism. This unity made liberation unionism a potent force in terms of numbers and its ability to shut down the colony and force negotiations.

Like in 1919, the 1937 general strike relied on and empowered people at the community level. According to one newspaper report, "People wholly unconnected with the strikers marched through the streets or assembled at street corners."[60] Other reports regularly noted "strikers and sympathizers."[61] Whole towns were shut down as businesses and shops closed their doors.[62] Still, shopkeepers provided food and resources to sustain the strikers, thereby allowing the strikes to carry on for a longer period. According to one newspaper report, "Fyzabad strikers are prepared to hold out indefinitely. They have pooled every penny of their savings to create a food fund, and have even arranged with local shopkeepers to supply them with eatables if and when their savings run out. Shopkeepers have agreed to cooperate with the strikers in this."[63] Shopkeepers and other strike supporters also erected "breakfast sheds" to provide meals and shop goods and give cash to strikers.[64] In addition, unemployed persons were active participants in the demonstrations.[65] Within just a few days of the start of the 1937 uprising, newspapers were reporting that the strike was now "island wide" with unrest "almost everywhere," involving workers and sympathizers across the length and width of the colony, from an array of industries and in multiple work activities, along with community sympathizers and the unemployed.[66]

Women and children remained actively engaged in militant action. One Indian woman sugar worker, Poolbasie, attended NWCSA meetings in the sugar estates, reported on sugar workers' living conditions and the sexual violence of overseers against young girls, and participated in the 1934 Hunger Marches.[67] Others, like Etherlin Roberts and Daisy Crick, were lead organizers and speakers in the oil belt. Crick turned her home into a headquarters for organizing activities.[68] According to reports of the 1937 unrest, gatherings "composed of men, women and children" and women workers were also demanding wage increases.[69] Another report described how "a mob of men, women and children, armed with sticks, bottles and stones stormed these places [public offices, provision shops, stores and schools] threatening the employees."[70] Young and old, these women, children, and men, "brandishing sticks, cutlasses and other weapons[,] walked from factory to factory in the district infecting workers with the striker fever which proved to be very contagious."[71] Domestic workers withdrew their labor, as captured in a *Trinidad Guardian* report: "In sympathy with the men who are engaged in the big 'sit down' strike, hundreds of women who were employed as cooks, washers and maidservants in the bungalows of the Senior Staffs on the various Oil Companies have also gone on strike. Their strike, however, is not a 'sit-down' strike, as the majority of them have deserted the bungalows for their own homes."[72] Women remained a central pillar of liberation unionism in this period.

The workers' demands in 1937 built explicitly on the transformative ones from 1919. Workers carried over and expanded the unfulfilled demands from the 1919 reforms into the 1930s. In terms of worker-specific economic issues, demands across industries included wage increases for "agricultural laborers, oil workers, and all workers generally."[73] Workers demanded double or almost double the wage rates per day; overtime pay; reduced regular working hours; the removal of racist barriers to promotions and better working conditions, including an end to victimization and blacklisting; and the elimination of racial pay gaps.[74] One striker commented, "I am a poor man . . . and I have a wife and three children. What do I get?—Seven cents an hour! We are [d]emanding 14 cents."[75] In keeping with the diasporic unity, some demands specified that Caribbean immigrant workers be paid the same wages as Trinbagonian workers.[76] In addition, workers in the 1930s pushed for the nationalization of foreign oil and sugar company assets.

In the 1930s, workers intensified the call for political transformation. As part of this working people's nationalism, strikers demanded the end of colonial rule, national independence, and self-determination. For example, in various bicycle processions during the uprising (one involving about 130 cyclists), demonstrators carried placards that read "We want more pay," as well as "Home Rule party[,] no Labour Party."[77] Workers also demanded the right to meaningful collective bargaining.[78]

Workers also expanded their demands for social legislation in the 1930s to include the ability of married people to seek legal separation or divorce, a dole and tax relief for the unemployed, free employer-provided medical attendance and benefits for employees, health insurance for the population at large, more institutions for enhancing educational and technical training, and pensions and gratuities.[79] Workers also pressed the colonial state for more children's playgrounds and public lavatories throughout the cities.[80] Many reforms such as these reflected women's concerns.

Employer and Colonial State Repression

The colonial state and white capital in Trinidad and Tobago persisted in their refusal to recognize and accept the will of the people. Just like in 1919, their immediate response was to deny and downplay the existence of discontent and worker agitation.[81] The governor continued to blame outside agitators for inciting the unrest: "I have recorded my anxiety regarding the activity of agitators. Trinidad is, generally speaking, devoid of any sense of discipline, and it affords fertile ground for the mischief maker.... Stringent orders have been given to disperse meetings in public spaces and to arrest all persons who attempt to stir up trouble."[82] It was surprising to them that the working people of the colony could coordinate and organize. The colonial state also continued to project that racial divisions would prohibit cross-racial alliances. For example, with respect to Rienzi being president of the OWTU, the governor reportedly said he saw "no prospect that he will be able to control and guide the Oilworkers Union which is composed almost entirely of [N]egroes."[83] Workers proved this to be untrue as they had, in this historical moment, overcome the racial divide-and-rule-and-exploit strategy of the ruling class.

Employers continued to resist negotiations in 1937. They felt that workers were making "extraordinary demands," that many were already well compensated, and that therefore "there [was] really no reason why they should demand more money."[84] Likewise, United British Oilfields management issued a statement ten days into the 1937 uprising stating, "(1) Under no circumstances will there be any change in the present wage scale until everyone is back to work; (2) The Management will have no discussions with anyone on the question of wages or conditions until everyone is back to work; (3) When work has started again, any genuine grievances will be thoroughly investigated with representatives from our own employees."[85] In 1937 the governor spent weeks pleading with strikers to return to work, repeating the employers' refrain that there could be no settlement unless the workers agreed to go back to work.[86] As if learning nothing from 1919, the colonial state initially refused to meet with workers, encouraging them to take their grievances and demands to employers directly without state involvement.

Predictably, as they had in 1919, the white settlers and business elite advocated for an intensification of white violence to repress the masses. In one letter to the Colonial Office, one local white elite man reiterates, "To my mind it is most essential that White troops should be stationed there for years, and I know that that is the opinion of all right thinking men in the colony."[87] The colonial state again implemented a range of repressive tactics once the movement erupted. A series of measures were passed to restrict movement and the press. Police arrested striking men and women and ordered the closing of liquor stores "as a safety measure."[88] The governor dispatched police, special constables, the Trinidad Light Horse, and the Trinidad Light Infantry Volunteers to the oil fields, sugar factories and estates, and towns.[89] Police fired into crowds, killing several people, including children.[90] Governor Arthur George Murchison Fletcher continued the dangerous precedent of allowing armed white vigilante volunteers to protect the major export industries. These vigilantes included lawyers, merchants, clerks, civil servants, and ex-soldiers, and, among those, even some pensioners.[91] The groups they formed included the Mounted Volunteers of Trinidad (a white militia group comprising primarily businessmen) and the Colonial Vigilantes (members of a whites-only club). White American oil and asphalt workers were given arms by their company managers.[92] The colonial state deployed naval platoons and armed guards, and it passed "anti-intimidation" measures to protect strikebreakers and prevent workers from encouraging others to go on strike.[93] Navy planes frequently flew low over towns to intimidate strikers, and other planes dropped government pamphlets asking people to return to work as a precondition for the governor to pursue settlements.[94]

The British warship HMS *Ajax* arrived on June 23, 1937, and about 150 Blue Jackets and Marines descended on the strikers, followed by the HMS *Exeter*, which arrived the day after.[95] It took three thousand troops (local police and British armed forces), according to some estimates, plus volunteers and assistance from two warships to put down the uprising.[96] In these ways, the colonial state aligned with the white settler and business elite's view concerning the use of external and internal white repressive force to crush the uprising, at least in the short term. Together, the economic elite class and the colonial state deployed a range of strategies similar to those used in 1919 to suppress the movement.

Political Opportunities Still Open

The state's repressive capacity relative to the size of the movement, state–elite conflict, and the strategic importance of Trinidad and Tobago's oil together produced relative restraint in the British colonial repression of liberation unionism. One would think that after the 1919 uprising, the colonial state would have invested in strengthening the local police force to prevent future recurrences. But the police force remained small. Workers, knowing this, further frustrated police efforts by disrupting communications, such as cutting telephone and telegraph lines, and blocking roads by felling large trees, digging large ditches, and strewing coconuts along the roadway.[97] According to Martin Thomas, colonial police forces "proved unable to cope" with the strikes, and their responses "were inadequate, sometimes disproportionate," such as live firing into crowds, which indicated panic more than some planned strategy.[98] The overall weakness of the state's coercive apparatus, its difficulty in mounting a powerful, coordinated repressive force, allowed the strikes to continue longer and to grow stronger, compelling the colonial state and capital to concede.

Further, state–elite rivalry, which included interethnic antagonisms among these Europeans, continued to produce relative restraint. Governor Fletcher, who had been in office for only approximately a year before the June 1937 uprising, and his colonial secretary, Howard Nankivell, expressed a similar disdain for the local white elite as Fletcher's predecessor had in 1919.[99] Fletcher reported, "Local white creoles were a degenerate lot. They did not mix with the 'imported' Europeans whom along with others they called 'foreigners' and drew a very strict color line. . . . They had an inferiority complex vis à vis the English. Even the Wardens were a poor lot—no discipline, lack of energy and suspicion of corruption. English personnel was needed in the districts."[100] Fletcher also criticized the local white elite for "blackballing" one unofficial Legislative Council member, whom he described as "only very slightly colored," from their club.[101] With this view, Fletcher did not always act in harmony with the white elites, which workers took advantage of to expand liberation unionism.

For example, the colonial state was hesitant to arrest Butler. In the early days of the protests, Governor Fletcher walked in step with the dominant class. He repeated the notion expressed by the manager and attorney at Apex Oilfields, Lt. Col. H. C. B. Hickling, that Butler was "mentally deranged," and, seven days into the uprising, even though "arrest [of Butler] may lead to great disorder," he found it "essential" and reported that every effort was being made to arrest him.[102] Workers made it clear that Butler was their undisputed leader and threatened even more revolt should the colonial state capture him. One banner read "We want Uriah Butler. Don't touch him. If you touch him, Fire, Blood."[103] Another read "No other representative but Butler."[104] Given the potential fallout of arresting Butler, just days after initially advocating for Butler's arrest, Governor Fletcher reneged, concluding that finding and arresting Butler would spell disaster in the colony. Fletcher reported, "In view of the desirability of avoiding bloodshed during strike negotiations no immediate steps are being taken for his [Butler's] capture but he is aware that he must surrender or be arrested at all costs."[105] Governor Fletcher also feared how African and Indian workers would respond to white volunteer troops: "To call them out would always be regarded as setting class against class."[106] Thus, the colonial officials' fear of the tenacity of the workers, combined with their animosity toward the local white elite and the authoritarianism embedded in the Crown Colony structure, coalesced to enable colonial officials to carve out a space of autonomous action, however tenuous. An imperial state investigation into the uprising supported Fletcher's relative prudence. The report recommended against the introduction of a permanent garrison of white troops, arguing that it "would create a feeling of bitterness and suspicion among the working people and would inevitably render more difficult the already difficult task of settling industrial disputes by normal industrial methods."[107]

The colonial officials used the eruption of liberation unionism to assert their authority over the local elite. Fletcher admitted that the protests were rooted in legitimate economic problems, a fact capital would never confess. According to Fletcher, "[Butler] was somewhat extravagant in his views and definitely extravagant in his mode of expressing them, yet there was sincerity. . . . [Butler's] speeches were at first intemperate in time, and became inflammatory as time went on; but there still was running through them all and through his letters an undercurrent of sincere appeal."[108] Nankivell went further and, according to Thomas, "castigated the oil and sugar companies for paying starvation wages, for valuing their workers less than their machinery and for repatriating their profits."[109] Nankivell's speech in the Legislative Council on July 9, 1937, is worth quoting at length:

> In the past we have had to salve our consciences with humbug and we have had to satisfy labour with platitudes. Those days have gone by: we can no longer say to labour we recognize your hardships but we cannot afford to remedy them. . . . Today government is collecting large revenues and the oil companies are paying big dividends. Even sugar is now to a considerable extent more than paying its way. . . . There can be no question today of these three employing groups, Government, the oil industry, and the sugar industry, being able to pay a fair wage and to provide decent conditions for its labour. . . . I would stress very strongly the point of view that an industry has no right to pay dividends at all until it pays a fair wage to labour and gives the labourer decent conditions. . . . A decent wage for labour and decent conditions should be a first charge on industry and there should be no question of paying dividends until those requirements are satisfied. I may remind the sugar industry, as they know very well, that they are a subsidized industry, subsidized by the Imperial Government, and subsidized by the local government, and that being the case, those who subsidize them have a right to intervene to a certain extent in their affairs. . . . I would remind the sugar industry also that the sugar industry was not subsidized in order to enable them to pay dividends to their shareholders; it was subsidized because it is the largest employer of labour. . . . [A]nd not only must we keep them [the workers] employed, but we must keep them employed in decent conditions

and not in conditions of economic slavery. . . . I feel that any transfer of profits from the shareholders' pocket to the pockets of the wage earners will be entirely in the interest of this colony.[110]

Needless to say, Fletcher's and Nankivell's comments and perceived restraint made them enemies of white capital. In the aftermath of the 1937 uprising, seventeen representatives of the Sugar Manufacturers' Association of Trinidad, the Petroleum Association of Trinidad, and the Trinidad Chamber of Commerce passed a resolution that "by far the greater portion of the responsible section of the community in this colony" had lost confidence in Governor Fletcher.[111] Their inflammatory letter charged that Fletcher was too lenient toward the supposed perpetrators of "barbarism." They wanted "an administrator endowed with firmness, steadfastness, and continuity of purpose."[112] These disagreements between the state and local elite ultimately led to Fletcher's and Nankivell's early removal from office in the colony but provided critical political openings that workers exploited.

Workers, keenly aware of the balance of power in the colony, saw Fletcher as perhaps the more reasonable among the authoritarian options. The executive committees of the sugar and oil unions (ATSEFWTU and OWTU) sent their resolution to the secretary of state for the colonies in London, stating that they were aware that the "reactionary vested interests" of the colony disagreed with Fletcher's stance toward addressing the economic problems in the colony. They hoped, they continued, that Fletcher's departure from office was not intended "to deprive the colony of an able, impartial and liberal minded administrator." They further noted, "The Unions would resent and oppose by every constitutional means any attempt on the part of the Colonial Office to recall Administrators or other Administrative Officials at the behest of Capital, solely because such Officials have endeavored to pursue a policy calculated to benefit the Colony as a whole by holding the scales of justice evenly between Workers and Employers."[113] Working people were demanding the separation of the colonial state and the white capitalist class, or, in other words, greater colonial state autonomy.

The third contextual factor shaping relative worker power was the even greater importance of Trinidadian oil to the British Empire in the lead-up to World War II. By the early 1930s, it accounted for 40 percent of imperial production and played a primary role as an aviation fuel supplier, providing about 25 percent of the Royal Air Force's total annual requirements for high-octane aviation fuel; it was one of the few sources of 100-octane gasoline in the British Empire.[114] In the late 1930s, the British Oil Board deemed Trinidad's oil of primary significance to British national security interests.[115] The local white elite, the colonial state, and the workers all attempted to use the importance of the colony's oil to advance their own interests. The white elite cited the colony's importance to the British Empire to call for permanent troops in the colony: "Of supreme importance to our Country [is]: The adequate protection of Trinidad, as the largest and most important Oil producing center in the Empire, and of vital importance to the Navy. It is vulnerable in the event of war or of internal disturbances, such as have just taken place.... We [the oil, sugar, and other industrial companies] feel that, if for reasons of Policy, Troops cannot be stationed in the Colony, it is essential that either a Naval or Aeroplane Base should be established in Trinidad."[116]

Trinbagonian workers understood their structural power. As Butler noted, the oil companies endeavored "to get more and still more oil because the Empire needs every drop we can produce because of war."[117] According to a 1936 article in a working-class newspaper:

> The local worker is not a churlish creature and in his heart of hearts he delights in plain speech and an honest deal. He realizes that the local oil companies that already can contrive to pay fairly handsome, or at any rate, assured dividends to their shareholders are hoping to be in a position to pay more enhanced dividends than they do now.... The contention of the workers is that their support in this matter must be one of bargaining.... It is not enough, they seem to say, for them to be given a mere verbal promise of benefits which will accrue to them from increasing activities or the larger operations which would be undertaken, as these would come, even in some small measure, as a matter of course. As the accumulation of funds for the award of dividends and the payment of labor are somewhat opposing conditions, those who supply the latter and by whose efforts the former are procurable demand that their share in the partnership should meet with more ample remuneration.[118]

Likewise, one waterfront worker and strike organizer said, "We are aware that labor is the foundation on which capital stands, therefore we make our demands."[119] Working people understood that they occupied a strategic position in the British Empire and that their mobilization would threaten British imperial expansionary interests and company profits.

The imperial state and colonial officials sought solutions to the labor crisis that would make for lasting peace in the colony, especially to secure oil supplies.[120] Earl Hugh William Fortescue, government spokesman in the House of Lords, expressed the importance of a measured response:

In 1936 Trinidad produced over 60 per cent of the oil produced from British Empire sources, but this was only 0.92 per cent of the world's production. None the less, on account of its quality and geographical position, it is of very real significance to the Empire as a whole, and in both peace and war the Royal Navy and the Royal Air Force have a vital interest in the development and modern scientific refining of Trinidad oil. Accordingly the security both from external and internal danger of the various oil plants, including the pipe lines and refineries, has become a matter of imperial concern. It is important to us all that good relations between capital and labor in the Trinidad oilfields should be built up and maintained.[121]

After the strikes ended, the secretary of state for the colonies, William Ormsby-Gore, echoed this sentiment:

The strike is now over and the men are back to work, but I have special reasons for desiring that such unfortunate incidents should not recur. The Trinidad oil field is one of the few Empire oil fields on which the Admiralty and Air Ministry will have to rely in time of war. Already there are large Admiralty and Air Force contracts for the supply of different types of oil fuel which are got and refined in Trinidad, including arrangements for the putting up of a new 3/4 million pound plant to produce a special spirit of the highest grade for our fast fighter aeroplanes for the defence of London. Oil wells and refineries with their complicated machinery are singularly vulnerable to sabotage, and if fires started millions of pounds worth of damage can be done. It therefore behooves Government in the interest of the State, even more than in those of property, to take all such steps as are humanly possible to prevent the causes—and especially the legitimate causes—of trouble arising.[122]

Ormsby-Gore said he was "determined to forestall the possibility of future disturbances by a settlement acceptable to the workers."[123] Trinidad's geostrategic significance to the British empire therefore opened up a political space for liberation unionism and shaped its success in stimulating state reforms.

Liberation unionism in the interwar years flourished and attained relative success because of the confluence of these factors. The strength of the movement relative to that of the police, the imperial interest in reliable oil supplies, the friction between the colonial state and capital, and the Crown Colony administrative structure provided the opening that labor seized on to successfully force concessions.

The 1937 uprising in Trinidad and Tobago was one of many labor protests across British colonies during these years. The British government put together a commission led by John Forster to investigate the uprising in Trinidad and Tobago, as well as the West India Royal Commission, led by William Edward Guinness (Lord Moyne), for a Caribbean-wide inquiry. Trade union representatives served as witnesses and testified to the economic, social, and political oppressions facing the masses. The recommendations from both the Forster Report (1938) and the Moyne Report (1945) reiterated the conditions and plight of labor.[124] Some scholars emphasize that working people won few tangible results from the general strike, as "the substance of colonialism remained intact."[125] Indeed, while workers did not overthrow the capitalist system and its attendant racial and colonial structure, this 1937 uprising forced the colonial state to undergo a second wave of reforms to address the recommendations from these colonial reports and the movement that sparked the investigation in the first place. These reforms further increased the state's orientation and capacity for progressive policies, which improved the well-being of working people.

State Autonomy

Worker mobilization compelled the state to further enhance its relative autonomy from the economic elite. After the 1919 uprising, the colonial state passed legislation to establish an Industrial Court in 1920 but never actually set up the institution.[126] After the 1937 movement, the colonial administration accepted the need to further extract itself from the arms of the white elite and build structures to address the racial and class tensions between nonwhite (African and Indian) workers and white capital. Governor Fletcher conceded, "There was a clear-cut racial demarcation between employers and workers, so that there was a pressing need for establishing and maintaining government contact with both sides."[127] In the immediate term, the colonial state put together a mediation committee comprising Acting Colonial Secretary Howard Nankivell, Collector of Customs and Excise A. E. V. Barton, and T. M. Kelshall to receive representations from any group of workers.[128] Hundreds of workers availed themselves of the mediation committee.[129]

For the long term, the colonial state institutionalized mediation with the construction and empire-wide diffusion of the Trinidad Trade Disputes (Arbitration and Inquiry) Ordinance of 1938. This ordinance legislated a system of arbitration to enable workers and employers to settle labor disputes and replaced a former 1920 ordinance that, according to one colonial official, was "useless for all practical purposes as a piece of machinery for settling trades disputes."[130] The new ordinance was hashed out during contentious negotiations among representatives of local labor unions, British colonial administrators, and private capital.[131] The resulting "Trinidad Ordinance" or "Trinidad model," as colonial officials called it, was subsequently adopted by twenty-three colonies across the British Empire.[132] Despite employers' unwillingness, a 1938 joint conference of employers and trade unions was "the first time in the history of this Colony" that both parties had been brought together in a formalized institutional structure to negotiate. Industrial Adviser A. G. V. Lindon described his efforts to encourage employers to accept the new state structures:

> Neither of the industries were prepared nor did bargain, or even attempt to,—neither oil nor sugar made the slightest advance towards the T.U. [Trade Unions] either in cash or in spirit.... The attitude of some of the Employers towards the T.U. fellows was superciliously cynical and overbearing, and at some stages they even sniggered at the inexperience of the employees' representatives.... Quite frankly, if English employers adopted a similar attitude to T.U. officials, the latter would not stay in conference five minutes, and proceed to organize stoppages.... And even I would feel justified in loosing the end of the rope and leave the Employers to learn good taste by experience. But here the material is far too inflammable. So I clung on until the Oil Companies agreed to the principle of arbitration pending authority from London.... All the Welfare schemes in the works will fail to produce the desired result while the workers and the T.U. representatives are conscious of an implied sense of inferiority.[133]

This quote shows that capital remained resistant to negotiations and that the employers' sense of superiority over the workers stemmed from a combination of racism and their antilabor stance. It also demonstrates that colonial state officials understood that they now needed to play a more active, interventionist, and mediating role. As the *Vanguard* acknowledged, "[Then Governor] Sir Hubert Young did a large part in persuading the oil companies to alter their original stand."[134]

After 1937 workers won another wave of wage increases and better working conditions in a wide range in private industries and the public sector. For all state employees, the Legislative Council unanimously decided to set a minimum wage for "unskilled (non-agricultural)" workers (an increase to nine cents per hour for city laborers and seven and a half cents per hour for those in the rural areas) and an eight-hour working day.[135] Despite the protestations of the private companies, industrial agreements reached with workers—between the Seamen and Waterfront Workers Trade Union and the Shipping Association of Trinidad and Tobago in 1938, and between the Oilfields Employers' Association and the OWTU in 1939 and 1940—increased wages and improved working conditions and governed these industries throughout World War II.[136]

Between 1938 and 1945, the colonial state passed several laws to ameliorate conditions for working people. The 1938 Shop (Hours of Opening and Employment) Ordinance stipulated seats for female workers and prohibited keeping shops open outside of specified operating hours, effectively providing an eight-hour workday for shop assistants and clerks.[137] The old Master and Servants Ordinance of 1846 was replaced with one (with the same name) that conformed to labor on the basis of a civil contract and omitted penal sanctions for worker breach of contract. Other postuprising worker protection ordinances restricted the employment of women in industries at night; regulated the system for recruiting workers; amended the Workmen's Compensation Ordinance to include agricultural and domestic workers; expanded the Trade Union Ordinance to recognize peaceful picketing and immunity from actions in tort; established trade boards; and extended the labor bureau system.[138] Liberation unionism therefore struck down a number of labor-repressive laws and stimulated the passage of legislation prohibiting a number of labor-repressive practices.

Bureaucratic Expansion and Infrastructural Reach

In the post-1937 period, the state further expanded its bureaucracy and infrastructural reach to meet labor's demands. Committees and agencies were established to review, recommend, create, and/or implement new developmental priorities. Throughout the 1940s, OWTU union members served "and played their part in influencing decisions taken on these bodies."[139] These included the Franchise, Agriculture Policy, Labor Recruitment, Unemployment, Health Insurance, Public Works Advisory, Full Employment, Demobilization, Resettlement, Social Welfare, Trade Unions Ordinance Amendment, Price Control, and Reserved Occupation Key Industries Committees. They also served on several commissions, such as the Planning and Housing Commission; the Trinidad and Tobago Joint Sugar Board; and several other boards, such as those for transport, poor relief, beef, and industrial training, among others.[140]

The civil service expanded to staff the new state agencies and structures. The number of positions in the public service establishment increased from 1,028 in 1935 to 3,960 in 1956.[141] The Mines Department was one of the prime units targeted for strengthening. From 1938, several pieces of legislation were introduced to generate more revenue from oil mining and operations, increase refining capabilities, collect more data on operations, and improve safety.[142] Reorganized by ordinance in 1948, the Mines Department abolished the position of inspector of mines and petroleum technologist and more effectively distributed the duties between the senior inspector of factories and the petroleum technologist. The same year, other ordinances were passed to simplify accounting procedures, channel more money from the petroleum sector to the general revenue of the colony, institute new methods of assessing royalties, and impose new regulations on operators in the industry.[143] After the removal of wartime price controls, the royalty rates were reexamined, and new rates negotiated.[144] Income tax for limited liability companies was also increased from 12.5 percent in 1935 to 37.5 percent in 1946 to 40 percent in 1949.[145] These reforms, together with greater oil production in the war years, produced an overall increase in the percentage of direct revenues contributed by the oil industry to the colonial state, from approximately 20 percent in 1938 to just over 30 percent in 1950.[146]

Infrastructural reach expanded as the colonial state devised and implemented a comprehensive development program for 1939 to 1944 that significantly extended the state's administrative presence throughout the colony. Per many of the workers' demands, the plan listed the intent to build "houses for the working classes," hospitals, and medical buildings; construct an aerodrome; improve and extend roads, the railway, water supplies, an electricity scheme, and public offices; and improve irrigation and drainage, antimalarial and sanitation works, and more.[147] The development program was financed from the colonial government's own surplus balances and loans. Acting Governor John Huggins projected that it could be implemented "without any additional taxation," as the colony had been in a healthy financial position, with ordinary revenues exceeding ordinary expenditure, since 1936.[148] Furthermore, in response to the labor movements all across the Caribbean in the 1930s, the 1929 Colonial Development and Welfare Act was extended in 1940, 1945, and 1950. On the need for the colonial state to pursue this more active developmentalist agenda, one colonial official urged, "The moral and political effect of doing something in Trinidad, and doing it quickly, is more important than a haggling over details. Trinidad has suffered for years from good intentions that have never been carried out. This development scheme has inspired new hope in the Colony and I think it is very important that we show that the Secretary of State is strongly supporting the Governor in his efforts to improve conditions there."[149] Liberation unionism forced the state to channel more of its resources to the masses and therefore stimulated capacity building to make this possible.

After the 1937 unrest, infrastructural reach with respect to education and apprenticeships expanded alongside an increase in local hires for higher-paid jobs in industry, two issues on which liberation unionism had pressed capital and the colonial state. The Moyne Report recommended that the government pay teachers, administer staffing issues, and control all new schools.[150] Net education expenditure (excluding school buildings) doubled from $878,499 in 1937 to $1,911,398 in 1944 (in local currency).[151] In 1937 there were 293 primary and intermediate schools (45 of them government run) serving 72,766 students, who maintained a 69.8 percent attendance rate.[152] By 1948, about a decade after the 1937 uprising, there were 301 primary and intermediate schools (of which 50 were government schools) serving 103,668 pupils, with a 75 percent attendance rate.[153] Likewise, the number of government or government-assisted secondary schools also steadily increased from nine to fourteen over the same period.[154] A board of industrial training maintained a full-time technical school and conducted evening classes at ten different centers distributed throughout the colony; these served about three thousand students pursuing trades with the City and Guilds of London Institute. The board worked with oil and sugar companies to conduct in-service training and workshops. The state also opened a government technical college in 1954 in San Fernando, and the Department of Education conducted evening classes for adults.[155] These efforts aimed at increasing local workers' expertise and ability to fill higher technical jobs in industry.

Worker mobilization spurred investments in health services. Health expenditure tripled from 1938 to 1948 (although still representing about 8 percent of the total expenditure).[156] The colonial state also invested in expanding and refurbishing the colonial/general hospitals, projects that were completed in the 1950s. Infant mortality generally decreased over the 1940s, and targeted programs at the community level to address the hookworm disease among laboring people reduced deaths from 119 in 1936 to 54 in 1946.[157] These examples provide evidence of how liberation unionism stimulated an increased state capacity for progressive social policies.

Housing became a top priority for the colonial state. While the governor viewed all the major works of the 1939–44 development plan as "of an equally urgent nature" and intended for the colonial state to undertake them concurrently, "housing for the working classes of the colony" was highlighted as being "of prime importance" and "a matter of great urgency."[158] In 1938 the colonial state passed three pieces of legislation to facilitate the construction of homes for working people and the poor—the Slum Clearing and Housing Ordinance, the Trinidad Town and Regional Planning Ordinance, and the Land Acquisition (Amendment) Ordinance. The state cleared and/or repaired unhealthy and unsanitary living areas in working-class communities and constructed new neighborhoods with schools, community centers, play areas, health centers, shops, and more, all subsidized from the general government revenues. It called for a planning and housing commission or planning authority to be set up to execute and enforce the development of land, cities, and towns in urban and rural areas. By 1940 the commission had demolished many decrepit barracks in Port of Spain and built five hundred homes. By 1956, 2,175 families were rehoused in new schemes in Port of Spain and San Fernando, and sugar estate workers were progressively rehoused into new communities.[159] Trinidad and Tobago's housing development scheme was later "taken as a basis" for implementation elsewhere in the British Empire.[160] Reflecting on the increased role of the state in providing proper housing, one Colonial Office memorandum noted, "Housing is now generally recognized as a problem of government and the ancient legacy of employer responsibility for housing is fast disappearing. The legislative and administrative advances which have been made in recent years should ensure that future development is sound and well founded."[161] Liberation unionism stimulated the will and enhanced the capacity of the state to deliver proper housing to the masses. Despite some problems with implementation, the labor movement shifted housing from the private sector to the public sector and laid a foundation for the state's role in land management, use, and distribution.[162]

The introduction of universal adult suffrage in 1946 undoubtedly shaped local government as plans for democratization overlapped with concerns about administrative efficiency. In 1946, for the first time since the Ward Ordinance of 1847, advances were made in reforming the local government sector. The counties became electoral districts (the total was still eight: Nariva and Mayaro were combined, and Tobago was added), each further subdivided into electoral divisions. Also in 1946, county councils were established as elected advisory bodies to the warden to communicate the needs of their districts and consider and advise on matters such as housing, public health, transport and communication facilities, and social services.[163] Thus, the administrative reach of the state extended throughout the colony in a unified and decentralized system that harnessed community voices and enhanced mass participation in democratic governance and formal local government.

Especially relevant for women and children, the colonial state also established a post of secretary for social services in 1937 and a social welfare department in 1939 to coordinate social services. Governor Fletcher had a new stance: "Such matters as the House of Refuge, Orphanages, Young Offenders, Discharged Prisoners, Charitable Institutions, and Child Welfare all required co-ordinated control."[164] The Department of Social Welfare initially focused on providing assistance to the aged, chronically sick, and children in poverty. Although this department struggled for state support relative to other areas of government and was closed from 1943 to 1948, the training of a corps of local officers, its emphasis on "women's work" (which involved childcare and nutrition), and the establishment of village councils that extended the state into rural areas were major accomplishments that were well received by local communities. When revived, the department extended into the 1950s, and by further enhancing ties with communities through such activities as folk arts, it gained widespread support from communities across the colony.[165] Village councils proliferated and flourished throughout the colony, upholding community-level democracy and enhancing state-society ties. These purely voluntary associations comprised elected members from those designated communities who represented village members' interests in economic, social, and cultural welfare and state improvement. Other social protections, such as noncontributory old-age pensions and public assistance (replacing the Poor Relief Ordinance of 1931), were introduced in 1939 and 1951, respectively. The state's infrastructural reach expanded through the proliferation of these councils.

Expansion of Political Participation

In accordance with worker demands for universal suffrage and local control of the state, the Moyne Report recommended greater local participation and representation in governance structures.[166] The Executive Council, which advised the governor, was rearranged in 1940 to include three nominated unofficial Legislative Council members and two elected members. This was altered again in 1943, and the number of nominated members was reduced to two and the number of elected members increased to three.[167] The Legislative Council was reformed to establish greater parity between the colonial officials and representatives of capital on the one hand and elected locals on the other. There were now nine seats for elected members, six for governor-appointed nominees, and three for colonial officials, with the governor retaining the casting vote and therefore maintaining colonial power.[168] In addition, the Legislative Council established a Franchise Committee in 1941 comprising thirty-three members, three of whom were trade unionists, to investigate and make recommendations for constitutional reform. Trade union representation on this body was crucial, for labor representatives vociferously contested attempts by the white economic elites to retain control of the state and keep it out of the hands of the masses. For example, the thirty men on the committee drawn from commerce and law signed a majority report in 1944 listing proficiency in English as a condition for voter registration, and they reduced but retained some level of income and property qualifications for holding office in the Legislative Council. The three trade unionists on the committee submitted minority reports contesting these restrictions.

Given that, in 1946, 50 percent of the Indian population was illiterate in English, compared with 9 percent of Africans and 8.5 percent for those racialized as "mixed," the English literacy requirement would have prohibited a large proportion of the population, disproportionately Indian, from voting.[169] Rienzi vigorously opposed this measure.[170] In solidarity with the Indian voting cause, *The Vanguard*, the official publication of the predominantly African OWTU, noted that "the trade unionists have not abandoned their stand and will press for the abolition of the language test."[171] After a six-week campaign led by Indian organizations for the abolition of the English requirement, during which they held community meetings and wrote letters to the press and to colonial authorities, an order in council refused to allow the discriminatory requirement.[172] In addition to challenging the English literacy requirement, the trade unionists on the committee fought against the income and property qualifications for voting. For example, Albert Gomes, FWTU vice president, stated, "The poor man and woman who would be denied the vote—it is they who suffer now from neglect; it is they who need the vote as an instrument to compel their needs to be attended to."[173] With pressure from labor on the committee and outside the state, the Legislative Council (Elections) Ordinance of 1946 was passed, despite the strong opposition of the white landed and business elite. It adopted adult franchise, including the right of women to vote; reduced qualifications for membership in the council, which was also open to women; increased the electoral districts from six to nine; and eliminated the English language requirement, instead incorporating the use of symbols to facilitate voting for those illiterate in English.

In addition, union representatives succeeded in winning several elected offices and nominated positions. These included positions on the Legislative Council (Rienzi was the newest elected labor representative in 1938, alongside several other reelected labor representatives), the Executive Council (Rienzi in 1943, resigned February 1944), and multiple local government positions (Rienzi in various roles as borough councilor, mayor, deputy mayor, or alderman from 1937 to 1944; Ralph Mentor as borough councilor, mayor, or deputy mayor from 1942 to 1946; and more).

Conclusion

The liberation unionism of the 1930s precipitated a second wave of structural and policy changes within the colonial state that, in turn, further enhanced social and economic development in Trinidad and Tobago. Even though workers organized themselves into separate unions by industry, labor leaders still collaborated across sectors. The movement remained united, internationalist, and transformation oriented. The colonial state, with insufficient repressive capacity relative to the movement, frictions with the local white elite, and dependence on Trinidad's oil, was compelled to substantively address labor's demands. Consequently, relative autonomy from the ruling class increased, political participation of the masses expanded at both the national and local levels, and the state's bureaucratic strength and infrastructural reach expanded as new agencies were created and new staff recruited to devise and manage the various new development priorities. The achievements of liberation unionism in improving the quality of life of the masses were numerous, profound, and long-lasting. Thus, in the late colonial period, Trinidad and Tobago was comparatively well poised for constitutional independence.

4

Decolonization and Fortuitous Failures

At the 1946 Legislative General Elections . . . the Union failed to secure a single seat on that body for any of its actual members. The results of the election provided a curious lesson in the irony of history. The elections were the first to be held under the basis of universal adult franchise. For years the Union had been conspicuous in its persistent agitation for the grant of this measure. Its representatives on the Franchise Committee played no mean role in persuading that body to recommend it. In point of fact the resolution [regarding universal adult franchise] . . . was actually moved by our General Secretary. At the elections a combination of forces and circumstances conspired to produce at the polls positive reverses for the cause of trade unionism in South Trinidad. From the Union's standpoint the results were disappointing, but they provided additional evidence of the mercurial uncertainties of local politics.
—*Vanguard*, August 2, 1947

Significant world transformations followed World War II. While Britain and the West celebrated their victory against Nazism and fascism at home, they were losing their centuries-long hold on their colonies. Explicit claims to rule based on racial superiority lost (some) legitimacy within Europe, claims long discredited among the colonized. Anticolonial movements gained momentum worldwide, advocating for national independence; self-determination; an end to the metropoles' expropriation and exploitation of land, labor, and resources; the elimination of racial oppression; and the erasure of the global color line.[1] Trinidad and Tobago's development trajectory was shaped by the events and processes that unfolded during this period.

Contrary to Frantz Fanon, the long nationalist struggle in Trinidad and Tobago was not led by a revolutionary peasantry assisted by intellectuals while a self-interested apolitical labor aristocracy stood on the sidelines.[2] The working people were undisputedly at the vanguard since liberation unionism first emerged in 1919, advancing a radical vision of an anticolonial Pan-African self-determination and possessing a historical track record of tangible wins for the masses. By 1945, as in other parts of the colonized world, working people had won the battle for universal suffrage and the severing of colonial chains. One might have expected, given the astounding strength of this movement and its presence within the colonial state bureaucracy, that unions would have won national elections, taken control of the state, and advanced the equitable development project that the movement had long envisioned. Yet, in the transition to postindependence democracy, workers and unions failed to win state power. Instead, the heretofore politically lethargic African and Indian petty bourgeoisie organized into political parties and successfully took over the independence movement and the state, with the temporary consent of large sections of the working people, and perpetuated racialized capitalist social relations and foreign control of the economy. This chapter examines the dramatic fall of liberation unionism from the end of World War II to Trinidad and Tobago's independence in 1962 and its consequences for the state apparatus and equitable development.

The marginalization of trade unions and the masses during the historic transfer of power from the colonizers to the colonized is a common pattern observed from the Caribbean to Africa to Asia. Many studies of decolonization focus on the role of elites in the transition to independence: their efforts to mold movements, protect their interests, inherit states, and shape international institutions.[3] Other scholars emphasize the importance of examining the contestations between elites and the opposing voices of youth, working men and women, peasants, and other marginalized groups, which shaped elite strategies and orientations.[4] The actions, policies, and maneuvers of colonial and imperial states also cannot be ignored, as these powers sought to control the terms of the transition to constitutional independence in order to preserve the local and global arrangements of domination and exploitation.[5] Thus, decolonization was shaped by a complex struggle between different groups with competing interests. Scholars examining the fate of labor typically trace its downfall to co-optation by middle-class nationalist politicians and state repression.[6] This chapter argues that the weakening of trade unions and liberation unionism during decolonization was due not only to labor–party and labor–state relations but also to broader global and local processes.

In keeping with the Black radical analytic framework of this book, I attend to Trinidad and Tobago's place in the white capitalist system, especially in the context of a shifting postwar political and economic terrain. My combined attention to race and class reveals the importance of new political actors, namely, the African and Indian petty bourgeoisie, and the new alliances and conflicts that shaped the relative strength (or weakness) of labor. I also examine how workers and unions responded to and shaped the social changes unfolding at the time, including decolonization and party politics. Liberation unionism was weakened and labor ultimately excluded from the state apparatus due to events and processes that were occurring at the global and local levels in this conjuncture. As studies in other contexts have shown, colonial state repression and political manipulation opened space for the emergence of petty bourgeois–led nationalist political parties, whose racial divisiveness and co-optation of trade union leaders indeed weakened the movement in the postwar years. Exogenous forces and intramovement dynamics, however, also contributed to the fragmentation of liberation unionism. Externally, the decline of the British Empire and the ascendancy of the United States on the global stage reduced the structural power of Trinbagonian workers. Internally, within the movement, postwar democratization had a disintegrative effect on union coherence. Together, these factors led to the relative demobilization of the labor movement, which in turn allowed local political elites and foreign capital significant control over economic policies and certain aspects of state building. While state structures expanded to promote social welfare and political participation, relative state autonomy from capital in industrial and trade policies was severely constrained, ultimately giving rise to a neocolonial state. This type of state, as defined by Kwame Nkrumah, has all the appearances of international sovereignty but, in reality, is directed from the outside by imperial powers.[7] Thus, institution building in this critical juncture diverged markedly from what workers had originally envisioned.

Some may view liberation unionism during this conjuncture as a noble yet ultimately failed endeavor or a less than ideal outcome. For Black radical thinkers, it represents a missed opportunity—a pivotal moment of struggle that could have refashioned the social order, eradicated inequities, and set a new course. On the other hand, contemporary scholars interested in the origins of democracy and welfare states in peripheralized economies would likely have predicted this "social democratic" or "power resources" model of development, as some segment of organized labor struck a compromise with capital and aligned with a middle-class, left-leaning political party. Nevertheless, these scholars argue that had a powerful labor party emerged and won state power, business interests would have had less influence over economic and social policies, and redistribution would have been more expansive.[8]

The inability of working people to win control of the Trinidad and Tobago state should not be entirely lamented, however. Labor radicalism never totally disappeared. The fragmentation of liberation unionism, the uneven incorporation of different unions into the ruling political party apparatus, and the overall failure of labor parties to win state power was ironically fortuitous, for it enabled radical elements of the movement to remain independent of parties and the state. The preservation of this autonomy was essential to prevent the entrenchment of demobilization and enabled liberation unionism to continue to serve as a formidable force stimulating state capacity for development after independence.

British Imperial Decline, US Hegemony, and Trinbagonian Worker Power

Walter Rodney maintained that understanding the process of formal decolonization requires analyzing changes in the form and direction of imperialism in the centers and peripheries.[9] Aspiring hegemons seek to capitalize on periods of crisis and change to seize control of global regimes of capital accumulation and reorganize the world capitalist system, and World War II marked the collapse of British hegemony over the world system and the United States' assumption of world hegemonic power.[10] Across the Caribbean, the relations of neocolonial dependency shifted predominantly from the United Kingdom to the United States.[11] Trinidad and Tobago occupied a relatively less prominent position in US imperial interests as a source of oil. Still the colony was important to the United States as a geostrategic location and as a site of increased investments in US oil refining. Thus, the structural power of workers was reduced relative to what they had in the British imperial system during the wars, albeit not entirely wiped out. These global changes weakened liberation unionism during this period.

The United States was a different imperial beast from the United Kingdom, which impacted the potency of liberation unionism in the early years after World War II. Among the many differences between the two, crucially, the United States possessed abundant natural resources; it both produced and exported domestically sourced raw materials *and* exploited foreign raw materials through multinational structures.[12] This included oil. Consequently, unlike the United Kingdom, the United States did not need Trinidad and Tobago for its oil. Between the two world wars, the US oil industry became a global industrial giant. US field oil production went from an average of 1,037,000 barrels per day in 1919 to 3,464,000 in 1939.[13] Exports of crude oil went from 6,019,000 barrels in 1919 to 72,073,000 in 1939.[14] According to Robert Vitalis, despite claims of scarcity, between 1939 and 1945, the United States was "by far the most resource self-sufficient of the Allied powers."[15] With a minuscule market share of world oil production, Trinidad and Tobago was negligible to the United States as an oil supplier. As a result, workers' structural power declined.

However, Trinidad and Tobago was still a part of US geostrategic imperial interests in the Caribbean region. As the world wars dragged on, the British and French navies suffered enormously, which increased US concerns about protecting the Panama Canal, the prime conduit linking the Atlantic and Pacific for the US Navy. Ninety-five percent of American oil supplies passed from the Gulf ports to the US East Coast refineries. Tankers also carried oil from Venezuela to Dutch refineries in Aruba and Curaçao. Trinidad stood at the crossroads of these routes.[16] The sea lanes between Trinidad and Curaçao were the "most profitable waters," as eight to ten vessels arrived in and departed from Trinidad daily.[17] Concerns escalated when the Caribbean Sea became a launching pad for German attacks. In 1941, the German navy targeted this zone in the Caribbean Sea as a "soft spot" where several US and British ships could be sunk in a short space of time.[18] This would disrupt vital oil lanes and thereby cripple British and American war capabilities. "The Battle of the Caribbean," as the Allied forces called it, occurred right at Trinidad and Tobago's doorstep. In the waters around Trinidad, average U-boat operation sinkages stood at 43.3 vessels per U-boat, compared with the worldwide average of 9.2 vessels per U-boat.[19] Between 1942 and 1943, the highest concentration of shipping losses during World War II occurred within a 250-kilometer radius of Trinidad and Tobago.[20] Furthermore, the United States also viewed Trinidad and Tobago as an ideal location for launching US Army operations in South America.

Consequently, the United States made it a top priority to establish a military presence in the Caribbean and in this British colony.

In a major signifier of weakened labor and the decline of British hegemony in the region, the United Kingdom and the United States struck two major deals despite opposition from labor unions and the local colonial government. In the Destroyer-Bases Deal of 1940 and the United States Bases Agreement in 1941, the United Kingdom received fifty US warships in exchange for allowing the United States to establish naval and air bases throughout British Caribbean colonial territories. According to US officials, the ninety-nine-year lease on the Chaguaramas site in northwestern Trinidad and Tobago was "designed to be the key to United States defense planning for the entire Caribbean and South Atlantic area."[21] The construction of the bases produced its own economic boom and Dutch disease effects as thousands abandoned agricultural labor for significantly higher "Yankee dollars," wages surpassing anything workers had seen before, and large amounts of money circulated in the economy.[22] Trinbagonian labor leaders opposed the deal. To Albert Gomes, for example, the military bases constituted a "threat not only to the prestige and the self-respect of West Indians but . . . to their aspirations along the line of federation and self-government."[23] However, workers failed to mount a movement to challenge it. Eric Williams, historian and aspiring politician at the time, rather than the unions, would later take up the issue of sovereignty and the Chaguaramas site as a rallying cry in the anticolonial nationalist movement, reflecting the weakened organizing capacity of liberation unionism during the post–World War II period.

The decline in workers' structural power was relative rather than absolute in nature as the Caribbean became an important site for US oil refining. The US multinationals invested in refineries and transshipment centers in multiple Caribbean territories throughout the 1950s, in Trinidad and Tobago, Aruba, Antigua, St. Lucia, and the Bahamas, to process global sources of crude (mostly from Venezuela and Mexico) and ship the refined oil on to the United States. Oil refineries became the largest recipient of foreign investment in the Caribbean, one of the region's largest employers, especially in the construction phases, and a significant source of state revenues.[24] In the Caribbean, Trinidad and Tobago was the largest oil and gas producer and one of the largest transshipment centers.[25] According to anthropologist David Bond, the enclave refinery modality of empire replaced the plantation modality across the region.[26] Whatever worker power stemmed from increased oil refining and the country's geostrategic importance to US empire would later shape postindependence worker struggles. But in this 1940s and 1950s conjuncture, the decline of the

United Kingdom and emergence of the United States as the world hegemonic power negatively impacted worker power and liberation unionism in Trinidad and Tobago.

Democracy's Disintegrative Effect on Unions

While the political landscape in the colony between 1945 and 1962 showcased some of the greatest achievements of liberation unionism, those very wins paradoxically precipitated conflicts that weakened the movement. Workers won universal suffrage and widespread political participation, democratic political process and party politics, and greater collective bargaining with new trade union legislation. As a result of these hard-won political developments, trade unions and labor parties proliferated. However, the unintended or unanticipated consequences of a movement's success have the potential to subvert its survival.[27] Democratization, scholars have shown, can have a demobilizing effect on movements as activists compete with each other, get co-opted into more conservative parties, and pursue institutionalized forms of collective action rather than direct confrontation.[28] In Trinidad and Tobago, liberation unionism was weakened in the 1940s and 1950s as unions in this new, more politically open environment succumbed to infighting, disunity, and a lack of coordination as they competed among themselves for members and for voters.

Unions Competing for Members

Unlike the spirit of active collaboration that characterized the different unions in the 1930s, with more liberal trade union legislation, the number of unions multiplied, and leaders fought among themselves to represent the workers. The number of registered unions increased from five at the apex of labor mobilization in 1937 to sixty-seven twenty years later.[29] In the sugar sector, for example, six different trade unions claimed to represent sugar workers in 1952. According to one labor organizer, "Everybody had a sugar union in those days. . . . [E]very Tom, Dick and Harry had a union."[30] This fragmentation persisted well into the mid-1950s.[31]

Leadership struggles among these unions undermined oil worker unity. When Tubal Uriah Butler was released in 1939 after two years of imprisonment, he initially joined forces with the Oilfield Workers' Trade Union (OWTU), which was then under the presidency of Adrian Cola Rienzi (1937–44; later John Rojas was president from 1944 to 1962). Optimism was in the air for a revival of the liberation unionism that had been so effective in the 1930s. According to a report in *The People* describing one of the demonstrations, "Men, women and children of the Afro and Indo West Indian races mixed together as never before, reminding one of the unity which was born as a result of the struggles and sacrifice of these two downtrodden races during the general strike of June 1937."[32] However, a deep chasm emerged between Butler, on the one hand, and the OWTU executive, on the other, over union strategy. For Butler, gains came only from direct confrontation, so he endeavored to mobilize workers for militant action. Conversely, the OWTU executive under Rienzi and Rojas favored a collective bargaining approach and, as such, disapproved of Butler's tactics. Like Arthur A. Cipriani's Trinidad Workingmen's Association (TWA) in the early 1930s, the OWTU and some other unions started tending toward bureaucratic conservatism. In 1939 Butler supported a worker strike at the Trinidad Lake Asphalt Operation Company, but the OWTU executive condemned it and expelled Butler from the union. In response, a significant portion of OWTU members left the union and joined Butler's newly formed British Empire Workers' Peasants and Ratepayers Trade Union (registered in June 1946).[33] Again, in December 1946 oil field workers went on strike at Butler's call for a substantial wage increase and improved working conditions.[34] However, the strike did not last, as the OWTU leadership "issued an instruction telling oil workers not to strike . . . [and when that did not work] openly recruited people to break the strike!"[35] This was a far cry from the coherence and coordination of the 1919 and 1937 uprisings. This within-sector union strife weakened worker solidarity during this period.

The rich tradition of cross-sectoral organizing also suffered in the late 1940s and 1950s. For example, in 1947, when sugar workers dissatisfied with the All Trinidad Sugar Estates and Factory Workers' Trade Union (ATSEFWTU) leadership decided to strike over their wages, they called in Butler's union for assistance. The sugar companies and colonial government refused to recognize Butler. Around the same time, laborers for the city council and workers in the public service and at the Port of Spain waterfront were already on strike. During the interwar years, these government and waterfront workers in northern Trinidad had joined forces with the oil and sugar workers of the south. This time, however, the waterfront workers accepted the capitalists' offer and returned to work. This capitulation averted a nationwide strike the likes of 1919 and 1937. The colonial state raided Butler's headquarters, beat and arrested hundreds of demonstrators, and crushed the strike.[36] Thus, union solidarity just after World War II was demonstrably weaker relative to the heydays of liberation unionism in the interwar years.

Ideological disagreements also ensued, affecting unity with regional and international worker organizations. One example was the fragmentation of the Trinidad and Tobago Trades Union Congress (TTTUC), established in 1938 on the advice of Walter Citrine and modeled on the British Trades Union Congress.[37] With Rienzi as its first president, the TTTUC was a central labor organization uniting some twenty-seven registered labor unions in different sectors and had a combined membership of some twenty thousand workers by 1948.[38] However, divisions within the TTTUC arose regarding communism, due to a combination of red-baiting and anticommunist repression by the colonial state and a genuine rejection of communism by many working people. The TTTUC affiliated with the World Federation of Trade Unions (WFTU), which was formed in 1945 as an organization to unite all the world's trade unions. In 1949 Cold War tensions and acute ideological differences caused the US, British, and other liberal-oriented unions to break off and form the International Confederation of Free Trade Unions, leaving the communist-oriented unions in the WFTU. Mirroring conflicts at the international level, the TTTUC also split: the moderates who wished to join the International Confederation broke off and formed the Federation of Trade Unions, while the radical trade unionists who wanted to retain the WFTU affiliation remained in the TTTUC. The TTTUC remained divided over this issue until 1957.[39]

Similar debates weakened regional labor solidarity. The Caribbean Labor Congress (CLC), for example, was established in 1945 to unite labor across the Caribbean and promote the West Indian federal government and welfare concerns within it. The TTTUC actively participated in the West Indian Labor Conferences and held seats on the executive committee of the CLC. The CLC was largely ineffective, however, and eventually disbanded in 1952 because of disagreements both within the CLC executive and with local unions about the details of the West Indies Federation, self-government, and affiliation with the WFTU and the communist bloc.[40]

Overall, the trade union unity that characterized liberation unionism declined during decolonization due to union competition for workers and ideological divisions. Admittedly, workers continued to strike, and unions gained significant expertise in handling negotiations with employers. For example, in 1945 the OWTU won a major industrial agreement with concessions benefiting fourteen thousand workers, which included increased wages, annual leave based on years of service, reduced work hours, and enhanced recognition of the OWTU as the authorized negotiator for oil workers.[41] In 1960 Carl Tull successfully led a long four-month strike of the Communication Workers Union, which pushed the colonial government to assume part ownership of the then British-owned telephone company.[42] That same year, the OWTU halted operations in a massive strike in the oil fields of Texaco, Shell, British Petroleum (BP), Apex, and other companies over Texaco's measly offer of a 4 percent wage increase and subsequently won a 22 percent wage increase and reduction of work hours from approximately seventy-two per week in 1937 to forty-four hours.[43] Even the governor admitted the significance of these wins. He (condescendingly) noted, "When it is remembered that the trade union movement in this colony is only seven or eight years old, it is a very hopeful sign that in such a short time its leaders have acquired a technique of negotiations, a debating skill and a breadth of judgement of which more experienced trade union officials at home might well be proud."[44] Some interunion collaboration also occurred during the period. For instance, the OWTU negotiated and executed industrial agreements for asphalt workers in 1939, steel workers in 1942, and sugar workers with the ATSEFWTU, which they called the "brother union" of the OWTU, in 1944–45.[45] Still, despite these achievements, this was not the liberation unionism of the interwar years. The internal conflicts within and among unions fragmented the entire movement. Further, with the introduction of party politics, labor leaders competed to organize not only workers but also voters.

Unions Competing for Voters

Another source of disunity among workers after the arrival of representational politics and universal suffrage was the emergence of labor parties and competition among them for voters. Between 1945 and 1962 (when Trinidad and Tobago won its independence), four general elections were held with universal suffrage—in 1946, 1950, 1956, and 1961—and one in 1958 to elect local representatives to the regional West Indian Federation. Five major political parties contested the first election of July 1, 1946, four of which claimed to represent organized labor (the fifth was a pro-business party). These labor parties all ran a multiracial slate of candidates and advanced similar platforms—the fight against racial discrimination, nationalization of the major industries, mass education and social security, self-government, and support for the West Indian Federation.[46]

In the 1920s, when the TWA was the only union, it successfully amassed resources and voters and placed labor leaders on the Legislative Council. In the 1940s and 1950s, by contrast, the proliferation of labor parties and competition between them split up the worker votes, thereby weakening labor's unity and its ability to win control of the state. In the 1946 election, no single labor party won a majority, and as such, labor had little collective influence in the Legislative Council. In addition, no single racial group dominated among the winners. People of African, Indian, Portuguese, and Syrian descent won council seats. And interestingly, none of the party leaders won the seats they contested in their constituencies, including parties headed by trade union leaders.[47] According to John La Guerre and Cherita Girvan, these elections revealed "the vast interplay of the many influences on voting behavior of superstition, Hindu-Moslem rivalries, family feuds and finance."[48] In these authors' assessment:

> The Indians were divided between Moslems and Hindus, between urban and rural dwellers; the Negroes were divided on a "class" basis and between revivalist movements and Christians; the Europeans were divided as between French and English and both and the Portuguese. So too was the working class. The sugar workers were as apart from the industrial proletariat as they are to this day; and the industrial proletariat, in turn, was divided as between workers in Port of Spain and those of San Fernando; between those involved in tertiary trades as against those whose incomes derived from oil.[49]

Thus, 1940s party politics in Trinidad and Tobago had less to do with race (being Indian or African) than with the intersections of a multiplicity of cross-cutting factors and the union movement's lack of coherent organizational capacity.

The 1950 elections were only marginally clearer. Constitutional changes introduced a quasi-ministerial system and expanded the number of seats on the Legislative and Executive Councils. The competition was fierce, as a total of 141 candidates registered to contest eighteen seats! This time, the Butler Party won six seats, making it the only party with a significant bloc within the Legislative Council.[50] Still, none of the Butlerites was accepted on the Executive Council.[51] In effect, even though labor successfully secured more seats at the table, the colonial state continued to marginalize them, blocking them from the highest decision-making positions (more on this later). Similar to the 1946 election, in 1950 racialized voting patterns separating Africans and Indians had not yet emerged due to the importance of other factors such as leadership and charisma, ideology, levels of organization, and financial resources.[52] The only clear pattern was that in the era of representative democracy, the white local elite and white elite-affinity parties failed to win mass electoral support, as they represented the old repressive colonial order—the enemy of the racialized colonial toilers.[53] Labor parties were undoubtedly successful in turning out the vote. Voter turnout was 52.9 percent in 1946 and 70.1 percent in 1950.[54] But the multiplicity of labor parties and the wide array of factors influencing voting meant that no single labor party clearly dominated.

At the same time, labor was also divided on whether entry into the state should even be an aspiration. Some leaders felt that getting elected to the council would make meaningful differences in the lives of the masses. For example, Butler maintained a commitment to keeping militant worker mobilization alive but also saw the value of occupying the state apparatus: "When elected to the Council, we are the ones to pass laws, for the benefit of every man, woman and child in Trinidad and Tobago, get justice and compensation for the strikes and gain Home Rule. Monies derived from the produce of the colony shall then remain within for the benefit of the people of Trinidad and Tobago and the strangers within our gates."[55] Other labor leaders discussed the real dangers of moving into the state apparatus. They were acutely aware of how the Legislative and Executive Councils exerted a conservative pull on labor representatives. Cipriani was an early example of a labor leader who became increasingly moderate once integrated into the governing apparatus, and he lost favor with the working classes as a result. Similarly, of Rienzi's move into the Executive Council in 1944, labor organizer E. R. Blades wrote, "He has a great love for politics, even more than real trade union work, and has a tendency to mix the two issues. He did much valuable work . . . but the higher he goes the less the workers see of him. . . . [S]ince he has reached the top of the ladder he is a changed man, and neglects his trade union work."[56] For labor leaders like Blades, state entry was no replacement for grassroots organizing. Albert Gomes, a labor leader turned pro-capitalist politician, also described in his autobiography both the government's stifling effect on labor representatives and the reaction of the masses to those who entered the upper echelons of the state apparatus:

> Popularity eroded rapidly once you became a member of the Executive Council, a result which I suspect was intended in the case of an elected representative. Membership there provided the government with its most effective means of stripping the people's idols of their halos. The discipline it imposed on their demagogic proclivities was severe but cunningly unobtrusive. Indeed, it seemed designed to persuade the victim that he was being sacrificed to worthy ends. Yet cruel as it was to the aspirations of the elected representative, it was in one sense benevolent: it brought him into close contact with those disenchanting realities of government from which his free-wheeling activities in opposition divorce him.[57]

Gomes's remarks also acknowledge that public support in the context of radical trade union struggles did not automatically translate into public support for labor party candidates. Thus, tensions existed within the movement and among the masses after 1945 as to the efficacy of labor parties and state entry for advancing worker interests. In sum, despite every attempt by labor to win control of the state, infighting and disagreements within the movement weakened the effectiveness of labor as both an organizing force for workers and a political force to win state power.

The Emergence of Racialized Party Politics Led by the Petty Bourgeoisie

C. L. R. James, Frantz Fanon, Walter Rodney, Amílcar Cabral, and others have argued that perhaps the most significant set of contradictions shaping the transition to constitutional independence derived from how the national and/or petty bourgeoisie (both the commercial and bureaucratic arms) consolidated itself as a class around the state. But this class did not come to dominate the state by its ingenuity alone. A debilitated labor movement and competition between unions and labor parties opened space for these actors to gain ground in the political arena. Contrary to scholars who argue that the middle classes can play a progressive role in democratizing the political system and disciplining capitalists in service of generating national prosperity, the Trinidad and Tobago middle strata was only barely left of center and sought to carry forward colonial ideologies and economic arrangements.[58] By 1956, the petty bourgeoisie, with the help of colonial officials, spearheaded the development of racialized party politics and usurped the heretofore preeminent role of liberation unionism in colony-wide political and economic struggles, further excluding labor from the state apparatus and retaining the extractive economic policies of the colonial regime.

Just a few years before independence, two political parties captured the political arena. Eric Williams's People's National Movement (PNM) came to be seen as the party representing the African population. Williams, a preeminent historian and author of the seminal book *Capitalism and Slavery*, was born in 1911 to a middle-class family, earned his PhD at Oxford University, and taught at Howard University before returning to Trinidad in 1948. In 1955 he started delivering public lectures and launched the PNM in 1956. Bhadase Sagan Maraj's People's Democratic Party (PDP), later renamed the Democratic Labour Party (DLP), came to be seen as the party representing the Indians. Maraj also had no roots in labor organizing. He was born in the sugar belt in 1920 to a Hindu village leader who operated a small shop. Maraj started a small operation mining sand for construction and grew enormously wealthy by supplying sand for the construction of the US base in the colony and speculating in surplus material left at the military base when the US presence ended.[59] These African- and Indian-dominated petty bourgeois parties used the worker movement as their base and were elected to the "decolonizing" and postindependent state.

Spawned by capitalist imperialism and colonial rule, both the economic and political factions of this petty bourgeois class were subordinate to and dependent on the imperial core. The middle stratum was small, with commerce, finance, public administration, defense, and professional occupations accounting for 7.7 percent of the total employed workforce in 1931.[60] The small group of Syrians, Lebanese, and Jews who had migrated to Trinidad and Tobago in the late nineteenth century rose to economic prominence during the 1940s and 1950s almost exclusively through commerce.[61] By 1930 about 10 percent of Indians were merchants, professionals, managers and overseers, teachers, public officers, and peasant proprietors (the other 90 percent were laborers in agriculture and other areas).[62] The local bourgeoisie was content with their position as junior partners with the international bourgeoisie and a neocolonial state that, in guaranteeing favorable conditions for foreign capital, would also benefit smaller-scale local economic pursuits.[63] The professional and managerial class, mostly Black and mixed race, had salaried positions in the foreign multinational corporations (MNCs). The *Vanguard* later described them as agents who "refuse to be identified with the negro": "These 'black bosses' were good colonials and were rewarded for spying, reporting their fellow blacks and assisting in every way in bringing their downfall."[64] The bureaucratic arm of the petty bourgeoisie was predominantly Black (mostly civil servants, professionals, and political careerists). This segment, as in other peripheralized countries, heavily depended on the state apparatus for their own reproduction.[65] Their means of life, according to James, "spring from participation, direct or indirect, in the government, or circles sympathetic to or willing to play ball with the government."[66]

Party incorporation (when political elites seek to mobilize labor's support for a political party) and political incorporation (asymmetrical formal and informal linkages between ruling parties and trade unions where unions sacrifice autonomy for privileges and benefits from the ruling party) are consequential for party structures and regime dynamics.[67] But in former colonies like Trinidad and Tobago, unions predated parties. With the introduction of majoritarian politics, the aspiring middle class sought to capture the state and guarantee their own sustenance and resources, but their politicians lacked a large-enough base to win elections against the more popular labor parties. Moreover, in James's analysis, they were "political *nouveaux-riches*," because "they have no actual political experience, they have no political tradition."[68] Middle-class politicians' strategies to win state power involved infiltrating and exploiting working-class organizations, co-opting the nationalist discourse and agenda, and advancing a racially divided party politics, which together contributed to the overall disintegration of liberation unionism in this period.

Liberation unionism suffered as middle-class political aspirants, like nationalist elites elsewhere, infiltrated and exploited workers' organizing infrastructure and radical ideology to gain working-class support, only to turn around and betray the workers.[69] Some joined unions and labor parties, where they received political education, were trained in organizing and public speaking, and developed extended networks among labor organizers and workers, before branching off to pursue their own interests. Albert Gomes, for instance, described his tenure with the Negro Welfare Cultural and Social Association as a "political apprenticeship" that allowed him to build up the working-class base that he "desperately needed" for his own political ambitions.[70] Likewise, a number of Indian business actors and educated elites hitched themselves to the revered Butler, such as Ranjit Kumar, Chanka Maharaj, Stephen Maharaj, Bhadase Maraj, Mitra Sinanan, and Ashford Sinanan.[71] Whether they were longstanding Butler devotees, recent financiers of the Butler Party, or just outright opportunists, the common thread was that once they won seats in the Legislative Council in the 1946 and 1950 elections and gained entry to the state, they distanced themselves from Butler and labor. Chanka Maharaj, for example, abstained from voting on bills and motions supported by Butler.[72]

Others formed informal alliances with unions to garner worker support without formally incorporating labor into the party structures, thereby excluding labor from the party apparatus and, in turn, the state. Such alliances between labor movements and nationalist parties render the former vulnerable to political incorporation after independence.[73] This was the strategy of Eric Williams and the PNM. The People's Charter of the PNM reiterated worker demands such as immediate self-government, a British Caribbean federation, a comprehensive labor code, expanded infrastructure, housing, schools, medical and social services, a national health insurance scheme, the abolition of racial discrimination in employment, the expansion of agriculture and industry, and more.[74] Williams and the PNM's "Afro-creole nationalism" also drew on other rituals and symbols of the Black working people, including dialects, dress, and forms of worship, and Williams spoke at locations that were centers for union organizing in the interwar years, such as Woodford Square.[75] All this symbolism enabled Williams to become revered by the African masses, and from this basis, he launched the PNM. Over time, the PNM increasingly vocalized support for foreign capital and local subordination to imperial interests. The PNM called socialism and communism "ridiculous economics," and Williams condemned the oil worker strikes of 1960, blaming "irresponsible elements . . . [who] talked about emulating Castro."[76] The PNM aimed to subordinate labor under petty bourgeois party leadership. According to Williams, "With the experience of the British Labour Party before us, we were careful not to allow our movement to be dominated by the trade union block vote. But we made provision for affiliation of any democratic trade union."[77] In this way, labor was increasingly pressed into the service of petty bourgeois and metropolitan goals.

Other unions were totally subsumed by parties. Unions in the sugar industry had already been weakened by infighting, and Bhadase Sagan Maraj and the PDP further debilitated them through coercion and capture in order to secure Indian sugar workers' votes. In 1953 Maraj spearheaded the amalgamation of the two main formerly competing unions—the ATSEFWTU and the Sugar Industry Workers Union—into one ATSEFWTU and made himself president of the combined union.[78] Maraj, who had no history or experience with unions, was a "muscular philanthropist" who used a combination of strong-arm tactics and patronage (using his personal wealth to directly cover requests by Indian laborers, such as medical expenses) to take control of the union and gain the legitimacy to lead.[79] He even reportedly paid the dues of all union members and, together with pandit and solicitor Simbhoonath Capildeo, financed a sugar strike in 1956.[80] By 1961 he was reportedly on the payroll of the sugar company to keep labor contained: "Bhadase used to get an allowance in Trinidad, for his movement, from Tate and Lyle."[81] According to Fred Dalley, the British Trades Union Congress (TUC) adviser who had been sent to the colony, "Bhadase Maraj then appeared on the scene and having made himself popular in several ways the two registered unions agreed to federate under his Presidency. . . . I had no evidence of Mr. Maraj's qualifications as a trade union leader. I particularly disapprove of any idea of members' contributions being paid for them [by Maraj] as has been suggested."[82] This union takeover by these political actors occurred partly because liberation unionism was so weak during this time. Maraj's PDP initially did not even have a written manifesto. Like the PNM, the PDP party platform for the 1958 elections for the West Indian Federation included such promises as welcoming foreign capital, promoting free enterprise, and reducing taxation. The above-mentioned Ashford Sinanan, a staunch Butlerite turned deputy leader of the PDP, proclaimed, "We are inflexible in our advocacy at all times that the only hope of the entire West Indies is the belief in private enterprise."[83] The symbolic embrace of working-class nationalist rhetoric, combined with the disorganization of working-class organizations, made space for petty bourgeois–led parties to usurp unions and take over the state.

Importantly, some key unions resisted these parties' attempts to incorporate and subsume them, which enabled at least a segment of the working class to retain its independence and militance. When the leader of the West Indian National Party aimed to unite and subordinate Butler Party industrial, agricultural, and peasant workers under his leadership, Butler declined, declaring, "I am no lackey. . . . Nobody will ride on my back," and insisted on other organizations joining under the Butler Party banner and Butler's leadership.[84] Even the then reformist OWTU continued to prize its organizational autonomy from political parties. In a speech for the ten-year anniversary of the OWTU in 1947, President General John Rojas reminded the audience (even if through lip service) that the OWTU "has never been a merely materialist institution. It has throughout its history been imbued with a high idealism. . . . The Oilfields Workers' Trade Union has always maintained and remained an independent force. It is known to cooperate with Government. It has accepted a share of responsibility for industry, but it has never become a part of machinery of the State or of the industrialist. . . . Unless we have a conception of human rights belonging to all human beings and not to any particular race, we shall fail to secure industrial peace, and eventually world peace."[85] Radical segments of the rank and file held their leaders to this standard, to avoid becoming an extension of parties and the state. For the 1961 election, for example, the National Trades Union Congress (NTUC) with Rojas as president announced its support of the PNM and organized a pro-PNM demonstration in the capital city.[86] Rojas was also appointed senator while still president of the NTUC, which, according to one worker, was "most probably because of his brilliant manoeuvre in obtaining a then free and independent trade union movement to demonstrate openly its support for the People's National Movement."[87] The oil workers, however, would ultimately reject the entanglement of labor leaders with the system of racialized party politics advanced by the PNM and DLP (formerly PDP). "It was not long after however," the same writer continues, "that the trade union leaders realized their folly, and having seen through Mr. Rojas's game, quickly removed him and his satellites from office."[88] While the tendency toward incorporation and co-optation was strong, the autonomy of these structurally powerful workers from the political party that would ultimately have hegemonic control over the state (the PNM) was crucial for postindependence state building.

Finally, party politics became increasingly racialized with the rise of Indian- and African-dominated petty bourgeois parties, which, in turn, drove a wedge between Indian and African workers and weakened liberation unionism as a political force. An intraclass racial competition for the state emerged within the middle class between the Africans, who viewed themselves as the rightful heirs of the state apparatus, and the Indians, who saw state power as crucial to their own accumulation and expansion. As Black radical thinkers have shown, this class inherited from the colonizers the tendency to view racism as within their class interests. In their quest for state power, their strategies and actions, according to Fanon, "become increasingly tinged with racism," eventually switching "from nationalism to ultranationalism, chauvinism, and racism."[89] As Rodney theorized, each stressed African or Indian racial identity in order to be seen as insiders within their respective racial groups rather than as the exploiters they were.[90] Thus, in this postwar conjuncture, race consciousness and solidarity served as a mechanism to mask petty bourgeois interests in accumulation and state power, rather than as a way to invigorate class consciousness and multiracial unity, as it had in the interwar years.

The petty bourgeoisie politicized racial identity through racial political articulation. Cedric De Leon and colleagues define *political articulation* as the creation of political valence out of shared racial, ethnoreligious, gender, and other circumstances to build powerful voting blocs.[91] The Indian petty bourgeoisie made the politicization of Hinduism central to their political goals, and in just a few years in the late 1950s, Maraj and the PDP consolidated their leadership and the rural Indian Hindu voting base. Like the colonial state and capital before them, the PDP minimized the ethnolinguistic, caste, and class diversity among the Indians (described in chapter 1), bringing them together under the umbrella of a "Hindu" voting bloc, which, over time, they expressed in racial terms. In 1952 Maraj coalesced the two main factions within the Sanatan Dharma community in the colony into one organization called the Sanatan Dharma Maha Sabha as "the sole religious body representing the Sanatanist Hindus of the Colony."[92] The Maha Sabha was remarkably successful in achieving its objectives, which included propagating and teaching Hinduism throughout the colony, building and running Hindu schools and providing cultural training, promoting the observance of Hindu festivals, and giving aid to Hindu temples and schools.[93] According to historian Steven Vertovec, the highly coordinated "schools, temples, publications, collective celebrations, and the participation of almost every Brahman pundit" allowed for Hinduism to be standardized and routinized, gradually replacing all other religious practices among the Hindu Indians.[94]

In 1953, just one year after the Maha Sabha was formed, Maraj installed himself as the president of the Indian-dominated sugar workers' union—the ATSEFWTU. Later that same year (1953), Maraj and fellow Indian business and professional elites launched the PDP. Unlike the PNM, the PDP did not develop organizational independence as a political party. According to Vertovec,

"Under the strong-arm tactics of Bhadase Maraj, the leadership and support of the People's Democratic Party (later becoming the Democratic Labour Party) was virtually indistinguishable from that of the Maha Sabha."[95] It was well reported that pandits made Hindus swear on the lotah (a holy vessel) to support PDP candidates or face religious consequences.[96] Thus, the Maha Sabha branches, pandits, and the sugar union were the organizational apparatus of the party, enabling the PDP to politicize Hinduism and creating a voting bloc out of Indian workers ahead of the 1956 elections.

Similarly, Williams and the PNM appealed to racial solidarity to consolidate an African voting bloc. For Williams, Hindi education did not fit into the hegemonic Afro-creole "national" identity; he argued that the education system was already fragmented due to religious diversity and that "it would be suicidal to aggravate this religious diversity and religious difference by a linguistic differentiation."[97] In a public lecture, Williams roared, "This so called desire for cultural independence must end somewhere. . . . It was the denominational school yesterday, it is Indology today, what will it be tomorrow? The communal vote?"[98] To the Indian middle class seeking to promote Indian identity, Williams's position on this issue paralleled the historical role of the colonial oppressors who, just ten years earlier, advocated for English literacy as a voting requirement.[99] To them, Williams and the PNM intended to continue marginalizing Indians.

The racially divisive party politics would rear its head in a number of debates about Trinidad and Tobago's future, including in the West Indies Federation. Indian middle-class legislators sent a petition to the secretary of state as early as 1946 opposing the formation of a federation: "We as representatives of the East Indian community in Trinidad protest against federation being granted to the people of the West Indies because it would mean that the Negroes—NEGROES—will have the upperhand over the Indians, the persons who labored to build up this colony."[100] Other delegations, Maraj among them, went to London to prevent the establishment of the West Indies Federation.[101] Williams initially adopted a discourse of interracial unity. However, when the PNM lost the 1958 election for representatives to the federal parliament, while the DLP (formerly PDP) won, he verbally attacked the Indian population. In what would become the most controversial and criticized speech of his political career, entitled "The Danger Facing Trinidad, Tobago and the West Indian Nation," Williams conducted a racial analysis of the voting patterns, which he claimed reflected "the DLP campaign and the DLP's appeal that Indians should vote for DLP so as to ensure an Indian Governor and an Indian Prime Minister."[102] He charged that a letter signed "Yours Truly, Indian," and addressed to "My Dear Indian Brothers" was circulated in Indian communities;

it contained "nothing of taxation or government policy. . . . It was sheer race."[103] He denounced those who were supposedly pushing "an Indian nation" as "the recalcitrant and hostile minority of the West Indian nation masquerading as 'the Indian nation' and prostituting the name of India for its selfish, reactionary political ends."[104] The pejorative language racialized the Hindu voting bloc as Indian and contributed to the divisive racial politics that was developing. Williams's race-baiting dog whistles to the Black population in the speech were unmistakable: "We sympathize deeply with those misguided unfortunates who, having ears to hear, heard not, eyes to see, saw not, who were complacent, for whom everything was in the bag, who had the DLP covered, who were too tired too busy to vote. . . . They will understand hereafter that he or she who stays home and does not come out to vote PNM, in effect votes DLP. They have learnt their lesson. Today, they regret it bitterly, and they are already swearing that it must never happen again."[105] Maraj responded by proclaiming that Williams would have to "destroy every East Indian in Trinidad because we do not intend to sit with our arms folded and let him do what he wants."[106] In the aftermath of the PNM's defeat in the 1958 federal elections, the party, with the help of colonial officials, moved quickly to secure wins in the 1961 national elections by increasing the number of seats from twenty-four to thirty and redrawing electoral districts in ways that effectively favored the PNM.[107] Through racial political articulation led by the middle class, the party system in Trinidad and Tobago became split along racial lines, as did the laboring masses.

Labor party leaders deployed a racial discourse that emphasized unity, as they had in the interwar years. However, in this postwar period, race consciousness without working-class organizational coherence could not buck the developing trends in the political arena. For instance, one Butler Party rally in 1949 included slogans and placards such as "Butler Policy on Indian African Unity," "Long Live African-Indian Unity," "Long Live the Indian Republic," "Long Live Pundit Nehru," "Down with Racial Discrimination," "India Today Africa Tomorrow," and "We Want a United West Indian Republic."[108] In Butler's words, the colonial government wanted to prevent him from "'mixing freely' with the thousands and thousands of Indians and Creole workers in the sugar belt of the country who now hail me as 'Trinidad's Mahatma Gandhi'."[109] Likewise, in a speech to the oil workers and sympathizers, Butler repeated aims that mirrored those he proclaimed in the 1930s: "I, Tubal Uriah Butler by the Grace of God and the will and expressed desire of thousands of Trinidad history making Indians and Negroes, Supreme Commander of the biggest Army of Warrior-Workers and legitimate sufferers at the hands of Capitalist-Imperialist-Exploiters and their friends in the ranks of the now quite definitely unwanted, undemocratic and unconstitutional Butler-Baiting Shaw Government [seek to build a force that is] ever organized into a single militant movement in the whole history of the colony of Trinidad and Tobago."[110] As this quote shows, Butler and other labor parties attempted to rally workers through a discourse of multiracial working-class unity against all forms of oppression.

But this discourse was overpowered by the rising racial hostilities developing out of the racial political articulation of the petty bourgeois parties. Butler, recognizing the unfolding processes, warned:

> Here we are together living in what can be rightly considered a place bought with the slave labor of Africans, indentured East-Indians. We have made this country, and if we start anything racial we are going to use our part of the juice while the God's [*sic*] smile. So let us dwell together in love and unity respecting each other's religion, cultures, and habits. Let us respect each other's views on all matters for the day we start to fight each other, we by that suicidal act, will be committing ourselves and the country to an eternity of oppression and exploitation from the hands of Imperialism.[111]

This plea fell on deaf ears. The political conflicts stoked and exacerbated by the African and Indian middle class in their intraclass race contest for control of the state greatly eroded the unifying tendencies of liberation unionism. The local white elite was staunchly opposed to the PNM but felt that they could not openly get into conflict with a party that was so popular. While they initially supported the DLP, DLP leaders' calls for violence around the elections caused them to defect. The Chamber of Commerce reconciled itself to political impartiality and urged both parties not to antagonize foreign investors.[112] Working people's interests remained in the lurch as liberation unionism disintegrated, and racialized voting became consolidated.

Colonial State Repression and Imperial Institutional Designs

Colonial state repression is an enduring theme in this book and indeed across this time period. At every instantiation of liberation unionism where working people organized and directed themselves toward changing the order of their existence, cutting off the colonizers from their source of wealth and validity, and establishing a society with greater egalitarianism and dignity for all, their mobilization elicited violence, of multiple forms, and economic and political maneuvers from privileged actors as they scramble to preserve their interests.[113] This is why Fanon asserted, "[decolonization] cannot be accomplished by the wave of a magic wand, a natural cataclysm, or a gentlemen's agreement."[114] As we have seen, at times repression was less effective in debilitating liberation unionism. However, between 1945 and 1962, it succeeded. Fanon and Rodney both highlight how imperial interests intervene in the local arena if necessary, using instruments such as the army or police force and electoral fraud to ensure that their preferred leaders inherit the state.[115] In Trinidad and Tobago, the colonial state used these strategies and more to demobilize labor and realize their desired outcome.

The colonial state continued to rely on measures it had long used to suppress liberation unionism, all of which involved the suspension of political and civil liberties. Arrests, imprisonments, curfews, raids, and bans followed the 1937 insurrection.[116] Elma François, Jim Barratt, and Butler were among those who were tried for sedition; the latter two were found guilty and sentenced to imprisonment.[117] When released, they remained targets of the state. The colonial state banned Butler from certain areas and detained him in 1946 for "anti-war activities" because he supported an oil worker strike where two oil wells were set on fire.[118] As mentioned earlier, the OWTU had condemned this strike. States of emergency remained an instrument of labor repression, and they were invoked every time there was an acute threat of a labor uprising, for instance, in response to the 1947 and 1948 agitations by oil and sugar workers, respectively.[119] Throughout the 1940s the white capitalist class also relied on their regular tool kit. Victimization, retrenchments, and dismissals discouraged many workers from union involvement. In one area where the labor force was three hundred workers, the OWTU had only eighteen members at that branch.[120] Therefore, on the way to independence, the colonial state persisted in repressing labor activity.

The colonial state further contributed to the fragmentation and frailty of liberation unionism by using labor organizers from the metropole to moderate worker militance. The secretary of state for the colonies and the colonial government called in Walter Citrine and Fred Dalley from the British TUC to assess the state of industrial relations and provide financial assistance and "technical expertise" to help create "responsible," that is, conservative, unions in the colony. The imperial state and colonial administration favored "constitutional trade unionism," which meant amicable relations between the government and labor, and the use of the newly constructed institutions for settling disputes "without recourse to stoppage of work and all the disastrous consequences which flow therefrom," according to the governor.[121] Dalley drew a sharp contrast between "Butlerism" and "Trade Unionism" and declared them incompatible.[122] In a speech delivered to the TTTUC in 1947, Dalley similarly urged strike avoidance: "A wise Trade Union only used it [a strike] as a last resort. . . .

If a strike was to be embarked upon it should be only as a last resort and after very great consideration. It must not be spontaneous or undertaken lightly or inadvisably; but soberly and discreetly."[123] The historical record of liberation unionism shows that workers had always used strikes only after exhausting all other possible avenues. They nevertheless viewed striking as a necessary strategy for success. Dalley and the colonial administration actively sought to deter striking and delegitimize radicalism in the movement.

The colonial administration also elevated their favored amenable labor leaders to state positions while excluding the more radical ones. As Rienzi's political ambitions grew, he increasingly adopted the conciliatory approach advocated by the colonial administration, which, in turn, the colonial state rewarded. Colonial officials described the once reviled radical socialist agitator Rienzi as "exceedingly helpful in . . . placating his colleagues."[124] Orde Browne reported that he found Rienzi to be "more conciliatory than I should have expected."[125] In 1943, Rienzi was appointed to the Executive Council and accepted, which radical elements in the labor movement marked as "the final capitulation . . . a logical step from the politics of compromise he had been practicing for some time."[126]

Butler, by contrast, was the biggest threat to the colonial state and capital. In 1937, the governor described him as a "lunatic" who had "a history of mental derangement in his family" and was "deficient in judgement."[127] In 1939 the acting governor called him "a religious fanatic," whose "megalomania" stirred trouble for the colonial government.[128] Alexander Rocklin argues that this discourse reflects the colonial administration's deliberate strategy to stigmatize, delegitimize, and crush Afro-Caribbean traditions of grassroots mobilization and resistance. More explicitly, colonial officials saw him as a "potential danger to peace and good order in the colony" and an immediate threat to "the oil industry which has been declared an essential service."[129] They were especially concerned about the "disproportionately large number of women [who] were included among his more enthusiastic supporters," since repressive forces were said to face "greatly increased difficulties . . . when large numbers of women take part in actual disturbances."[130] In other words, women's involvement not only increased the size and militance of the movement but affected repressive methods in ways that tipped the balance power in favor of the movement. Given Butler's popularity and militance, colonial administrators expressed "hope that the more responsible leaders of the Trade Union movement will retain their control."[131] The colonial state did more than hope. As officials embraced moderates like Rienzi in the state ranks, they targeted, policed, and excluded more militant labor organizers like Butler, which contributed to splitting workers into conservative and radical segments.

Finally, when worker disunity, racial articulation, and repression failed to produce a clear petty bourgeois leader acceptable to colonial officials, imperial powers, and metropolitan capitalists, the colonial state resorted to actively orchestrating the installation of political puppets to ensure, as Rodney put it, "favorable political decisions by remote control."[132] The colonial state actively prevented Butler and the Butler Party from occupying the highest decision-making positions in the state and from taking the colony into independence. They were too militant and popular and would never be subservient to any reformist party. Thus, even though the Butler Party won the majority bloc of seats in the 1950 elections to the Legislative Council and, in accordance with the new quasi-ministerial system, should have won appointments to the Executive Council, colonial officials refused to appoint Butler or any of the Butlerites to the Executive Council.[133] The colonial administration also pushed out Butler's allies. For example, the governor removed Timothy Roodal from the Executive Council because of his affiliation with Butler, explaining, "Mr. Roodal's reputed wealth and status in the East Indian community, will make him a welcome reinforcement to Butler and, as such, his nuisance value will be considerable."[134] Through this method of colonial repression, the colonial state actively prevented labor parties from occupying the state even when they won legitimate seats at the table through the democratic electoral process.

The colonial administration also blocked Maraj and the PDP from state power, fearing both Maraj's efforts to foment a Pan-Indo-Caribbean movement and his affiliation with Butler. Together, those forces would increase worker power and the potential for industrial unrest. Colonial officials viewed Maraj as a suspicious character and an unpredictable opportunist whose consolidation of Indians would have had tremendous economic and political consequences. According to one official, "The signs of the increasing organization of the East Indian community as a political force are disturbing."[135] To Governor Hubert Rance, "If he [Maraj] felt strong enough to do this [stage a strike throughout the sugar industry], it might be dangerous."[136] Colonial agents feared Indian political organization not only locally but also regionally. Maraj had been actively communicating with Cheddi Jagan in Guyana, a powerful Marxist-Leninist Indo-Guyanese labor organizer and political figure. Jagan had even written to Maraj for financial assistance to build up the opposition to his political rival, Forbes Burnham.[137] Maraj had also been forging connections between the Maha Sabha in Trinidad and Tobago, Guyana, and Suriname. Colonial officials feared a merger into what the governor termed "a single powerful unit" to advance the "plans for East Indian domination, not only in Trinidad, but on a regional basis."[138] The regional unity of Indian workers would undoubtedly elevate worker power vis-à-vis white capital and the colonial state. As such, colonial officials even sought to cut Indians in Trinidad off from the commissioner for India and considered banning the importation of anticolonial publications from India.[139] The colonial state suppressed Maraj and the development of Pan-Indo-Caribbean solidarity.

Colonial administrators also feared an alliance between Maraj and Butler, or what the acting governor called "a dangerous and irresponsible combination," for similar reasons.[140] If Maraj joined forces with Butler—leader of the working people writ large—a racially united working class could coalesce and win state power. According to the governor, "It became known that plans had been made for a political campaign aimed at securing at least 10 East Indian seats in the Legislative Council should the present Council be dissolved and a new General Election held. It was hoped that with the support of the Butler Party and several other independents in the new Council, the East Indian element would be assured of the political domination of the Colony."[141] Terrified of the consequences of a Maraj-Butler alliance for the state and industry, colonial administrators worked to prevent Maraj and the PDP from inheriting the state apparatus.

Of all the candidates for state power, among whom Butler, Maraj, and Williams were most prominent, the colonial state came to view Williams as the most favorable inheritor of the postindependence Trinidad and Tobago state, thereby excluding labor from state power. To be clear, the colonial state was not enamored with Williams. Officials viewed his anticolonial nationalist speeches and his leadership of the late 1950s anticolonial struggle as vitriolic and dangerous. Still, they saw him as the more predictable candidate with a reliable record of supporting metropolitan interests and a dependable "transmission line," in Fanon's words, between the colony and metropole. In 1956 he supported the Texaco takeover of Trinidad Leaseholds, opposing labor's call for nationalization.[142] In explicitly refusing to establish formal links with unions, condemning worker strikes, and denouncing Cuba, communism, and socialism, Williams and the PNM assuaged imperial concerns. In Williams, colonial officials saw someone who "has expressed anti-white views" and "anti-British sentiments" and was "very learned but not so shrewd as is generally believed."[143] The colonial preference for Williams was clear.

As such, colonial state political interference in the 1956 elections ensured that labor was kept out of the state and Williams was given the reins. The PNM won a majority of the elected seats—thirteen—but to have a working majority, the party needed sixteen seats. Williams was faced with three choices: (1) join with Butler and form a coalition with labor; (2) join with the PDP, which would create a more multiracial party; or (3) incorporate the independents.

He preferred the third option, as the PNM would then retain control of the party vis-à-vis labor and the Indian population. The governor and the Colonial Office, however, having decided that the PNM was their preferred inheritor of the administrative and military apparatus, stepped in and offered Williams an entirely different path to power: two more seats from the nominated members of the Legislative Council, whom the governor instructed to vote with the government.[144] Despite his calls for nationalism and autonomy from colonial interference, Williams accepted this path to power, thereby aligning himself with the colonial oppressors. Thus, one year before independence, the state was well consolidated in the hands of the PNM with the DLP in opposition. The African and Indian petty bourgeoisie assumed their role as the guarantors of capital accumulation for foreign interests, and labor was shut out from state power.

State Capacity, 1945–1962

The demobilization of labor, the exclusion of the masses from the state, and the emergence of neocolonial politics had uneven consequences for state capacity during the years of formal decolonization. Pre-1945 liberation unionism had established a firm foundation for social welfare priorities and structures on which the colonial state expanded. However, the petty bourgeois–occupied state was not oriented around enhancing state autonomy from capital. The resulting state at the time of what Rodney called "flag independence" was well positioned for positive economic and social development with respect to bureaucratic and infrastructural reach and political participation, but also for conflict due to its relationship to capital.

In the postwar era, developmentalism increased across late colonial states, but in Trinidad and Tobago, the strong labor movement and earlier institution building led to more expansive infrastructural reach. The colonial state extended the 1939–44 development plans that were spurred by the 1937 general strike into the post–World War II period. In 1950 the colonial state created another Five-Year Economic Program to develop water supplies, electricity, roads, medical services, and educational facilities.[145] As in the 1920s, labor advocates on government committees ensured new policies prioritized working people. As shown in table 4.1, infant mortality decreased by 68 percent between 1937 and independence, and the overall death rate dropped by 49 percent. School enrollment more than doubled, with attendance also showing a marked increase.

Building on prior civil service reforms, a public service commission was created in 1950 under the Trinidad (Constitution) Ordinance as an independent advisory body to the governor on appointments, promotions, transfers, train-

TABLE 4.1. Changes in Trinidad and Tobago's Social Development over Time

Year	Infant mortality (per 1,000)	Maternal mortality (per 1,000)	Death rate (per 1,000)	Primary school enrollment	Primary school attendance
1937	120.0	6.1	15.8	74,833	69.5%
1948	75.0	3.2	12.3	103,668	76%
1958	63.0	2.1	9.2	167,294	–
1962	38.0	–	8.0	175,260 (1960)	–

Sources: B. Mitchell, International Historical Statistics, 84, 86; De Barros et al., Health and Medicine, table 11.1; Harding and Gent, Dominions Office and Colonial Office List for 1940, 496; Great Britain Colonial Office, Colonial Office List 1950, 361; Great Britain Colonial Office, Colonial Office List 1962, 209.

ings, and dismissals of civil servants and government schoolteachers. More Trinbagonians attained higher-level positions within the colonial state. Admittedly, this benefited the African educated middle class far more than the Indians, who continued to be disproportionately excluded from the state via racism and the legacies of constrained educational opportunities.[146] In addition, as part of reorganizing the public service, the public service commission was granted executive authority in 1962, which was intended to serve as a safeguard against political and government interference. This, combined with impressive voter turnouts for national elections (80.1 percent in 1956 and 88.1 percent in 1961), boded well for postindependence participation in the political life and structures of the newly independent country.[147]

The colonial state's administrative presence extended further into rural areas. In 1952 county councils were granted executive powers and took charge of maintaining local roads, sanitation, burial grounds, recreational facilities, markets, and water distribution in their respective counties.[148] This move facilitated the deconcentration of major functions originally held within the state. County councils remained linked to the state via the warden and funding, since, unlike the town councils, they could not collect their own revenue to implement local development projects.[149] In addition, the village and community councils created after the 1937 uprising multiplied throughout the colony. By 1955 there were 170 village councils and thirty-one community centers built by volunteer labor.[150] These councils were incorporated under the administrative umbrella of the Trinidad and Tobago Association of Village and Community Councils in the late 1950s.

These enhanced linkages between the state and local communities facilitated the colony-wide implementation of development campaigns and priorities. For example, health expenditures increased from $3,149,135 in 1948 (in local currency; 8 percent of total expenditure) to $16,764,039 in 1960 (about 11 percent of total expenditure), which, paired with colony-wide coordination of health programs at the county levels and the help of community councils, facilitated the mitigation of diseases that had long plagued working people.[151] The implementation of a malaria eradication program in this manner, involving island-wide spraying, drug treatments, improved drainage, and enhanced case-finding systems, successfully reduced deaths from the disease such that by 1960 the World Health Organization determined that the colony had met the criteria for malaria eradication.[152] The expanding bureaucracy coupled with the increased embeddedness of the state in communities enabled the success of such development initiatives.

The education system also stretched into nonurban areas. Between 1948 and 1958, the colonial state built an additional eighteen primary schools, bringing the total number of government primary and intermediate schools to sixty-eight. Together with government-assisted schools, the total number of primary schools distributed throughout the colony was 415 in 1958.[153] In terms of postprimary education, two more technical colleges were added, and the number of government and government-assisted secondary schools went from ten with 4,958 pupils in 1948 to twenty-two with 12,839 pupils in 1960.[154] Furthermore, as of 1960, secondary education was also made available free of cost, further enhancing pupils' access to education.

Increased state rationalization also weakened the community voice in other ways. Friendly Societies, for example, suffered a drastic blow as the state increased bureaucratization. Despite government officials' initial verbal support for nurturing the institution and establishing it as an instrument of social and economic policy, the state invested much more in cooperative societies and credit unions in terms of staff and training.[155] In 1953 an updated Co-operative Society Ordinance was passed, and the number of registered cooperative societies increased from 8 in 1948 to 383 in 1960, with 35,295 members (over 4 percent of the population) and total assets of $3,125,933.[156] The number of Friendly Societies went from 340 in 1953 with 153,939 members (just about 22 percent of the population) to 334 with about 94,000 members in 1962, and they continued to fade thereafter.[157] The lack of institutional support for Friendly Societies as the state apparatus became increasingly rationalized contributed to the ultimate downfall of this community-run institution.

Without the powerful forces of liberation unionism, the resulting flag-independent state reinforced strong ties with foreign capital at the expense of labor. The Afro-creole neocolonial state and its industrial policies facilitated free trade, increased exports, and allowed profit repatriation for foreign capital and, by extension, the enrichment of a fast-emerging local capitalist class. Such an orientation depended on the continuation of racialized labor superexploitation and peripheralization. The Pioneer Industries Ordinance and the Income Tax (in Aid of Industry) Ordinance, both passed in 1950, confined the state's role in development to attracting foreign capital by creating a favorable environment for investment (extraction), such as generous tax concessions, easy expatriation of profits, low worker wages and worker docility, and the necessary infrastructure for foreign multinationals. Albert Gomes worked closely with colonial officials to develop this plan.[158]

Eric Williams amended this industrialization strategy with elements from Arthur Lewis's Puerto Rico model, including the creation of an industrial development corporation in 1959 to make recommendations for new industries, identify land for industrial estates, plan housing schemes, and issue business loans. This adjusted model was instituted in the PNM's first Five-Year Development Plan (1958–62).[159] As such, labor's dreams of self-determination were crushed as the bureaucratic petty bourgeoisie consolidated itself around the state, enabling the smooth continuation of the expatriation of surplus by foreign multinational corporations. A neocolonial state was born.

Conclusion

According to Walter Rodney, "The people of Trinidad and Tobago advanced towards independence with a purposefulness which was not matched in any other part of the British Caribbean; and, consequently, few observers within Trinidad or the West Indies failed to be struck by the rapid onset of neocolonial politics."[160] This chapter has described the factors and processes that contributed to the disorganization and disintegration of liberation unionism. Some reasons were internal to the movement itself, namely, the infighting between leaders about who would represent workers and constituents, and others were exogenous, such as decreased worker power as world hegemony shifted from the United Kingdom to the United States, the emergence of racialized petty bourgeois political parties, and colonial state repression and political interference. It is difficult to ascertain which of these were more consequential than the others, as these developments occurred simultaneously. However, I have shown the ways in which these factors together contributed to fragmentation and worker disunity.

In this context, the severely weakened liberation unionism was incapable of mounting an effective effort to capture the state. Instead, the Afro-creole bureaucratic petty bourgeoisie replaced the colonial administrators and became the dominant group in control of the state, and the Indian middle class positioned itself as a forceful race-based and pro-capital opposition party. State capacity in terms of bureaucratic reach and political participation carried forward from the earlier period, but the result was a neocolonial state that had little autonomy from foreign capital.

Some argue that the failure of labor parties to win state power was an unfortunate missed opportunity. According to historian Gordon Lewis, "For that entire period [1946–56], the local political scene was a wild circus of electoral independents and trade union 'czars' having nothing to unite them in a national front . . . save a common passion for the spoils of office." Lewis continued, "It all portrayed a scandalously low level of political intelligence and a complete failure to think out in any coherent way long range answers to the colonial problems."[161] I interpret this period differently. The defeat of labor parties and the floundering of liberation unionism produced two ironically favorable conditions for postindependence democratic and redistributive development. First, the loss prevented labor from becoming entrenched in the oligarchic leadership and reformist political agendas that come with state power. Cipriani in the late 1920s and early 1930s and the OWTU leadership post-1945 are two examples of the moderating effect of state power on once radical labor leaders and the internal divisions that emerge within the movement when leaders gravitate toward political unionism. As Robert Michels wrote, "Political organization leads to power. But power is always conservative."[162]

Second, the mutual resistance by some unions and the PNM to incorporating unions into the organizational apparatus of what would eventually become the ruling party preserved the autonomy of at least a significant proportion of the working people. The sugar unions and their predominantly Indian membership, conversely, lost their independence when Indian middle-class politicians infiltrated and took over the organization. However, as we shall see, Maraj's hold on sugar workers was fragile and temporary, and the relationship fell apart soon after independence. The relative autonomy of labor from petty bourgeois–led political parties and the state was crucial to the survival and revival of liberation unionism in the early postindependence period. Its renewal as a powerful counterbalance to state power and a force for more equitable development is the subject of the next chapter.

5

Postindependence Resurgence
of Liberation Unionism

The temper of the people in this country is rising. They have seen year after year oil being extracted and shipped away—the wealth of the country. They know that what has gone out exceeds what was brought in by thousands of times. They see that now our new country is in a real crisis of unemployment the oil industry is unwilling to help but thinks only of its profits. The whole country is in a ferment. Particularly among the employed and unemployed young people this ferment is working. And it has the sanction of all those intellectuals who have not yet been bought by business. There is a spirit abroad here now, similar to the spirit that was abroad in Fyzabad and Trinidad in 1937.... Read the history of what happened here in 1937 and beware.
—George Weekes, 1968

The people of Trinidad and Tobago celebrated their flag independence in 1962 with joy and jubilation. However, the euphoria of this historic occasion masked a far less cheerful reality. Also in 1962, the number of industrial disputes reached its highest level in a decade.[1] Strikes, demonstrations, protests, and boycotts were unrelenting, with workers mobilizing in almost every sector of the economy.[2] Popular agitation also arose from multiple other quarters—radical university students and intellectuals, youth groups, community organizations, and the unemployed masses. The National Joint Action Committee (NJAC) was formed in 1969 by Khafra Kambon and Makandal Daaga as a loose confederation of these unions and these groups, with the goal of pressing for economic and political change and a Black cultural revolution. The resulting Black Power Movement, as it was called, gained momentum in the late 1960s. The *Vanguard*, the official newspaper of the Oilfield Workers' Trade Union (OWTU), described the labor situation in 1969 as "not only critical, but potentially explosive.... [It] could create a general social and political crisis 1000 times more dangerous than 1937–'38."[3] Liberation unionism had reemerged.

This revolutionary spirit culminated in what came to be called the February Revolution in 1970, when for the first time in the postindependence period of both Trinidad and Tobago and the anglophone Caribbean, a mass movement came closest to toppling the state. The movement was actually sparked by racial discrimination against Caribbean students in Canada; in response, in the first few months of 1970, radical students in Trinidad and Tobago, with the support and participation of militant unions, organized massive demonstrations against the persistence of the colonial and racial order.[4] Radical unions called on "Black proletarian warriors" to unite and set April 21, 1970, as the date for a general strike of African and Indian workers in sugar, oil, transport, and electricity, with the allyship of the NJAC, youth groups, and the unemployed.[5] To avert the strike, the government declared a state of emergency and imprisoned several labor leaders and Black Power activists, precipitating a mutiny of a group of army officers who supported the mass movement. Fortunately for the state, the mutiny was contained, and the NJAC fizzled out as their leaders were arrested, but the crisis was not over.[6] From his prison cell, George Weekes, then president general of the OWTU, wrote, "BLACK PEOPLE WILL WIN BACK THIS COUNTRY OR DIE."[7]

Remarkably, liberation unionism returned with a fury not witnessed since 1937 and 1919. As chapter 4 illustrated, after World War II, liberation unionism faced significant setbacks, due not simply to the continued exploitation of labor by the state, foreign/metropolitan capital, and a rising local business elite. The movement was also divided and weakened by bureaucratic conservatism, political incorporation, and the divisive politicization of race by Indian and African middle-class politicians. This chapter explores how working people rebuilt liberation unionism and resumed their historic role as the vanguard of the revolutionary struggle. It also documents how the movement precipitated a third wave of reforms within the postindependence neocolonial state, further propelling the economic and social development of Trinidad and Tobago. The timing of the mass mobilization was crucial, as the 1960s movement nearly crippled the state just before it received significant oil windfalls from the 1973 and 1979 oil booms, shaping how the state invested these revenues.

The chapter addresses several key questions: Given that liberation unionism had been so severely weakened in the decolonization period, what accounts for its resuscitation in the 1960s? The global political economy in the 1960s was different from the interwar years. What were the political, economic, and institutional conditions under which working people were organizing? What strategies did workers and unions use to rebuild liberation unionism in the new context? What were the impacts of this mobilization on the state and development?

These are the burning questions that currently preoccupy labor unions, labor movements, and the left in general. Previous works have shown that labor unions can reverse oligarchic tendencies and regain militance. They can address internal dynamics, that is, reorganize internally by embracing new leaders, radical outsiders, and a different organizing culture. Labor militancy can also be revived by external forces, such as the spillover effects of other social movements.[8] These strategies certainly contributed to the revival of liberation unionism in postindependence Trinidad and Tobago.

But the revitalization of unions and the labor movement was driven by more than reorganizing relations internally within the union/movement and externally with other unions and social movements. Unions regained their militance, unconventional disruptive tactics, and commitment to organizing the unorganized by reaching back in time and returning to the deep historical ideological and organizational traditions of working people. They consciously and intentionally excavated principles, institutional knowledge, and tactics that were successful in the interwar years and innovated on them to develop new creative solutions to contemporary challenges to advance the movement. This was another iteration of what Cedric Robinson has called the "Black Radical Tradition"—"an accretion, over generations, of collective intelligence gathered from struggle."[9] This tradition was the product not of an innate African culture of resistance, as Robinson asserts, but rather of knowledges, tools, and strategies birthed, developed, and transmitted in direct response to centuries of European aggression.

Working people recovered and reworked traditions of Black working-class radicalism and deployed several strategies that challenged the actors, discourses,

FIGURE 5.1. March of Resistance, June 3, 1967. *Source: Vanguard*, March 30, 1968.

and structures responsible for the incapacitation of the movement. Groups of militant workers reclaimed union leadership from conservative agents. They also severed ties with co-opted labor organizations and forged ties with other radical unions. And they countered racial divisions between workers through a racially inclusive Black Power ideology. As we shall see, not all the strategies were successful. Labor parties continued to fail at the polls. Still, the agency of working people in energizing race consciousness, class consciousness, anti-imperial fever, and interracial worker unity succeeded in resuscitating liberation unionism in the postindependence political field (see figure 5.1). The resulting movement forced the state and capital to accede to many demands within its broad-based transformative agenda. As part of the compromise, the state further carved out some autonomous policy space from foreign capital and underwent yet another series of intensive institution-building efforts toward enhancing the masses' well-being.

Postindependence Liberation Unionism: Recovering and Rebuilding

Figure 5.2 shows the number of strikes and lockouts between 1953 and 1985. The early years of little worker agitation reflect labor's demobilization during the decolonization period. However, the number of strikes increased dramatically from just three in 1955 to seventy-five in 1962 and seventy-one in 1971.[10] Work-

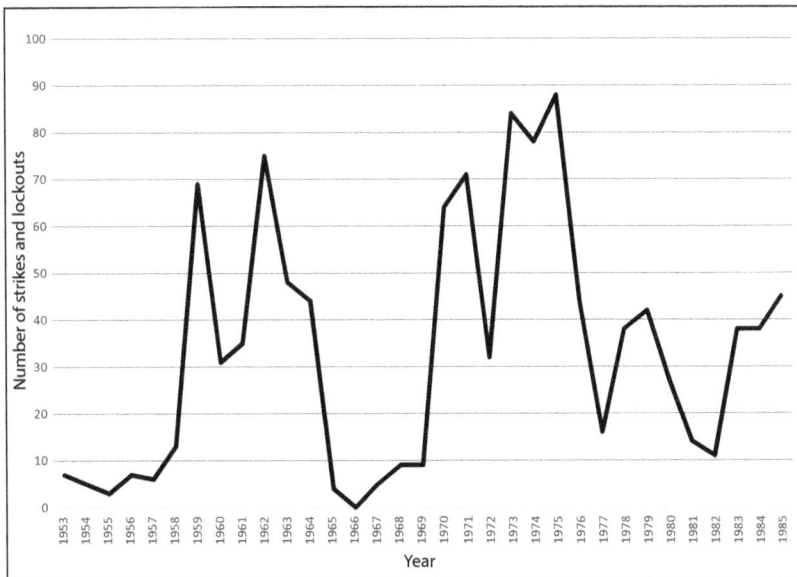

FIGURE 5.2. Strike activity in Trinidad and Tobago, 1953–85. *Sources:* International Labour Organization, *Year Book 1970*, 826; International Labour Organization, *Year Book 1973*, 793; International Labour Organization, "ILOSTAT Indicators and Data Tools."

ers mobilized against old challenges in new guises. The state's first five-year development plan (1958–62, released 1958) defined the state's role in the economy as follows: "What Government has to do is to create a framework which is favorable for investment, and to try to persuade as many persons as possible, home and overseas, to create new employment opportunities."[11] Foreign direct investment flowed in, and the country registered an impressive annual growth rate, averaging 8 percent between 1963 and 1968.[12] However, the plan resulted in significant unemployment, dispossession, and dislocation for working people. Oil exports accounted for more than 40 percent of total exports, but the oil industry employed relatively few workers.[13] Agriculture employed far more labor, but its contribution to the gross domestic product (GDP) declined significantly in the first decade of independence.[14] The modest growth in the manufacturing sector did not significantly increase employment.[15] Unemployment averaged around 14 percent between 1964 and 1973, and about the same percentage was classified as underemployed.[16] Inflation increased from 2.1 percent in 1960 to 14.8 percent in 1973.[17]

Multinationals and the state engaged in profit-maximizing strategies, including increasing mechanization, retrenching workers and hiring from the unemployed on a contract basis, and reducing some of the hard-won provisions from the 1937 uprising, such as medical services.[18] Moreover, the anti-Black and anti-Indian racism of white multinational company managers continued to shape workers' everyday work experiences and advancement opportunities.[19] Expansion of the tourism industry in Tobago pushed Tobagonians off their land and into licit and illicit service labor, such as waitressing and sex work.[20] The state's generous tax concessions to foreign companies accompanied increased "indirect" taxes on the masses, such as bus fares, fees for vehicle licenses and driver permits, taxes on gasoline and tires, and higher electricity and sewage rates.[21] Inequality worsened, as evidenced in the GINI coefficient, which went from 0.43 in 1957 to 0.51 in 1971.[22] Meanwhile, the conspicuous consumption of the metropolitan and local business elite only further incensed workers and the poor.[23] The African and Indian masses felt the brunt of the state's industrialization strategy.

The political and institutional environment also frustrated workers. The state passed the Industrial Stabilization Act (ISA) of 1965, which repealed and replaced the hard-won 1938 Trade Disputes (Arbitration and Inquiry) Ordinance. The provisions of the ISA, such as compulsory arbitration through the Industrial Court and limits on direct trade union action, restricted collective bargaining and union power.[24] Further, the Industrial Court ruled so often in favor of multinational corporations that workers came to see the court as "a weapon of the capitalists" and expressed "no confidence" in the institution.[25] In sum, the economy, the state, and arbitration institutions were failing working people.

Militant workers revitalized the movement through three main strategies: wresting unions from oligarchic leaders, abandoning conservative unions and organizationally uniting with radical ones, and mobilizing and uniting Indian and African workers with Black Power discourse.

Taking Back Oligarchic Unions

Bureaucratic conservatism and the co-optation of union leaders were widespread in the early 1960s. Some of these pseudo–trade unionists—union leaders who "ride the backs of the workers for their own ends"—acted in the employers' interest to control and demobilize workers in exchange for monetary compensation.[26] One such example was allegedly Bhadase Maraj, whose All Trinidad Sugar Estates and Factory Workers' Trade Union (ATSEFWTU) was the only union sugar companies recognized.[27] Others received rewards from the ruling party, such as appointments on legislative bodies, statutory boards, committees, and government delegations. For instance, Carl Tull of the Communication

Workers Union, John Rojas of the OWTU, W. W. Sutton of the Amalgamated Workers Union, and Nathaniel Critchlow of the National Union of Government Employees, who all supported the People's National Movement (PNM), accepted appointments as state senators while they were union and labor federation leaders.[28] The *Trinidad Guardian* described them as "both top-flight trade unionists and party colleagues in the ruling People's National Movement."[29] Thus, one approach to restoring radicalism was to oust these leaders.

The main archetype for this strategy was the militant oil workers' revitalization of the OWTU. After World War II, oil workers were divided between the militant Butlerites and the more conciliatory Rojas-led OWTU. After the failure of the 1947 oil strike, Tubal Uriah Butler moved to London to agitate for home rule. Butlerites still needed protection in the context of deteriorating conditions. Further, some OWTU members were frustrated with Rojas's leadership and started recruiting Butlerites to help refashion the union.[30] The return of radical Butlerites changed the makeup and tenor of the OWTU. They joined forces with the anti-Rojas union members to form "the rebels" and transformed the OWTU by waging internal campaigns against the executive, organizing to win branch elections, and engaging in and supporting strikes that were unsanctioned by the OWTU leadership. They ultimately succeeded in forcing Rojas to resign through a vote of no confidence.[31] According to the *Vanguard*, Rojas became a "*persona non grata*, as he represents no one but himself. . . . Mr. Rojas through his actions, has permanently and irrevocably ex-communicated himself from the councils of the workers."[32]

In June 1962 the rebels were elected by popular vote, ushering in a new radical executive committee and president, George Weekes. Weekes was born and raised in a small, remote fishing village called Toco. After primary and intermediary school, he served as a noncommissioned officer with the Caribbean Regiment in the United States, Italy, and Egypt. His exposure to Garveyism and socialism was nurtured during his travels. When he returned to Trinidad and Tobago, he took a job as a pipe fitter in the oil industry in 1949 and formed a relationship with Butler.[33] Weekes joined the OWTU in 1952.[34] As soon as the rebels took the executive, Weekes and the OWTU immediately went to battle with Texaco, BP, and Shell and organized a series of strikes for better wages, working conditions, and job security; the strike against BP in 1963 lasted as long as fifty-seven days and involved 2,600 oil workers.[35] What occurred in the OWTU in 1962 was reminiscent of the Trinidad Workingmen's Association (TWA) in 1917, when the militant faction organized to win control of the union executive and successfully swept aside leaders who favored narrower agitations for political reforms and nonconfrontational methods (see chapter 2). This rank-and-file reclamation of the OWTU, completed just two months before Trinidad and Tobago won its independence, restored radicalism to the union.

The resurgence of disruptive tactics was the result of deliberate efforts by radical leaders to retrieve the ideological roots and institutional foundations of interwar liberation unionism. Unity, Pan-African internationalism, and transformation—the core tenets of liberation unionism—were recentered alongside militancy and democracy within the union as hallmarks of OWTU organization and strategy. The new rebel leaders of the OWTU saw themselves as disciples of Butler who were returning to the union's founding principles. Weekes reminisced, "I got my political education as a Butlerite. In fact, I was so fired by the Chief's ideas on 'Home Rule,' nationalization of the main industries, the redistribution of wealth, and the raising of the standard of living of the workers that I became an active speaker on his platform."[36] Weekes saw it as his duty "to continue the work started by the 'Chief' [Butler]."[37] Under the rebels' leadership, the OWTU reclaimed Butler, honored him with the union's highest award and a statue, became his main benefactor, and designated June 19 as Butler Day in honor of his role in the 1937 unrest.[38] Butler's legacy, his commitment to confrontation, and the expansiveness of the demands lived on through the new leaders.

Workers also revived interracialism as an important tradition and a key movement goal. According to one article in the *Vanguard*, "Butler was not the great almost. He achieved in his own time what has come to be known as interracial solidarity, and taken it to a pitch none of the present political parties has done. . . . Uriah Butler stirred Indian sugar workers and Negro rig workers into action whether this was going on strike for better conditions or of paying their pennies for the Butlerite campaign."[39] The specific strategies used to rebuild a multiracial movement are discussed later in this chapter.

The unions also drew on the organizing knowledge and skills of the women in liberation unionism. Daisy Crick, for example, started as a lead organizer in the TWA under Arthur A. Cipriani in the 1920s, continued to organize in the oil belt in the 1937 uprising (see chapter 3), after which she went on to serve as president of the La Brea OWTU branch (1946–52) and an OWTU trustee (1952–62).[40] The OWTU recognized Crick's leadership and revered her as "the doyen of women's group activities," and she trained many women activists before and after independence.[41] Through organizers like Crick, working people actively passed down their traditions of liberation unionism through the generations, enabling the movement to survive into the postindependence era.

Like in the TWA and the 1930s unions, the organizational openness of the OWTU facilitated an inclusive membership, which, in turn, further increased women's participation and leadership, the multisectoral and multiracial character of the union, and its embeddedness in communities. For instance, Crick had never been an employee in the oil sector or any of the allied industries represented by the OWTU. She was a housewife.[42] Further, many women who were not union members were incorporated into the work of unions and movement building. For instance, one organizer, Yvonne Joseph, asserted, "When workmen are out of jobs, we, the women suffer. . . . The Union's business is our business, don't mind we are not members of the Union."[43] Women also held leadership positions in the branch executives, worked as union clerks and other staff, and, in the OWTU, maintained a vibrant Women's Section.[44] Other unions also had many active trade unionists who were women, such as Audrey Forde of the Transport and Industrial Workers' Union (TIWU) and Rookmin Rampersad of the ATSEFWTU.[45] These women organized and advocated not only for unionized women workers but also for youth, nonunionized women (e.g., housewives), and other working people who were not covered by regular industrial agreements.[46] As a result of women's organizing work, liberation unionism enhanced union-community linkages, more people joined the marches and protests, and the scope of demands was broadened.

Unions also re-embedded themselves into communities through other methods. The OWTU, for example, encouraged, sponsored, and supported local arts and culture, such as children's essay competitions, film screenings, calypsonians, and a steel orchestra.[47] Branch buildings opened their doors for use not only by oil workers but also by members of the community.[48] The children of prominent labor organizers also formed their own organizations and discussion groups. For instance, two secondary school students—Ayesha Johnson and Josanne Leonard (daughter of Indo-Trinbagonian OWTU and NJAC/Black Power revolutionary Winston Leonard)—started the National Organization of Revolutionary Students.[49] Progressive unions were also heavily involved in a monumental NJAC-led long march into the sugar belt in 1970 under the banner "Indians and Africans Unite Now," which drew in schoolchildren alongside young and old men and women (see figures 5.3 and 5.4). Members of the predominantly Indian communities along the route in the sugar belt opened their doors, served food and refreshments to the marchers, and offered them a place to rest.[50] It was a testament to the multisectoral, multiracial, women-involved, community-supported unity of liberation unionism that was revived through the radicals' reclamation of unions and return to the traditions of organizing characteristic of the interwar years. This approach to resisting political co-optation and pacification enabled postindependence liberation unionism to become a formidable countervailing force to state power and to advocate for a developmental agenda.

FIGURE 5.3. The Long March to Caroni, Trinidad, March 1970. *Source: Vanguard,* March 21, 1970.

FIGURE 5.4. The Long March to Caroni, Trinidad, March 1970. *Source: Express,* March 17, 1970.

The rank and file were not always successful in reorganizing unions internally. When these efforts failed, they adopted a different approach: abandoning co-opted unions and forging alliances with more radical ones. For example, this strategy proved effective for sugar workers frustrated with ATSEFWTU leader Bhadase Maraj. In the early 1960s, sugar workers voiced numerous complaints against Maraj and the ATSEFWTU executive, including failing to represent workers' grievances to employers, frequently betraying workers through side deals with employers, bringing in strikebreakers to undermine strikes, maintaining authoritarian control of the union, and singlehandedly withdrawing from the centralized union federation—the National Trades Union Congress (NTUC).[51] Maraj was also a tyrannical leader who used violence to suppress worker agitation. The sugar workers reported, "Anyone who crossed him ... was given a rough time."[52] That included shooting up their cars and homes, throwing gas and gelignite bombs into their homes, and puncturing their car tires.[53] They even tried forming alternative unions under different leadership but were unsuccessful.[54]

In a letter entitled "SOS to NTUC," the sugar workers appealed to the NTUC, "particularly the Oilworkers' Trade Union," to aid them in dealing with "the unbearable state of dissatisfaction and uneasiness ... plaguing our everyday working lives, due to the undemocratic, dictatorial, victimizing and unconstitutional behavior" of the ATSEFWTU executive committee.[55] Some unions in the NTUC did not support the sugar workers. Others who did—like Weekes and the OWTU, the TIWU, and the National Union of Foods, Hotels, Beverages, and Allied Workers (NUFHBAW)—decided to break off from the central organization and aid the sugar workers, forming their own Council of Progressive Trade Unions (CPTU) in 1965.[56] The oil workers' position on supporting the sugar workers was clear: "The sugar workers need the help of the Oilfields Workers' Trade Union and the members should be proud to allow George Weekes to help do for sugar what he has done for oil."[57]

In fact, the OWTU played a key role in embracing workers who were seeking militant representation and, in doing so, enhanced the multisectoral, multiracial character of the movement. Many workers in other industries sought the OWTU, as well as the TIWU and the NUFHBAW, as their recognized union due to their militance, negotiation expertise, capacity to handle grievances, and overall liberatory mission.[58] Oil workers recognized that they were the highest paid and had the best contracts.[59] Nevertheless, the OWTU saw itself as "the Vanguard of the working class struggle in this country," proclaiming, "[We] shall continue to fight not only the cause of the oilworkers, but that of the labour movement as a whole. We shall continue to be labour's democracy, equality, and independence."[60] In 1967 the OWTU constitution was formally amended to allow non–oil workers to join the union.[61] Mottos like "A Blow to One Is a Blow to All" reinforced the principle of solidarity across industrial sectors.[62] The unity of oil and sugar was particularly important, as workers predicted it would "result in a fundamental alteration of the distribution of political and economic power in this country. The authoritarian power-structure—with its alliance of Afro-Saxon politics and metropolitan economics—will be substantially democratized as a result of the unification of the workers in the two major props of the neo-colonial economy."[63] In 1970, again, sugar workers appealed for and received the help of the OWTU. The alliance between sugar and oil workers, combined with unity across other sectors, nearly brought the state to its knees.[64]

Likewise, when electricity workers sought OWTU recognition in 1969, the OWTU responded, "Unity of oil and electricity workers into one union is not only in the interest of the oppressed and exploited workers in oil and electricity but in the interest of our divided trade union movement. . . . The OWTU stretches out its Mighty Arm of Spartan Leadership and Membership Solidarity to their Brothers in the Electricity Commission in answer to their Cry for Protection and Justice! The merging of these two 'Sources of Power' (Oil and Electricity) will create a lasting confluence along the course of Working-class Endeavor to Generate a Greater Flow of Progress and Achievement!"[65] The merger of these strategically important industries increased the bargaining strength of the entire movement and helped revive liberation unionism.

Furthermore, the radical labor leaders spoke on each other's platforms and held joint public meetings, and multiple officers held key positions in more than one of these unions, which further strengthened movement unity.[66] They pledged to support each other through financial assistance and solidarity strikes, and they also co-organized joint strikes and demonstrations, such as the 1968 March of Resistance.[67] All of this collaborative work mirrored the strategies that militant workers had developed in the early 1930s to overcome the increasing bureaucratic conservatism of Cipriani and the TWA. Such multisectoral and multiracial unity of the rebels—the warrior workers—across the individual unions facilitated the reemergence of liberation unionism in the early postindependence period.

Even before the sugar workers' SOS divided the NTUC, conflicts arose between the politically incorporated unions and the militant unions over the central labor organization's strategy—whether to negotiate with the government, as favored by the former, or to engage in direct action, as insisted on by the latter. For example, in 1964, when the NTUC debated whether to engage in talks with the government, radical unions took an uncompromising position of nonengagement. In 1964 this disagreement led to a split, and some of the co-opted unions withdrew from the NTUC and formed their own National Federation of Labor.[68] One article in the *Vanguard* reflected on these different orientations to the state and the way this impacted worker unity: "Leaders of the largest and most important unions are hostile to each other. Any getting together of these leaders cannot produce lasting unity. The differences between them are too deep. What is more, the differences do not arise out of trade union matters or trade union activity. They are political differences. This fact must be faced squarely."[69] As such, radical unions saw the centralized national labor organizations like the NTUC and the Labor Congress as a "marriage of convenience," according to one organizer, or more aptly, "a marriage of incompatibles."[70]

Interunion collaboration did not encompass all unions in the country; therefore, the movement was not as large in numbers as it otherwise would have been. However, loyalties to different political parties and the state risked the depoliticization of liberation unionism as a whole. As one organizer wrote, "Trade union unity, nice as this sounds, is meaningless and worthless if we think simply in terms of organizational structure. Trade union unity can be achieved on the basis of a pervasive philosophy and concern."[71] Butlerism, the author asserted, needed to be the basis for such a philosophy. As such, the unrelenting position on union autonomy from the parties and the state stemmed from reflections on the trajectory of unions since the revolutionary 1937 movement. Otherwise, "unity for unity sake is stupid," as one writer bluntly put it.[72] Similarly, Weekes noted, "Twenty-eight years of experience has taught us oil workers many things. . . . But . . . above all, this lesson, a lesson that needs to be underlined. . . . *That lesson is that we must do our own independent thinking*."[73] The independence of and unity between militant unions enabled a significant portion of the working people to retain their radicalism and press developmental demands on the state.

Worker autonomy from ruling parties is crucial for preserving not only workplace democracy but also democratic institutions more broadly.[74] With this independence, the radical trade union movement carved out space to mercilessly attack Williams, racialized party politics, and the state-capital relationship, as they had done in the interwar years. In an analysis similar to Frantz Fanon's, one article in the *Vanguard* admonished the petty bourgeois political leadership for betraying working people: "The three Parliamentary parties

[PNM, Democratic Labour Party (DLP), and Liberal Party] are based on the middle class of Trinidad, a class whose limitations and outlook have been created and represented by generations of Colonial Rule. The PNM successfully used the Trade Union Movement on two occasions to secure power and deliberately used the said power to stab the very workers in the back."[75] Likewise, the Indian-dominated opposition party, the DLP, was also hostile to the workers' cause and lacked a coherent alternative plan for industry and development. The DLP, in the eyes of workers, was "unwilling to develop any sort of criticism of Government's inept policy."[76] One John La Rose wrote that the "revealed incapacity of West Indian middle class political leadership" could only be solved by "POWER TO THE MASSES" and the "action of the Trinidad workers in outbidding the middle class for the leadership of the national revolutionary struggle."[77]

Labor leaders framed Afro-creole state officials' orientation to metropolitan interests as racial betrayal. Workers saw the latter as "willing accomplices" in racialized exploitation, as "black stooges," who were "whiter than the whites themselves."[78] The president of the Industrial Court was called "Enemy No.1 of the Working Class" and a "Ruling Class Lacey [sic]."[79] Militant workers bore a particular disdain for Eric Williams, however. Campaigns against Williams referred to him as "The Puppet," "The Butcher," "The Snake," and a "White man in a Black body."[80] The *Vanguard* had a column called "The Doctor Said," where excerpts from Williams's book *Capitalism and Slavery* and his nationalist speeches were printed to illustrate the inconsistencies between his intellectual work and his political praxis. According to one trade unionist, "It has taken an expert on slavery to re-impose slavery on his own people."[81] In a lecture entitled "The Problems of Unemployment," Weekes linked these individual actions to the lineages of colonialism in the neocolonial state structure: "[Trinidad and Tobago's economic problem] is a result of our country's original structure as a colonial possession of the British Empire. True we have won our political freedom, but it is equally true that nothing has substantially changed. Instead of outright colonialism of yesterday we now have neo-colonialism through the collaboration of the present black government serving their white masters."[82] The government consistently intervened to protect (white) foreign and local capital.[83] However, workers were clear: "We want the Prime Minister to act as a black man in defense of the black oppressed masses. (Applause)."[84] This mobilization against Williams, the neocolonial state, and the docile opposition party was possible only because radical unions had the independence to hold leaders accountable. As summed up in the words of trade unionist Alston Salandy, "Political independence is of great importance to the working class."[85] In sum, workers combated the co-optation and political incorporation that had resulted in movement demobilization by breaking away from employer- and government-controlled unions and labor organizations and coalescing with other progressive unions. This autonomy helped foment the mass movement.

Countering Racial Political Articulation

Liberation unionism also flourished after independence as working people countered the divisive racial identity politics of the major political parties with their own racial and class-based politics. Through Black Power—"a global Pan-African phenomenon"—unions enlivened Black racial consciousness and combined it with union demands.[86] Labor leaders also redefined the term *Black* to fit the context of Trinidad and Tobago and the Caribbean in ways that embraced Indians and fostered the resurgence of a multiracial movement.

Even though Marcus Garvey and the Universal Negro Improvement Association (UNIA) were long gone by the 1960s and 1970s, Black racial pride, Pan-African unity, and the Black self-determination of Garveyism remained deeply interwoven into the fabric of Black diasporic political culture. "Black Power" became the new slogan for this deeply historical ideology and political movement that evolved from Garveyism.[87] As Kate Quinn notes, Black Power represented "the long historical struggle for black liberation rooted in slavery and the transatlantic trade."[88] The term originated with activists—the Afro-Trinbagonian Kwame Ture (formerly known as Stokely Carmichael) and African American Willie Ricks—in 1966 at a Student Nonviolent Coordinating Committee rally in Mississippi. Others, such as Brinsley Samaroo, have already noted the historical connections between Black Power and interwar labor movements in Trinidad and Tobago.[89] Here, I highlight how Black Power was articulated to class and multiracial collective action in liberation unionism.

First, like the use of Garveyism in interwar labor organizing, workers' deployment of Black Power discourse heightened Black racial consciousness and linked it with union demands. Rejecting the use of Black Power to mean tokenism and symbolic representation, radical workers emphasized Black racial pride, Pan-Africanism, economic independence, and self-determination.[90] Using terms like *neo-slavery*, labor leaders drew direct parallels between African enslavement and the multinational corporations' treatment of workers:[91] "The slave was given what his master thought good for him, and the slave had no choice but to take it and keep on working. Today, nearly 132 years after Emancipation the oil workers are offered what Texaco thinks is good for them, and the workers must take it and keep on working or else! . . . Today, behold the Company acts as if it owned the workers like cattle just as their likes owned our forefathers like cattle. . . . OIL WORKERS ARE BACK IN CHAINS TO BE TRAMPLED UNDERFOOT BY HEAVY COWBOY BOOTS FROM TEXAS!!"[92] In public speeches, labor leaders conjured up global histories of emancipation, the Haitian Revolution, and Abyssinia as a source of inspiration.[93] For instance, Weekes highlighted the importance of recovering this knowledge "of Daaga of Trinidad, Sam Sharpe of Jamaica, Accrebreh of Guyana, Henri Christophe, Dessalines and Toussaint L'Ouverture of Haiti. And memory of these leaders would have carried knowledge of their deeds. Deeds which when recalled would have made it even more difficult for our imperial masters to hold us down in the bondage of indenture and wage slavery."[94] Such imagery stirred the crowds and kindled the Pan-African revolutionary spirit that was so effective in challenging capital and the colonial state.

In postindependence liberation unionism, workers also linked these racial concerns to class consciousness. Black Power was not a singular ideology; it was a diverse movement encompassing a range of shared and divergent political positions and concerns under the umbrella of the pursuit of Black liberation.[95] In Trinidad and Tobago, some, especially among the student organizers, viewed racism (the political economy of racism, not just interpersonal bias and discrimination) as the most important determinant of one's conditions and life experiences. Others, like C. L. R. James, recognized racism as a central dynamic that cannot be ignored but is ultimately secondary to class. Still others viewed race as the medium through which capital is accumulated and class relations are experienced and reproduced, aligning with Stuart Hall's later formulations. These divergent positions would eventually contribute to the fragmentation of the Black Power movement. However, during the 1960s–1970s, labor organizers avoided getting bogged down in these distinctions. Instead, they, as with Garveyism in the interwar years, merged the racial uplift discourse of Black Power with the fight for workers' rights, thereby intertwining two crucial phenomena: race and class. The OWTU described the specific racial ideology of the worker movement as follows:

> In our West Indian society of yesterday the white plantation owners used the racialist or ethnic ideology to rationalize and consolidate their class rule and economic domination. And by the inevitable dialectic of history in Trinidad and Tobago society of today we in turn utilize a **specially defined racial and ethnic ideology** to CONSOLIDATE AND RATIONALIZE the ranks of the oppressed in our struggle for economic emancipation and people's rule. . . . [T]he call for Black Power in Trinago is the same as the call for Proletarian Power; the cause of our black

brothers and sisters in our beloved country at present occupied, not by foreign troops but, by foreign capital is the same as our proletarian cause; the task of our black proletarian kith and kin who want work and meaningful intellectual employment is the same that our historical mission as the organized Vanguard of the oppressed commands us to perform.[96]

This quote reflects how these "Black Working Class Liberators," as they called themselves, conceptualized the link between race and class, and between Black Power and worker power.[97] There was a compatibility between these different forms of consciousness that motivated and energized working people.

Like for Garvey's UNIA and the TWA, the organizational ties between Black Power–promoting organizations and the militant unions also facilitated the circulation of expertise and resources and embedded the movement in communities, which also helped revitalize liberation unionism and broaden working people's demands. Militant unions pledged human and financial resources to NJAC's and university students' campaigns, and they joined together for strikes and demonstrations.[98] According to one TIWU resolution, the union saw solidarity with the students in their fight against racism as a necessary step toward the "eventual destruction of racism and its creator capitalism."[99] Additionally, some trade unionists, such as Clive Nunez of the TIWU, were also members of the NJAC. These key interlocutors transmitted information between the two organizations, including intelligence that helped preserve liberation unionism from infiltration and co-optation by conservative elements.[100] After years of organizing in and supporting the Black Power movement, on April 4, 1970, the OWTU General Council officially announced its support for the movement.[101] The statement partially explained the reasons behind OWTU's resolution: "We know and see that it is being massively supported by the oppressed citizens of our country who are not only our black brothers and sisters but are also our class comrades and allies. We take this stand because we are convinced that it is our bounden duty to the thousands of our black proletarian kith and kin . . . **as well as in the interest of our own dear skins**—to see and ensure that they are gainfully employed all year round on productive and meaningful undertakings."[102] Joining forces with Black Power enabled the union to connect with the grassroots Pan-African revolutionary spirit and expand the movement's membership, demands, and sympathizers.

Radical labor organizers in Trinidad and Tobago advanced a formulation of Black Power that challenged the political parties' politicization of race that lumped Indians together as an integral community with different interests from Africans and vice versa in order to prevent worker unity. According to

Weekes, they wanted to "turn black men against black, Negro against Indian, but those who benefit most from this are not Black and they are neither Negro nor Indian."[103] Indeed, many Indian workers saw little difference between the African workers with whom they were meant to coalesce and the African petty bourgeoisie who monopolized the state. Likewise, the mostly Christian African workers seemed not to fully understand or appreciate the central role Hinduism occupied in the majority of Indian laborers' lives.[104] Generalizations and stereotypes attributed to racial and cultural differences abounded.[105] The construction of opposed race-based interests remained a threat to worker unity through the postindependence period.

Nonetheless, interracialism remained a crucial component of liberation unionism. As in the interwar years, it was not simply a by-product of sectoral unity but a deliberate strategy. To working people, achieving African-Indian unity was "the historical role of the workers in oil and sugar," as only workers had "the real power to bring about that concrete unity between Indians and Negroes," not parties, not the middle class, "only at the level of labor, because this is where most of our Indians and Negroes belong."[106] Labor organizers met this challenge by reformulating the *Black* in Black Power into a political term that referred to the shared histories of racial, colonial, and imperial subjugation of African and Indian labor within the Caribbean plantation system. As Walter Rodney explained, Indians in the Caribbean were taken there to be exploited, were reduced to racist stereotypes, and met with the same racist hatred that whites applied to Africans; "Black Power in the West Indies, therefore, refers primarily to people who are recognizably African or Indian."[107] Indian and African organizers went door-to-door, to "nightclubs, bars and communities," to build relationships, shape worldviews, and weave solidarities.[108]

The evidence of this inclusive racial political construction is plentiful. In a piece entitled "East Indians and Black Power" in the *Vanguard*, an author using the pseudonym "Indian" wrote that while Indians may feel closer to and aspire to whiteness because "of the texture of their hair, 'straight' noses, thin lips etc," "YOU Mr. INDIAN, have got to realize that YOU ARE BLACK! BLACK!!!" because Indians were brought to the colony to replace African labor and faced similar racist oppression on the plantations. The writer ends, "Coolie or nigger, we are both BLACK. Let us be proud, let us unite, let us fight for our true identity."[109] Thus, workers remade the connection among race, phenotype, and shared material interests in a manner that opposed hegemonic racializations in pursuit of a common political goal. Another example of the political Blackness construct comes from a report in 1969 about some thousand African and Indian workers who downed their tools against rampant racism at Texaco: "Black workers, Indians and Negroes, united in protest, risking their jobs and their freedom defying the law in the protection of a black brother against the attack of a foreign white racist."[110] Statements from the OWTU Women's Section also reflected the construction of political Blackness: "The employers by and large are white people mostly foreigners; the employed are black people—Indian and Negroes."[111] The OWTU also awarded "certificates of meritorious service" to workers who struck in solidarity with each other; the award read, "Unity and Strength among all Black People, Africans and Indians... for TRUE and TOTAL LIBERATION."[112] The historic bonds between Africans and Indians necessitated a unified front: "It is our sacred duty to struggle to the death if necessary to put an end to the exploitation and discrimination to which we the blacks of this world, Africans and Asians, have been and are still being subjected."[113] Thus, for labor organizers, Black Power was not incompatible with multiracial unity.

The combination of political Blackness and the anti-imperialism of Black Power was a crucial component of the organizing framework through which labor demanded that Trinidad and Tobago "delink," in Samir Amin's sense, from the imperatives of the white capitalist system.[114] Weekes, for example, expresses this race consciousness, interracialism, and anti-imperialism in the following excerpt: "Today in our struggle for Economic Liberation, BP must mean one thing—'Black Power.' Oil is black, oil is Black Power, so when we advise the Government of Trinidad and Tobago to acquire BP holdings, what we are actually advocating is the transfer of power—White Power—into the hands of Black People. That is to say, Africans and Indians principally in our country."[115] Thus, for workers, race, class, and empire were deeply imbricated, and Black liberation required, first and foremost, a recognition of these interconnections and organizing to challenge them.

How Indian workers internalized this renovation of the term *Black* varied. Some Indian workers perhaps never came to see themselves as Black.[116] Still, the evidence of multiracial unity in the movement indicates that political Blackness and Black Power discourse, like the Black pride of Garveyism before it, did not repel Indian workers from liberation unionism. Others fully embraced political Blackness. Winston Leonard, for example, an Indian organizer in both labor unions and the NJAC, also deployed this formulation when he spoke of "the struggle for Black Liberation."[117] In addition, unions maintained some level of multiracial leadership, for example, among the executive, branch officers, and staff of unions such as the National Union of Government Employees, OWTU, and TIWU.[118] Unions also commemorated and attended cultural events of importance to their members, including Diwali, Eid, and Christmas.[119]

In his annual Diwali greetings in 1965, Weekes stated, "The Trade Union in the modern world is concerned not only with raising and protecting the economic position of its members, but also their educational, social and religious welfare. . . . May we continue to respect one another's religions and views and struggle together for the uplift of the working class and the progress of the Nation."[120] Thus, the institutionalization of multiracial representation and the visibility of Indian and African unity among labor leaders were consistent with the political Blackness discourse. Together, this organizational and ideological consonance united Indian and African working people.

The diasporic character of liberation unionism and its connection to Black Power was also reminiscent of interwar labor organizing. The postindependent movement continued to build and connect with global circuits of Pan-African and other anti-imperial revolutionary labor and social movement organizers around the world. Political Blackness also appears in the Black Consciousness Movement led by Steve Biko in South Africa and in UK movements in the 1960s as an umbrella term for the common experience of racial and colonial domination that unites African, Caribbean, and Asian immigrants.[121] Interestingly, some of the Afro-Trinbagonian activists in the United Kingdom had connections with unions and Black Power in Trinidad and Tobago, such as Darcus Howe and Altheia Jones-LeCointe.[122] In fact, Darcus Howe had visited and collaborated with the labor unions in Trinidad with a letter of recommendation from C. L. R. James, who himself was another key example of transnational organizing.[123]

Liberation unionism forwarded its Pan-African internationalist orientation, continually seeking to support Black liberation struggles abroad and to build a united global revolutionary movement. Local unions forged links with other unions and labor organizations abroad, which was useful for both receiving and providing technical assistance, expertise, and financial support for struggles against multinational corporations and other employers.[124] Workers followed news on the war in the Congo, the Vietnam War, and labor struggles around the world.[125] Throughout the late 1960s, the *Vanguard* printed writings and speeches by and articles about local and international Black Power, civil rights, and anticolonial activists and revolutionaries like Kwame Ture, Miriam Makeba, and James Boggs.[126] They vehemently critiqued the anti-Blackness of other Afro-creole neocolonial states, such as the Jamaican government's banning of Walter Rodney.[127] The ultimate goal was to build international working-class solidarity and Black liberation.

In sum, working people displayed creative agency in countering the racial disunity stoked by electoral party politics. The parallels between the roles of

FIGURE 5.5. Working people march to support bus workers' strike, 1969.
Source: Vanguard, May 3, 1969.

Garveyism and Black Power in labor organizing demonstrate the centrality of race and Pan-Africanism to working people in different conjunctures (see figure 5.5). Together with the undeniable role of women and embeddedness in communities, militant workers managed to successfully break out of the arms of pseudo–trade unionists, employers, and parochial racial identity politics and bring liberation unionism back to life in the 1960s and 1970s.

While it is important to understand the strategies that were successful, it is also important to assess those that failed. Radical unions also sought to combat insularity and political incorporation by forming labor parties, but these efforts were largely unsuccessful. Workers generally rejected the involvement of trade unions in party politics.

Many labor leaders saw the importance of politics, lawmaking, and policies as a path to social change. As expressed in the *Vanguard,* "Only legislators who understand and are sympathetic to their [workers'] cause can pass laws which will benefit them. Who then is better qualified to do the job than able trade union leaders?"[128] In admiration of Antigua, Barbados, Jamaica, St. Vincent, and St. Kitts, where unions and parties were intertwined, radical labor leaders in Trinidad and Tobago sought to establish or form alliances with labor parties to advance policies that met the demands and interests of the masses.[129] In 1965 radical unions threw their full weight behind the Workers and Farmers Party (WFP), led by C. L. R. James and Stephen Maharaj (who defected from the DLP), from its launch, including campaigning and even putting up candidates.[130] But in the 1966 election, the WFP failed miserably. Despite a 66 percent voter turnout, the WFP won only 3 percent of the popular vote and no elected seats.[131]

The reasons for the defeat of labor parties mirrored many of the challenges they faced in 1945–62: different ideological positions, lack of financial resources comparable to those of the PNM, red-baiting, and state repression.[132] Yet the issue was more fundamental. Trinbagonian workers viewed unions and parties as somewhat incommensurable. As other scholars have noted, labor leaders' popularity among workers in union organizing did not transfer into popularity in national electoral politics.[133] Worker attendance and participation soared at strikes and demonstrations organized by the OWTU, the TIWU, sugar workers, and so on, but was feeble at party rallies organized by the same unions during the same year.[134] In sum, the form of labor organization mattered for working-class participation. Where liberation unionism successfully stitched together a unified multiracial worker movement, the same strategies, when deployed by labor in the arena of electoral politics, failed to overcome the racial political articulation of the PNM and DLP.[135] Labor parties were simply not as successful as labor unions.

Toward Transformation

Posters from two demonstrations in 1968—the March of Resistance and the Confrontation March—read "SO MUCH TO DO AN [sic] YOU STILL RETRENCHING?," "Not A Man Must Go," "WE DEMAND THE RIGHT TO STRIKE," "UNEMPLOYMENT IS THE KEY TO STARVATION," and "WILLIAMS MUST GO."[136] Posters called on working people to come out to "Confront the Foreign Oppressors and Exploiters—the Local Lackeys and Traitors"; to march against "Oppression of Black People, The Economic System, Unemployment, Industrial Genocide, Corruption, Invisible Governments, Neo-Colonialism, The ISA ... RACISM"; and to press for "Work, Food, Justice, Democracy, Job Security, Higher Wages, Economic Liberation, Higher Living Standards."[137]

As they did in the colonial era, workers framed their concerns as broader than just those affecting the workplace. According to one Ronald Hoolasie writing in the *Vanguard*, "A unified trade union movement cannot afford to limit its activities to bargaining for higher wages and more fringe benefits.... We have got a nation to build and a revolution to carry out."[138] One labor leader even said explicitly, "Our problems are in three main heads, namely, political, sociological and economic."[139]

Economically, the movement demanded not just better wages and working conditions, as well as improved vacation and maternity leave, but also a nation-wide reorganization of ownership and control. This included the nationaliza-tion of industries, agrarian reforms to ensure the sector was "not controlled by expatriates and the privileged few," land redistribution to benefit agricul-tural workers, full-employment policies at the national level, legislation and regulation of contract work, institutions for cooperative savings, investment in small-scale industries to combat unemployment and economic stagnation, and national control of trade with protection from imperialist domination.[140]

Nationalization, a goal of liberation unionism since the colonial period, involved establishing a national oil company (demanded in 1963) and taking over the factories and refineries to use them "for the good of our nation."[141] In some cases, the unions suggested acquisition with "reasonable compensation," for instance, for BP in 1967, and in others, they demanded acquisition with no payment, particularly for Texaco.[142] They also pushed the government for "an independent foreign policy that would tie us in with the third world coun-tries" as a base for trade, rather than continue the dependence on imperialist countries.[143] To the unions, nationalization accompanied by greater integration with other Third World countries would mitigate unemployment, contract labor, and retrenchment.[144] Unemployment was seen as a destructive force. Liberation unionism sought the "complete eradication of unemployment and under-employment in the country," because foreign companies thrived on a vast mass of unemployed and underemployed racialized workers.[145]

Postindependence liberation unionism also included political demands. Unions fiercely opposed legislation that curtailed political and civil rights. They fought the ISA (and the subsequent Industrial Relations Act), for example, because it not only constrained collective bargaining by workers but also im-pinged on the "fundamental freedoms of the individual" that were enshrined in the constitution, thereby impacting both workers and the general popula-tion at large.[146] Workers demanded the right to work and the right to withhold labor, greater democratization of the state, and the mobilization of national forces to fight against imperialism. They also pushed for greater checks and balances against government corruption, as well as increased worker and union participation in development planning and programs.[147]

Social demands were equally all-encompassing. Working people sought greater social security and social insurance, including coverage for the unemployed and unemployment relief; improved pension plans; medical and health schemes; expanded educational opportunities for technical, professional, and university education; and more affordable and improved housing.[148] Additionally, women advocated for reforms that would address the triple exploitation—on the basis of race, class, and gender—and therefore benefit the entire population. These included promotion of locally grown food over imports, job security, land settlement schemes, favorable credit policies, price guarantees, nutrition programs, abortion rights and proper medical care for abortions, and access to family services and contraception.[149] As the woman organizers later put it, "All political and economic struggles are ultimately social struggles . . . to be settled by fundamental questions of relationships between people and people. Again, this is a lesson that women, because of their particular position within capitalist society, seem to understand more readily than men."[150] In addition, for the radical unions, skills training and political education were both seen as critical components of education. According to the OWTU education secretary, "In the process of revolutionizing the economic, social and cultural structure of a society, Workers' Education is paramount as it would seek to make the worker have a better, fuller, richer, and meaningful life; equip him to solve his problems; expose him to his rights and responsibilities and so make him a creative member of society."[151] Accordingly, in addition to internal programs to educate workers on trade union matters and socioeconomic and political issues, unions also sought to expand meaningful vocational training and promote the "raising of our cultural standard."[152] To that end, the unions established a labor college in 1968, called the College of Labour and Industrial Relations.[153] Unions like the OWTU and the NJAC organization formed alliances with the Steelband Association, which saw the objectives of Black Power and the Steelband movement as overlapping. Together, they pushed for a government ministry to handle funding and grants to support the steelpan and the wider arts sector.[154] Importantly, it was the unions, building on campaigns that started in the 1930s, that started celebrating Emancipation Day on August 1 and pushed for it to replace Columbus Day as a public holiday.[155] What was at stake was far greater than workplace concerns. One editorial outlined the goals thoroughly:

> Labor's struggle is essentially more than just a struggle against individual employers, but a struggle against a whole system which gives the employer class an unfair advantage over the working class. The fight is therefore not against the employer class as such, but against the inequality in the relationship between the two parties. And the roots of this inequality lie within the political and economic system which we have inherited

from colonialism. Once we understand who or what the real enemy is, it automatically broadens our ideas about what the real task of the progressive union must be. The role of the trade union movement must be, not just to extract as many concessions as possible from the employer class under this system, but to work towards the abolition of the system completely, and towards its replacement by a society in which the relationship between employer and employee is completely transformed.[156]

This Black radical trade unionism carried forward its comprehensive approach to social change, emphasizing not only economic and political dimensions but also local cultural autonomy and community enrichment.

Elites and State Responses

In peripheral societies, the lack of space for self-centered, autonomous economic activity, the colonial manner in which economic reproduction was brought forth, and mass protest, especially an offensive by labor, that threatens the politically weak petty bourgeoisie can draw the state toward authoritarianism.[157] In Trinidad and Tobago, the relatively underdeveloped military infrastructure and foreign capital's waning interest in the oil sector created favorable conditions for liberation unionism to pull against the state's authoritarian leanings. Like their predecessors in the interwar years, postindependence liberation unionism interrupted production and profits, bringing the state to the brink of downfall. Company managers, the Trinidad Chamber of Commerce, the Trinidad Manufacturers Association, the Ministry of Labor, and the Industrial Court often ignored calls for negotiations or held labor in endless unproductive meetings.[158] The state hosted three tripartite talks between labor, government, and business in 1964, 1966, and 1968 in response to labor's repeated requests, but these meetings produced no positive outcomes for workers.[159] State officials also resorted to simply acceding to some aspects of the workers' demands, such as no further retrenchments without government consent, and then later reneging on their agreement.[160] When delaying, co-opting, and double-crossing were insufficient to suppress dissent, the state ramped up repression. However, as in the interwar years, repression was somewhat moderated by the persistent weakness of the state's repressive capacity relative to the movement and a lack of foreign intervention, both of which continued to provide space for liberation unionism to positively impact state capacity for development.

State repression in the 1960s and 1970s was brutal. Armed state and company police officers beat, intimidated, arrested, fired at, and wounded strikers and protesters.[161] Police raided union headquarters, and private companies banned *Vanguard* circulation at the workplace and fired militant workers.[162] Propaganda by capitalist- and state-owned media red-baited labor leaders and aimed to delegitimize and demonize the movement, especially Black Power.[163] Williams repeatedly asserted that Black Power was a foreign import, "American phraseology and practices and philosophy which have no local relevance" and which supposedly alienated "other sections of the population," most certainly meaning the Indians.[164] The 1965 ISA and the declaration of a state of emergency every time a multisectoral general strike loomed—in March 1965, April 1970, and October 1971—empowered the police to search without warrants and limited freedom of movement and association.[165] According to Williams, the 1965 state of emergency was to prevent "an open attempt to link the trade unions in oil and sugar."[166] Williams even placed his former mentor C. L. R. James under special curfew and prevented him from leaving his neighborhood.[167]

Labor vigorously opposed this repression. In fact, the ISA completely backfired as it stimulated a coalition of several radical unions in different industrial sectors and mammoth demonstrations in opposition to this state repression.[168] More than a negotiation-related issue, the unions viewed the ISA as a version of US McCarthyism, "a violation of human rights," an abrogation of "economic democracy and social justice," and *"a reversion to slavery and indenture . . . and the prelude to the establishment of totalitarian fascism in Trinidad and Tobago."*[169] Even the *Trinidad Guardian* noted that the workers were in "a political confrontation with the government, with the ISA as a rallying point, using the strike as a political weapon for the repeal of the Act."[170] The opposition party, the DLP, did not forcefully object to the state's repression. About half of the party supported the legislation, including Lionel Seukeran and Ashford Sinanan, who had once been involved in the labor movement and members of labor parties fighting alongside Butler.[171]

State investments in the police force increased the repressive capacity of the state to some extent. In 1965 the force consisted of 60 officers, 70 inspectors, and 2,247 personnel with other ranks.[172] In 1970 the police force consisted of 63 officers, 72 inspectors, and 2,446 personnel with other ranks.[173] Quantitatively, the ratio of the population to police officers in both 1965 and 1970 was about 383:1, which indicates a stronger repressive capacity than around 1919, when the ratio was approximately 522:1. In addition, some of the police officers and army soldiers in the 1960s had been active in containing the 1937 uprising.[174] Still, the police force and army as a whole continued to have grievances about low pay, insufficient officers and personnel, long hours, and poor working conditions.[175]

Likewise, similar problems plagued the army—the Trinidad and Tobago Defence Force—which weakened the state's response to liberation unionism and generated sympathies with the Black Power ideology and movement. The army was created in 1962 as a prerequisite for independence, but the state never invested significantly in the institution.[176] For years after independence, the mostly African soldiers worked in unsanitary conditions and experienced victimization and racism, whereas British privates and other white soldiers in the local force continued to enjoy relative privileges. Consequently, officers resigned, disobeyed orders, and aligned themselves with workers and the Black Power movement, ultimately leading to a mutiny in April 1970. According to one private, "We are for Black Power. . . . We can achieve Black Power. . . . We can have it tomorrow morning."[177] Lieutenants Raffique Shah and Rex La Salle were among the most outspoken in highlighting the officers' grievances and Williams's state repression.[178] This configuration of factors left the state open to insurgent challengers.

Another political opportunity for labor that shaped its impact on the state was the lack of imperial military intervention in support of the Williams regime. The United Kingdom adopted a noninterventionist approach to the political upheavals occurring in the now independent Trinidad and Tobago. While United Kingdom officials expressed willingness to send weapons, they explicitly refused to send British soldiers, even if requested (which Williams did not). In addition to requesting weapons, Williams also asked the United Kingdom to act as an intermediary to request soldiers from Nigeria, Tanzania, or Zambia. In Williams's view, the recruitment of African troops was crucial, as deploying white soldiers or involving the Organization of American States, dominated by the United States, would only further inflame the Black Power and anti-imperial worker movement. UK officials hesitated on this request as well. According to British Prime Minister Harold Wilson, Nigerian leaders were "very conscious of their reputation as an independent African state" and would likely be more receptive to requests "that did not pass through our channels."[179] Wilson told Williams, "No one is better qualified than you to handle the situation," adding, "I am sure that your wise statesmanship will enable you to overcome successfully this emergency."[180] Ultimately, Williams withdrew the request for weapons, saying he had already received a shipment (purchased from the United States). Overall, the former British colonial overlords were not committed to rescuing the Williams regime.

Without British willingness to intervene, Williams appealed to the United States and Venezuela. The American ambassador was willing, asserting, "There can be no compromise with the rebels if his government is to survive for long."[181] Still, the actual US response was limited, and it agreed only to sell some weapons to the Williams government.[182] The United Kingdom, the United States, and Venezuela all sent vessels to the waters around Trinidad and Tobago, ostensibly to evacuate UK and US citizens. In the case of Venezuela, that government preferred the Williams "kind of government" as opposed to "the subversive threat of a Black Power kind."[183] They even offered to send armed guards to Williams's residence to protect him, but he refused for fear that the optics would worsen the situation. Williams even appealed to other Caribbean leaders, in Jamaica and Guyana, but those state officials worried that any actions to suppress Black Power abroad would further enrage their own Black Power revolutionary forces at home.[184] Guyanese labor leader and revolutionary Eusi Kwayana had already voiced objections to President Richard Nixon regarding the US postings in Trinidad waters.[185] In the end, the foreign forces never landed on Trinidad and Tobago soil because loyalist Coast Guard officers quickly contained the mutiny. Still, the Trinidad and Tobago state had to face the insurrectionary movement largely on its own.

The Williams regime was also forced into a concessionary approach because of the changing interests of foreign capital. While in the interwar years the British imperial state had entrenched interests in Trinidad and Tobago oil and encouraged conciliation in order to restore smooth access to the resource, in the 1960s and 1970s foreign capital operating in Trinidad and Tobago was less interested in the country than in previous decades. In the late 1960s, major multinational oil companies—BP Trinidad and Shell—cut back investments and announced plans to eliminate operations in the country in favor of more profitable areas, most notably the North Sea.[186] Texaco was deliberately running down its own facilities and reducing refinery utilization. Sugar giant Tate and Lyle also expressed its intention to withdraw.[187] Liberation unionism, operating within these contextual factors of the overall declining interest of foreign capital in the country coupled with relatively insufficient repressive capacity, effectively cornered state officials into conceding to some worker demands.

To be sure, the threat of US invasion was a looming possibility. Given the record of Central Intelligence Agency (CIA) infiltration of trade unions, engineered racial and civil strife, military interventions, and support for dictators across Latin America and the Caribbean in service of US capitalist imperialism, such as in Guyana, Trinidad and Tobago may have taken a very different path had Williams actually been deposed.[188] US vessels were certainly poised and awaiting instructions to intervene. However, with the insurrection averted, restrictions on political and civic freedoms remained in place for one year, and all except the five mutineers who were imprisoned for striking and protesting were freed. At the same time, the state's precarious position prompted yet another wave of reforms.

State Capacity Building

Working people, building on their revolutionary foundations from the colonial period, rebuilt liberation unionism from the ground up, threatened the interests of capital and the state, and spurred another wave of state capacity building. In May 1970, in a televised address to the country, Williams confessed, "It was only when the total breakdown of the trade union movement was imminent that I decided to act," noting that the immediate question subsequently facing the state was "the reconsideration of the Development Program for 1970 and 1971 in light of what has happened, so as to accelerate the creation of job opportunities and encourage the greater involvement of the people in economic development . . . [as well as] the reorganization of the governmental machine . . . a drastic reconstruction of the Government and its administrative arm."[189] The decade of struggle from 1962 through the 1970s forced the state to take a more active role in the economy and to strengthen the bureaucratic structure to be able to fulfill its new role. Oil prices spiked in 1973 due to the Arab oil embargo, gradually increased from 1975 to 1978, and jumped again from 1979 to 1981 due to the Iranian Revolution.[190] Even though Trinidad and Tobago was not a member of the Organization of the Petroleum Exporting Countries (OPEC), the country benefited enormously from high oil prices, combined with the 1940s state reforms that had instituted a new petroleum taxation regime.[191] Trinidad and Tobago's oil revenues increased from TT$494 million in 1973 to TT$7,118 million in 1982.[192] The oil windfalls entered into a deeply rooted and long-established set of relations between the state and the working people, where the latter moved the state toward a more developmental and redistributive agenda and shaped how the state invested the windfalls. Liberation unionism pushed the state to become more autonomous from foreign capital, to take a more interventionist approach to development, and to develop greater bureaucratic capacity to manage and distribute the country's resource wealth; it also served as a safeguard against the state's authoritarian tendencies. Together, this institution building promoted broad-based economic and social development. As table I.1 in the introduction shows, the average well-being of working people increased significantly after independence.

Postindependence liberation unionism pushed the state to increase its autonomy from foreign capital and its involvement in the economy by taking greater local control over the commanding heights of the economy. During decolonization and in the early years of independence, the state confined its role in the economy to creating favorable conditions for capital. By the Third Five-Year Plan (1969–73) for national development, the government admitted the weaknesses of the former approach and signaled its intent to reckon with the structural problems in the economy: unemployment, oil dependence, the persistent problems with proper housing, the undue burden of increasing indirect taxes on the population, and the lack of local decision-making in vital economic and social matters.[193] The state admitted that "the economy has been acted upon, with the local Governments and people playing a passive dependent role in the process," and proclaimed that its development approach would be "modified as a result of the nationalist movement."[194] The state announced its decision to shift from economic dependence to "economic interdependence," defined as retaining integration into the global economy via trade, technology, and capital flows but with greater local control and internal generation of economic change and/or reactions to external changes.[195]

As part of this plan, the 1972 budget speech and two reports, both titled *White Paper on Public Participation in Industrial and Commercial Activities* (published in 1972 and 1975), listed no new 100 percent foreign-owned companies in key economic sectors. Instead, there would be "meaningful" state participation in new joint ventures with foreign-owned enterprises, the stimulation and support of local industry, and a leading role for the state in expediting national control and ownership.[196] Economic interdependence is not what workers demanded, but it became the outcome of the conflict between labor, on one side, and capital and the state, on the other. The state now viewed the establishment of public companies as an "urgent requirement" to compensate for a private sector that was unresponsive to both incentivizing and disciplinary industrial policy instruments, given that foreign companies responded to metropolitan governments and head offices rather than to national interests.[197] State participation in industries expanded from a total of twenty-one companies in 1972 to sixty-six in 1983.[198] The cost of this state participation increased from approximately TT$31 million in 1973 to TT$505 million in the first half of 1980.[199] According to state documents, its new role was to be the "prime mover in the national economy" and the "principal force to increase the extent of local control, and to ensure that needed private foreign investment would make its maximum contribution to overall national development."[200] Liberation unionism pushed the state toward this role.

With this new orientation, workers had finally achieved their historic goals of state nationalization of the major industries. In April 1967 the OWTU delivered a proposal entitled *Oil in Turmoil and OWTU Memorandum on the Formation of a National Oil Company* to the Williams government calling for nationalization of BP through the purchase of its assets, including a pledge by the OWTU to commit financial resources and technical expertise toward the acquisition.[201] The vigorous campaign that paired proposals with protests and strikes bore fruit in July 1969, when the state bought BP and established a new state-owned enterprise (SOE) called the National Petroleum Company to formulate energy and industrial policy and act as a holding company for wholly state-owned or joint ventures in the oil sector.[202] The Ministry of Petroleum and Mines announced, "Government has manifested its awareness of the need for greater participation in the workings of the industry by deciding to form a National Petroleum Company."[203] The state did not accept many other OWTU suggestions from the memorandum. For example, concerned about its lack of technical, managerial, or international marketing capacity to run this enterprise, the state elected to partner as the majority shareholder with Tesoro Petroleum Company of Texas to form Trinidad-Tesoro, which operated what were formerly BP's assets. In response, the OWTU criticized the state's impulse "to hold hands with foreign corporations—the very thing that the Union was protesting against."[204] Still, this acquisition represented a historic win for the worker movement as it thrust the state into a more active interventionist role. The state later bought out Tesoro and established full ownership of the company in 1985.

Similarly, in 1974 the state bought Shell operations and established a new SOE called the Trinidad and Tobago Oil Company (TRINTOC). In 1985 the state finally acquired some of Texaco's assets and, through TRINTOC, took control of Texaco's oil refinery, land operations, reserves, and real estate. The government cabinet acknowledged that an OWTU letter detailing Texaco's worker safety record, environmental pollution, labor force reduction through retrenchment and attrition, and deliberate underproduction, as well as exposing Texaco's ties to South Africa and Rhodesia, prompted the state to launch the commission of inquiry that ultimately led to the state's decision to intervene.[205]

In the sugar industry, the state purchased shares in Tate and Lyle in 1970 and used the oil windfalls to acquire total ownership in 1975, resulting in a new SOE, Caroni (1975) Limited. According to the minister of finance in 1974, "Government will use oil to assist agriculture," and the state injected large amounts of revenue into the failing sugar industry.[206] The state established the Agricultural Development Bank, advanced land settlement through the Crown Lands Program, and increased subsidies to fishers and farmers to expand local food production, which was a long-identified issue related to food security and economic diversification.[207] The state announced plans to localize the entirely foreign-owned financial sector in the budget speech of 1969. Foreign banks and insurance companies were urged to sell shares and incorporate locally.[208] By the early 1980s, the banking industry became almost entirely locally owned.[209]

With this new orientation to the economy, the state also invested in a massive resource-based industrialization plan to develop higher-value-added liquefied natural gas, petrochemical, and iron and steel industries that would run on natural gas reserves.[210] Between 1975 and 1984, the Point Lisas Industrial Complex was established and included a gas pipeline company (National Gas Company), the wholly state-owned Iron and Steel Company of Trinidad and Tobago, and two state-owned companies—Trinidad Nitrogen Company and Fertilizers of Trinidad and Tobago—that partnered with Federation Chemicals, W. R. Grace, and Amoco for the production of ammonia, methanol, urea, and melamine. The state created the National Energy Corporation in 1979 as a holding company for state investments in energy.[211] By the turn of the twenty-first century, Trinidad and Tobago emerged as the world's largest exporter of ammonia, the second-largest exporter of methanol, and the sixth-largest exporter of liquefied natural gas.[212] Based on these investments, Trinidad and Tobago entered the twenty-first century with natural gas rather than oil as its main revenue source.[213]

Across the private and public sectors, liberation unionism produced significant gains for workers in terms of wage increases and better working conditions. The OWTU won an agreement with Texaco after a decade of negotiations, the longest in the history of the union, which brought the highest wage increase up to that time both in dollars and as a percentage.[214] The union won OWTU-like benefits for workers in other industries across the country, such as some in sugar and electricity. This included securing a forty-hour workweek, subsistence and meal allowances, disturbance allowances (when an employee is transferred from one location to another), maternity leave, housing benefits and social security schemes from companies, pensions, and funeral leave of up to four days for oil workers, and an extension of vacation leave from two weeks in 1947 to five weeks in 1977.[215] According to the OWTU General Council, OWTU agitation and negotiations "set standards and precedents for other Unions to follow. We have, therefore, been responsible in 'pulling up' the standard of living of workers outside the general membership of the OWTU—yet another benefit for the country."[216] Sugar laborers' average weekly earnings went from TT$50 in 1971 to TT$108 in 1975 and TT$217 in 1979, and government manual workers in agriculture went from TT$51 in 1973 to TT$82 in 1975 and TT$189 in 1979.[217] Operators, clerks, and workers in manufacturing and services also won significant wage increases.[218] Furthermore, nationalization did not lead to the depoliticization of labor. Workers continued to press their claims to their new employer—the state.[219] In the first nine months of 1974, organized labor had successfully negotiated or renegotiated forty-three industrial agreements and obtained salary increases.[220] Liberation unionism forced the state to alter its relationship to private capital and the economy.

Bureaucratic Expansion and Infrastructural Reach

The size of the state expanded rapidly to meet its new priorities, roles, and responsibilities. Government employment went from 18.3 percent of total employment in 1975 to 24.5 percent in 1982, not including SOEs, making the state the largest employer.[221] State departments, such as the Ministry of Petroleum and Mines, mushroomed to fulfill the new mandates that came with the introduction of new legislation in the energy sector. The first petroleum legislation under the newly independent government was passed in 1969, and then the Petroleum Regulations of 1970, Petroleum Production Levy and Subsidies Act of 1974, and Petroleum Tax Act of 1974 incentivized petroleum exploration and land-based operations; updated the provisions for the granting of licenses for exploration and operations, including licensing fees, fees for the ministry's administrative costs, and revised royalties; introduced competitive bidding; altered the oil taxation structure; appointed local managers; constructed refineries based on proven reserves; and stimulated production-sharing contracts.[222] The state created the Energy Planning Division within the Ministry of Petroleum and Mines in 1975 with a team of professionals and technicians for project planning and development.[223] In addition, new units were created to regulate the industry, such as a pipeline inspection unit, which would be responsible for oil and gas pipeline safety.[224]

The state also invested in strengthening its personnel and technical competence in order to successfully manage its new activities. For instance, the state admitted that the expertise and staffing requirements of the Ministry of Petroleum and Mines up to the mid-1960s had "been in an acutely unsatisfactory condition."[225] The rapid expansion of petroleum policy and the substantial increase in the role and activities of the ministry required "highly trained personnel fully knowledgeable about all aspects and phases of the industry—national and international, technical and economic."[226] To meet these increased needs, the ministry enlarged its staff through an "expansion program," which involved hiring more local petroleum inspectors and engineers. It also coordinated and funded training programs for Trinbagonian nationals in relevant fields such as computer technology, mathematics, and engineering; provided scholarships for petroleum-related degrees; and introduced and expanded postgraduate courses in petroleum engineering at the University of the West Indies (UWI).[227] Not only would this education and training create a more effective ministry, but it also enabled "greater participation at the higher technical and managerial levels of the industry" and the replacement of expatriate personnel with nationals (yet another of the new mandates of the ministry).[228] In 1979 the ministry was renamed the Ministry of Energy and Energy-Based Industries to capture the expanded roles and responsibilities of the unit.

Similar to the interwar years, radical unions placed representatives in key positions within the expanding state bureaucracy, while at the same time retaining autonomy and continuing to apply external pressure. This helped guard against political incorporation and depoliticization. For instance, Williams offered Weekes a position as the director of the National Petroleum Company. In a letter to Weekes, Williams admitted that this decision "was motivated solely by the initiative taken by the Oilfield Workers' Trade Union in general, and by yourself [Weekes] in particular" in campaigning for the company.[229] After intense deliberation the OWTU membership voted to allow Weekes to accept the position but retained the right to advance its vision for the company's policy and to withdraw their representative if "the policy being following by the Board runs counter to what we conceive to be the correct policy for a National Oil Company."[230] Likewise, two members of the Canefarmers Association were appointed to the board of the new government-run sugar company.

Along with enhancing bureaucratic capacity, the state also further extended its infrastructural power into communities, thereby improving the population's access to education, health, and social services throughout the country. Government expenditure on social and community development, sewage, health, water, education, electricity, drainage, public buildings, transport and communications, agriculture, forest and fisheries, and industry and tourism increased.[231] The state also repaired and constructed new roads and bridges.[232] Since there was almost universal primary education at independence, only twenty-one additional primary schools had been added by 1985. The greatest expansion occurred in postprimary education as the number of secondary schools increased from thirty-four in 1964 to ninety-five in 1985.[233] The Black Power movement also spurred the revision of the curriculum to emphasize more Caribbean history and literature and more African and Indian diasporic studies.[234]

Health care access also widened, and care improved as the state constructed new health centers, delivery units, and community health centers, and upgraded the general hospital facilities.[235] Infant mortality dropped from fifty-three (per thousand live births) in 1962 to twenty-seven in 1990.[236] Through direct confrontation and proposals for new safety laws, workers succeeded in pressuring the government to update legislation and enforce health and safety practices in petroleum and allied industries.[237] In 1974 the state launched an extensive housing program to offer low-interest loans for mortgages and home construction in an effort to provide better housing for working people.[238] The National Housing Authority, originally established in 1962 to construct and distribute homes to low- and middle-income working people, was "modified" to mitigate former inefficiencies and stimulate private sector efforts in housing and land development within the stated goals.[239]

Liberation unionism also prompted the state to shift taxation policy to relieve working people of heavy tax burdens. Whereas, before the boom, the state was increasing indirect taxation, in 1973, 1974, and 1979, the state provided income tax relief through a system of increased tax rebates. The range of allowances also expanded to include a personal allowance as well as allowances for housewives and working wives, children, education and books, and life insurance. Taxes were also reduced on some items, such as on purchases of motor vehicles, refrigerators, stoves, garments, and so on.[240] In addition, the state aimed to reduce the cost of living by increasing subsidies for food, fuel, public utilities (e.g., electricity, water), and transportation. It also increased welfare provisions, such as old-age pensions, public assistance, and food stamps.[241] The state introduced the National Insurance Scheme in 1971.[242]

In line with its increased infrastructural reach, the state also sought to improve processes for community groups to voice complaints and grievances related to the delivery of public services. It created interministerial committees to better coordinate between ministers in charge of housing, public information, and citizens' grievances; appointed investigation teams comprising state officials from the Office of the Prime Minister and Ministry of Finance to go to affected areas and speak with people directly; and strengthened disaster relief services.[243] Liberation unionism was also a check against state corruption. For example, in addition to encouraging the state to disseminate reports such as *Accounting for the Petrodollar* (one published in 1980 and another in 1984), which detailed the use of the oil windfalls, workers also targeted state officials who reportedly accepted bribes from foreign companies and funneled money to secret bank accounts abroad.[244] Through these measures, liberation unionism stimulated the state to increase its engagement with larger segments of the population, thereby promoting redistributive reforms.

Political Participation

Liberation unionism both elicited and countered the authoritarian leanings of the state. As previously described, the state sought to suppress the voices and demands of the working class. At the same time, liberation unionism was equally central to dismantling undemocratic measures and restoring political rights and civil freedoms. Workers continued to organize after the 1970 February Revolution. Lower-ranked union officers took the reins when their leaders were detained and imprisoned.[245] On release from prison, those labor leaders immediately returned to the battlefield against employers and the repressive state.[246] Through their incessant struggle, the ISA was repealed. Still, state efforts to create favorable conditions for capital persisted. Officials created new antilabor legislation, such as the Industrial Relations Act in 1972 and the Public Order Act in 1972, which were so draconian that they were forced to scrap it due to widespread public outrage. And in response to a worker march in 1975, the police were so violent that it earned the name Bloody Tuesday.[247] Still, liberation unionism served as an important force protesting state abuses and advancing democracy. According to Freedom House data on political rights and civil liberties, in contrast to many other countries in the Global South, especially the oil and mineral exporters, the Trinidad and Tobago state has maintained relatively competitive elections, the independence of the judiciary and media, and freedom of expression, assembly, and association.[248] Liberation unionism played a critical role in promoting and preserving democratic institutions.

Conclusion

As one worker in 1965 wrote, "The spirit of 1937 lives on."[249] Postindependence development in Trinidad and Tobago clearly followed a trajectory that had begun during the colonial era when liberation unionism first stimulated the construction of state institutions, which produced more democratic and redistributive outcomes. During decolonization and after independence, workers had to contend with new players and processes that sought to uphold the structures and ideologies of racialized labor exploitation and capital accumulation—racialized party politics, political incorporation of labor by the ruling party and neocolonial state, and bureaucratic conservatism within unions. Still, workers managed to reach back to the wisdom and tactics of the interwar years and reactivate liberation unionism's core elements of unity, Pan-Africanism, and the push for transformation through Black Power ideology and "political Blackness," internal reorganization, and the severing of ties with conservative unions. The upswell of worker militance, combined with the autonomy of radical unions from parties and the state, was crucial for preserving and expanding the gains won in the interwar years.

The reemergence of this movement after an almost twenty-year period of disunity and demoralization was impressive. Deprivation alone cannot explain why liberation unionism resurged and why it had the effect of encouraging relative state autonomy from foreign capital, bureaucratic capacity to deliver health and social services, and democracy. These investments had real impacts on life expectancy, health, education, and the overall quality of life in the country. Only by tracing the long historical arc of Trinidad and Tobago's position in the white capitalist system and workers' agency in building a movement with the goal of liberating themselves from oppressive structures and ideologies can we begin to make sense of this country's remarkable trajectory.

Labor leaders were not always successful in all their pursuits. The failure of labor parties to win over the electorate is one glaring example of the ways in which working people distinguished between different means to the same end goal—liberation. They treated labor unions and labor parties as separate entities, even though they were constituted by the same people, who held the same ideologies and deployed similar strategies for mass mobilization. Workers generally rejected union participation in party politics. This is why the word *union* in the concept *liberation unionism* is central. This orientation characterizes Trinbagonian electoral politics to this day as we have yet to see a labor party triumph.

In addition, while some state policies in response to liberation unionism were guided by the transformational aspirations of the movement, others were simply meant to placate the masses and retain support for the ruling party. Alongside increased state capacity for implementing progressive reforms, state support for small businesses (self-employment, that is) was a politically rewarding way to reallocate the labor force made redundant or refused entry by capital-intensive industrialization policies.[250] Patterns of patronage also emerged to help secure what Percy Hintzen calls "regime survival" in the face of the powerful organized internal threat, in this case liberation unionism.[251] A 5 percent unemployment levy on petroleum companies was instituted in 1970 to finance government jobs for the large numbers of unemployed in short-term community works and beautification projects, and for housing and urban renewal schemes. This Special Works Program, first initiated in the colonial era (1950s), went by many subsequent names—Development and Environmental

Works Division in the 1960s and 1970s, then Labor-Intensive Development Program in the 1980s, Unemployment Relief Program in the 1990s, and the Community Environmental Enhancement Program in the early 2000s. However, this program was a short-term economic relief program for the surplus labor population and a patronage mechanism to maintain and/or gain electoral support.[252] Likewise, patronage also benefited the local business elite, who gained enormous profits from access to subcontracts and high-paying jobs in SOEs.[253]

Still, Trinbagonian working people significantly impacted state structures and policies. Like many other countries in the Global South, Trinidad and Tobago borrowed heavily to finance these transformations. By the mid-1980s, Trinidad and Tobago succumbed to exhausted foreign exchange reserves and turned to the International Monetary Fund and the World Bank in the late 1980s and early 1990s for debt restructuring and external financing, ushering in neoliberal policies that increased economic pressure on working people for a decade. Still, consistent with "time-to-build" lags, or the time between investment and output, the decade of investments in industry and state building between the oil booms and the 1980s bore fruit ten years later, when, in the mid-1990s, the Trinidad and Tobago economy experienced impressive and consistent economic growth alongside welfare expansion.[254] The institution building that stemmed from the legacy and upsurge of liberation unionism enabled Trinbagonian working people to reap appreciable gains in income, health, and well-being, and the expansion and maintenance of democracy, compared to those in many other oil producers facing similar challenges of resource dependence, such as Gabon and Nigeria.[255] Today Trinidad and Tobago has high levels of human development; its population is, on average, among the wealthier and healthier across the Global South and enjoys comparably more political and civic freedoms.[256] Working people may not have taken down the white capitalist system, but they achieved much more than if they had not organized at all. Trinidad and Tobago provides a dramatic example of how relatively effective state-led development can be created and reproduced by formerly colonized people and highlights the long historical roots of those state-building activities in the mass mobilization of workers from below.

6

Comparing Worker Movements

A common question around single case studies is the extent to which the findings are generalizable. This book does not offer generalizability in the positivist social science sense. I do not aim to make universal claims about development paths across the Global South. Instead, following Black radical thinkers like W. E. B. Du Bois and Walter Rodney on the question of generalizability, I conduct a historically specific comparative analysis and discuss implications for other cases. I recognize that the formulations may differ depending on particular historical conditions, variations in racial or ethnic relations within and across classes, and the different ways in which countries are integrated into the overall white capitalist system.[1] With the concept of liberation unionism, as developed from the case of Trinidad and Tobago, this book offers an analytic device with which to think about working-class movements and their effects on state building and development in other sites.

With this objective, I compare Trinidad and Tobago to the former British colony of Guyana over the course of the twentieth century. Based on secondary readings of other cases, liberation unionism appears to have been the dominant form of unionism across other British Caribbean colonies during the interwar years, albeit becoming consolidated at different times during that period and with varying degrees of militance and persistence.[2] This likely stems from the British Caribbean colonies' shared histories of plantation slavery based on

African labor, immigrant labor from within the region and from afar (e.g., Asia), subjugation under the British Crown, and structural dependency in the white capitalist system. Garveyism, with its Pan-African and anti-imperial elements, was deeply embedded across the region; many labor leaders were followers of Marcus Garvey, and some had direct experience in the Universal Negro Improvement Association (UNIA).

Of these cases, Guyana is most similar to Trinidad and Tobago. The two countries share similar colonial histories of imported and racialized labor, mostly from Africa and India, for plantation slavery, indentureship, and natural resource exploitation. Guyana was also a strategic resource supplier, of bauxite in this case, to the British Empire during the war years. Theoretically, racialized labor in Guyana should have had similar structural power to working people in Trinidad and Tobago. Many comparative historical studies of these two cases explore their similarities and variations in racial antagonisms and racial politics.[3] Those that compare economic and social development outcomes tend to emphasize the similar structural constraints on transformation in both former colonies.[4] Percy Hintzen, for example, argues that Trinidad and Tobago and Guyana largely ended up in the same place, developmentally, as political elites used similar strategies to win and maintain state control, which in both cases privileged narrow interests over collective needs.[5] Yet the development outcomes differ markedly between the two countries. Table 6.1 shows a comparison of economic and social indicators for the two countries between 1960 and 2019. Although these colonies shared the aforementioned similarities during the colonial period, Trinidad and Tobago ultimately outperformed Guyana on almost every measure. The few studies that have attempted to explain the divergence typically attribute Guyana's underperformance relative to Trinidad and Tobago to "bad governance."[6] In terms of this book's argument, liberation unionism should have emerged there, stimulated state capacity building, and produced long-run equitable development.

In fact, liberation unionism did emerge in Guyana during the interwar years, perhaps with even more force than in Trinidad and Tobago. According to historian O. Nigel Bolland, "the history of persistent labor militancy and labor organizations is longer in Guyana than elsewhere in the British Caribbean."[7] How, then, despite this history of liberation unionism in colonial Guyana, did the country end up having weak state capacity to direct development, with less redistributive and more authoritarian orientations, and "one of the poorest development performances in the Western Hemisphere" from the 1960s to the early 2000s?[8] Despite its brevity, this case study assesses the features of libera-

TABLE 6.1. A Comparison of Social Development Indicators for Trinidad and Tobago and Guyana

	T&T	Guyana
GDP per capita (constant 2015 US$)		
1960	4,291	2,734
1980	8,612	3,248
2000	10,027	3,760
2019	17,401	6,279
Human Development Index		
1990	0.656	0.496
2019	0.813	0.711
Literacy rate, adult total (% of people ages 15 and above)	98 (2000)	85 (2009)
Life expectancy at birth, total (years)		
1960	63	58
1980	67	61
2000	69	64
2019	74	69
Mortality rate, infant (per 1,000 live births)		
1960	56	67
1980	34	53
2000	25	37
2019	15	24
Mortality rate, under 5 (per 1,000 live births)		
1960	68	93
1980	39	71
2000	28	47
2019	17	29
Maternal mortality (deaths per 100,000 live births)		
2000	74	190
2019	26	110
Gender Inequality Index, 2019	0.269	0.433
Political rights		
1973	2	4
1980	2	5
2000	2	2
2019	2	2

(continued)

TABLE 6.1. (*continued*)

Civil liberties			
1973		2	2
1980		2	4
2000		2	2
2019		2	3

Population			
1960		847,063	571,990
2019		1,363,985	807,665

Sources: Freedom House, *Freedom in the World 2024*; United Nations Economic Commission for Latin America and the Caribbean, CEPALSTAT: Statistical Databases and Publications, 2024; UNDP, Human Development Index dataset, 2024; World Bank, World Development Indicators, 2024.
Note: Freedom House indices of political rights and civil liberties are on a seven-point scale ranging from 1 (least democratic) to 7 (most democratic).

tion unionism in Trinidad and Tobago and helps to pinpoint the decisive causal factors and processes linking liberation unionism to development outcomes.

This chapter contends that the concept of liberation unionism is indeed useful for understanding varied development outcomes. The findings lend support to my assertion that a strong tradition of liberation unionism stimulates the kind of state capacity building needed for long-term equity-enhancing development, within the constraints of being peripheralized in the global capitalist system. I trace Guyana's divergence from Trinidad and Tobago to more interventionist imperial and violent colonial state repression of liberation unionism, precisely because of its potency and threat to the interests of the colonial state and capital. In Guyana the worker movement that emerged in the interwar years exhibited all the characteristics of liberation unionism—it was united, was internationalist in orientation, and had a transformational agenda—and it successfully pushed the colonial state to attain some capacity for development. This movement was so powerful and deeply embedded in society that it survived the decolonization period and, through a labor party, won state power. However, foreign intervention by imperial powers, unwilling to concede to the will of the people, thwarted Guyanese working people's socialist aspirations. These powers supported middle-class politicians in stoking racial divisions and installed an authoritarian regime that halted the construction of state capacity for redistributive economic and social development.

This case comparison reveals the importance of the political opportunities in which liberation unionism operates. Guyana shows that liberation unionism was not unique to Trinidad and Tobago. However, where geopolitical forces and state repression outweigh the strength of the movement, this can impede the building of state capacity for enhancing the well-being of the masses. Guyana shows us the constraints on liberation unionism in the white capitalist system and the ways in which the imperial containment of Black self-determination inhibited the kind of state building that promotes equity-enhancing development.

Guyana

Guyana's colonial history and race-class structure are very similar to Trinidad and Tobago's. At first, under Spanish colonial rule, the French also had a presence in the colony, but it was the Dutch who established many settlements and gained significant control over the region over the course of the seventeenth century. The British took permanent control in 1796 and formally established the Colony of British Guiana in 1831.[9] Similar to Trinidad and Tobago, Guyana's population in 1910 was predominantly Indian (42.7 percent) and African (39 percent). The rest of the population was classified as "Mixed" (10.2 percent), Indigenous Amerindians (2.3 percent), Chinese (0.9 percent), Europeans and other whites (4.7 percent) and "not stated" (0.1 percent).[10] The colonial history and social hierarchy were similar to those in Trinidad and Tobago: the white plantation-owning and business elite possessed economic power and political privileges, and the Africans (enslaved Africans and their descendants), Indians (Indian indentured laborers brought to replace African plantation labor after emancipation, as well as their descendants), and Amerindians were relegated to the bottom of the social ladder. Similar to Trinidad and Tobago, capital concentration in sugar increased in the late nineteenth and early twentieth centuries.[11] The Guyanese economy was dependent on agricultural production, specifically sugar and rice, and on Indian labor after emancipation.

A geological survey reported bauxite deposits in 1910. Bauxite, the raw material used to make aluminum (and some other products), grew in strategic military importance for the manufacture of aircraft, wiring, and munitions during the wars. The mining industry was primarily dominated by North American capital. The Aluminum Company of America (ALCOA), a US company, was an early entrant in 1914, and the Demerara Bauxite Company (Demba; a subsidiary of a Canadian company) was incorporated to operate ALCOA's concessions in 1916 in keeping with British Crown stipulations that exploitation be undertaken by British or British Commonwealth entities.[12] US-owned Reynolds Metals exploited smaller concessions in 1952.[13] The mining industry drew African workers who were both fleeing plantations and being actively undercut by the white plantation-owning class.

By the end of World War I and continuing through the interwar years, Guyana had already become a major producer, accounting for about 9 to 10 percent of world bauxite production. By World War II, the colony became the second-largest bauxite producer in the world with 19 percent of world production.[14] France was another major bauxite producer, from which the British sourced most of its bauxite, but France's defeat by Germany in 1940 prompted the British to turn to Guyana for its supplies. The United States had vast domestic deposits of its own and was the global leader in bauxite production. Still, Guyanese bauxite was central to the rapid expansion of US aircraft manufacturing, and the latter sought to protect bauxite carriers, which were targeted by German U-boats during the war and signed agreements with the British to establish military bases near bauxite plants in Guyana in the early 1940s.[15]

The colonial state in Guyana bore some structural differences from that in Trinidad and Tobago, but the orientation and activities were similar. While the British imposed a Crown Colony system in Trinidad and Tobago in 1831, they did not introduce this in Guyana until 1928. All that time, the Guyana legislature, called the Combined Court, retained holdovers from Dutch rule. The governor presided over the Dutch Court of Policy, where five officials and five representatives of plantation (and later merchant) interests sat together on equal terms, along with six financial representatives who were elected by the 1 percent of the population who were eligible to vote.[16] According to Walter Rodney, the Combined Court "was the political fulcrum of planter power."[17] The plantocracy and merchants dominated the colonial state apparatus, including the budgets and the various boards that regulated roads, sanitation, transport, and so on.[18] The court's activities revolved around creating the laws and organizing society to guarantee capital accumulation and white control. Similar to Trinidad and Tobago, the decision to impose Crown Colony rule stemmed from a desire to wrest control from the local white elite and to prevent the Guyanese middle class from entering the colonial legislature in large numbers. The latter agitated for such constitutional reform and relied heavily on worker support in their campaigns and petitions.[19] The British responded to these political demands by instituting a proper Crown Colony system in 1928, with a minority of fourteen elected members outnumbered by the governor, his officials, and his nominees.[20]

During the colonial period, labor unrest in Guyana was frequent and persistent. There were more numerous large-scale disturbances and strikes in the later decades of the nineteenth century in Guyana (one in 1869, six in 1870, one in 1872, more than fourteen in 1873, a hundred between 1886 and 1889, forty-nine between 1895 and 1897, sixty between 1899 and 1903, and one in 1905) than in Trinidad and Tobago (one in 1903).[21] Between 1900 and 1950, there were over 250 strikes, resulting in the deaths of forty-seven workers.[22] In addition to labor militance, formal recognition of labor organizations preceded that in Trinidad and Tobago. The first recognized trade union in the English-speaking Caribbean, the British Guiana Labour Union (BGLU), was launched in 1919 by then eighteen-year-old African waterfront worker Herbert Critchlow after a strike in 1905 and was registered in 1922. By the end of 1919, the BGLU had about seven thousand members.[23] Similar to Trinidad and Tobago, unions proliferated by sector in the 1930s. The ManPower Citizens' Association (MPCA) of mostly Indian sugar workers was the next most significant union in Guyana after the BGLU. Formed in 1937 by Indian middle-class actors, such as Ayube Edun (the MPCA president; a jeweler and journalist) and Charles R. Jacob (the MPCA treasurer; a merchant), the MPCA claimed ten thousand members by 1939 and twenty thousand by 1943, making it the largest union in terms of numbers.[24]

Evidence from secondary sources confirm that the Guyanese working people's movements shared the characteristics of liberation unionism seen in Trinidad and Tobago. Like the Trinidad Workingmen's Association (TWA) in Trinbago, the BGLU's membership was predominantly of African descent, but it was nonetheless united across racial and sectoral lines and deeply embedded in local communities. Its membership included African industrial employees in urban areas and Indian sugar estate workers, and the BGLU actively assisted sugar workers' strikes.[25] Women were also central to liberation unionism in Guyana.[26] The movement was also diasporic and dominated by Garveyites and Pan-Africanism.[27] According to Rodney, the Guyanese workers' emphasis on racial identity coexisted with powerful upsurges of class consciousness.[28] Finally, the Guyanese worker movement also pushed for universal adult suffrage and societal transformation.[29]

Also similar to the situation in Trinidad and Tobago, certain conditions in Guyana facilitated liberation unionism's expansion. The relative weakness of the colonial police force mirrored that in Trinidad and Tobago: in 1917 the ratio of the population to police was 456:1, compared with 537:1 in Trinidad and Tobago; in 1937 the ratio in Guyana was 514:1, which was even weaker than the 387:1 in Trinidad and Tobago.[30] In addition, the white colonial elite was characterized by ethno-national differences, notably between the Dutch and the British, which may have shaped the colonial state's responses to worker mobilizations.[31] Liberation unionism brought remarkable gains for the Guyanese working people. Public provisioning of health care and sanitation, education, and water supplies, for example, began to manifest in the improved health and well-being of the population during the interwar years.[32] In 1950 infant mortality (per 1,000 live births) in Guyana was 85.0 compared with 80.3 for Trinidad and Tobago. The crude death rate (per 1,000 mean population) was also comparable, at 14.6 for Guyana and 12.2 for Trinidad and Tobago. The expenditures of both colonial states on health and education in 1951 were around 10 or 11 percent, with similar numbers of primary schools and beds at the general hospitals.[33] Based on comparing secondary evidence of Guyanese labor organizing to the case of Trinidad and Tobago, we can confidently call the Guyanese worker movement liberation unionism.

In the early years after World War II, the political landscape in Guyana was similar to Trinidad and Tobago's. Unions proliferated, and competition between unions for workers and voters threatened to tear apart a once united worker movement. The first election in Guyana with universal suffrage took place in 1953, and Guyana became independent in 1966. In the first postwar elections of 1947 (not yet with universal suffrage but with reduced property requirements), the Indian-dominated MPCA and African-dominated BGLU launched political parties that competed against each other in the same constituencies. While this signaled both the intertwining of labor with political parties and an emergent racial differentiation of labor in party politics, workers were not yet voting along racial lines, as the BGLU won five seats (including in Indian-dominated constituencies) and the MPCA one.[34] In addition, many felt that MPCA leaders were too close to the sugar companies and suspected that they were collaborating with capital rather than representing the interests of sugarcane cutters. In response, many Indian sugar workers abandoned the Indian middle-class MPCA leaders in 1948 for the new Guiana Industrial Workers Union, organized and led by Marxist-Leninist and US-trained Indian dentist Cheddi Jagan.[35]

Members of another group—the Political Affairs Committee (PAC)—ran as independents, and its leader Jagan was successfully elected to the Legislative Council. The PAC was formed in 1946 by a group of middle-class Marxist-Leninist radicals comprising mostly overseas-trained professionals and intellectuals.[36] The Marxist-Leninist emphasis was a noteworthy departure from the Pan-African Black nationalist frames of earlier years. According to historian Clem Seecharan, core organizers Moses Bhagwan and Eusi Kwayana had warned that the color-blind approach, which presupposed that ameliorating economic conditions would inevitably solve social problems, including racial ones, was not well suited to addressing the Guyanese African-Indian racial dynamic.[37] Still, the masses latched on to the PAC's call for a multiracial movement to destroy the capitalist system in Guyana and create a classless society based on "a well-planned collective industrial economy."[38] The PAC founders played a leading role in organizing and supporting worker strikes in the late 1940s and managed to win over the trade union movement.[39] Forbes Burnham, a young African lawyer who had been studying and working in London, returned to Guyana and became the BGLU's new chairman in 1949. From this multiracial, multisectoral base, the PAC launched a cohesive radical multiracial working-class party—the People's Progressive Party (PPP)—in 1950. The PPP was vehemently anticolonial and predominantly communist in ideology, and "declared open war upon the colonial economic-political alliance that dominated the territory."[40]

At the time when labor in Trinidad and Tobago was internally fragmented and unable to form a cohesive labor party, the PPP in Guyana dominated the political landscape, reflecting a consolidation of radical trade unionism and party politics. In the first general election with universal adult suffrage in 1953, the PPP beat other contenders and won eighteen of twenty-four seats.[41] The PPP's win marks the divergence in trajectories between Trinidad and Tobago and Guyana. The trade union movement had won state power, and the PPP began ushering in the highly anticipated socialist state.

However, this was not to be. Imperial intervention into Guyanese politics through the colonial state destroyed democracy and interrupted the state capacity-building process. Jagan and the PPP's pro-Soviet Marxist Leninism, their affiliation with communists, and the popularity of Jagan's radical policies distressed the colonial government, local elites, and the US imperial state.[42] In 1953, after the PPP had been in office for just 133 days, the United Kingdom suspended the Guyanese constitution.[43] British troops forcibly removed the PPP from government and instituted an even more despotic form of Crown Colony government with wholly nominated Executive and Legislative Councils for the next five years.[44] British imperial forces reversed democracy in Guyana.

In addition, as part of their post–World War II war on communism, the British and US governments sought to remove Jagan through several channels, one of which involved exploiting emerging fissures among PPP members during the first general elections. The PPP victory belies some disagreement within the party about contesting this many seats. Eusi Kwayana argued that even though the PPP was projected to win the election, the party needed more time to further ground and cement African-Indian racial unity, especially in the context of what he later called "racial insecurity," that is, the collective sense of uncertainty or fear felt by certain racialized groups about their future welfare, status, and safety compared to other groups.[45] Kwayana's predictions came to pass. Burnham, desiring to be the leader of the party, started to challenge Jagan for the position as early as 1953. In addition, Jagan's development policies—favoring agriculture over urban development, assistance to small and medium business (and therefore Indians), increased Indian representation in the civil service, and so on—appeared to Burnham and other Africans in the party as benefiting the Indian-descended community more than those of African descent.[46] According to Kwayana, the PPP became guided more by a motivating force of "Jaganism," or the Indian drive for preeminence in the state and society, than by "Marxism-Leninism."[47] Burnham was expelled from the party in 1955 for maneuvering to oust Jagan, and several African leaders also resigned, giving the appearance that race was a motivating factor for the split.[48] Burnham contested the 1957 election under his new party, the People's National Congress (PNC). This party was forged in alliance with the leaders of a Black and light-skinned middle-class cultural organization, and its base became the African workers and middle class.[49]

During these years of infighting within the party, imperial forces sought to exploit the wedge and supported the UK/US-aligned Burnham over the Marxist Jagan. The United States also attempted to get Britain to suspend the Guyanese constitution a second time and worked to depoliticize unions through organizations such as the Institute of Free Labor Development.[50] The Central Intelligence Agency (CIA) actively involved itself in inciting protests and later in sustaining race riots.[51] When Jagan's PPP again won the 1957 election, the British refused to accept the results, postponed Guyana's transition to independence, and held three subsequent elections hoping that their preferred candidate, Burnham, would win. However, this only served to increase racial political articulation by both PNC and PPP politicians as they competed for state power.

The combination of imperial electoral interventions and petty bourgeois racialized party politics ultimately produced "a war between the races" in the early 1960s.[52] Racial violence, rioting, race-based murders, arson, beatings, and looting spread across the country and took over a hundred lives, injured hundreds of people, and dislocated tens of thousands.[53] British troops intervened in 1964 to supposedly restore order and peace for the upcoming elections, after having incited the violence in the first place. Jagan, cornered by both internal and external pressures, ultimately relented to British/US and PNC pressure to introduce a system of proportional representation, and Burnham's PNC succeeded in ousting the PPP in the 1964 elections.[54] With US and British backing, state building in Guyana followed a decidedly despotic course, resulting in low levels of economic and social development.

Whereas workers in Trinidad and Tobago were able to rebuild liberation unionism after its demobilization in the postwar period, in Guyana institutional investments in the repressive apparatus of the state, racialized party politics, and political incorporation of unions thwarted Guyanese workers' efforts. Strikes remained a common feature of the Guyanese landscape.[55] However, they were isolated and company-specific, lacking the unified multisectoral character they had in the pre–World War II colonial period or in 1960s Trinidad and Tobago. Workers persisted in their efforts to rejuvenate the movement, for example, through organizations like the African Society for Cultural Relations with an Independent Africa (ASCRIA), the Organization of Working People (formed by bauxite workers), the Indian People's Revolutionary Association, and the Working People's Alliance. Eusi Kwayana—a labor organizer, founder of ASCRIA, and member of the PPP (before breaking with the party)—did not describe it as a Black Power organization but did see its goals of racial pride, the defeat of imperialism, and economic and cultural advancement of Africans as similar those of the Black Power movement. Kwayana, Walter Rodney, Andaiye, and others worked to articulate Pan-African pride and a working-class consciousness that would bind African and Indian men and women to a unified liberatory project.[56] Rodney in particular worked through a framework of political Blackness.[57] Multiracial, multisectoral strikes began to blossom in the 1970s.[58]

However, the Guyanese state attacked the worker revitalization efforts through a combination of co-optation and force. Observing the mounting threat to the state in Trinidad and Tobago when workers mobilized with the Black Power movement, and the risk of Eric Williams's downfall, the Burnham regime announced the establishment of the Co-operative Socialist Republic in 1970.[59] According to Kwayana, the idea for a cooperative republic in Guyana originated with ASCRIA but was "coopted and sabotaged by the PNC."[60] It was a strange cocktail of a seemingly leftward turn toward elements of economic nationalism from Black Power alongside the consolidation of an authoritarian repressive state. It involved increasing local ownership and control in the economy, including of mineral and forest resources; self-sufficiency in food, clothing, and housing; economic development through cooperatives of ordinary people; alignment and diplomatic relations with Cuba, China, the Soviet Union, and left-leaning African countries such as Tanzania and Angola; and the "paramountcy of the party," which made Burnham and the ruling PNC party the supreme authority over the state, parliament, the political process, and the judiciary. This petty bourgeois-led state socialism, as opposed to a worker-directed and worker-controlled socialist project, wreaked havoc on the Guyanese working people.

Despite a colonial history of strong liberation unionism, Guyana experienced limited economic and social development after independence. The state remained closely tied to foreign capital, its bureaucratic capacity and infrastructural reach remained limited, and it repressed and excluded the masses, leading to the squandering of the country's resource wealth rather than the promotion of equitable development. First, Burnham nationalized the key sectors of the economy, including the bauxite and sugar industries, giving the state control over about 80 percent of the economy.[61] Greater state control of these industries coincided with upsurges in the international market prices of bauxite and sugar, which, like the oil boom did for Trinidad and Tobago, allowed the state to accrue significant revenues.[62] However, without a robust independent counterforce to state predation like the liberation unionism in postindependence Trinidad and Tobago, redistribution that would benefit the masses was comparably more limited than in Trinidad and Tobago. The External Trade Bureau, established in 1970, dispensed licenses to favored businesspeople and PNC officials.[63] This rendered large proportions of the population dependent on the PNC and the state. Corruption was rampant, and there were few checks and balances, which served to enrich the PNC elite. Under Burnham's 1974 "Party Paramountcy" policy, which gave the ruling party greater powers over other political parties and state institutions, the PNC gained direct access to state revenue without having to account for the use of these funds. This and other legislative changes allowed Burnham and his cronies to consolidate power and fill their pockets with state monies.[64]

Furthermore, Burnham's establishment of diplomatic relations with Cuba and the Soviet Union, and Guyana's votes against US resolutions at the United Nations, angered the United States and United Kingdom. The United States retaliated by reducing its loans to Guyana and blocking loans from other international agencies to the Guyanese government. The United States also excluded Guyana from preferential trade agreements to which other Caribbean countries were privy.[65] Thus, Guyana's external debt grew burdensome, and foreign exchange reserves were depleted by the late 1970s. In addition, citing human rights violations, economic instability, and election rigging, the IMF barred Guyana from using its financial resources in 1985, all of which translated into heavy burdens on the working people.[66]

Second, bureaucratic capacity remained weak. According to John Gafar, "Under Burnham's rule, qualifications, merit and experience were sacrificed in determining public sector employment, and the basis, in most cases was political party affiliation and race."[67] The result was widespread economic and administrative mismanagement, which caused frequent electricity outages and breakdowns in the water supply; increased rates of gastrointestinal diseases due to lack of sewage system maintenance; flooding as a result of poorly maintained seawalls, canals, and drainage; soaring inflation; surges in unemployment; and increased food shortages.[68]

Finally, state officials channeled institution-building energy and resources toward increasing the state's military apparatus to repress the masses and their political activities. Electoral fraud, patronage, and repression plagued the country's political institutions and limited civil freedoms. Irregularities included dubious increases in the number of voters in PNC strongholds, voter rolls padded with nonresidents, and inconsistencies in voter counting.[69] Burnham expanded the armed forces from about two thousand personnel in 1964 to twenty-two thousand in 1977, and the defense budget increased from 2 percent of the national budget to over 14 percent in the same period.[70] The PNC state crackdown on any opposition was brutal, and arrests, terror, murder, intimidation, and violent attacks were a constant struggle for working people.[71] The attempted and executed political assassinations, including of the revolutionary Walter Rodney, further increased fear in the population and demobilized the movement.

This history frames Guyana's relative underperformance compared to Trinidad and Tobago and its trajectory into the neoliberal era. Burnham died in 1985, and Desmond Hoyte, a leading member of the government, inherited the presidency. The IMF and World Bank oversaw sweeping structural adjustment programs in 1988, involving the familiar cuts in already relatively limited social expenditure, declines in wages, and increased taxes and inflation, wreaking havoc on working people.[72] Under mounting domestic pressure due to economic problems and international pressure, Hoyte called elections in 1992. While the Working People's Alliance conducted a vibrant campaign with multiracial membership and leadership in the party, it could not overcome the entrenched racial political articulation of the PNC and PPP, and won only two seats in parliament. Jagan and the PPP returned to state power, but the difficult conditions for working people have largely persisted. Together with the establishment of multiparty democracy in 1992, the discovery of oil in Guyana in 2015 might have signaled an optimistic future for democratic and redistributive development. However, the weakness of the state's structural and legal infrastructure, combined with a labor politics that was significantly gutted by neoliberal restructuring and divided by racial conflicts and party co-optation, has only reproduced economic hardships, political exclusion, and social dislocation.[73] Guyana illustrates the constraints on the full potential of liberation unionism in the context of a global system of white supremacy and capitalist imperialism.

Conclusion and Implications for Other Cases

The findings from this chapter reinforce the general argument that liberation unionism enhances state capacity for long-run democratic and redistributive development. The comparison between Trinidad and Tobago and Guyana exposes the crucial contextual factors that can enable or constrain the developmental potential of liberation unionism, such as imperial repression. During the interwar years, Guyanese working people achieved significant gains through liberation unionism and the state investments in health, education, and well-being that worker mobilization precipitated. Unlike in Trinidad and Tobago, the Guyanese working people won state power through the PPP during formal decolonization. However, British and US imperial interests intervened to reverse these political developments through force and constitutional maneuvers, aiding petty bourgeois leaders to construct racialized voting blocs. This led to antidemocratic and anti-redistributive state building, which persisted after Guyanese flag independence. Efforts to rebuild liberation unionism were systematically obstructed by racially divisive parties and an authoritarian state that had built up the willingness and capacity to co-opt, maim, and kill any opposition in order to remain in power. Guyana shows that liberation unionism is not unique to Trinidad and Tobago, but it can be derailed. Guyana's experience also supports this book's argument: Without the independent, organized countervailing force of working people to compel the state to meet people's needs, the developmental consequences can be quite disappointing.

Imperial aggression, racial political articulation, and party/political incorporation are not isolated threats to liberation unionism. They operate simultaneously, with one sometimes becoming more prominent than the others, and the sequence unfolding differently in each case. In Guyana imperial interference and repression were the critical factors that derailed the movement and created space for racialized party politics and party co-optation of unions. In Trinidad and Tobago, none of these three major demobilizing forces reached the levels of overt influence seen in Guyana, allowing militant workers to maintain some independence, which was crucial for postindependence movement building.

For heuristic purposes, even more concise comparisons of Trinidad and Tobago with two other cases of strong worker power in the interwar years—Jamaica and Zambia—further support my argument regarding the centrality of liberation unionism for equitable development. Jamaica demonstrates that the neutralization of liberation unionism might be triggered by yet another configuration of the aforementioned factors. In Jamaica unions in the 1930s were as strong as in Trinidad and Tobago, according to O. Nigel Bolland.[74] The Jamaican movement also resembled liberation unionism in Trinidad and Tobago, and a labor rebellion there in 1938 shook the colonial order.[75] But the postrebellion unionism followed a slightly different trajectory than in Trinidad and Tobago and Guyana. The previously unified trade union movement became divided between two main political parties after the labor uprising—the Jamaica Labour Party (JLP), led by Alexander Bustamante, the undisputed leader of the working people in 1930s Jamaica, and the People's National Party (PNP), established by Bustamante's cousin Norman Manley in 1938 as a reformist middle-class-oriented party (and therefore also attracting the lighter-skinned educated and wealthier population).

Over time, an intense rivalry developed between Bustamante and Manley over control of the state. Bustamante won the first two elections with universal suffrage in 1944 and 1949.[76] As minister of communication (1949–55), Bustamante effectively served as chief minister and, in the competition with the PNP to retain state power, used his position to dole out funds, jobs, and contracts to JLP supporters. Additionally, with the commencement of bauxite mining in the 1950s, the state began accruing significant revenues from taxes on mining companies.[77] This new revenue compounded the already emergent system of patronage and cemented long-lasting patterns of unions' party allegiance and animosity, replete with inflections of colorism, which often erupted in violence between JLP and PNP supporters.[78] The trade union movement remained divided along JLP/PNP lines during the Black Power movement in Jamaica in the late 1960s. Pro-government union members even had physical clashes with anti-JLP Black Power demonstrators.[79] This political fault line undoubtedly weakened worker unity. As discussed in chapter 2, unionism comes in many forms. The liberation unionism of the interwar years in Jamaica morphed into political unionism after the 1938 rebellion. In fact, party and political incorporation served as the main force demobilizing liberation unionism across British Caribbean colonies.

State building in Jamaica therefore produced mixed results. Some scholars describe it as a "paradox" or a "confounding" case where high levels of poverty and precarity exist alongside high levels of health and education.[80] Despite all the (often inconsistent) anti-imperialist rhetoric from both parties, the leaders of both the JLP and the PNP promoted foreign interests and private capital accumulation at the expense of working people.[81] Bureaucratic capacity building was uneven. The state invested in public goods, such as health and education, but infrastructural reach was significantly inhibited by patron-client and personalistic ties. And Jamaica maintains a relatively democratic system of government that is competitive and offers some basic political rights and civil liberties, but the rigidity of the two-party system and political violence around national elections do not offer much choice to the voting population.[82] The Black Power movement was able to move the state toward greater capacity building and social investments through the electoral victory of Michael Manley and the PNP's adoption of democratic socialism from 1974 to 1980. However, the unions allied with the PNP were not in an independent position to challenge Manley's more conservative tendencies, and the United States embarked on a series of efforts to destabilize the Jamaican economy while covertly supporting the JLP.[83] In the economic turbulence that followed, Jamaica turned to the IMF in the late 1970s. The implementation of structural adjustments and neoliberal policies further inhibited state building for broad-based development. Thus, political and party incorporation of unions divided the working people and inhibited state capacity building for development. Jamaica's trajectory represents the intractability of institutions inherited from the British, as Orlando Patterson has emphasized, precisely because of the uneven gains and ongoing struggle of Jamaican working people to refashion the state to serve their needs.[84]

Given that liberation unionism existed in other cases but did not always lead to equity-enhancing development, some may ask which factor is more important in driving a positive developmental outcome—the worker movement or the political opportunity context? The reality is that neither the colonial officials nor the local political careerists demonstrated any inherent impulse to advance redistribution and democracy that would truly transform life for the working people. Therefore, it is unlikely that the state would have undergone reforms on its own initiative. Thus, liberation unionism must first be constituted to push the state toward a developmental agenda.

The example of Zambia is instructive here. Zambia, formerly called Northern Rhodesia by the British colonizers, occupied a strategic position, especially during the buildup to World War II and the war itself, as the only source of copper under direct British control.[85] Significant worker unrest erupted in the Northern Rhodesian Copperbelt in 1935 and 1940 as African mine workers went on strike over tax increases, wages, benefits, working and living conditions, food shortages, and racial wage gaps and managerial practices.[86] However, this worker movement did not fit our definition of liberation unionism. It was much more fractured, as European mine workers organized to keep Africans underpaid and subordinated, and as the strikes remained confined to specific sectors and geographic areas as opposed to the multisectoral striking in Trinidad and Tobago.[87] Further, the workers were less transformation oriented in their demands. They focused on wages and workplace issues, and engaged less with broader political struggles and community-based issues relative to working people in Trinidad and Tobago and Guyana. This is perhaps because while women participated in and supported strikes, the formal labor organizations that were formed in the 1950s were heavily male dominated, and men demanded a "family wage," which reinforced the male-breadwinner ideal and the lack of compensation for women's labor.[88] During decolonization the Zambian worker movement began to gain momentum, but it was then demobilized by political incorporation and state repression. Zambia's worker movement, powerful as it was, did not have the features of liberation unionism in Trinidad and Tobago.

The unity of the movement and the breadth of worker demands set the agenda for the reforms that the state would undertake—the narrower the demands, the narrower the reforms. Workers gained few immediate concessions out of the 1935 strike: a compound manager was fired, committees were formed, and the Rhodes-Livingstone Institute (a social science center to investigate the conditions of the masses) was founded.[89] Some bureaucratization of the state did occur, but strong resistance by capital and colonial administrators slowed the pace of institutional change, and the state remained closely allied with private companies.[90] The infrastructural reach of the state was barely extended. Investments in health, education, water and sanitation, and social welfare remained paltry. Furthermore, the colonial state underwent few political reforms to broaden representation and participation. After all, workers had not demanded it. Thus, African workers would not gain seats on the Legislative Council until 1948, more than twenty years after workers in Trinidad and Tobago.[91]

During formal decolonization, Zambian labor leaders did not seek to form labor parties, as they viewed unions as nonpolitical organizations exclusively devoted to negotiations over wages and working conditions, even if their rank and file disagreed.[92] The worker movement underwent several splits and mergers over debates concerning the union-party relationship.[93] Zambia gained its independence in 1964, with Kenneth Kaunda winning the presidency in the first elections with universal suffrage. Workers reorganized and engaged in a wave of persistent striking in the immediate postindependence period (1964–69).[94] However, labor was progressively demobilized over its divided and politically ambivalent relationship with the ruling party. Whereas in Trinidad and Tobago, the most powerful union, the OWTU, remained independent of the ruling party and state throughout the 1960s, the Zambian Mineworkers' Union became incorporated into the state-controlled union federation in 1966.[95] In 1972 Kaunda announced the official introduction of a one-party state, which lasted until 1991, and state building proceeded in ways that did not significantly enhance the well-being of the masses. For instance, despite some increase in schools and health services, there was overcrowding of facilities in urban areas, and rural populations remained severely underserved.[96] Zambia underperforms relative to Trinidad and Tobago and Guyana on every measure of economic and social development listed in table 6.1.[97] The case of Zambia shows that while political opportunities may be conducive for worker movements to emerge, not all worker movements are equally developmental. If liberation unionism or unionism of a similar form has not developed in the first place, state building is less likely to proceed along the lines of constructing institutions that significantly raise the living standards of the masses.

Before I conclude this chapter, it is important to address how countries are integrated into the global capitalist system. Some may argue that a country's specific commodity export influences its developmental fate. Indeed, the spike in oil prices in the 1970s provided Trinidad and Tobago with the resources to address worker demands. However, we should not overemphasize commodity prices as an *independent* determinant of development. Other oil-dependent countries, such as Gabon and Nigeria, experienced similar oil booms, yet they lacked the state capacity needed for development due to the absence of a social force like liberation unionism, which is crucial for pushing the state to restructure itself in pro-developmental ways.[98]

The overall results of the comparison between Trinidad and Tobago and Guyana support the argument that improvements in state capacity and development, or the lack thereof, hinge on the legacies of colonial labor movements. They provide evidence that within the constraints of the white capitalist system, liberation unionism fosters the construction of state institutions that improve the well-being of working people. Where liberation unionism either emerges and is dismantled or does not emerge at all, the consequences for working people can be disastrous.

Conclusion

Almost fifty years ago, Walter Rodney wrote, "Probably the most important conclusion which can be drawn from contemporary political trends in the English-speaking Caribbean is that working class power is the only guarantor for economic growth and political democracy which precede and accompany socialism as a system of social justice."[1] For the case of Trinidad and Tobago, this statement rings true. The main question motivating this book is: What accounts for Trinidad and Tobago's relatively impressive levels of economic and social development? Analyzing archival data, government documents, and secondary sources using this framework, this book develops an institutional angle on Black radical theories of race and capitalism to answer this question. These thinkers force attention to the agency of racialized colonized subjects in effecting social transformation, and to the ways in which the structures and subjectivities of race and class interact to shape conflicts, politics, and the relationship of the state to the white capitalist system. Fusing this attention to system and struggle with the examination of the institutional architecture of the state, in terms of agencies, policies, and orientations, this book links the study of mass mobilization to development outcomes. In what follows, I review what we have learned about the key operative forces driving equity-enhancing development in Trinidad and Tobago over the course of the twentieth century. I then discuss how working people in Trinidad and Tobago have fared in the neoliberal twenty-first century and what this book's argument might mean for making sense of the country's contemporary situation and future development trajectory. Then we can consider more broadly the lessons that follow from the book's findings.

Summation

In this book I have argued that a specific form of unionism—liberation unionism—was the dominant and decisive force shaping broad-based economic and social development in Trinidad and Tobago, through enhancing the state's capacity to meet the needs of the people. Through an in-depth historical case analysis, I identify the specific features of liberation unionism and discuss how such a movement emerged out of the structures of racial and colonial oppression and the agency of working people. Liberation unionism was based on unity across industrial sectors and race and was inclusive of women; it was internationalist in terms of Pan-African racial uplift, diasporic ties, and anti-imperial resistance; and it pressed for total social, economic, and political change. The historic achievements of liberation unionism in Trinidad and Tobago since its first eruption in 1919 are undeniable. The Trinidad and Tobago state did not move by itself toward democracy and redistributive development. Liberation unionism forced the state to organize a class compromise between working people and their employers (the state itself and the reluctant capitalist class), which, in turn, required altering state-capital relations and building the structures needed to promote the welfare of the masses.

Liberation unionism forced state officials to act more independently of the interests of foreign and local capital, to develop new agencies and mediation machinery, and to alter the laws and build the regulatory structures to mitigate labor superexploitation. Working people demanded that the state channel the country's natural resource revenue to the masses and not the few foreign corporations or local elites whose raison d'être was to amass disproportionate wealth and status from the labor of the people. Liberation unionism also stimulated an increase in the bureaucratic strength and infrastructural power of the state. In calling on the state to improve not just wages and working conditions but also social protections, health and sanitation services, education, housing, infrastructure, and transportation across the entire territory, liberation unionism compelled the state to pass new legislation, invest revenues differently, and construct and staff the agencies necessary for providing such developmental services to the population at large. Finally, this movement made it less tenable for state officials to keep aloof from the masses. In response to liberation unionism, the state developed structures to be more responsive to the needs of working people and the unemployed and to improve transparency and accountability. Further, it promoted more democratic ties between the state and society, including the extension of political participation and civil liberties.

The abbreviated comparative case study of Guyana demonstrates the importance of the geopolitical and repressive context. In Guyana, like Trinidad and Tobago, liberation unionism emerged in the interwar years, and working people won significant gains. Unlike in Trinidad and Tobago, the movement in Guyana survived into the postwar period, and working people successfully elected a multiracial mass party representing their interests to the state. But US and British powers would not allow it. The imperial-aided colonial state repression that followed crushed worker dreams, reappropriated the state, and set Guyana on a postindependence path of weak redistributive and democratic development. Had working people in Trinidad and Tobago won state power, they may have suffered a similar fate. The comparison of Trinidad and Tobago to Guyana demonstrates how geopolitical conditions can constrain liberation unionism and derail equitable development. Further, this case study demonstrates the open space for more comparative research on worker movements and their impacts on state capacity and development.

Neoliberalism and the Unfinished Project of Liberation

Trinidad and Tobago's development up to the mid-1980s, as impressive as it was, still occurred from a position of dependency in the global political economy. Consequently, like in other states across the Global South, including the so-called miracles of East Asia, the transformative potential of state-led interventionist strategies was constrained. In countries across the world system, postwar social compacts that aimed to promote both social welfare and profitability contributed to tightening returns for capital. Policies intended to resolve the crisis of profitability for capital, in addition to blows to US imperialism such as its defeat in Vietnam, the demands of Third World states for a "New International Economic Order," and the raising of oil prices by OPEC (the Organization of the Petroleum Exporting Countries) in the 1970s, provoked a broader US-led imperial core shift away from development planning, guarantees of social protections, and Keynesian strategies to policies that foiled Third World development projects.[2] Trinidad and Tobago's economy, like so many other peripheralized economies, faced significant challenges in the mid-1980s. The subsequent global neoliberal economic restructuring thrust Trinidad and Tobago into crisis, weakened unions, and stalled liberation unionism. This book's analysis, however, shows that it is not so easy to bury liberation unionism. Before we write labor's obituary, we must situate the past forty years within the long history of worker struggles.

For Trinidad and Tobago, the increased revenues that came with the short-term spikes in oil prices in 1973 and 1979 were not enough to finance the movement-inspired reforms, and the state turned to external borrowing. In addition, foreign multinationals punished the state for 1970s reforms that exacted from them more revenues for the masses and engaged in a range of retaliatory actions, such as pursuing court actions, reducing investments, evading taxes, and requesting that the US State Department pressure the Trinidad and Tobago state.[3] Refineries suffered declines in production due to US protectionist policies favoring refineries located in the United States.[4] In addition, state-owned enterprises (SOEs) in Trinidad and Tobago lacked the networks and infrastructure of the multinational corporations, which they needed to access the necessary inputs and technology and to market oil products abroad. Moreover, imperial countries have removed multilateral trade "protections" and "preferences" for small economies in the past few decades.[5] These structural problems, combined with rapidly falling oil prices in 1981, spelled economic crisis for the country. By the mid-1980s, Trinidad and Tobago had exhausted its foreign exchange reserves.

Like other countries riddled with debt during this period, the state turned to the International Monetary Fund (IMF) in 1989 and 1990 and the World Bank in 1990 and 1991 for debt restructuring and external financing. Trinbagonians experienced a decline in per capita gross domestic product (GDP) and a decade of economic stagnation and hardship. Following IMF prescriptions, the state implemented measures to attract foreign capital, reduced corporate taxes, devalued the currency, and significantly privatized government assets.[6] Neoliberal economic restructuring and imperial aggression further constrained the range of options available to the state for managing the economy.[7] The US invasion of Grenada in 1983 to crush the socialist aspirations of the people, according to Norman Girvan, "was one of the final nails in the coffin that signaled the end of the experimentation with radical and alternative avenues to decolonization, and the consolidation, simultaneously, of the neoliberal paradigm."[8]

Debt and restructuring in the 1980s and 1990s spurred a number of political and social problems. In the realm of party politics, the economic downturn ended the thirty-year rule of the People's National Movement (PNM). This ushered in a musical-chair rotation of different parties in government and the heightening of racial political articulation, but there has still been remarkable consistency in the neoliberal orientations of these successive administrations.[9] These challenges even led to a failed attempted coup in 1990 by the Jamaat al-Muslimeen, a small group of Muslims of African descent, triggered by a land dispute with the government and by general frustration with the economic malaise. Out-migration increased in the mid-1990s as workers sought employment opportunities in the United Kingdom, the United States, and Canada, and their remittances helped buttress their families and the struggling economy.[10] Further, crime rates rose following the mid-1980s economic recession. While crime remained steady in the 1990s, and even declined on some measures such as murder rates, it has once again resurfaced in the twenty-first century as an issue of grave concern due to the rapid increase in violent crimes. Most experts trace the recent spike in crime to the country's location within transnational networks of gun trafficking.[11] Thus far, the state demonstrates little capacity to address this public concern.

Also consistent with global trends, the Trinidad and Tobago labor movement has been severely weakened over the past few decades. Workers continued to organize throughout the 1980s and into the present but are nowhere near the levels of the 1960s and 1970s strike activity. Apart from one spike in strikes in 2001, which was confined to the transport, storage, and communication sectors, the average number of strikes has declined significantly since the late 1970s.[12] The neoliberal shift to contract, part-time, and seasonal work in the private and public sector has drastically reduced union membership.[13] The most significant blows to worker power came with the fall of King Sugar and the restructuring of state-owned Petrotrin, the largest oil refinery in the country, as natural gas has come to dominate twenty-first-century revenues. Unstable sugar prices on the international market, the elimination of trade preferences for sugar, reduced sugar and oil output, and increased indebtedness of SOEs forced the state to address the drain on public resources. Despite workers' valiant efforts to save the sugar industry and the oil refinery and enact dreams of worker-owned oil and sugar industries, the state closed Caroni (1975) Limited in 2007 and began restructuring Petrotrin in 2018.[14] Of the affected ten thousand predominantly Indian sugar workers, some remained farmers or leased their plots, while others moved into construction, low-wage work (becoming landscapers or security guards), and government jobs, or opened small businesses.[15] For the thousands of retrenched oil workers, early reports show they have also struggled to find secure alternative employment and/or are now engaged in nonunionized contract work, including in the natural gas sector.[16]

In addition, state repression has also weakened unions. State efforts to trammel a historically effective organized worker movement have produced one of the most highly regulated and restrictive compulsory arbitration models in the Caribbean, severely constraining legal strike action.[17] Infighting within unions, the lack of coordination across racialized groups and sectors, and racialized two-party politics are inhibiting worker unity. Together, the contemporary challenges that liberation unionism faces are reminiscent of those workers faced after World War II.

Still, the infrastructure and social welfare investments that came out of the long history of open confrontations between workers, on the one hand, and employers and the state, on the other, had long-lasting positive impacts on human conditions. The middle class was significantly enlarged through the struggles waged by working people in the colonial and postindependence periods. Even when per capita income declined in the latter half of the 1980s, developmental priorities around people's well-being continued to be reflected in outcomes such as health, education, and other welfare measures, and in the state's resistance to fully embracing the private sector. Once constraints on financing eased after 2002, the state reasserted its role in the economy, especially in housing and infrastructure, with all the politics that entails, and new state agencies were created (sometimes replacing older ones) to coordinate these tasks.[18] Without the infrastructure building and institutionalization in response to twentieth-century liberation unionism, the conditions of working people would have most likely been far worse.

Furthermore, far from promoting a unilinear development thesis, the study of labor and development in this book is attentive to both advances and reversals. In situating Trinidad and Tobago's development within the long historical arc of labor struggles and various reorganizations of global capitalism, the downturn in liberation unionism in this neoliberal era is one period in a longer history of the waxing and waning of worker mobilization and state building. Liberation unionism was also significantly divided and diminished during decolonization, but it made a remarkable comeback after independence. Thus, the fate of liberation unionism is not given. Just as working people reactivated and retooled the movement in the 1960s conjuncture, they might revive liberation unionism in the future.

Liberation Unionism: Implications for Development
Theory and for the Future

Twentieth-century liberation unionism in Trinidad and Tobago provides some useful lessons for development theory, contemporary leftist debates, and liberation struggles. First, Trinidad and Tobago's experience reiterates that the collective action of working people matters for enhancing the living standards of the masses. Enslaved, indentured, and superexploited, these working people were subjected to harrowing degradation and squalid conditions. From this subjugation, they resisted, persisted, envisioned a better future, and acted with intention in pursuit of collective well-being.

As I demonstrated in chapters 2, 3, and 5, working people in Trinidad and Tobago built a unionism rooted in Black liberation struggles. They constructed the class awareness that labor scholars have emphasized.[19] However, they did so through and alongside the race-conscious discourse and organizational infrastructures of Pan-Africanism. Similar to C. L. R. James's analysis of "Negro struggle" in the United States, it is not easy to subsume liberation unionism in Trinidad and Tobago under the Comintern, communism, or class struggle alone: it had "an organic political perspective" and "a vitality and a validity of its own."[20] Similarly, George Padmore's 1956 assessment of African national liberation was true of Trinbagonian working people in the colonial period and the 1960s: "Africans do not have to wait for Communists to 'incite' them. The realities of their status have infused their determination to be free. And they prefer to attain freedom under the standard of Pan-Africanism, a banner of their own choosing."[21] That Pan-African banner in Trinidad and Tobago was primarily a pragmatic Garveyism and Black Power that drew on the organizational networks and resources of those movements. Working people both produced these global scripts and also fashioned them to suit their local movement-building needs. This creative agency might not be acknowledged "in the pages of capitalist historians," as C. L. R. James quipped, but it is the force that altered the character of the state to promote democracy and enhance welfare.[22] As the discussion of Zambia showed, the absence of liberation unionism had negative consequences for development. However, I am not arguing that only worker organizing in the form of liberation unionism will bring forth state capacity for progressive social policy and redistributive development. Other studies have shown that around the world, other forms of labor, peasant, and social movements have, to varied extents, also stimulated similar processes of institution building and socioeconomic and political outcomes, depending on how elites respond to that collective mass agitation.[23] This book extends this body of work by exposing one kind of movement that was consequential for welfare, democracy, and well-being that has been overlooked and undertheorized relative to other forms of organizing in the studies of mass movements and development.

Contemporary global Black liberation struggles, such as Black Lives Matter and prison abolition movements, continue to demonstrate the efforts of racially dehumanized and superexploited people to create their own history. How these movements interact and intersect with workers and unions and across different countries remains the subject of ongoing research.[24] If the findings of this book hold, the size and scale of any state capacity-building efforts that are born out of confrontations between these movements, on one hand, and states and capital, on the other—and, in turn, the improvements in human welfare that are exacted—will depend on the size, scale, and demands of these working people's movements.

The argument in this book therefore diverges from those that give primacy to European colonial agents as the drivers of broad-based economic and social development.[25] European colonizers may have been "disseminators and enforcers" of the administrative institutions they elected to "transmit" and "uphold."[26] However, an equity-enhancing developmental agenda is rarely the result of self-directed or innately benevolent state officials. Subjugated peoples were not merely passive recipients or inheritors of colonial institutions. They were also not simply "initial conditions," "mediating mechanisms," or contingency factors shaping the colonizer's strategies of rule and state-building practices.[27] This book shows that working people were an active agent—a cause—of significant economic and social improvements. This argument therefore pushes the scholarship on colonial institutional legacies to take seriously the role of racialized laboring classes in institutional outcomes.

Second, I have shown how, for ordinary folks who sit at the intersection of racialized, gendered, colonial, and imperial oppressions, the emancipatory struggle is not solely against labor exploitation. Organizing for liberation involved articulating demands that linked these interlocking systems of oppression, and in doing so, workers broadened the scope and power of the movement. Working people and unions in Trinidad and Tobago pushed a broad-based developmental agenda that included but went far beyond the narrow focus on wages and workplace issues that characterizes business unionism, as well as the agenda of the conservative and "parasitic" labor aristocrats that Frantz Fanon critiqued. This agenda also went beyond the demands for political reforms or the pursuit of alliances with political parties that is characteristic of political unionism. *Fueling Development* shows that liberation unionism, similar to social movement and social justice unionism, also involved linking up with communities to challenge the social order. Extending their challenge even further, the breadth of the demands, actions, and relations in liberation unionism was not tied just to materiality. Racialized workers were anchored to a freedom-seeking tradition of asserting their humanness against European architectures of enslavement, production for empire, and a domineering colonial system that defined and treated them as subhuman. The expansiveness of the demands shaped the extensiveness of the concessions and reforms. This book therefore extends the typology of trade unionisms in labor studies and provides a basis for future comparative work on labor and labor movements.

Third, Trinbagonian workers have shown us that unity across race, gender, and geographic lines is not just a utopian dream. This book provides more empirical evidence that it is not only conceivable but also achievable.[28] Unity among the working people—Africans and Indians; men, women, and children; immigrants and persons born locally—was crucial not just for increasing the numerical size of the movement but also for promoting the broad distribution of gains. The involvement of women and children in liberation unionism, for instance, and the specific demands targeting issues such as food production, women's health, childcare, women's political rights, and community development, produced remarkable gains in the welfare and well-being of the population writ large, just as Black Marxist feminist, Black feminist, and development scholars alike have established.[29] The wins were not always evenly spread, to be sure. Gendered exploitation and exclusions persist even as Trinidad and Tobago's measures of gender equity, in addition to broader indicators of well-being, are impressive relative to other countries in the Global South.[30] This book shows that movement unity is crucial to forestall the unequal apportioning of concessions and promote a broad-based developmental impact.

This book shows that to achieve worker unity and mobilization, workers do not need to de-emphasize their racial identity. The popular notion among some academics, labor organizers, and activists alike that racial or gender identity politics is irreconcilable with class consciousness, that it hinders coalition building and anticapitalist struggles, and/or that it fails is overblown.[31] Relatedly, the notion that racial or ethnic diversity hinders development simply because the salience of these identities provokes competition and conflicts that weaken state capacities for directing development and the provision of public goods is also incomplete. Scholars have found instances of successful multiracial organizing in Communist Party–affiliated unions, and while many have attributed this unity to the reduction of race consciousness in favor of heightening class consciousness, some argue that the two can coexist quite harmoniously.[32]

Just as this book demonstrates that organizations and ideologies outside of the Communist Party also served as a framework for multiracial worker unity, it also shows that workers and sympathizers came together across racial lines without detaching from or suppressing their racial and gender identities.

Whether and when race becomes constructive or obstructive in interaction with materialist politics is an empirical question that must be answered with robust research into concrete events, processes, and discourses. The Trinidad and Tobago case shows that different racialized groups deployed colonial racial categories, sometimes to sow divisions and maintain domination and sometimes to build solidarities and challenge the social order. For example, the Pan-Africanism of Marcus Garvey and Black Power successfully aroused Black consciousness and solidarity. At the same time, through the anti-imperial and anticolonial fervor of Pan-Africanism, workers knit together a narrative about the shared histories of racialized subjugation and exploitation that inextricably bound together Indian and African working people. Paired with the organizational structure and resources within the radical unions that supported multiracial involvement and nonexclusionary politics, workers successfully brought the African-Indian worker movement into being. By contrast, the salience of race with the emergence of middle-class-dominated party politics contributed to worker disunity in the postwar period. In other words, there is a difference between a race consciousness that promotes harmony between racial pride and interracial cohesion and a race consciousness that is divisive, uncooperative, and based on notions of superiority and inferiority. This distinction is underappreciated. This book encourages us to think beyond *whether* racial pride and identity politics should be mobilized and consider *how* it could be mobilized to advance the goals of contemporary progressive and liberatory movements.

Fourth, this book also forces us to adopt a more nuanced view of the relationship between natural resource dependence and development. Just as resource-curse scholars now recognize that not all raw material exporters are beset by similarly weak state institutions and development outcomes, oil- and mineral-dependent states, too, are much more varied and multifaceted than the majority of this literature has acknowledged. This book adds Trinidad and Tobago to the list of cases of relatively robust resource-led redistributive development. However, my explanation for its performance goes beyond a focus on elite conflict versus cooperation and challenges arguments that attribute this outcome to the victory of capitalist forces that promote extraction and private property over progressive movements.[33] Equitable development in Trinidad and Tobago was the product of ordinary people organizing and extracting concessions from capital and states, not only in terms of per capita income, but also in terms of the wider collective interests in health, well-being, and democracy.

My argument is consistent with evidence from Norway, which is perhaps the most praised among petrostates as a case that escaped the deleterious effects of oil wealth. Resource-curse scholars largely overlook the fact that infrastructural development, wealth redistribution, expansive social welfare, democracy, and heavily state-subsidized farming were underwritten by a labor party that answered to a powerful alliance of trade unions and farmers.[34] Unionism and the labor movement in Norway, where white workers are racially and economically at the center of the white capitalist system, can hardly be fairly compared to workers' plight in Trinidad and Tobago. Still, Norway supports my general point that powerful worker movements are a force for democratic redistributive development. This is why it is crucial to situate any investigation of the effects of natural resources on development within longer histories of labor and/or social agitation and state-society relations of protest and concession. As Gwenn Okruhlik reminds us, "Life did not begin, as many imply, in 1973 with the quadrupling of oil prices. Rather, oil enters into an ongoing process of development and into a constellation of identities."[35] For future research, rather than treating oil dependence (or racial diversity or forms of colonial rule, for that matter) as determinants of weak state capacity and, in turn, poor development outcomes, these factors are better conceptualized as contexts in which the motives and agency of working people might intervene and refashion the state, thereby forcing it onto a path that promotes equitable development.

As chapters 2 and 3 showed, oil production opened up political possibilities for Trinbagonian working people. They sought to make the most of the structural power they possessed on account of their strategic position at a choke point, both spatially, in terms of their location in oil production, and temporally, during a time of war when the British imperial power felt acutely vulnerable. Like the coal workers in Timothy Mitchell's *Carbon Democracy*, Trinbagonian worker power from oil production not only propelled the emergence of democracy but upheld it against the state's authoritarian proclivities. With the restructuring of world capitalism, the relocation of industrial activities around the world, and the increased complexity of global commodity chains, more racialized workers in the periphery today are engaged in labor beyond primary commodity production.[36] Despite predictions that these workers will be even more powerless as a result of the reorganization of low-wage work, many labor scholars have already pointed out that workers' bargaining power may have in fact increased due to their ability to cause greater disruptions in chains of production and transportation.[37] Even with transitions to natural gas and green energy, movements for resource sovereignty and an anticapitalist socio-ecological order are alive around the world.[38] As such, racialized peripheralized labor still has the potential to exploit political openings to extract concessions and spur institutional changes that enhance working people's welfare.

Finally, this book addresses the complex relationship between trade unions, political parties, and states while emphasizing the crucial role of state capacity in development. It reinforces the position of Black radical thinkers and contemporary scholars of labor and development that worker mobilization is necessary but not sufficient for improving welfare. In addition to worker mobilization, the argument confirms the conclusions of earlier Weberian ideas that the bureaucratic capacity of the state and the nature of state-society ties also shape development outcomes.[39] A functional and cohesive administrative apparatus is required for coordinating reforms and delivering housing, health care, and education.

However, the mere occupation of the state by a labor party does not guarantee democratic governance or welfare for the masses, especially in dependent economies in the white capitalist system. History is littered with examples like Guyana, where imperial powers have overthrown labor-led governments, thwarting efforts to delink from the white capitalist system and achieve self-determination. Even if labor parties are not deposed from the state apparatus by foreign forces, as in Jamaica, the lack of union autonomy to hold party leaders accountable can lead to the erosion of radical agendas. Economic downturns and pressure from imperial states can push labor parties toward conservative policies that harm working people. This is evident even in cases like postrevolutionary China and Cuba, Hugo Chávez–era Venezuela, and the widely praised social democratic state of Mauritius, where tightly interwoven labor-party-state connections brought remarkable redistributive transformations but also gave rise to debates over union autonomy and how to preserve welfare gains amid imperial subversion efforts.[40]

Trinidad and Tobago offers a different model. Here, labor parties never fully occupied the state apparatus. Instead, the limited presence of representatives of the worker movement inside the state apparatus afforded liberation unionism a degree of independence that allowed working people to press a broad set of demands, force compromises, and stimulate the kind of state building that afforded them some protections from the full ravages of the white capitalist system. This book thus contributes to ongoing debates about the relationship between labor, parties, the state, and imperial forces, emphasizing that the independence of working people is crucial, regardless of who controls the state.

Trinidad and Tobago's state structure differs from the East Asian developmental state type, which typically relied on the extreme exclusion and repression of working people for rapid economic growth. While the state may be social democratic, it differs from the structures in Kerala, where worker-peasant mobilization resulted in the installation and hegemony of the Communist Party regime in the state apparatus. In Trinidad and Tobago, the relative independence of the movement from the state helped preserved its militance, preventing radical segments from becoming a casualty of conservative reformism or imperial aggression. This book does not assert that working people should abandon revolutionary goals or prioritize concession, conciliation, and social democratic arrangements over confrontation. In fact, this book presents substantial evidence that the labor-capital-state configuration upon which class compromises rest were unstable and heavily dependent on ample state revenues to redistribute, which in this resource-dependent peripheral economy translated to international oil and gas prices. *Fueling Development* shows the practical realities of worker organizing and the range of internally generated and externally imposed difficulties that working people faced when they organized to challenge the white capitalist system. The outcome of these struggles in the case of Trinidad and Tobago, short of revolution, increased state capacity for progressive social policies, which in turn raised working people's living standards and enabled them to live longer, healthier lives.

Certainly, these reforms may be seen as part of the "ideological state apparatus" that reproduces the conditions necessary for capital accumulation by organizing consent through seemingly neutral processes and institutions.[41] The state also tried to maneuver its way out of implementing the reforms demanded by the movement. Still, working people forced those concessions and institutional changes and, in doing so, improved their own material conditions. Thus, the state remains important to enhancing well-being, but only insofar as worker mobilization reoriented state officials to act in the interests of the masses.

In sum, because capital accumulates in racist, gendered, and spatial ways, these fissures have often impeded successful worker organizing the world over. Liberation unionism can serve as a blueprint for future labor organizing. United, Pan-Africanist, and transformation oriented, working people's collective action stimulated the creation and expansion of the institutional infrastructure of the state, which has real tangible effects on the enhancement of human well-being. Protecting the integrity of such movements from middle-class reformers, state co-optation and repression, and the backlash of capital is also part of the ongoing struggle. To build and maintain a movement that can push states toward truer democracy and greater egalitarian distribution of material conditions is certainly no easy feat, but African and Indian working people in Trinidad and Tobago show that it is possible. It is in that kernel of possibility that we might find inspiration for emancipatory politics today.

Appendix
Methodology

This book seeks to capture the economic and social outcomes pertaining to the conditions of life for ordinary people and the deep historical and dynamic processes that explain Trinidad and Tobago's economic and social development over the course of the twentieth century. Given Trinidad and Tobago's deviation from conventional expectations of development, this case allows for building and reformulating the content of development theory.[1] Methodologically, this book follows the historical and dialectical materialist analysis deployed by the Black radicals who embraced, or critically engaged with, Marxism, and for whom explaining capitalist development required attending to imperial domination and the political economy of race and colonialism. It begins from the premise that contemporary institutions and outcomes can be understood only by tracing out how past structures, events, and processes inform the present. In tracing out the causal mechanisms, I use a narrative strategy characteristic of both Black radical political economy and historical-comparative research methods in North American sociology.[2] I lay out the temporal order, the sequence of events, the interplay between structure and agency, and the conjunctures and contingencies over time *and* space. Like C. L. R. James, W. E. B. Du Bois, and others in the Black radical tradition, I aim to combat what recent scholars have termed *methodological nationalism*, or the treatment of the nation-state as a bounded container isolated from wider relations. When, why, and how things happened in Trinidad and Tobago was inextricably tied up with when, why, and how things happened in the British Empire and wider white capitalist system and vice versa. In this way, this book heeds recent calls in comparative-historical works for "relational" and "*dynamic time-space*" analyses.[3]

Documenting and assessing the material existence of working people requires data on economic conditions, human health, and well-being. This book follows Walter Rodney's approach to assessing economic and social development. He noted that dominant development indicators, such as the gross national income (GNI) and gross domestic product (GDP), are part of the capitalist ideological language and instruments of Western institutions and occlude the racialized, gendered, and colonial exploitation that constitutes economic growth.[4] "Nevertheless," he stated, "the per capita income is a useful statistic for comparing one country with another," *in combination* with indicators of how people are faring in terms of basic welfare and needs, such as calorie consumption; provision of social services, including schools and hospitals, in relation to the population size; and the extent to which people can access them, as indicated by life expectancy, deaths among children, malnutrition rates, literacy rates, and the occurrence of preventable diseases.[5] I have utilized a wide range of datasets and government records to obtain these economic and social indices, levels of inequality and poverty, and standards of living. Table A.1 shows how Trinidad and Tobago's development indicators compare to other commonly studied cases in the development literature, including widely praised examples of equity-enhancing development (Costa Rica, Kerala, and Mauritius).

In addition, to understand development planning and policy implementation in the postindependence period, I have relied on a number of published and unpublished government documents, such as the proceedings of investment negotiations, budget speeches, and government development planning and policy documents. The Trinidad and Tobago government collects and archives this information in the government ministry libraries and databases, such as those of the Ministry of Finance, Ministry of Energy and Energy Industries, Ministry of Trade and Industry, and Ministry of Planning and Development. I supplement these records with data from other sources, such as World Bank and International Monetary Fund reports.

To understand the historical structure and conditions of Trinbagonian society, the racial and class conflicts, working-class desires and strategies, and the administrative capacity of the state for development, I have turned to a range of archival sources. To excavate the voices and agency of the colonized, I analyzed local newspapers, speeches, letters, oral histories, and the documents of local organizations, in particular, worker organizations and trade unions. These primary documents are housed in the National Archives of Trinidad and Tobago, the Alma Jordan Library at the University of the West Indies, and the library of the most dominant local trade union during my period of investigation, the Oilfield Workers' Trade Union. To examine and understand the perspectives, strategies, actions, and policies of the British colonial officials and imperial interests, I used colonial correspondence and reports housed in the National Ar-

TABLE A.1. A Comparison of Social Development Indicators, 2019

	Trinidad and Tobago	Costa Rica	Kerala	Mauritius	Botswana	Brazil	India	South Africa	LIC
GDP per capita (constant 2015 US$)	17,401	12, 878	1,783	10,957	6,952	8,771	1,936	6,032	718
Human Development Index	0.813	0.811	–	0.806	0.703	0.764	0.638	0.741	–
Literacy rate, adult total (% of people ages 15 and above)	98 (2000)	97 (2011)	94 (2011)	93 (2016)	87 (2013)	93 (2018)	69 (2011)	95 (2019)	62
Life expectancy at birth, total (years)	74	79	75	74	65	75	71	66	63
Mortality rate, infant (per 1,000 live births)	15	7	10	14	34	13	30	28	49
Mortality rate, under 5 (per 1,000 live births)	17	8	12	16	43	15	34	36	71
Maternal mortality (deaths per 100,000 live births)	26	19	42	49	118	61	116	118	416
Gender Inequality Index	0.269	0.239	–	0.328	0.458	0.396	0.476	0.408	–
Political rights	2	1		1	3	2	2	2	
Civil liberties	2	1	–	2	2	2	3	2	–
Population (millions)	1.4	5.0	33 (2011)	1.3	2.3	208	1,389	60	661

Sources: Freedom House, *Freedom in the World 2024*; Government of Kerala, *Economic Review 2019*; UNDP, Gender Inequality Index dataset, 2024; UNDP, Human Development Index dataset 2024; World Bank, World Development Indicators, 2024.

Notes: Freedom House indices of political rights and civil liberties are on a seven-point scale ranging from 1 (least democratic) to 7 (most democratic); Gender Inequality Index is on a scale ranging from 0 (women and men fare equally) to 1 (gender inequality is high on all measured dimensions); LIC = low-income countries; Trinidad and Tobago's Human Development Index rank in 2019 was 67 out of 189 countries.

chives in the United Kingdom (UK) and the British Library.[6] As much as was possible, these records were cross-checked with and supplemented by secondary sources (books and articles) by historians, sociologists, political scientists, and country specialists. This book relies on significant archival research. Still, those well versed in Trinidad and Tobago labor history will be familiar with the general facts presented here. Indeed, the large body of work by labor scholars of and from Trinidad and Tobago was indispensable to this analysis. My overall aim is sociological: to identify analytical patterns within and resulting from labor upsurges, and to convince readers of the recurring causal configurations in Trinidad and Tobago's history that, in turn, shaped the country's trajectory over time.

For the abbreviated case study comparison with Guyana, I used data from secondary sources. In comparing across cases, I aim neither for theoretical generalization nor solely historically specific descriptions. Rather, the comparison enables me to refine the concept of liberation unionism and assess the accuracy and limits of my causal claims from the in-depth case study. As such, the book offers a "historically conditional" account of development using the Trinidad and Tobago case.[7]

Notes

INTRODUCTION

Epigraph: *The People*, May 18, 1935, 7.

1. I use Walter Rodney's term *working people* and *working class* interchangeably to refer to urban and rural wage workers and peasants, and the not-so-stark distinction between worker and peasant in the Caribbean colonies. See Rodney, *History*; Rodney, "Class Contradictions in Tanzania." For a more recent theorization, see Shivji, "Concept of 'Working People.'"

2. *Wages Committee, 1919–1920 Report*, November 5, 1920, The National Archives (TNA), Colonial Office (CO) 295/531; *Trinidad and Tobago Disturbances 1937 Report of Commission* (Forster Report), TNA, CO 295/601/2.

3. Harding and Gent, *Dominions Office and Colonial Office List for 1937*; Harding and Gent, *Dominions Office and Colonial Office List for 1940*; Mercer and Collins, *Colonial Office List for 1919*; Mercer, Harding, and Gent, *Dominions Office and Colonial Office List for 1930*; Forster Report, 30–41.

4. UNDP, Human Development Index (HDI) dataset, accessed December 3, 2024. https://hdr.undp.org/data-center/human-development-index#/indicies/HDI.

5. World Bank, "World Development Indicators" databank, accessed December 5, 2024, https://databank.worldbank.org/reports.aspx?source=2&country=TTO.

6. Pan American Health Organization, "Trinidad and Tobago."

7. World Bank, "World Bank Country and Lending Groups," accessed June 15, 2024, https://datahelpdesk.worldbank.org/knowledgebase/articles/906519-world-bank-country-and-lending-groups.

8. Freedom House, *Freedom in the World 2024*, Country and Territory Ratings and Statuses, 1973–2024, accessed December 5, 2024, https://freedomhouse.org/report/freedom-world.

9. These literatures are vast. For just a few examples concerning the developmental legacies of colonialism, see Acemoglu et al., "Colonial Origins"; Kohli, *State-Directed Development*; Lange, *Lineages of Despotism*; Mahoney, *Colonialism and Postcolonial Development*. On the problems of dependence on oil, see Karl, *Paradox of Plenty*;

Mahdavy, "Patterns and Problems"; Ross, *Oil Curse*. On challenges related to racial or ethnic diversity, see Alesina et al., "Fractionalization"; Churchill and Smyth, "Ethnic Diversity and Poverty"; Easterly and Levine, "Africa's Growth Tragedy."

10. Evans, "Constructing the 21st-Century Developmental State"; Evans, *Embedded Autonomy*; Evans and Heller, "Human Development"; Heller, *Labor of Development*; Lange, *Lineages of Despotism*; Mann, *Sources of Social Power*; Mkandawire, "Thinking About Developmental States"; Sandbrook et al., *Social Democracy*; Weir and Skocpol, "State Structures."

11. Acemoglu et al., "Colonial Origins"; Boone, "States and Ruling Classes"; Gerring et al., "Direct and Indirect Rule"; Lange, *Lineages of Despotism*; Mahoney, *Colonialism and Postcolonial Development*; Migdal, *Strong Societies and Weak States*; Patterson, *Confounding Island*. For related arguments about institutions created by colonizers, see also Kohli, *State-Directed Development*; Mamdani, *Citizen and Subject*; Miles, *Hausaland Divided*; and Owolabi, *Ruling Emancipated Slaves*; Woodberry, "Missionary Roots"; Young, *African Colonial State*. Following Julian Go in *Postcolonial Thought and Social Theory*, the term *post-colonial* (with the hyphen) connotes a period following the end of formal colonial domination or after a colony attained constitutional independence, whereas *postcolonial* (without the hyphen) refers to a body of writings and thought that seeks to challenge and transcend imperial epistemes.

12. Auty, *Sustaining Development*; Humphreys et al., *Escaping the Resource Curse*; Isham et al., "Varieties of Resource Experience"; Ross, *Oil Curse*; Sachs and Warner, "Natural Resource Abundance"; Lederman and Maloney, *Natural Resources*; Vicente, "Does Oil Corrupt?"

13. Auty and Gelb, "Political Economy of Resource-Abundant States"; Beblawi and Luciani, *Rentier State*; Bellin, "Robustness of Authoritarianism"; Chaudhry, "Economic Liberalization"; Jensen and Wantchekon, "Resource Wealth"; Karl, *Paradox of Plenty*; Mahdavy, "Patterns and Problems "; Ross, *Oil Curse*; Sachs and Warner, "Natural Resource Abundance."

14. Scholars argue that Botswana, Chile, Indonesia, Malaysia, and Kazakhstan escaped the resource curse. See Acemoglu et al., "African Success Story"; Jones Luong and Weinthal, *Oil Is Not a Curse*; Rosser, "Escaping the Resource Curse."

15. Banerjee et al., "History, Social Divisions," 639. See also Alesina et al., "Fractionalization"; Easterly and Levine, "Africa's Growth Tragedy"; La Porta et al., "Quality of Government"; Montalvo and Reynal-Querol, "Ethnic Diversity"; Pribble, "Worlds Apart."

16. Baldwin and Huber, "Economic Versus Cultural Differences"; Cederman et al., "Why Do Ethnic Groups Rebel?"; Chandra, *Why Ethnic Parties Succeed*; Franck and Rainer, "Does the Leader's Ethnicity Matter?"; E. Lieberman and McClendon, "Ethnicity–Policy Preference Link"; Posner, *Institutions and Ethnic Politics*.

17. The white population was 1.9 percent in 1960. Abraham, *Labour and the Multiracial Project*, 19; Brereton, *History of Modern Trinidad*; M. John, *Plantation Slaves of Trinidad*, 6; MacDonald, *Trinidad and Tobago*, 146; A. Robinson, *Mechanics of Independence*; Williams, *History of the People*; Wood, *Trinidad in Transition*.

18. Titus, *Amelioration and Abolition*; Trotman, *Crime in Trinidad*.

19. The minimum threshold for resource dependence, according to Terry Karl, is where oil and gas account for more than 40 percent of exports and 10 percent of resource rents. See Karl, *Paradox of Plenty*.

20. Based on a comparison of HDI indices for 2019 (before the 2020 COVID-19 pandemic). UNDP, Human Development Index dataset, accessed December 3, 2024, https://hdr.undp.org/data-center/human-development-index#/indicies/HDI. For a detailed comparison of the development indicators of Trinidad and Tobago and Botswana, see table A.1 in the appendix.

21. On the role of labor in universal suffrage, decolonization, and democracy, see Bonilla, *Non-Sovereign Futures*; Collier and Collier, *Shaping the Political Arena*; Hart, *From Occupation to Independence*; Kiely, *Politics of Labour and Development*; Ledgister, *Class Alliances*; Plys, *Brewing Resistance*; Post, *Arise Ye Starvelings*; Ramdin, *From Chattel Slave*; Reddock, *Women, Labour and Politics*; Rennie, *History of the Working-Class*; Rueschemeyer et al., *Capitalist Development and Democracy*; Samaroo, *Adrian Cola Rienzi*; Samaroo and Girvan, "Trinidad Workingmen's Association"; Seidman, *Manufacturing Militance*; Teelucksingh, *Labour*; Zeilig, *Class Struggle*. On the role of labor in creating and expanding welfare states, see Agarwala, *Informal Labor*; Esping-Andersen, "Power and Distributional Regimes"; Huber and Stephens, *Development and Crisis*; Korpi, *Democratic Class Struggle*; Selwyn, *Struggle for Development*. And on the role of labor in better institutions of governance, see Lee, "Labor Unions"; see also Quadagno, "Social Movements." The literature on social movements and development also argues that collective mass agitation shapes state structures and industrial policies, depending on the elite responses to those movements. See Doner, *Politics of Uneven Development*; Kuhonta, *Institutional Imperative*; Slater, *Ordering Power*; Vu, *Paths to Development*.

22. Bergquist, *Labor in Latin America*; Gray, *Labour and Development*; S. Kale and Mazaheri, "Natural Resources."

23. Heller, *Labor of Development*.

24. Kiely, *Politics of Labour and Development*.

25. Amsden, *Asia's Next Giant*; Chibber, *Locked in Place*; Evans, *Embedded Autonomy*; Chalmers Johnson, *MITI*; Kuhonta, *Institutional Imperative*; Rueschemeyer and Evans, "State and Economic Transformation"; Wade, *Governing the Market*.

26. Chang, "Labour and 'Developmental State'"; Deyo, *Beneath the Miracle*; Evans, *Embedded Autonomy*; Fishwick, "Labour Control"; Sen, *Development as Freedom*; Vu, *Paths to Development*. Richard Doner and colleagues argue that alongside violent repression might be significant "wealth-sharing" to pacify "restive popular sectors." Doner et al., "Systemic Vulnerability."

27. Amenta et al., "All the Movements Fit to Print"; Calhoun, "'New Social Movements' of the Early Nineteenth Century"; Clemens, *People's Lobby*; Doner et al., "Systemic Vulnerability"; Gamson, *Strategy of Social Protest*; McAdam et al., *Comparative Perspectives on Social Movements*; Morris, *Origins of the Civil Rights Movement*.

28. Matlon, *Man Among Other Men*; Paschel, *Becoming Black Political Subjects*; Perry, *Black Women*.

29. Bogues, *Black Heretics, Black Prophets*; Carole Davies, "Sisters Outside"; Henry, *Caliban's Reason*; Kelley, *Freedom Dreams*; Rabaka, *Africana Critical Theory*; Rabaka, "Revolutionary Fanonism"; Reddock, "Radical Caribbean Social Thought"; C. Robinson, *Black Marxism*; D. Scott, "On the Very Idea."

30. Hunter and Abraham, *Race, Class*, xvii–xlv; Reddock, "Radical Caribbean Social Thought," 499. On Black radical political economy, see Burden-Stelly, "Absence of

Political Economy"; Edwards, "Applying the Black Radical Tradition"; Rice, "Political Economy."

31. Cox, *Caste, Class, and Race*; Cox, *Capitalism as a System*; Du Bois, *Black Reconstruction in America*; Du Bois, *World and Africa*; James, *Black Jacobins*; Fields, "Slavery, Race and Ideology"; C. Robinson, *Black Marxism*; Rodney, *How Europe Underdeveloped Africa*; Williams, *Capitalism and Slavery*. See also Wynter, "1492." Contrary to these scholars, Cedric Robinson argues that race is an enduring relic of European feudalism.

32. Cox, *Capitalism as a System*, 158.

33. Amin et al., *Dynamics of Global Crisis*; Amin, *Imperialism*; Baran, *Political Economy of Growth*; Bornschier and Chase-Dunn, *Transnational Corporations and Underdevelopment*; Bunker and Ciccantell, *Globalization*; Cardoso and Faletto, *Dependency and Development*; Dos Santos, "Structure of Dependence"; Frank, *Dependent Accumulation*; Marini, *Dialectics of Dependency*; Wallerstein, *Modern World-System*.

34. Best, "Outlines of a Model"; Best and Levitt, *Essays*; Girvan, "Development of Dependency Economics"; C. Thomas, *Dependence and Transformation*; Meeks and Girvan, *Thought of New World*.

35. Antunes de Oliveira, "Who Are the Super-Exploited?"; Arrighi et al., *Anti-Systemic Movements*; Beckford, "Plantation System"; Girvan, *Aspects of the Political Economy*. Variations of the New World Group and dependency arguments concerning contemporary inequalities produced from structural hierarchy of the world system appear in other works that are not squarely part of these traditions but draw on them, while at the same time centering race. See, for example, Ramsaran, "'Myth' of Development."

36. "Racial capitalism" is used by Legassick and Hemson, *Foreign Investment*; and C. Robinson, *Black Marxism*. "Racial and colonial capitalism" is from Itzigsohn and Brown, *Sociology of W. E. B. Du Bois*. "Racist capitalism" is from Rabaka, *Africana Critical Theory*. "Racialized capitalism" is used by N. Fraser, "Expropriation and Exploitation"; and Virdee, "Racialized Capitalism." "Race and capitalism" is from Dawson, "Hidden in Plain Sight."

37. See, for example, Go, "Three Tensions."

38. Rodney, *How Europe Underdeveloped Africa*, 303; Rodney, *Groundings with My Brothers*, 63.

39. Rodney, *Groundings with My Brothers*, 9–13.

40. Fanon, *Wretched of the Earth*, 5.

41. Loveman, *National Colors*; Nobles, *Shades of Citizenship*; Telles, *Pigmentocracies*; Telles, *Race in Another America*.

42. Fanon, *Wretched of the Earth*, 5.

43. Du Bois, "Marxism and the Negro Problem"; Du Bois, *Black Reconstruction*; Du Bois, *Color and Democracy*; James, *Black Jacobins*; Padmore, *Pan-Africanism or Communism?* Marx did not theorize race, but there is evidence that he recognized how racial slavery operated to inhibit solidarity between workers and maintain the power of the capitalist class. In *Capital*, he wrote, "Labour in a white skin cannot emancipate itself where it is branded in a black skin" (414).

44. Fanon, *Wretched of the Earth*, 107–10; James, "Case for West Indian Self-Government," in *Life of Captain Cipriani*, 171–72.

45. Cabral, "The Weapon of Theory"; Fanon, *Wretched of the Earth*, 97–144; Nkrumah, *Neo-Colonialism*; James, "West Indian Middle Classes"; Rodney, "Contemporary

Political Trends"; Rodney, *How Europe Underdeveloped Africa*; see also Marable, *How Capitalism Underdeveloped Black America*.

46. Du Bois, *Black Reconstruction*, 700; see also Du Bois, "Class Struggle," and Padmore, *Life and Struggles*.

47. Du Bois, *World and Africa*, 27.

48. Cox, *Capitalism as a System*, 195. See also Rodney, *How Europe Underdeveloped Africa*, 176–77.

49. James, "West Indian Middle Classes," 256.

50. Du Bois, *Black Reconstruction*; James, *Black Jacobins*; James, *History of Pan-African Revolt*; Fick, *Making of Haiti*.

51. Rodney, *Decolonial Marxism*, 30.

52. Combahee River Collective, "Black Feminist Statement"; A. Davis, "Reflections"; Jones, *End to the Neglect*; Thompson, "Toward a Brighter Dawn." Intersectionality (Crenshaw, "Demarginalizing the Intersection of Race and Sex" and "Mapping the Margins"; Hill-Collins, *Intersectionality as Critical Social Theory*) is currently the dominant framework through which to study race-class-gender oppression and mobilization in the social sciences, but it is not the only one. In this book, I draw on the political economy approach to the integrated study of race, class, and gender as developed by Louise Thompson Patterson, Claudia Jones, Angela Davis, Andaiye, and other Black radical feminists. There are important shared ambitions and affinities between the two traditions—namely, a critique of racism and patriarchy. The political economy tradition, however, includes a critique of capitalist imperialism and centers the racialized and gendered superexploitative relations of production and reproduction that enable accumulation via the labors and bodies of people categorized as Black women. For more detailed discussions of the two approaches, see Edwards, "Beyond Intersectionality"; Burden-Stelly and Dean, *Organize, Fight, WIN*; Carole Davies, *Left of Karl Marx*; and C. Davies and Burden-Stelly, "Claudia Jones Research and Collections."

53. Fanon, *Wretched of the Earth*, 238; Rodney, *How Europe Underdeveloped Africa*, 17; see also Du Bois, *Dusk of Dawn*, 155.

54. Fanon, *Wretched of the Earth*, 238–39.

55. Du Bois, *Black Reconstruction*, 345.

56. James, *Every Cook Can Govern*. James also seemed to envision direct democracy coexisting with state power. See Quest, "'Every Cook Can Govern.'"

57. Meeks and Girvan, *Thought of New World*, 7.

58. Evans, *Dependent Development*.

59. Arrighi, "Development Illusion"; Bissessar and Hosein, "Role of the State"; Silver, "Contradictions of Semiperipheral Success."

60. Adams et al., *Remaking Modernity*; Aminzade, "Historical Sociology and Time"; Lange, *Comparative-Historical Methods*; Mahoney and Rueschemeyer, *Comparative Historical Analysis*.

61. Bhambra, *Connected Sociologies*; Boatcă, *Global Inequalities Beyond Occidentalism*; Go, *Postcolonial Thought*; Go and Lawson, *Global Historical Sociology*; Hammer and White, "Sociology of Colonial Subjectivity"; Itzigsohn and Brown, *Sociology of W. E. B.*

Du Bois; Magubane, "Overlapping Territories and Intertwined Histories"; Meghji, *Decolonizing Sociology*; Silver, *Forces of Labor.*

62. Goldfield, *Decline of Organized Labor*; Hattam, *Labor Visions.*

63. Caswell Johnson, "Emergence of Political Unionism"; Lambert, "Political Unionism"; Scipes, "Social Movement Unionism"; Seidman, *Manufacturing Militance*; Webster, "Rise of Social-Movement Unionism."

64. Basualdo, "Labor and Structural Change"; Bergquist, *Labor in Latin America*; Heller, *Labor of Development*; Jung, *Reworking Race*; Kelley, *Hammer and Hoe*; Seidman, *Manufacturing Militance*; Goldfield, *Southern Key*; Zeitlin and Weyher, "'Black and White.'"

65. Goldfield, *Decline of Organized Labor.*

66. Mahoney, "Comparative-Historical Analysis."

CHAPTER I. PROLETARIANIZATION, RACE MAKING,
AND CAPITAL ACCUMULATION, 1498–1914

1. Boomert, *Indigenous Peoples*, 88–103, 115.

2. F. Knight, *General History*; Mintz, *Three Ancient Colonies.*

3. By now it is widely acknowledged that attending to these dynamics corrects the methodological deficiencies common in so-called classic studies of working-class formation, such as E. P. Thompson's *Making of the English Working Class* and Eric Hobsbawm's *Labouring Men.* For just one example of this critique and a corrective, see Virdee, *Racism, Class and the Racialized Outsider.*

4. Loveman, "Is 'Race' Essential?"; Wimmer, "Race-Centrism"; Bonilla-Silva, "Essential Social Fact of Race"; Winant, "Race, Ethnicity."

5. Bashi, *Ethnic Project*, 10.

6. Braithwaite, "Social Stratification in Trinidad," 75; K. Singh, *Race and Class Struggles*, xx–xxi; Segal, "'Race' and 'Colour'"; Reddock, "Competing Victimhoods."

7. I refrain from using quotation marks around the various terms for racial groups so as not to interrupt the flow of the argument, but I do maintain that these and other races are socially constructed, not natural, categories.

8. There have been turns within contemporary African American racial politics and among Indian diaspora intellectuals to reclaim and redefine these respective terms. See, for example, Carter and Torabully, *Coolitude*; and Kennedy, "Who Can Say 'Nigger'?" However, both in the time period under analysis in this book and in contemporary Trinidad and Tobago, these terms are harmful racial epithets, and no such politically salient counterdiscursive movements have emerged at the grassroots level.

9. Brereton, *History of Modern Trinidad*, 96–115; Ryan, *Race and Nationalism*, 18–27.

10. On the effect of changes in the organization of production, see Bendix, *Nation-Building and Citizenship*; Heller, *Labor of Development*; Hung, "Labor Politics"; Seidman, *Manufacturing Militance*; and Rueschemeyer et al., *Capitalist Development and Democracy*; see also Tilly and Tilly, *Class Conflict.* On the effects of state repression, see Collier and Collier, *Shaping the Political Arena*; Deyo, *Beneath the Miracle*; and Jenkins and Perrow, "Insurgency of the Powerless"; see also Davenport, "State Repression"; Tarrow, *Power*

in Movement; Tilly, *From Mobilization to Revolution*. On economic conditions as catalysts, see Bergquist, *Labor in Latin America*; Seidman, *Manufacturing Militance*.

11. See also Bender and Lipman, *Making the Empire Work*; Casey, *Empire's Guestworkers*; Fink and Greene, "Builders of Empire"; Goldthree, "Greater Enterprise"; and M. Kale, *Fragments of Empire*.

12. Wynter, "1492." *First Peoples* emerged more recently as a self-identifying label. Forte, "Carib Identity," 190.

13. Forte, "Carib Identity," 176–79; Forte, "Writing the Caribs Out," 15–17, 25.

14. Boomert, *Indigenous Peoples*, 83–88, 103; Brereton, *History of Modern Trinidad*, 6, 15; Williams, *History of the People*, 2–5. Despite ongoing narratives of the extinction of Indigenous people in Trinidad and Tobago, Carib identity has been resilient, and there is a vibrant self-identified and nationally recognized Carib population today. For more, see Forte, "Carib Identity."

15. Williams, *History of the People*, 74.

16. Forte, "Writing the Caribs Out," 26.

17. Boomert, *Indigenous Peoples*, 151–53.

18. Brereton, *History of Modern Trinidad*, 88–95.

19. Khan, "What Is 'a Spanish'?"

20. Trinbago is a portmanteau of Trinidad and Tobago that became popular after independence.

21. Reddock, "Competing Victimhoods"; K. Singh, *Race and Class Struggles*.

22. M. John, *Plantation Slaves of Trinidad*, 12–14; Millette, *Genesis of Crown Colony Government*, 24. In Tobago, which was under French colonial rule in the early 1780s, the French used similar incentives to attract plantation owners.

23. C. Campbell, "Rise of a Free Coloured Plantocracy," 39. In Tobago the enslaved African population increased from 4,716 (plus 125 maroons) in 1771 to 14,170 in 1790. See Williams, *History of the People*, 58.

24. Millette, *Genesis of Crown Colony Government*, 80; Titus, *Amelioration and Abolition*, xv; Williams, *History of the People*, 86–101. The labor shortage argument was very successful in enabling enslavers in Trinidad to win higher compensation rates per enslaved person from the British government at emancipation than in many other colonies.

25. Brereton, *History of Modern Trinidad*, 45; C. Campbell, "Rise of a Free Coloured Plantocracy," 49.

26. Williams, *History of the People*, 67, 74–75.

27. Higman, *Slave Populations*, 159.

28. Brereton, *History of Modern Trinidad*, 55; Reddock, *Women, Labour and Politics*, 78–79.

29. Higman, *Slave Populations*, 310.

30. M. John, *Plantation Slaves of Trinidad*, 119; Williams, *History of the People*, 102–21.

31. M. John, *Plantation Slaves of Trinidad*, 103.

32. A. Davis, "Reflections"; Jones, *End to the Neglect*; Reddock, "Women and Slavery"; Reddock, *Women, Labour and Politics*, 16–27.

33. Brereton, *History of Modern Trinidad*, 61; Reddock, "Women and Slavery"; Trotman, "Women and Crime."

34. Reddock, *Women, Labour and Politics*, 16–17.

35. Cudjoe, *Slave Master of Trinidad*, 27–28, 32–33, 42–43, 89, 116; M. John, *Plantation Slaves of Trinidad*, 101.

36. Cox, *Caste, Class, and Race*; Williams, *Capitalism and Slavery*; Wynter, "1492."

37. Cudjoe, *Slave Master of Trinidad*, xvi, 76.

38. Quoted in M. Kale, *Fragments of Empire*, 46.

39. Quoted in Cudjoe, *Slave Master of Trinidad*, 113.

40. Brereton, *History of Modern Trinidad*, 77–79, 133; M. Kale, *Fragments of Empire*, 48–49; Trotman, *Crime in Trinidad*, 137–38.

41. Richardson, "Caribbean Migrations," 206.

42. Beginning in 1882, with depressed sugar prices and subsequent restructuring of production, African and Indian cane farmers could buy or lease land to grow and sell cane to sugar factories. Brereton, *History of Modern Trinidad*, 80–81, 86.

43. Brereton, *History of Modern Trinidad*, 80–81.

44. British High Commission Port of Spain to Secretary of State Foreign and Commonwealth Office, appendix to dispatch 12/1, "Oil and Natural Gas in Trinidad," October 28, 1971, The National Archives (TNA), Foreign and Commonwealth Office (FCO) 63/871; see also Holland, "Oil Industry of Trinidad: Report by Sir Thomas Holland" (Holland Report), 1928, 3, TNA, Ministry of Power and of related bodies (POWE) 33/397.

45. Higgins, *History of Trinidad Oil*, 35, 217, 403; Colony of Trinidad and Tobago, *Blue Book 1939*, 677–81, National Archives of Trinidad and Tobago (NATT).

46. Colony of Trinidad and Tobago, *Mines Department Administrative Report of the Inspector of Mines for the Year 1913–1914*, 6; Colony of Trinidad and Tobago, *Mines Department Administrative Report of the Inspector of Mines for the Year 1930*, 7.

47. Olivier, *Report of the West India Sugar Commission 1929–30*, 105.

48. Bergquist, *Labor in Latin America*, 210.

49. Besson, "Black Gold, the Real El Dorado," 22–24; Brereton, *History of Modern Trinidad*, 201–3; O'Connor, *Some Trinidad Yesteryears*, 86–88.

50. O'Connor, *Some Trinidad Yesteryears*, 84, 86.

51. M. Thomas, *Violence and Colonial Order*, 241.

52. Brereton, *Race Relations*, 112–14.

53. On Trinidad's attractiveness, see Richardson, "Caribbean Migrations," 206.

54. Brereton, *Race Relations*, 112–14.

55. Brereton, *History of Modern Trinidad*, 96–97.

56. Brereton, *Race Relations*, 130; see also Teelucksingh, *Labour*, 111–12.

57. Colonial officials and local academics and laypeople also use the term *East Indian*, but historically this term has been used "to deny the assimilability of the 'Indian,'" according to Viranjini Munasinghe. Munasinghe, *Callaloo or Tossed Salad*, 253.

58. M. Kale, *Fragments of Empire*, 48; Williams, *History of the People*, 85.

59. Cudjoe, *Slave Master of Trinidad*, 143–49.

60. Brereton, *History of Modern Trinidad*, 97–98; Williams, *History of the People*, 76.

61. Williams, *History of the People*, 74–75, 76. The indenture system for the Europeans was one year of service, and contracts were not enforceable under normal law of contract.

For the Indians who came later, indentureship involved five-year contracts enforceable by criminal law.

62. Quoted in Cudjoe, *Slave Master of Trinidad*, 91.

63. Quoted in Lowe, *Intimacies of Four Continents*, 30–31.

64. Quoted in Lowe, *Intimacies of Four Continents*, 24.

65. M. Kale, *Fragments of Empire*, 46–47; Williams, *History of the People*, 76–77, 86–101.

66. Williams, *History of the People*, 110–12.

67. Williams, *History of the People*, 111.

68. Cited in Cudjoe, *Slave Master of Trinidad*, 18.

69. Brereton, *History of Modern Trinidad*, 103.

70. Jha, "Indian Heritage in Trinidad," 29–30, 42.

71. Jayaram, "Metamorphosis of Caste," 46. Narayana Jayaram also notes that the colonial authorities did not keep robust records and that "caste passing" and name changes at the time of recruitment were common, as people would try to pass themselves off as of higher caste and, in some cases, of lower caste.

72. Jha, "Indian Heritage in Trinidad," 42.

73. Jayaram, "Dynamics of Language," 42–45.

74. Ambedkar, "Castes in India"; Cox, *Caste, Class, and Race*.

75. Jayaram, "Metamorphosis of Caste," 148–50.

76. Haraksingh, "Control and Resistance," 9.

77. Reddock, "Freedom Denied," ws85–86. From 1871 to 1891, there were about 2,100 men to every 1,000 women; from 1901 to 1911, it was about 3,000 men to every 1,000 women.

78. Vertovec, "'Official' and 'Popular' Hinduism," 135.

79. Jayaram, "Metamorphosis of Caste," 169.

80. Williams, *History of the People*, 99–100.

81. Brereton, *History of Modern Trinidad*, 110–15.

82. Brereton, *History of Modern Trinidad*, 113.

83. Brereton, *History of Modern Trinidad*, 113; Ryan, *Race and Nationalism*, 23.

84. Governor Lord Harris, quoted in Williams, *History of the People*, 111.

85. Besson, "Black Gold, Part 2," 45, 47–50; Williams, *Inward Hunger*, 17–19.

86. Williams, *History of the People*, 102–21; Williams, *Inward Hunger*, 16–21.

87. Mohammed, *Gender Negotiations Among Indians in Trinidad*, 105–6; Reddock, "Freedom Denied," ws83; Reddock, *Women, Labour and Politics*, 36–38, 74–75, 84; Brereton, *History of Modern Trinidad*, 61.

88. Teelucksingh, *Labour*, 89–94.

89. Brereton, "Historical Background"; Trotman, *Crime in Trinidad*.

90. Haraksingh, "Control and Resistance," 2.

91. Brereton, *History of Modern Trinidad*, 88–95, 105–6.

92. K. Singh, *Race and Class Struggles*, 78.

93. C. Campbell, "Rise of a Free Coloured Plantocracy," 39n26. Population records for 1765 show 1,277 (Indigenous) Indians, 401 whites, 608 coloreds, and 217 slaves (for a total of 2,503).

94. C. Campbell, "Rise of a Free Coloured Plantocracy," 47, 49–50.

95. Brereton, *History of Modern Trinidad*, 30.

96. Williams, *History of the People*, 72.

97. Brereton, *Race Relations*, 90.

98. Brereton, *Race Relations*, 34; Millette, *Genesis of Crown Colony Government*, 32.

99. Ferreira, "Madeiran Portuguese Migration," 78–80; Look Lai, *Chinese in the West Indies*, 15; Williams, *History of the People*, 76.

100. Up until the census of 1960, Portuguese appears as a separate ethnic group, after which they were incorporated as whites.

101. Brereton, *Race Relations*, 90; K. Singh, "Conflict and Collaboration," 230.

102. K. Singh, "Conflict and Collaboration," 231–32.

103. Brereton, *History of Modern Trinidad*, 129–30; Brereton, *Race Relations*, 100–101; K. Singh, "Conflict and Collaboration," 241.

104. Cabral, "Weapon of Theory"; Fanon, *Wretched of the Earth*; James, "West Indian Middle Classes"; Rodney, "Contemporary Political Trends." Following Cabral and Rodney, *petty bourgeoisie* in this book refers to educated professionals, state administrators, military/police officials, and small-scale entrepreneurs who are dependent on international capital; the term is used interchangeably with *middle strata* and *middle class* in the Caribbean and African contexts.

105. Brereton, *Race Relations*, 94; James, *Life of Captain Cipriani*, 15; K. Singh, "Conflict and Collaboration," 236.

106. James, "West Indian Middle Classes," 250.

107. MacDonald, *Trinidad and Tobago*, 146.

108. Brereton, *Race Relations,* 33–34.

109. Brereton, *Race Relations*, 37–47; Williams, *History of the People*, 47.

110. Brereton, *Race Relations*, 37–47.

111. Brereton, *History of Modern Trinidad*, 116–19, 122.

112. Ramdin, *From Chattel Slave*, 55.

113. O'Connor, *Some Trinidad Yesteryears*, 82–86.

114. Higgins, *History of Trinidad Oil*, 219–20.

115. Rennie, *History of the Working-Class*, 91; Teelucksingh, *Labour*, 108.

116. Bergquist, *Labor in Latin America*, 218; Brereton, *History of Modern Trinidad*, 204.

117. Chatterjee, *Nation and Its Fragments*, 10.

118. Brereton, *History of Modern Trinidad*, 4, 9–10, 20; Millette, *Genesis of Crown Colony Government*, 57; Williams, *History of the People*, 40–50, 68.

119. Millette, "Civil Commission of 1802," 30, 33–34; Millette, *Genesis of Crown Colony Government*, 39, 49, 53.

120. The population included 1,082 Amerindians, 10,009 enslaved people, 4,466 free coloreds, and 2,086 whites (for a total of 17,643). Williams, *History of the People*, 47; see also Millette, *Genesis of Crown Colony Government*, 25.

121. C. Campbell, "Rise of a Free Coloured Plantocracy," 39, 47, 49–50.

122. Picton (1802), quoted in Williams, *History of the People*, 69.

123. Williams, *History of the People*, 72.

124. The legislature consisted of the governor as head, six official members (the chief justice, the colonial secretary, the attorney general, the colonial treasurer, the protector of slaves, and the collector of customs) and six unofficial members selected by the governor from the principal proprietors of the colony. The Executive Council comprised the governor as head, the colonial secretary, the attorney general, and the colonial treasurer.

125. Brereton, *Race Relations*, 24–33.

126. Millette, *Genesis of Crown Colony Government*; A. Robinson, *Mechanics of Independence*, 9–10.

127. Cudjoe, *Slave Master of Trinidad*, 14–15.

128. On punishments, see Great Britain Colonial Office, *Trinidad and Tobago Report on the Blue Book for 1914–15*, TNA, CO 295/499/44; *Trinidad and Tobago Blue Book 1919*, NATT; *Trinidad and Tobago Blue Book 1935*, NATT; Millette, *Genesis of Crown Colony Government*, 55–63. On workers' understanding of state-elite collaboration, see Williams, *History of the People*, 88.

129. Brereton, *Race Relations*, 33.

130. Millette, *Genesis of Crown Colony Government*, 5–6, 45–47.

131. C. Campbell, *Young Colonials*, 11.

132. *Report of the West India Royal Commission* (1897), TNA, CO 137/584/15; Thomas Sanderson, *Report of the Committee on Emigration from India to the Crown Colonies and Protectorates, 1910* (Sanderson Report), India Office Records and Library, British Library (BL), IOR/L/PJ/6/885, File 2876; Great Britain, *Report of the Sugar Industry of The West Indies and British Guiana (West Indian Sugar Commission, 1929–30)*; *Trinidad and Tobago Disturbances 1937 Report of Commission* (Forster Report), TNA, CO 295/601/2.

133. C. Campbell, *Young Colonials*, 1–6, 29–48.

134. Great Britain Colonial Office, *Trinidad and Tobago Report on the Blue Book for 1914–15*, 16-17.

135. Brereton, *History of Modern Trinidad*, 122–27; C. Campbell, *Young Colonials*, 48–55.

136. Higman, *Slave Populations*, 260–62, 266; Jacklin, "British Colonial Healthcare," 82, 120–38.

137. Craig, *Community Development*, 174; Jacklin, "British Colonial Healthcare," 8, 86, 90–92.

138. Jacklin, "British Colonial Healthcare," 86.

139. C. Campbell, *Young Colonials*, 74.

140. Brereton, *History of Modern Trinidad*, 146–48; MacDonald, *Trinidad and Tobago*, 37–38; A. Robinson, *Mechanics of Independence*, 25–26.

141. Best, "Outlines of a Model"; Rodney, *History*, 19.

142. Brereton, *History of Modern Trinidad*, 82–88; Rodney, *History*, 20–21.

143. Brereton, *History of Modern Trinidad*, 106–7; Reddock, *Women, Labour and Politics*, 37–39.

144. Rodney, *History*, 25.

145. Brereton, *History of Modern Trinidad*, 82–83.

146. Jung, *Reworking Race*, 11–54; Kimeldorf, *Reds or Rackets*, 57–60.

147. M. John, *Plantation Slaves of Trinidad*, 17.

148. Brereton, *Race Relations*, 48.

149. Wood, *Trinidad in Transition*, 295.

150. Brereton, *History of Modern Trinidad*, 88–95.

151. Lans, "Plant-Based Traditions," 1429. Trinidad lost its position in 1921 due to a crop disease, the Great Depression, and the rise of West African cacao production.

152. Arrighi, *Long Twentieth Century*; Horne, *Apocalypse of Settler Colonialism*; Modelski and Thompson, *Seapower in Global Politics*; D. Spence, *Colonial Naval Culture*; Wallerstein, *Modern World-System III*.

153. W. Brown, "Royal Navy's Fuel Supplies," 41–42; Podobnik, *Global Energy Shifts*, 65–66.

154. W. Brown, "Royal Navy's Fuel Supplies," 49.

155. W. Brown, "Royal Navy's Fuel Supplies," 54.

156. Colin Davies, "British Oil Policy," 5–7.

157. Quoted in W. Brown, "Royal Navy's Fuel Supplies," 68.

158. Colony of Trinidad and Tobago, *Mines Department: Report of the Inspector of the Mines for the Year 1914–1915*, 4.

159. Holland Report, 4, 14, 16.

160. *Petroleum World* 12, no. 172 (1915): 18.

161. Waring, *Geology of the Island*, 157.

162. Higgins, *History of Trinidad Oil*, 184; Holland Report, 3.

163. Besson, "Black Gold, Part 2," 56.

164. Amin, "Imperialism and Globalization"; Amuzegar, *Managing the Oil Wealth*, 12; Paone, "Strategic Raw Materials"; Roush, "Strategic Mineral Supplies."

165. Bergquist, *Labor in Latin America*; Rodney, *How Europe Underdeveloped Africa*, 31; Silver, *Forces of Labor*.

166. J. Scott, *Weapons of the Weak*. See also Brereton, "Resistance to Enslavement"; Mahase, "'Plenty a Dem Run Away.'"

167. Brereton, "Resistance to Enslavement"; Cudjoe, *Slave Master of Trinidad*, 249–55.

168. L. Fletcher, "Politics, Public Policy."

169. K. Singh, "Conflict and Collaboration," 232.

170. Quoted in Samaroo and Girvan, "Trinidad Workingmen's Association," 212.

171. Samaroo and Girvan, "Trinidad Workingmen's Association," 207; Teelucksingh, *Labour*, 22–28.

172. Jung, *Reworking Race*, 60.

173. Rodney, *Decolonial Marxism*, 15.

CHAPTER 2. THE 1919 UPRISING AND THE EMERGENCE OF LIBERATION UNIONISM

1. *Trinidad Guardian* (*TG*), December 2, 1919, NATT.

2. *TG*, November 15, 1919; see also Elkins, "Black Power," 74.

3. Governor John Chancellor to Secretary of State for the Colonies (SOSC) Alfred Milner, secret dispatch, December 7, 1919, TNA, CO 295/523; *TG*, November 28, 1919.

4. Governor Chancellor to SOSC Milner, secret dispatch, December 7, 1919; *TG*, November 18, 1919; *TG*, November 19, 1919; *TG*, November 20, 1919; *TG*, November 21, 1919; *TG*, November 23, 1919.

5. *TG*, December 2, 1919; *TG*, December 3, 1919.

6. James, *History of Pan-African Revolt*, 98.

7. *TG*, December 3, 1919.

8. Governor Chancellor to SOSC Milner, secret dispatch, December 7, 1919.

9. Silver, *Forces of Labor*, 125.

10. Arrighi and Silver, "Labor Movements"; Bergquist, *Labor in Latin America*; Cooper, *Decolonization and African Society*; Jung, *Reworking Race*; Silver, *Forces of Labor*.

11. Katznelson, "Working-Class Formation," 17–20; Somers, "Narrativity."

12. Goldfield, *Decline of Organized Labor*; Hattam, *Labor Visions*; Moody, *Injury to All*.

13. Lambert and Webster, "Re-Emergence of Political Unionism"; Caswell Johnson, "Emergence of Political Unionism."

14. B. Fletcher and Gapasin, *Solidarity Divided*; Scipes, "Understanding the New Labor Movements"; Seidman, *Manufacturing Militance*; Webster, "Rise of Social-Movement Unionism."

15. Dawson, *Black Visions*; Fredrickson, *Black Liberation*; Jordan-Zachery, "Let Men Be Men"; Kelley, *Freedom Dreams*; Marable, *Black Liberation*; L. Spence et al., "True to Our Native Land."

16. Dawson, *Black Visions*, 2.

17. Great Britain Colonial Office, *Trinidad and Tobago Annual General Report for the Year 1918*, TNA, CO 295/522, 14.

18. Great Britain Colonial Office, *Trinidad and Tobago Annual General Report for the Year 1918*, 5.

19. Great Britain Colonial Office, *Trinidad and Tobago Annual General Report for the Year 1918*, 9–11.

20. Mercer, Collins, and Harding, *Colonial Office List for 1920*, 406.

21. Great Britain Colonial Office, *Trinidad and Tobago Report on the Blue Book for 1914–15*, 14, TNA, CO 295/499/44; Great Britain Colonial Office, *Trinidad and Tobago Annual General Report for the Year 1918*, 15, 19.

22. Owen, *Trek of the Oil Finders*, 1012.

23. Great Britain Colonial Office, *Trinidad and Tobago Annual General Report for the Year 1918*, 19.

24. K. Singh, *Race and Class Struggles*, 15.

25. Great Britain Colonial Office, *Trinidad and Tobago Annual General Report for the Year 1918*, 6.

26. Great Britain Colonial Office, *Trinidad and Tobago Annual General Report for the Year 1918*, 6.

27. Governor Chancellor to SOSC Milner, secret dispatch, December 7, 1919.

28. On soldiers' treatment, see Elkins, "Black Power"; *TG*, December 7, 1919. On the lack of remuneration and benefits, see Ramdin, *From Chattel Slave*, 54–55. European and Euro-creoles from Trinidad and Tobago were accepted into the British forces as officers, while nonwhite subjects had to join the separate British West Indies Regiment.

29. Brereton, *History of Modern Trinidad*, 159. Indentured laborers still on contracts had to serve out the duration of their term.

30. Habitual Idlers' Ordinance 1918, 1, TNA, CO 295/516/66.

31. McAdam et al., *Comparative Perspectives*, 6.

32. Samaroo and Girvan, "Trinidad Workingmen's Association," 211.

33. Samaroo and Girvan, "Trinidad Workingmen's Association," 213; Teelucksingh, *Labour*, 33.

34. Samaroo and Girvan, "Trinidad Workingmen's Association," 211.

35. Teelucksingh, *Labour*, 12–13.

36. Ramdin, *From Chattel Slave*, 46–47, 52.

37. Teelucksingh, *Labour*, 32–33.

38. Samaroo and Girvan, "Trinidad Workingmen's Association," 213; Teelucksingh, *Labour*, 33.

39. Bergquist, *Labor in Latin America*; T. Mitchell, *Carbon Democracy*; Rodney, "Class Contradictions in Tanzania"; Silver, *Forces of Labor*; Wright, "Working-Class Power."

40. Governor Chancellor to SOSC Milner, January 21, 1920, confidential dispatch, CO 295/526; *TG*, December 2, 1919.

41. K. Singh, *Race and Class Struggles*, 30–32; *TG*, November 25, 1919; *TG*, December 2, 1919; *TG*, December 11, 1919.

42. *TG*, December 2, 1919.

43. *TG*, November 22, 1919; *TG*, December 2, 1919; *TG*, December 10, 1919. See also Ramdin, *From Chattel Slave*, 58, 60.

44. *TG*, December 4, 1919; *TG*, December 5, 1919; *TG*, December 20, 1919; *TG*, December 21, 1919.

45. K. Singh, *Race and Class Struggles*, 27.

46. *TG*, November 25, 1919, 6.

47. *TG*, December 4, 1919.

48. Ramdin, *From Chattel Slave*, 61. One newspaper reported that the acting secretary of the TWA testified that the dockworkers had resolved to strike of their own accord independently of the TWA and that the TWA was simply playing a supportive role. See *TG*, December 3, 1919.

49. Ramdin, *From Chattel Slave*, 44, 48–54.

50. *TG*, December 4, 1919.

51. K. Singh, *Race and Class Struggles*, 132.

52. Ramdin, *From Chattel Slave*, 44, 53.

53. *The People* (*TP*), April 15, 1933. Estimates vary widely according to different sources.

54. K. Singh, *Race and Class Struggles*, 133.

55. Kelley, "Building Bridges," 43.

56. Petition and resolutions for the repeal of the ordinance submitted to SOSC Milner by the TWA (passed May 9, 1919), Manzanilla Literary and Debating Club (passed June 23, 1919), and Sangre Grande Mutual Help Friendly Society (passed June 16, 1919), CO 295/523.

57. *TP*, August 4, 1934, 2.

58. K. Singh, *Race and Class Struggles*, 27.

59. *TG*, December 5, 1919.

60. Jung, *Reworking Race*, 3.

61. Cabral, "Weapon of Theory."

62. K. Singh, *Race and Class Struggles*, 31.

63. *TG*, December 4, 1919.

64. Kissoon, "'Creole Indian,'" 184.

65. Samaroo, *Adrian Cola Rienzi*, 1–5.

66. Kissoon, "'Creole Indian,'" 237n81; K. Singh, "Adrian Cola Rienzi," 12; *TP*, August 2, 1934; *TP*, August 11, 1934.

67. Kissoon, "'Creole Indian,'" 184–85, 188.

68. Kissoon, "'Creole Indian,'" 184.

69. James, *Life of Captain Cipriani*; Teelucksingh, *Labour*, 38.

70. *TG*, November 19, 1919; *TG*, November 23, 1919.

71. *TG*, November 20, 1919.

72. A. Davis, "Reflections"; Joseph-Gabriel, *Reimagining Liberation*; Keisha-Khan Perry, *Black Women*.

73. Rennie, *History of the Working-Class*, 6; *TG*, November 25, 1919.

74. Reddock, *Women, Labour and Politics*, 149, 151–52.

75. *TG*, December 4, 1919.

76. *Port of Spain Gazette* (*POSG*), December 12, 1919, 7.

77. District Medical Officer Sgd. E. Hamil Smith, Sub-enclosure to Enclosure No. 1 in confidential dispatch, January 24, 1920, report, December 9, 1919, TNA, CO 295/526.

78. *TG*, December 10, 1919.

79. *TG*, December 31, 1919.

80. "Triple exploitation" is from Thompson, "Toward a Brighter Dawn"; "triple oppression" is from Jones, *End to the Neglect*. See also A. Davis, "Reflections."

81. Jones, *End to the Neglect*.

82. Reddock, *Women, Labour and Politics*, 122.

83. On their concern for working-class issues, see *TP*, May 18, 1935, 7, 10. On their concern for imprisoned women, see *TP*, October 21, 1933, 7.

84. Enclosure VII in Trinidad secret dispatch, March 13, 1920, TNA, CO 295/527.

85. *TP*, July 29, 1933; *TP*, March 30, 1935, 10; *TP*, May 25, 1935; Reddock, *Women, Labour and Politics*, 123, 126; K. Singh, *Race and Class Struggles*, 133.

86. *TP*, May 6, 1933, 6; *TP*, May 5, 1934, 1, 6, 7.

87. On the founding, see *TP*, February 2, 1935, 10. On the leadership, see *TP*, April 6, 1935, 5. On events organized, see *TP*, July 27, 1935.

88. *TG*, December 4, 1919.

89. Jung, *Reworking Race*; Padmore, *Voice of Colored Labor*; Padmore, *Life and Struggles*; Waterman, "Trade Union Internationalism." The term *Black internationalism*, according to Michael Oliver West and William Martin in "Contours of the Black International," is the "conscious interconnection and interlocution of black struggles across man-made and natural boundaries" (1). Garvey's Pan-Africanism, the Pan-African Congresses, Black Bolshevism, and the Rastafari movement are some of the different political formations within Black internationalism. For more, see Bedasse et al., "*AHR*

Conversation"; Burden-Stelly and Horne, "From Pan-Africanism"; and Makalani, *Cause of Freedom*.

90. Adi, *Pan-Africanism*; Heller, *Labor of Development*; Jung, *Reworking Race*; Seidman, *Manufacturing Militance*.

91. Stevens, *Red International*, 22, 146, 163–64.

92. Padmore, *Pan-Africanism or Communism?*

93. Teelucksingh, *Labour*, 20.

94. Adi, *Pan-Africanism*; H. Campbell, *Rasta and Resistance*; H. Campbell and Worrell, *Pan-Africanism*; Du Bois, *World and Africa*; Padmore, *Pan-Africanism or Communism?*

95. James, *History of Pan-African Revolt*, 92; Martin, *Marcus Garvey, Hero*, 161.

96. Bolland, *Politics of Labour*, 155–211; Ewing, *Age of Garvey*, 30; Martin, *Marcus Garvey, Hero*, 27, 59, 71–72; Martin, *Pan-African Connection*, 47–57, 63–83.

97. Quoted in Worcester, *C. L. R. James*, 14.

98. Elkins, "Marcus Garvey," 70.

99. K. Singh, *Race and Class Struggles*, 21.

100. K. Singh, *Race and Class Struggles*, 21–22.

101. Quoted in Elkins, "Hercules," 56.

102. Quoted in K. Singh, *Race and Class Struggles*, 21–22.

103. Quoted in K. Singh, *Race and Class Struggles*, 22.

104. Garvey, "The Negro, Communism, Trade Unionism and His (?) Friend," 69–71.

105. Bolland, *Politics of Labour*; Burnett, "'Unity Is Strength'"; Ewing, "Caribbean Labour Politics"; Harpelle, "Cross Currents"; Post, *Arise Ye Starvelings*; Putnam, "Nothing Matters but Color"; West, "Seeds Are Sown."

106. Teelucksingh, *Ideology, Politics, and Radicalism*, 13, 21–23.

107. Hall, "Race, Articulation."

108. Jim Barratt, in an interview with Jim Barrett and Christina King, Oral and Pictorial Records Programme of the University of the West Indies, 1983, Alma Jordan Library, University of the West Indies (UWI), St. Augustine, Trinidad and Tobago, 36–37.

109. Governor Chancellor to SOSC Milner, Record of James Brathwaite, Enclosure VII in Trinidad secret dispatch, March 12, 1920, TNA, CO 295/527.

110. Teelucksingh, *Ideology, Politics, and Radicalism*, 26, 28.

111. Ewing, *Age of Garvey*, 76–77, 133–36; Martin, *Pan-African Connection*, 64.

112. Quoted in Ewing, *Age of Garvey*, 145.

113. Quoted in Ewing, *Age of Garvey*, 135.

114. Cited in Teelucksingh, *Ideology, Politics, and Radicalism*, 29.

115. Jung, *Reworking Race*.

116. Martin, *Pan-African Connection*, 63–87.

117. Hill, *Marcus Garvey and Universal Negro Improvement Association* [UNIA] *Papers*, 11:cclxv; Teelucksingh, *Ideology, Politics, and Radicalism*, 12.

118. Martin, *Pan-African Connection*, 65; Teelucksingh, *Ideology, Politics, and Radicalism*, 12, 16; *Labour Leader* (LL), December 30, 1922.

119. Ewing, "Caribbean Labour Politics," 30.

120. Hill, *Marcus Garvey and UNIA Papers* 11:cclxv; TP, August 4, 1934, 2.

121. McAdam et al., *Comparative Perspectives*; Morris, *Origins*.

122. Ramdin, *From Chattel Slave*, 64.

123. Governor Chancellor to SOSC Milner, secret dispatch, March 12, 1920, TNA, CO 295/527; see also Hill, *Marcus Garvey and UNIA Papers*, 11:616; Reddock, *Women, Labour and Politics*, 121–22; Teelucksingh, *Labour*, 28, 38.

124. Kissoon, "'Creole Indian,'" 182.

125. Record of Reverend E. Seiler Salmon, Enclosure VI in Trinidad secret dispatch, March 12, 1920, TNA, CO 295/527.

126. Record of Reverend E. Seiler Salmon, Enclosure VI in Trinidad secret dispatch, March 12, 1920. Preachers also played a role in helping to mobilize workers. See Ramdin, *From Chattel Slave*, 15.

127. Martin, *Pan-African Connection*, 47–57.

128. Samaroo, *Adrian Cola Rienzi*, 31–37.

129. Ramdin, *From Chattel Slave*, 53–54.

130. K. Singh, *Race and Class Struggles*, 47.

131. Teelucksingh, *Labour*, 71.

132. Ramdin, *From Chattel Slave*, 44.

133. *LL*, December 9, 1922.

134. Ramdin, *From Chattel Slave*, 43; Teelucksingh, *Labour*, 145–73.

135. *LL*, October 21, 1922; see also Reddock, *Women, Labour and Politics*, 124.

136. *LL*, September 2, 1922; *LL*, November 18, 1922; see also K. Singh, *Race and Class Struggles*, 142; *TP*, May 6, 1933, 6.

137. *LL*, September 16, 1922; *LL*, October 21, 1922.

138. *TP*, September 16, 1933, 11–12; *LL*, July 28, 1934, 9.

139. Inspector of Constabulary Harold de Pass, report, Enclosure III in Trinidad secret dispatch, March 12, 1920, December 28, 1919, TNA, CO 295/527.

140. Inspector General of Constabulary Sgd. G. H. May to Colonial Secretary in Trinidad William Gordon, report by Commandant of Local Forces, Enclosure No. 2 in Trinidad confidential dispatch, August 7, 1919; August 5, 1919, TNA, CO 295/522; George Huggins et al. (powerful white elites) to Trinidad and Tobago Colonial Secretary William Gordon, July 30, 1919, TNA, CO 295/522.

141. "Agitators from elsewhere" is from *TG*, December 7, 1919; see also Sub-Inspector Tobago Division H. Cavenaugh, report, December 8, 1919, TNA, CO 295/526, and Inspector General of Constabulary Sgd. G. H. May to Colonial Secretary in Trinidad William Gordon, report by Commandant of Local Forces, Enclosure No. 2 in Trinidad confidential dispatch, August 7, 1919; August 5, 1919. "Acute racial feelings stirred up by returned soldiers," is from a folio comment by a colonial official, December 8, 1919, TNA, CO 295/523. See also Governor Chancellor to SOSC Milner, secret dispatch, December 7, 1919; Huggins et al. to Trinidad and Tobago Colonial Secretary Gordon, July 30, 1919.

142. James, *Black Jacobins*, 95.

143. Allen, *Invention of the White Race*; Du Bois, *Black Reconstruction*; Fields, "Slavery, Race and Ideology"; Virdee, "Racialized Capitalism."

144. Huggins et al. to Trinidad and Tobago Colonial Secretary Gordon, July 30, 1919.

145. Acting Governor Gordon to SOSC Milner, secret dispatch, September 10, 1919, TNA, CO 295/522.

146. Acting Governor Gordon to SOSC Milner, secret dispatch, September 10, 1919.

147. Mercer and Collins, *Colonial Office List for 1919*, 396; C. B. Franklin, *Trinidad and Tobago Yearbook 1919*, 220–22, NATT.

148. Jung, *Reworking Race*.

149. *TG*, November 28, 1919.

150. Governor Chancellor to SOSC Milner, secret dispatch, December 7, 1919.

151. *TG*, November 26, 1919; Governor Chancellor to SOSC Milner, secret dispatch, December 7, 1919.

152. Jung, *Reworking Race*; Rueschemeyer et al., *Capitalist Development and Democracy*; Seidman, *Manufacturing Militance*; Vu, *Paths to Development*. See also Davenport, "State Repression"; Tarrow, *Power in Movement*.

153. Governor Chancellor to SOSC Milner, telegram, received December 6, 1919, TNA, CO 295/523.

154. Huggins et al. to Trinidad and Tobago Colonial Secretary, July 30, 1919.

155. Huggins et al. to Trinidad and Tobago Colonial Secretary, July 30, 1919.

156. *TG*, December 7, 1919.

157. *TG*, December 31, 1919; *TG*, February 7, 1920.

158. *TG*, December 7, 1919; *TG*, December 10, 1919, 8.

159. *TG*, November 2, 1919; Governor Chancellor to SOSC Milner, secret dispatch, December 7, 1919; Governor Chancellor to SOSC Milner, secret dispatch, February 28, 1920, CO 295/526. By December 10, 1919, the Merchants' and Planters' Contingent stood at 270 members. *TG*, December 11, 1919.

160. Governor Chancellor to SOSC Milner, telegram, received December 6, 1919; *TG*, November 2, 1919.

161. Ramdin, *From Chattel Slave*, 62.

162. Governor Chancellor to SOSC Milner, confidential dispatch, January 27, 1920, CO 295/526; Record of Sidney de Bourg (Enclosure IV) and Record of Bruce McConney (Enclosure V) in Trinidad secret dispatch, March 12, 1920, TNA, CO 295/527; Governor Chancellor to SOSC Milner, secret dispatch, March 12, 1920.

163. Solicitor General, L. H. Elphinstone, minutes, Enclosure I in Trinidad secret dispatch, March 12, 1920, February 27, 1920, TNA, CO 295/527; K. Singh, *Race and Class Struggles*, 33–36.

164. Governor Chancellor to SOSC Milner, secret dispatch, March 12, 1920.

165. James, *Black Jacobins*.

166. McAdam et al., *Comparative Perspectives*; Meyer, "Protest and Political Opportunities"; Tarrow, *Power in Movement*. See also Seidman, *Manufacturing Militance*.

167. Extract from the *Administration Report of the Inspector General for the Constabulary for 1918*, Sub-enclosure to Enclosure No. 2 in Trinidad confidential dispatch, August 7, 1919, TNA, CO 295/522. "Official" standards for "ideal" police-to-population ratios vary widely across the world. A comparison of colonial police officers (per 1,000) can be found in Lange, *Lineages of Despotism*, 48. Quantitatively, Trinidad had more colonial police officers (per 1,000 people) than places like Zimbabwe and Nigeria. Unsurpris-

ingly, the colonial police force numbers are higher precisely in the colonies where labor rebellions were more frequent. While quantitative information is insightful, the qualitative understandings of the strength of the police force by colonial officials and working people is valuable: they reveal how the perceptions (and later the reality) of the state's capacity to repress shaped both the opportunities that the working people seized and the anxieties and responses of the colonial state to the movement.

168. Inspector General of Constabulary Sgd. G. H. May to Colonial Secretary in Trinidad William Gordon, Enclosure No. 2 in Trinidad confidential dispatch, August 7, 1919; August 5, 1919.

169. Governor Chancellor to sosc Milner, telegram, received December 6, 1919.

170. Governor Chancellor to sosc Milner, secret dispatch, December 7, 1919. Note that the returned soldiers in Tobago were reported to have assisted the colonial government in maintaining order during the December 6 strike. Governor Chancellor to sosc Milner, confidential dispatch, January 24, 1920, co 295/526.

171. Committee of Imperial Defense, *Trinidad Local Forces Annual Inspection Report*, 1928, 5, TNA, Cabinet Office records (CAB) 9/19.

172. Committee of Imperial Defense, *Trinidad Local Forces Annual Inspection Report*, 1928, 1, 4, 2–5.

173. Committee of Imperial Defense, *Trinidad Local Forces Annual Inspection Report*, 1928, 3.

174. Committee of Imperial Defense, *Trinidad Local Forces Annual Inspection Report*, 1928, 4.

175. Committee of Imperial Defense, *Trinidad Local Forces Annual Inspection Report*, 1928, 6.

176. Oversea Subcommittee of the Committee of Imperial Defense, *Trinidad: Report on Inspection of Local Forces*, 1921, 7, TNA, CAB 9/19. Despite these problems and against the advice of the Oversea Subcommittee of the Committee of Imperial Defense in 1919, this body was re-created in 1920 under a new name—the Defense Reserve, also known as the Volunteer Reserve.

177. Inspector General of Constabulary Sgd. G. H. May to Colonial Secretary in Trinidad William Gordon, August 5, 1919.

178. Inspector General of Constabulary Sgd. G. H. May to Colonial Secretary in Trinidad William Gordon, August 5, 1919.

179. Inspector General of Constabulary Sgd. G. H. May to Colonial Secretary in Trinidad William Gordon, August 5, 1919.

180. Acting Governor Gordon to sosc Milner, confidential dispatch, August 7, 1919, TNA, CO 295/522.

181. Solicitor General L. H. Elphinstone, minutes, Enclosure I in Trinidad secret dispatch, March 12, 1920, February 27, 1920.

182. Colonial official, folio comments, June 26, 1920, TNA, CO 295/527.

183. Cox, *Capitalism as a System*, 196.

184. Mercer, Collins, and Robinson, *Colonial Office List for 1915*, xlviii.

185. W. Brown, "Royal Navy's Fuel Supplies," 168n64.

186. Colin Davies, "British Oil Policy," 16n1.

187. Still, the 1918 Imperial War Conference resulted in no common imperial policy on oil exploration in the colonies with respect to restrictions on non-British/British Empire companies, due to debates around whether imposing restrictions on non-British investors could be perceived as hostile and invite retaliatory actions, especially by the US government. W. Brown, "Royal Navy's Fuel Supplies," 176–77. While South Africa, Australia, New Zealand, and some parts of the British Caribbean had no restrictions on the development of Crown lands by non-British interests, and Nigeria, Somaliland, and Canada allowed both British and non-British capital, Trinidad, along with British Guiana and India, restricted entry to British capital only. Colin Davies, "British Oil Policy," 68.

188. Holland Report.

189. SOSC Milner to Governor Chancellor, telegram, December 16, 1919, CO 295/523.

190. Steinmetz, "Colonial State," 591–92.

191. Millette, *Genesis of Crown Colony Government*; Young, *African Colonial State*.

192. Rodney, *How Europe Underdeveloped Africa*, 31.

193. *LL*, December 30, 1922, 2.

194. Frederick Douglass, "The Significance of Emancipation in the West Indies: An Address Delivered in Canandaigua, New York, on August 3, 1857," Frederick Douglass Papers Project, accessed July 1, 2024, https://frederickdouglasspapersproject.com/s/digitaledition/item/10509.

195. Esping-Andersen, "Power and Distributional Regimes"; Korpi, *Democratic Class Struggle*; Panitch, "Trade Unions and the Capitalist State."

196. Heller, *Labor of Development*, 45.

197. *TG*, December 3, 1919. The workers had originally proposed a body consisting of four representatives of the workers and four of the shipping agents.

198. Governor Chancellor to SOSC Milner, secret dispatch, December 7, 1919.

199. Governor Chancellor to SOSC Milner, confidential dispatch, December 22, 1919, CO 295/523.

200. Governor Chancellor to SOSC Milner, confidential dispatch, December 22, 1919.

201. The committee ultimately recommended minimum wage rates with a sliding scale based on the cost of living. See Ramdin, *From Chattel Slave*, 62–63.

202. Teelucksingh, *Labour*, 94. Though most likely an undercount due to initial problems with monitoring and enforcement, eleven cases of child labor were prosecuted by 1929.

203. Governor Chancellor to SOSC Milner, secret dispatch, January 27, 1920; R. Thomas, *Development of Labour Law*, 4–5.

204. Reddock, *Women, Labour and Politics*, 127.

205. Reddock, *Women, Labour and Politics*, 128; Ramdin, *From Chattel Slave*, 73–74. The legislation was amended to include clerks, shop assistants, and agricultural workers (except those employed on less than thirty acres of land), and the maximum compensation was raised.

206. Teelucksingh, *Labour*, 102–4.

207. *LL*, October 21, 1922; see also K. Singh, *Race and Class Struggles*, 138–39.

208. Bissessar, "Difficulty of Protecting Merit," 74.

209. Great Britain Colonial Office, *Trinidad and Tobago Annual General Report for the Year 1918*, 22–23; Harding and Gent, *Dominions Office and Colonial Office List for 1938*, 483–84.

210. See C. Campbell, *Young Colonials*, 137.

211. In 1918 there were 596 teachers with certificates, almost all nonwhite, and 36.4 percent of them were women. C. Campbell, *Young Colonials*, 169.

212. Mercer, Collins, and Harding, *Colonial Office List for 1920*, 416–17; Harding and Gent, *Dominions Office and Colonial Office List for 1935*, 478–79.

213. Medical Board Council Secretary J. R. Dickson, "A Review of the Medical and Health Sections of the Report of the Commission on the Trinidad and Tobago Disturbances, 1937, by the Trinidad and Tobago Branch of the British Medical Association," July 30, 1930, TNA, CO 295/614/4.

214. B. Mitchell, *International Historical Statistics*, 84.

215. Great Britain Colonial Office, *Trinidad and Tobago Annual General Report for the Year 1918*, 9; Colony of Trinidad and Tobago, *Trinidad and Tobago Blue Book 1921*, 542–86, NATT.

216. Williams, *History of the People*, 219–20. Wood reviewed and made recommendations concerning the call for representative government in the British Caribbean colonies. In his report, Wood wrote that enacting this demand in Trinidad "is more difficult than in any other Colony" because of the significant diversity of races, ethnicities, and "public opinion" (22–23). He therefore advised against the communal system of representation that the EINC wanted and also objected to granting self-government. See *Report by the Hon. E. F. L. Wood, M. P. (Parliamentary Under Secretary of State for the Colonies) on His Visit to the West Indies and British Guiana December, 1921–February, 1922*, Alma Jordan Library, UWI, St. Augustine, Trinidad and Tobago.

217. Williams, *History of the People*, 218.

218. Williams, *History of the People*, 218.

219. Reddock, "Early Women's Movement," 106–10.

220. Vithayathil, *Counting Caste*, 7.

221. Governor Chancellor to SOSC Milner, secret dispatch, December 7, 1919.

222. Colonial official, folio comments, June 26, 1920.

223. Colonial official, folio comments, January 9, 1920, CO 295/523.

224. Governor Chancellor to SOSC Milner, confidential dispatch, January 26, 1920, CO 295/526.

225. Governor Chancellor to SOSC Milner, December 22, 1919.

226. Phillips, *Renegade Union*.

227. Burden-Stelly, *Black Scare/Red Scare*; Foner and Lewis, *Black Worker*, vol. 3; Gerteis, *Class*; Foner, "IWW"; Goldfield, *Southern Key*; Jung, *Reworking Race*; Kelly, *Hammer and Hoe*; Trotter, *Workers on Arrival*; Zeitlin and Weyher, "'Black and White.'" See also Geschwender, *Class, Race, and Worker Insurgency* on the League of Revolutionary Black Workers in the late 1960s.

CHAPTER 3. THE 1937 GENERAL STRIKE AND
THE DEEPENING OF LIBERATION UNIONISM

1. Ramdin, *From Chattel Slave*, 101–2; Rennie, *History of the Working-Class*, 110–12.

2. *POSG*, June 22, 1937, 6; *POSG*, June 23, 1937, 6; *POSG*, June 24, 1937, 6.

3. *POSG*, June 22, 1937, 6; *POSG*, June 23, 1937, 2, 6; *POSG*, June 26, 1937, 6.

4. General Secretary of the British Empire Workers and Citizens Home Rule Party (BEW&CHRP) Tubal Uriah Butler to Barrister Adrian Cola Rienzi, July 1, 1937, Enclosure 1 in Trinidad dispatch no. 384, July 5, 1937, TNA, CO 295/599/14. For Butler's original intentions for the strike, see BEW&CHRP General Secretary Butler to Apex Oilfields Ltd. Attorney Lt. Col. H. C. B. Hickling, June 2, 1937, published in Jacobs, *Butler Versus the King*, 222–23; BEW&CHRP General Secretary Butler to Governor, June 2, 1937, published in Jacobs, *Butler Versus the King*, 224–25; BEW&CHRP General Secretary Butler to General Manager of Trinidad Central Oilfields Ltd. and the Petroleum Association Mr. Hunter, May 28, 1937, published in Jacobs, *Butler Versus the King*, 227–28.

5. Samaroo, *Adrian Cola Rienzi*, 56.

6. Higgins, *History of Trinidad Oil*, 113–14.

7. *Trinidad and Tobago Disturbances 1937 Report of Commission* (Forster Report), TNA, CO 295/601/2, 10–11.

8. Forster Report, 24.

9. *TG*, June 17, 1937.

10. *TG*, June 2, 1937.

11. Forster Report, 80; K. Singh, *Race and Class Struggles*, 36–40.

12. Forster Report, 54.

13. Forster Report, 49, 80.

14. Forster Report, 77–78.

15. Governor Arthur George Murchison Fletcher statements, Hansard: Debates in the Legislative Council of Trinidad and Tobago, July 9, 1937, 255, NATT; H. Beckett, report of conversation between SOSC William Ormsby-Gore and Governor Fletcher, December 8, 1937, TNA, CO 295/600/13; *Vanguard*, July 23, 1965, 5.

16. Ture and Hamilton, *Black Power*, 189.

17. Michels, *Political Parties*, 377; see also Piven and Cloward, *Poor People's Movements*.

18. Ewing, "Caribbean Labour Politics," 31–35.

19. *TP*, June 1, 1935, 9; Reddock, *Women, Labour and Politics*, 129–32, 135–38; Rennie, *History of the Working-Class*, 32–34, 64–65; K. Singh, *Race and Class Struggles*, 150, 162; Teelucksingh, *Labour*, 132–34. Cipriani's decision came after the colonial government adamantly refused repeated attempts by the TWA to amend the legislation to include the right to peaceful picketing and immunity against actions in tort. See Teelucksingh, *Labour*, 116–25.

20. Basdeo, "Indian Participation," 55.

21. On government workers, see *TP*, May 18, 1935, 7. On the demonstration against unemployment, see *TP*, August 3, 1935, 1–2. On the Apex oil workers, see Rennie, *History of the Working-Class*, 63–64.

22. Quoted in K. Singh, *Race and Class Struggles*, 162; Rennie, *History of the Working-Class*, 64–65. See also *TP*, November 6, 1937, 10.

23. Quoted in Reddock, *Elma François*, 22.

24. Reddock, *Women, Labour and Politics*, 135–38.

25. Brereton, *History of Modern Trinidad*, 180.

26. Brereton, *History of Modern Trinidad*, 180; Rennie, *History of the Working-Class*, 61, 119.

27. Reddock, *Elma François*, 23; Rennie, *History of the Working-Class*, 90, 175–76.

28. Rennie, *History of the Working-Class*, 119.

29. Rennie, *History of the Working-Class*, 39; Teelucksingh, *Labour*, 133–34.

30. Rennie, *History of the Working-Class*, 175–76; *TP*, December 28, 1935, 2; Teelucksingh, *Labour*, 133–34.

31. For an example of reports in the working-class newspaper on South Africa, see *TP*, June 15, 1935, 3. For reports on Jamaica, see *TP*, May 25, 1935, 11.

32. Martin, *Pan-African Connection*, 22-24; *TP*, September 4, 1937, 7.

33. *TP*, September 4, 1937, 7; *TP*, November 13, 1937, 6.

34. For the mass meetings, see *TP*, October 12, 1935, 2. On boycotts, see *TP*, July 13, 1935, 11; *TP*, October 12, 1935, 2; see also *TP*, August 31, 1935, 10. On fundraising, see *TP*, November 9, 1935, 4; Rennie, *History of the Working-Class*, 77.

35. *TP*, July 13, 1935, 11; *TP*, August 3, 1935, 8.

36. Reddock, *Elma François*, 18–21; Rennie, *History of the Working-Class*, 77.

37. "Hands Off Abyssinia," NWCSA resolution, *TP*, July 13, 1935, 11.

38. H. Beckett, report of conversation, December 8, 1937.

39. BEW&CHRP, "Mass Meeting of Citizens," pamphlet, 1937, TNA, CO 295/608/5.

40. This multiracial organizing predates the 1955 gathering of African and Asian national leaders in Bandung, Indonesia, which is widely celebrated as the first large-scale Afro-Asian conference to promote economic, political, and cultural unity and cooperation.

41. Quoted in *TP*, December 28, 1935, 2.

42. *TP*, November 9, 1935, 9.

43. BEW&CHRP General Secretary Butler speech in Notes by Lance Corporal J. Armstrong, May 16, 1937, quoted in Jacobs, *Butler Versus the King*, 199–200.

44. Quoted in Reddock, *Elma François*, 35–37.

45. Reddock, *Elma François*, 37.

46. On oil workers striking, see *POSG*, June 20, 1937, 6; *POSG*, June 22, 1937, 1, 6; *POSG*, June 23, 1937, 1; *TG*, June 20, 1937, 1. For agricultural workers striking, see *POSG*, June 22, 1937, 6; *TG*, June 24, 1937, 2, 6.

47. *POSG*, June 22, 1937, 6; *POSG*, June 24, 1937, 6; *TG*, June 25, 1937, 1; *POSG*, June 27, 1937, 6.

48. *POSG*, June 22, 1937, 4; *TG*, June 20, 1937, 1; *POSG*, June 24, 1937, 6; *POSG*, June 25, 1937, 6; *POSG*, June 26, 1937, 1.

49. *POSG*, June 25, 1937, 2, 6.

50. *POSG*, June 27, 1937, 6; *POSG*, June 29, 1937, 6.

51. *POSG*, June 29, 1937, 1.

52. *TG*, June 23, 1937, 1.

53. *TG*, June 23, 1937, 1.

54. Rennie, *History of the Working-Class*, 116–21.

55. Rennie, *History of the Working-Class*, 117. Rennie's summary is from an interview with NWCSA organizer Jim Barratt in 1973.

56. *Vanguard*, July 23, 1965, 6.

57. Brereton, *History of Modern Trinidad*, 185.

58. *POSG*, June 27, 1937, 6.

59. Brereton, *History of Modern Trinidad*, 185.

60. *POSG*, June 22, 1937, 6. Newspaper reports refer to the worker strikes as peaceful: "no evidence of violence anywhere" and "orderly behavior." *POSG*, June 22, 1937, 6; *POSG*,

June 23, 1937, 6. Reports also noted crowds unconnected with the strikers who were "bent on mischief" and some minor clashes "between sympathizers with the strikers and non-strikers." *POSG*, June 22, 1937, 1, 6; see also *POSG*, June 26, 1937, 6.

61. *POSG*, June 24, 1937, 1.

62. *POSG*, June 23, 1937, 6; *TG*, June 23, 1937, 2.

63. *TG*, June 24, 1937, 1.

64. *POSG*, June 30, 1937, 6.

65. *POSG*, June 24, 1937, 6.

66. *POSG*, June 24, 1937, 1; *POSG*, June 25, 1937, 1.

67. Reddock, *Elma François*, 14.

68. *Vanguard*, July 23, 1965, 3.

69. *POSG*, June 25, 1937, 6; see also *TG*, June 22, 1937, 2. On women workers' demands, see *POSG*, June 24, 1937, 6; *POSG*, June 26, 1937, 6.

70. *TG*, June 23, 1937, 2; see also *TG*, June 25, 1937, 2.

71. *TG*, June 25, 1937, 2.

72. *TG*, June 23, 1937, 2.

73. BEW&CHRP General Secretary Butler to the Governor, October 6, 1936, published in Jacobs, *Butler Versus the King*, 213–14.

74. On demands for higher wages, see *POSG*, June 24, 1937, 6. On removal of racist barriers to promotions and better working conditions, see *POSG*, June 23, 1937, 6; *POSG*, June 24, 1937, 6; *POSG*, June 25, 1937, 1, 6; *POSG*, June 27, 1937, 6; *POSG*, June 29, 1937, 6; *POSG*, June 30, 1937, 6; BEW&CHRP General Secretary Butler to Governor Fletcher, October 6, 1936, published in Jacobs, *Butler Versus the King*, 213–14. On elimination of racial pay gaps, see *POSG*, June 24, 1937, 6.

75. *POSG*, June 23, 1937, 6.

76. *POSG*, June 27, 1937, 6.

77. *POSG*, June 26, 1937, 6; see also *POSG*, June 30, 1937, 6.

78. *POSG*, June 27, 1937, 6.

79. *POSG*, June 24, 1937, 6; *POSG*, June 27, 1937, 6; *POSG*, June 30, 1937, 6; BEW&CHRP General Secretary Butler to Governor Fletcher, October 6, 1936, published in Jacobs, *Butler Versus the King*, 213–14; Butler Party pamphlet, December 13, 1937, cited in Jacobs, *Butler Versus the King*, 239; *Vanguard*, August 2, 1947, 8.

80. *TG*, June 2, 1937.

81. *POSG*, June 25, 1937, 6.

82. Governor Fletcher, cited in M. Thomas, *Violence and Colonial Order*, 248.

83. Quoted in Colonial official, memorandum, December 1937, TNA, CO 295/600/13.

84. *POSG*, June 25, 1937, 6; see also *POSG*, June 30, 1937, 6.

85. *POSG*, June 29, 1937, 6.

86. *POSG*, June 25, 1937, 6; *POSG*, June 29, 1937, 6.

87. George Huggins to Permanent Under-Secretary of State for the Colonies John Maffey, June 24, 1937, TNA, CO 295/599/13.

88. *POSG*, June 24, 1937, 6; see also *POSG*, June 25, 1937, 1; *POSG*, June 29, 1937, 6.

89. *POSG*, June 22, 1937, 6; *POSG*, June 23, 1937, 6; *POSG*, June 24, 1937, 6; *POSG*, June 25, 1937, 6; *POSG*, June 27, 1937, 6.

90. *POSG*, June 22, 1937, 1, 6; *POSG*, June 23, 1937, 1, 6; *POSG*, June 25, 1937, 6.

91. *POSG*, June 22, 1937, 6; *POSG*, June 23, 1937, 1.

92. M. Thomas, *Violence and Colonial Order*, 240.

93. *POSG*, June 25, 1937, 6; *POSG*, June 26, 1937, 6; *POSG*, June 27, 1937, 1.

94. *POSG*, June 26, 1937, 6; *POSG*, June 27, 1937, 6, 8; *TG*, June 24, 1937, 2.

95. *POSG*, June 23, 1937, 6.

96. Rennie, *History of the Working-Class*, 114; M. Thomas, *Violence and Colonial Order*, 245–46.

97. Jacobs, "Politics of Protest," 41; M. Thomas, *Violence and Colonial Order*, 244.

98. M. Thomas, *Violence and Colonial Order*, 213.

99. Colonial official, memorandum, December 1937.

100. In H. Beckett, report of conversation, December 8, 1937.

101. In H. Beckett, report of conversation, December 8, 1937. Fletcher is referring to Lennox O'Reilly, legal adviser to the companies in both major industries in the colony.

102. For discussion of Butler's mental state, see Governor Fletcher to SOSC Ormsby-Gore, confidential dispatch, June 26, 1937, TNA, CO 295/599/14. For attempts to arrest Butler, see Governor Fletcher, telegram of June 25, 1937, quoted in Colonial official, memorandum, December 1937.

103. *TG*, June 23, 1937, 4.

104. *POSG*, June 30, 1937, 6.

105. Governor Fletcher to SOSC Ormsby-Gore, telegram, TNA, 1937, CO 295/599/13.

106. In H. Beckett, report of conversation, December 8, 1937.

107. Forster Report, 90.

108. Hansard: Debates in the Legislative Council of Trinidad and Tobago, July 9, 1937, 249–50, NATT.

109. M. Thomas, *Violence and Colonial Order*, 247.

110. Hansard: Debates in the Legislative Council of Trinidad and Tobago, July 9, 1937, 263–66.

111. Members of Sugar Manufacturers' Association of Trinidad, Members of the Chamber of Commerce, and Members of the Petroleum Association of Trinidad to SOSC William Ormsby-Gore, December 22, 1937, TNA, CO 295/600/13; see also Colonial official, memorandum, December 1937, and Colonial official, memorandum, December 2, 1937, CO 295/600/13.

112. Members of Sugar Manufacturers' Association of Trinidad, Members of the Chamber of Commerce, and Members of the Petroleum Association of Trinidad to SOSC Ormsby-Gore, December 22, 1937.

113. OWTU General Secretary E. R. Blades to SOSC Ormsby-Gore, November 18, 1937, TNA, CO 295/600/13. Ultimately, owing to pressure on the SOSC from white business and plantation-owning interests, Fletcher was removed from office and replaced by Hubert Young, who had a reputation for his firm action against strikers when he was governor of Northern Rhodesia during the 1935 Copperbelt strikes. Nankivell was sent to be a colonial treasurer in Cyprus. All the evidence shows that Fletcher's actions were consistent with what was expressed by the imperial state. He repressed the labor uprising in every manner demanded by the white business and plantation-owing elite, except for

establishing a permanent garrison of forces. Thus, it appears he was scapegoated to appease the white business and plantation-owning elite.

114. Toprani, "Oil and Grand Strategy," 210–11.

115. President of Oil Board De La Warr, to Joint Secretary A. D. Nicholl, memorandum, "The Importance of the Trinidad Oil Supply in an Emergency: Memorandum by the Oil Board," November 1937, enclosed with A. D. Nicholl, "Trinidad: Degree of Importance as a Source of Oil Supply in Time of War," November 30, 1937, TNA, Cabinet Office Records (CAB) 50/6/13; Edgerton, *Britain's War Machine*, 186–87.

116. Chairman of the Associated West Indian Chambers of Commerce to UK Prime Minister Neville Chamberlain, July 3, 1937, TNA, CO 295/599/13.

117. BEW&CHRP General Secretary Butler, speech, December 9, 1937, 69, TNA, CO 295/608/5; see also Rennie, *History of the Working-Class*, 87–88.

118. *TP*, February 8, 1936, 7, 11.

119. *POSG*, June 27, 1937, 6.

120. See also H. Johnson, "Oil, Imperial Policy," 35–36; Samaroo and Girvan, "Trinidad Workingmen's Association," 215; M. Thomas, *Violence and Colonial Order*, 239–45.

121. Hansard: Conditions in West Indian Colonies, HL Deb. (5th ser.), vol. 107, cols. 863–65, February 23, 1938, https://hansard.parliament.uk/lords/1938-02-23/debates /5f267f13-8f3f-4b4d-b534-cfc612088d2c/ConditionsInWestIndianColonies.

122. SOSC Ormsby-Gore to British Trades Union Congress General Secretary Walter Citrine, July 10, 1937, TNA, CO 295/600/7.

123. Quoted in H. Johnson, "Oil, Imperial Policy," 37.

124. Great Britain Colonial Office, *West India Royal Commission Report 1938–1939* (Moyne Report), 1945. While this report was submitted in 1939, it was deemed so politically embarrassing to the British government that publication was withheld until 1945.

125. Craig-James, "Smiles and Blood," 81.

126. R. Thomas, *Development of Labour Law*, 18.

127. Cited in Colonial official, memorandum, December 1937.

128. *POSG*, June 27, 1937, 1, 6.

129. *POSG*, June 29, 1937, 1.

130. Governor's deputy to SOSC Ormsby-Gore, May 5, 1938, TNA, CO 295/608/3.

131. Governor's deputy to SOSC Ormsby-Gore, May 5, 1938. See also Extract from Hansard: Debates in the Legislative Council of Trinidad and Tobago, April 29, 1938, TNA, CO 295/608/3. Rienzi served as a trade union representative and Sir Lennox O'Reilly as an employer representative.

132. Colonial official, folio comments, July 4, 1939, TNA, CO 323/1543/5; Edwards, "Postcolonial Sociology."

133. Industrial adviser A. G. V. Lindon, sent to Trinidad by British Ministry of Labor, to SOSC Ormsby-Gore, April 13, 1938, TNA, CO 295/606/2.

134. *Vanguard*, August 2, 1947, 7.

135. *POSG*, June 30, 1937, 1, 6; see also *POSG*, June 22, 1937, 4.

136. Dalley, *Trade Union Organization and Industrial Relations in Trinidad*, 41; Great Britain Colonial Office, *Annual Report of the Social and Economic Progress of the People of Trinidad and Tobago 1938*, 30–32.

137. *Trinidad and Tobago Blue Book 1938*, 118, NATT.

138. Great Britain Colonial Office, *Annual Report of the Social and Economic Progress of the People of Trinidad and Tobago 1938*, 32–33; R. Thomas, *Development of Labour Law*, 24–28; *Vanguard*, August 2, 1947, 8.

139. *Vanguard*, August 2, 1947, 7.

140. *Vanguard*, August 2, 1947, 7.

141. Bissessar, "Determinants of Gender Mobility," 414, 416.

142. On revenues, see Colony of Trinidad and Tobago, *Mines: Report of the Inspector Mines and Petroleum Technologist for 1938*, 6. On refining capabilities, operations data, and safety, see Colony of Trinidad and Tobago, *Report of the Inspector Mines and Petroleum Technologist for the Year 1943*, 4; Colony of Trinidad and Tobago, *Mines: Report of the Inspector Mines and Petroleum Technologist for the Year 1945*, 3.

143. Colony of Trinidad and Tobago, *Administration Report of the Petroleum Department, 1948*, 8.

144. Colony of Trinidad and Tobago, *Administration Report of the Mines Department, 1947*, 8–9.

145. Great Britain Colonial Office, *Annual Report on the Social and Economic Progress of the People of Trinidad and Tobago 1936*, 53; Great Britain Colonial Office, *Annual Report on Trinidad and Tobago for the Year 1946*, 32; Great Britain Colonial Office, *Annual Report on Trinidad and Tobago for the Year 1949*, 47. The rate was 45 percent in 1948; see Great Britain Colonial Office, *Annual Report on the Colony of Trinidad and Tobago for the Year 1948*, 25, 68.

146. Colony of Trinidad and Tobago, *Administration Report of the Mines Department, 1947*, table 3, 13; Colony of Trinidad and Tobago, *Administration Report of the Petroleum Department for the Year 1950*, table 6, 22.

147. *Report of the Estimates Committee on a Comprehensive Development Program to Be Carried Out Within the Years 1939–1944*, TNA, CO 295/615/3.

148. Acting Governor John Huggins to SOSC Malcolm MacDonald, January 12, 1939, 3, 4, TNA, CO 295/615/3; see also C. G. Stevens, folio comments, February 2, 1939, TNA, CO 295/615/3.

149. A. Poyntin to Governor Huggins, folio comments, February 6, 1939, TNA, CO 295/615/3.

150. Moyne Report, 429.

151. Harding and Gent, *Dominions Office and Colonial Office List for 1939*, 495; Great Britain Colonial Office, *Colonial Office List 1946*, 211–12.

152. Harding and Gent, *Dominions Office and Colonial Office List for 1939*, 495.

153. Great Britain Colonial Office, *Colonial Office List 1950*, 361–62.

154. Great Britain Colonial Office, *Annual Report on the Social and Economic Progress of the People of Trinidad and Tobago 1938*, 37; Great Britain Colonial Office, *Colonial Office List 1950*, 361–62.

155. Great Britain Colonial Office. *Colonial Office List 1960*, 232.

156. *Trinidad and Tobago Blue Book 1939*, 55, NATT; Great Britain Colonial Office, *Colonial Office List 1950*, 361–62.

157. Great Britain Colonial Office, *Annual Report on the Social and Economic Progress of the People of Trinidad and Tobago 1937*, 8; Great Britain Colonial Office, *Annual*

Report on Trinidad and Tobago for the Year 1946, 49; B. Mitchell, *International Historical Statistics*, 84, 86.

158. C. G. Stevens, folio comments, February 2, 1939; Acting Governor Huggins to SOSC MacDonald, January 12, 1939, 6.

159. Home, *Of Planting and Planning*, 225.

160. Home, *Of Planting and Planning*, 188–91.

161. Quoted in Home, *Of Planting and Planning*, 190.

162. Home, *Of Planting and Planning*.

163. County Council Ordinance, 1946, no. 18, http://laws.gov.tt/ttdll-web/revision/byyear. In 1950 three-year terms were set for elected local authorities.

164. Cited in Colonial official, memorandum, December 1937.

165. Craig, "Political Patronage," 175–78.

166. Moyne Report.

167. Ledgister, *Class Alliances*, 101.

168. Samaroo, "1946 Trinidad Constitution," 12.

169. 1946 Census, cited in La Guerre and Girvan, "General Elections of 1946," 204.

170. Samaroo, *Adrian Cola Rienzi*, 112–21.

171. *Vanguard*, October 14, 1944.

172. Samaroo, "1946 Trinidad Constitution," 18–24; K. Singh, "Conflict and Collaboration," 232–43.

173. Quoted in La Guerre and Girvan, "General Elections of 1946," 185.

CHAPTER 4. DECOLONIZATION AND FORTUITOUS FAILURES

1. James, *History of Pan-African Revolt*.

2. Fanon, *Wretched of the Earth*, 74–76.

3. Bayart, *Politics of the Belly*; Chatterjee, *Nationalist Thought*; Dülffer and Frey, *Elites and Decolonization*; Getachew, *Worldmaking After Empire*; Hintzen, *Reproducing Domination*; Lawrence, *Imperial Rule and the Politics of Nationalism*; Lonsdale, "Emergence of African Nations"; Slater and Smith, "Power of Counterrevolution"; Young, *Post-Colonial State in Africa*.

4. Ahlman, *Living with Nkrumahism*; Bedasse, *Jah Kingdom*; Lal, *African Socialism in Postcolonial Tanzania*; Schmidt, *Cold War and Decolonization*.

5. Branch, "Loyalists, Mau Mau, and Elections in Kenya"; Nkrumah, *Neo-Colonialism*; Rabe, *U.S. Intervention in British Guiana*; Reed, "Gabon"; Rose, *Dependency and Socialism*; Yates, *Rentier State in Africa*.

6. Chibber, *Locked in Place*; Cooper, *Decolonization and African Society*; Curless, "Triumph of the State"; Larmer, *Mineworkers in Zambia*; Mawby, "Workers in the Vanguard"; McCann, "Possibility and Peril."

7. Nkrumah, *Neo-Colonialism*, ix. See also Fanon, *Wretched of the Earth*; Rodney, "Class Contradictions"; Rodney, "Contemporary Political Trends." The dependency and world-systems perspectives also discuss the constraints on the autonomy of peripheral states to pursue economic policies that might conflict with the interests of foreign capital. See Amin, *Delinking*; Amin, *Imperialism*; Frank, *Dependent Accumulation*; Wallerstein, *Capitalist World-Economy*, 20–21.

8. Esping-Andersen, "Three Political Economies of the Welfare State"; Heller, *Labor of Development*; Huber and Stephens, *Democracy and the Left*; Korpi, *Democratic Class Struggle*; Sandbrook et al., *Social Democracy*.

9. Rodney, "Contemporary Political Trends," 1.

10. Arrighi, *Long Twentieth Century*, 47–73.

11. Hintzen, *Reproducing Domination*, 96.

12. Bonini, "Complementary and Competitive Regimes"; Bunker and Ciccantell, *Globalization*; see also Silver and Arrighi, "Polanyi's 'Double Movement,'" 339–40.

13. US Energy Information Administration, "Petroleum and Other Liquids: US Field Production of Crude Oil," accessed December 15, 2024, https://www.eia.gov/dnav/pet /hist/LeafHandler.ashx?n=pet&s=mcrfpus2&f=m.

14. US Energy Information Administration, "Petroleum and Other Liquids: US exports of Crude Oil," accessed December 15, 2024, https://www.eia.gov/dnav/pet/hist /LeafHandler.ashx?n=pet&s=mcrexus1&f=a.

15. Vitalis, *Oilcraft*, 25.

16. Kelshall, *U-Boat War*.

17. Maingot, *United States and the Caribbean*, 58.

18. Maingot, *United States and the Caribbean*, 57.

19. Baptiste, "Exploitation of Caribbean Bauxite," 144; Maingot, *United States and the Caribbean*, 58.

20. Baptiste, "Exploitation of Caribbean Bauxite," 144.

21. Quoted in Palmer, *Eric Williams*, 82–83.

22. Brereton, *History of Modern Trinidad*, 192.

23. Quoted in St. Pierre, *Eric Williams*, 94.

24. Bond, "Oil in the Caribbean," 601.

25. Maingot, *United States and the Caribbean*, 58.

26. Bond, "Oil in the Caribbean," 607.

27. Suh, "What Happens to Social Movements."

28. Hipsher, "Democratization and the Decline"; Paret, *Fractured Militancy*; Robertson, "Leading Labor."

29. Smith, "Enduring Unfreedom," 159.

30. Basdeo Panday, interviewed by Devant Maharaj et al., June 2000, in Maraj, *Hostile and Recalcitrant*, 194.

31. Smith, "Enduring Unfreedom," 158–59.

32. *TP*, June 24, 1939.

33. *Vanguard*, June 19, 1965, 6.

34. See also *Vanguard*, June 19, 1965, 6.

35. OWTU, *Oilfield Workers' Trade Union July 1937–July 1977* (40th anniversary booklet), 21, OWTU library.

36. Rennie, *History of the Working-Class*, 185–87.

37. *Vanguard*, August 2, 1947, 8.

38. Bolland, *Politics of Labour*, 491.

39. Bolland, *Politics of Labour*, 491–93; Ramdin, *From Chattel Slave*, 167–68.

40. Bolland, *Politics of Labour*, 483–506; Teelucksingh, *Labour*, 166–73.

41. *Vanguard*, December 22, 1945, 1.

42. Parris, "Joint Venture I."

43. OWTU, 40th anniversary booklet, 25–26.

44. *Vanguard*, December 22, 1945, 2.

45. *Vanguard*, August 2, 1947, 7.

46. La Guerre and Girvan, "General Elections of 1946."

47. La Guerre and Girvan, "General Elections of 1946."

48. La Guerre and Girvan, "General Elections of 1946," 194.

49. La Guerre and Girvan, "General Elections of 1946," 198–99.

50. La Guerre, "Race Factor," 325; Ryan, *Race and Nationalism*, 89-90.

51. Figueira, *Tubal Uriah Butler*, 40.

52. La Guerre, "Race Factor," 324.

53. Ryan, *Race and Nationalism*. See also Albert Gomes's autobiography, *Through a Maze of Colour*, in which he laments his fall from popularity.

54. For the 1946 elections, see Ryan, *Race and Nationalism*, 77. For 1950, see La Guerre, "Race Factor," 328.

55. Cited in La Guerre, "Race Factor," 325.

56. Blades to Citrine, April 21, 1943, quoted in Bolland, *Politics of Labour*, 417.

57. Gomes, *Maze of Colour*, 118.

58. D. Davis, *Discipline and Development*; MacDonald, *Trinidad and Tobago*.

59. Maraj, *Hostile and Recalcitrant*, FW2–FW7; K. Singh, "Conflict and Collaboration," 244.

60. *Census of the Colony of Trinidad and Tobago, 1931*, 13, NATT. The data for occupations are disaggregated by race only for the Indian population.

61. Hintzen, *Costs of Regime Survival*, 26–27.

62. *Census of the Colony of Trinidad and Tobago, 1931*, 32.

63. Allahar, "False Consciousness"; Sudama, "Class, Race."

64. *Vanguard*, December 14, 1968, 3, 6.

65. Cabral, "Weapon of Theory"; Rodney, "Class Contradictions in Tanzania"; Rodney, "Contemporary Political Trends"; see also Göçek, *Rise of the Bourgeoisie*.

66. James, "West Indian Middle Classes," 250.

67. Collier and Collier, *Shaping the Political Arena*; C. Davis and Coleman, "Labor and the State."

68. James, "West Indian Middle Classes," 251, 254. See also Rodney, "Aspects of the International Class Struggle in Africa."

69. Hintzen, *Costs of Regime Survival*, 42; Rodney, "Contemporary Political Trends"; see also Chatterjee, *Nation and Its Fragments*; Fanon, *Wretched of the Earth*; Rodney, "Class Contradictions in Tanzania."

70. Gomes, *Maze of Colour*, 161, 37.

71. K. Singh, "Conflict and Collaboration," 250nn32–33. Kumar was born in Punjab in India, earned an engineering degree in England, and arrived in Trinidad in 1935. He imported Indian films to Trinidad and Guyana and founded the Maha Sabha, an Indian Hindu cultural organization.

72. Figueira, *Tubal Uriah Butler*, 56.

73. Bellin, *Stalled Democracy*.

74. Williams, *Inward Hunger*, 144–45.

75. Hintzen, *Reproducing Domination*, 55; *TG*, December 4, 1919; *TP*, October 12, 1935, 2.

76. Williams, *Inward Hunger*, 146. For Williams's comments about Castro, see Kambon, *For Bread, Justice and Freedom*, 46.

77. Williams, *Inward Hunger*, 146.

78. Maraj allegedly placed a gun on the table in a meeting with union leaders while telling them the unions would be brought together under his leadership. See Basdeo Panday, interviewed by Devant Maharaj et al., June 2000, in Maraj, *Hostile and Recalcitrant*, 194.

79. Oxaal, *Race and Revolutionary Consciousness*, 9; Maraj, *Hostile and Recalcitrant*, 2, 7–8.

80. Figueira, *Simbhoonath Capildeo*, 7.

81. Lionel Seukeran, speech tribute on Maraj's death, October 1971, in Maraj, *Hostile and Recalcitrant*, 131.

82. Dalley, *General Industrial Conditions*, 9.

83. Quoted in C. Singh, *Multinationals*, 55.

84. Quoted in Rennie, *History of the Working-Class*, 202.

85. *Vanguard*, August 2, 1947, 2.

86. G. Lewis, "Trinidad and Tobago General Election," 20; Ryan, *Race and Nationalism*, 257–58. The NTUC was formed in 1957 when the TTTUC reunited with the Federation of Trade Unions.

87. *Vanguard*, July 30, 1965, 6.

88. *Vanguard*, July 30, 1965, 6.

89. Fanon, *Wretched of the Earth*, 103; see also Rodney, "Race and Class."

90. Rodney, "Race and Class."

91. De Leon et al., "Political Articulation"; M. Desai, "Relative Autonomy of Party Practices"; Eidlin, "Why Is There No Labor Party."

92. Quoted in Figueira, *Simbhoonath Capildeo*, 5.

93. Figueira, *Simbhoonath Capildeo*, 6.

94. Vertovec, *Hindu Diaspora*, 56.

95. Vertovec, *Hindu Diaspora*; see also Ryan, *Race and Nationalism*, 141.

96. Ryan, *Race and Nationalism*, 141.

97. *TG*, May 20, 1955, 6.

98. Eric Williams, "Federation in the World Today," lecture, February 25, 1955, quoted in Palmer, *Eric Williams*, 263.

99. By 1960 Williams was expressing some empathy for teaching Hindi and attention to Indian culture. See Palmer, *Eric Williams*, 274. But the racialized political landscape had already been painted.

100. Hansard: Debates in the Legislative Council of Trinidad and Tobago, May 13, 1949, 927, NATT.

101. Proctor, "East Indians and the Federation."

102. Eric Williams, "The Danger Facing Trinidad, Tobago and the West Indian Nation," speech, *PNM Weekly*, April 21, 1958, 3.

103. Eric Williams, *PNM Weekly*, April 21, 1958, 3.

104. Eric Williams, *PNM Weekly*, April 21, 1958, 3.

105. Eric Williams, *PNM Weekly*, April 21, 1958, 4.

106. *TG*, April 23, 1958.

107. Figueira, *Simbhoonath Capildeo*.

108. Figueira, *Tubal Uriah Butler*, 111–12.

109. *TP*, February 14, 1948.

110. *TP*, February 14, 1948.

111. Quoted in Figueira, *Tubal Uriah Butler*, 54.

112. G. Lewis, "Trinidad and Tobago General Election," 9, 15.

113. James, *History of Pan-African Revolt*; Rodney, "Contemporary Political Trends,"
1. Engaging Fanon and Latin American Marxist dependency theorists, Inés Valdez calls
this the "paradox of dependent democratic founding"—where the demand by anticapitalist movements in dependent contexts to appropriate the *common*wealth is met with
repression and authoritarianism, which in turn undoes the emancipatory project. Valdez,
"Capitalism, Imperialism, and the Paradox."

114. Fanon, *Wretched of the Earth*, 2.

115. Fanon, *Wretched of the Earth*; Rodney, "Contemporary Political Trends."

116. *Vanguard*, June 19, 1965, 2.

117. Jacobs, *Butler Versus the King*; Reddock, *Elma François*. In addition, the natural
deaths of towering radical labor figures, like that of François in 1944, certainly dented the
movement.

118. Rennie, *History of the Working-Class*, 178.

119. *Vanguard*, June 19, 1965, 2.

120. *Vanguard*, July 23, 1965, 7.

121. *Vanguard*, August 2, 1947, 10.

122. *Vanguard*, June 19, 1965, 2.

123. *Vanguard*, May 31, 1947.

124. Industrial adviser A. G. V. Lindon, Enclosure in Trinidad dispatch no. 175, May 31,
1940, report of the first meeting of the Joint Conciliation Board for the oil industry,
May 31, 1940, TNA, CO 295/619/11.

125. Orde Browne, folio comment, July 19, 1940, TNA, CO 295/619/11.

126. OWTU, 40th anniversary booklet, 20.

127. Governor Murchison Fletcher, Hansard: Debates in the Legislative Council of
Trinidad and Tobago, July 9, 1937, 249, 276, NATT.

128. Acting Governor John Huggins to SOSC Malcolm MacDonald, confidential
dispatch, May 25, 1939, TNA, CO 295/614/11.

129. For Rocklin's analysis, see Rocklin, "Making the Chief Servant Mad." For colonial
responses, see Acting Governor Huggins to SOSC MacDonald, confidential dispatch,
May 25, 1939; Governor Hubert Young to SOSC Malcolm MacDonald, telegram, November 24, 1939, TNA, CO 295/614/11.

130. Governor Young to SOSC MacDonald, secret dispatch, December 7, 1939, TNA,
CO 295/614/11.

131. Acting Governor Huggins to SOSC MacDonald, confidential dispatch, May 25, 1939.

132. Rodney, *How Europe Underdeveloped Africa*, 33.

133. Figueira, *Tubal Uriah Butler*, 40.

134. Governor John Shaw to SOSC Arthur Creech Jones, April 6, 1948, TNA, CO 537/3810.

135. Colonial official Wallace, folio comment, June 10, 1953, TNA, CO 1031/127.

136. Governor Rance to SOSC Oliver Lyttelton, report, January 15, 1954, TNA, CO 1031/1804.

137. Cheddi Jagan to Bhadase Sagan Maraj, December 20, 1959, in Maraj, *Hostile and Recalcitrant*, 109.

138. Governor Rance to SOSC Lyttelton, report, April 13, 1954, TNA, CO 1031/1804.

139. Governor Rance to SOSC Lyttelton, report, June 18, 1953, TNA, CO 1031/127; Governor Rance to SOSC Lyttelton, report, March 16, 1954, TNA, CO 1031/1804.

140. Acting Governor Maurice Dorman to SOSC Alan Lennox-Boyd, report, September 14, 1954, TNA, CO 1031/1804.

141. Governor Rance to SOSC Lyttelton, report, May 29, 1953, TNA, CO 1031/127.

142. Figueira, *Tubal Uriah Butler*, 43; La Guerre and Girvan, "General Elections of 1946," 193; *PNM Weekly*, June 25, 1956, 1.

143. Trinidad and Tobago Intelligence Committee, "Note on the Political Situation in Trinidad and Tobago as at Nomination Day, 6th September 1956," TNA, CO 1031/1805.

144. Ryan, *Race and Nationalism*, 165–67.

145. Great Britain Colonial Office, *Colonial Office List 1955*, 204.

146. Bissessar, "Difficulty of Protecting Merit," 76–79; Stephenson et al., "Race Relations in the Caribbean."

147. Elections and Boundaries Commission, *Trinidad and Tobago Report on the Legislative Council General Elections 1956*, table 2, 26, accessed June 1, 2024, https://ebctt.com/wp-content/uploads/Report-on-the-Legislative-Council-General-Elections-1956-24th-September-1956.pdf; Elections and Boundaries Commission, *Trinidad and Tobago Report on the General Elections 1961*, table 1, 47, accessed June 1, 2024, https://ebctt.com/wp-content/uploads/Report-on-the-Parliamentary-General-Elections-1961-4th-December-1961.pdf#page=45.00.

148. Bissessar, "Local Governance Structures," 132–33.

149. Ragoonath, "Shifting Nature of Decentralisation," 692–93.

150. Craig, "Political Patronage," 177.

151. Great Britain Colonial Office, *Colonial Office List 1950*, 361–62; Great Britain Colonial Office, *Colonial Office List 1962*, 209; Great Britain Colonial Office, *Annual Report on Trinidad and Tobago, B.W.I. for the Year 1947*, 44–48.

152. Pan American Health Organization, *Register of Malaria Eradication*, 1–2. The criteria for malaria eradication in the report is no autochthonous cases for more than three years.

153. Great Britain Colonial Office, *Colonial Office List 1950*, 361; Great Britain Colonial Office, *Colonial Office List 1960*, 232.

154. Great Britain Colonial Office, *Annual Report on the Colony of Trinidad and Tobago for the Year 1948*, 52–53; Great Britain Colonial Office, *Colonial Office List 1962*, 209.

155. L. Fletcher, "Decline of Friendly Societies," 71–75.

156. L. Fletcher, "Decline of Friendly Societies," 68; Great Britain Colonial Office, *Colonial Office List 1962*, 210.

157. Great Britain Colonial Office, *Colonial Office List 1955*, 206; L. Fletcher, "Decline of Friendly Societies," 62.

158. Clarke, "Industrialisation Programme for Trinidad," 132, 135–40.

159. Clarke, "Industrialisation Programme for Trinidad," 140–49.

160. Rodney, "Contemporary Political Trends," 2.

161. G. Lewis, *Growth*, 214–15.

162. Michels, *Political Parties*, 333.

CHAPTER 5. POSTINDEPENDENCE RESURGENCE
OF LIBERATION UNIONISM

Epigraph: Weekes, speech at the opening session of negotiations between Texaco and the OWTU, September 3, 1968, printed in *Vanguard*, September 7, 1968, 2.

1. International Labour Organization, *Year Book 1970*, 826.

2. *Express*, April 3, 1970, 3; *Express*, April 6, 1970, 2; *Express*, April 20, 1970, 1; *TG*, March 1, 1965, 3; *TG*, March 4, 1965, 2; March 10, 1965, 1; *TG*, March 13, 1965, 1; *TG*, March 16, 1965, 1; *Vanguard*, July 23, 1965, 7; *Vanguard*, November 26, 1965, 4; *Vanguard*, December 23, 1965, 4, 5; *Vanguard*, January 13, 1968; *Vanguard*, May 3, 1969, 4.

3. *Vanguard*, May 3, 1969, 4.

4. See the following sources for the chronology of specific events leading up to the February Revolution: *Vanguard*, March 7, 1970, 3–6; Austin, "All Roads Lead to Montreal"; Meeks, "1970 Revolution"; Oxaal, *Race and Revolutionary Consciousness*; Pantin, *Black Power Day*.

5. "Black proletarian warriors" is from Weekes, "The Revolutionary 70s Have Begun," *Vanguard*, January 3, 1970, 8.

6. Meeks, "Rise and Fall"; Salandy, "Contestations of Memory."

7. *Vanguard*, July 11, 1970, 7.

8. Clawson, *Next Upsurge*; Isaac and Christiansen, "How the Civil Rights Movement Revitalized Labor Militancy"; Milkman and Voss, *Rebuilding Labor*; Voss and Sherman, "Breaking the Iron Law." Note that the trade union movement in Trinidad and Tobago in the early 1960s was by far the most dominant movement, predating the later emergence of the Black Power movement.

9. C. Robinson, *Black Marxism*, xxx. See also G. Johnson and Lubin, *Futures*.

10. International Labour Organization, *Year Book 1970*, 826; International Labour Organization, *Year Book 1973*, 793.

11. Quoted in Ramsaran, "'Myth' of Development," 125.

12. Farrell, *Underachieving Society*, 108.

13. GOTT, *Third Five-Year Plan 1969–1973*, 4, 11–12.

14. GOTT, *Third Five-Year Plan 1969–1973*, 12; Farrell, *Underachieving Society*.

15. Carrington, "Industrialization in Trinidad and Tobago," 37–43; GOTT, *Third Five-Year Plan 1969–1973*, 4, 12–13.

16. GOTT, *Third Five-Year Plan 1969–1973*, 1, 4, 11; Farrell, *Underachieving Society*, 108.

17. World Bank, World Development Indicators, Inflation, Consumer Prices (annual %), accessed August 1, 2024, https://data.worldbank.org/indicator/FP.CPI.TOTL.ZG ?locations=TT.

18. On retrenchment and use of contract workers, see *Vanguard*, December 23, 1965, 5; *Vanguard*, January 13, 1968, 1, 8; *Vanguard*, February 8, 1969, 3; *Vanguard*, February 10, 1968, 8; *Vanguard*, March 16, 1968, 1, 7; *Vanguard*, March 22, 1969, 6; *Vanguard*, March 30, 1968, 1; *Vanguard*, May 11, 1968, 3. On reductions in medical services, see *Vanguard*, October 29, 1965, 6.

19. *Vanguard*, November 2, 1968, 5, 6; *Vanguard*, November 16, 1968, 2; *Vanguard*, March 22, 1969, 1, 6.

20. *Vanguard*, April 18, 1970, 8.

21. *Vanguard*, December 23, 1965, 7; *Vanguard*, January 13, 1968, 2, 8; *Vanguard*, January 27, 1968, 4.

22. Farrell, *Underachieving Society*, 110.

23. *Vanguard*, March 2, 1968, 5; *Vanguard*, September 7, 1968, 1.

24. R. Thomas, *Development of Labour Law*, 43–47.

25. *TG*, March 18, 1965, 1; *Vanguard*, February 17, 1968, 1; *Vanguard*, December 21, 1968, 9.

26. *Vanguard*, November 26, 1965, 5; see also *Vanguard*, November 12, 1965, 5; *Vanguard*, October 24, 1970, 5.

27. *TG*, March 10, 1965, 1; *Vanguard*, October 29, 1965, 1, 7, 8; *Vanguard*, November 12, 1965, 5. Union recognition under industrial law required an employer to recognize and bargain with a trade union where more than 50 percent of employees were members. See R. Thomas, *Development of Labour Law*, 43–44.

28. *TG*, March 12, 1965, 1; *Vanguard*, June 22, 1968, 2; *Vanguard*, July 25, 1970, 3; *Vanguard*, January 9, 1971, 7; *Vanguard*, April 17, 1971, 6.

29. *TG*, March 12, 1965, 1.

30. Kambon, *For Bread, Justice, and Freedom*, 51–53.

31. Kambon, *For Bread, Justice, and Freedom*, 55–56, 61–65.

32. *Vanguard*, July 30, 1965, 6.

33. Kambon, *For Bread, Justice, and Freedom*.

34. Kambon, *For Bread, Justice, and Freedom*.

35. OWTU, *50 years of Progress: 1937–1987*, 1988, 20, booklet, OWTU library.

36. Quoted in Jacobs, *Butler Versus the King*, 155.

37. Quoted in Jacobs, *Butler Versus the King*, 155.

38. On the award and statue, see OWTU, 40th anniversary booklet, 34; *Vanguard*, May 28, 1965, 3; *Vanguard*, June 19, 1965, 1. On the union as Butler's benefactor, see OWTU, *General Council's Report by the General Secretary to the 37th Annual Conference of Delegates 1937–1976*, December 4, 1976, 11, report, OWTU library. On Butler Day, see *Vanguard*, July 9, 1965, 4; *Vanguard*, July 23, 1965, 3, 5.

39. *Vanguard*, June 19, 1965, 6.

40. *Vanguard*, July 23, 1965, 3.

41. *Vanguard*, July 23, 1965, 3; *Vanguard*, August 6, 1965, 5; *Vanguard*, September 3, 1965.

42. *Vanguard*, July 23, 1965, 3.

43. *Vanguard*, May 11, 1968, 3.

44. OWTU, 40th anniversary booklet, 63–67; *Vanguard*, June 25, 1965, 4; *Vanguard Supplement*, July 23, 1965, 3, 8; *Vanguard*, August 6, 1965, 7; *Vanguard*, September 3, 1965.

45. *Vanguard*, May 14, 1965, 3; *Vanguard*, May 1, 1968, 3.

46. *Vanguard*, May 14, 1965, 3; *Vanguard*, July 23, 1965, 3; *Vanguard*, January 13, 1968; *Vanguard*, October 5, 1968, 8; *Vanguard*, July 11, 1970, 3; *Vanguard*, July 25, 1970, 5; *Vanguard*, August 25, 1978, 3. On the women members of NJAC, see Pasley, "The Black Power Movement in Trinidad."

47. OWTU, 40th anniversary booklet, 72; OWTU, *General Council's Report by the General Secretary to the 39th Annual Conference of Delegates,* November 4, 1978, 24, report, OWTU library; *Vanguard*, November 12, 1965, 5.

48. *Vanguard*, February 10, 1968, 5.

49. Teelucksingh, "Black Power Movement," 170–71.

50. *Vanguard*, March 21, 1970, 3, 8.

51. *Vanguard*, May 1, 1968, 3; *Vanguard*, October 29, 1965, 7; *Vanguard*, December 23, 1965, 5; Weekes, *The Trade Union Congress and the Sugar Workers' Strike: Why I Resigned*, booklet, March 1965, OWTU library.

52. *Vanguard*, October 29, 1965, 7.

53. *TG*, March 10, 1965, 1; *Vanguard*, October 29, 1965.

54. *Vanguard*, July 30, 1965, 1; *Vanguard*, November 12, 1965, 5; *Vanguard*, November 26, 1965, 3; *Vanguard*, December 10, 1965, 2; *Vanguard*, December 23, 1965, 5.

55. *Vanguard*, October 29, 1965, 1.

56. Weekes, *Why I Resigned*; *TG*, March 12, 1965, 1; *TG*, March 13, 1965, 3; *TG*, March 16, 1965, 1.

57. *Vanguard*, August 6, 1965, 5; see also *Vanguard*, October 29, 1965, 5.

58. *Vanguard*, July 6, 1968, 2, 7.

59. OWTU, *General Council's Report by the General Secretary to the 34th Annual Conference of Delegates 1937–1974*, March 10, 1974, 13, report, OWTU library.

60. *Vanguard*, May 28, 1965, 8.

61. OWTU, 40th anniversary booklet, 8–9.

62. *Vanguard*, September 8, 1978, 1; Weekes, *Why I Resigned*.

63. *Vanguard*, February 7, 1970, 1. The term Afro-Saxon in this context was popularized by radical Trinbagonian economist and New World Group founder Lloyd Best and referred to global Africans who internalize, embrace, and reproduce European norms and value systems and white supremacist ideology.

64. *Vanguard*, February 7, 1970, 8.

65. *Vanguard*, March 8, 1969, 6; see also *Express*, April 4, 1970, 3; *Vanguard*, March 22, 1969, 2; *Vanguard*, April 19, 1969, 1; *Vanguard*, May 3, 1969, 2; *Vanguard*, August 23, 1969, 1; *Vanguard*, October 25, 1969, 1. In 1970 the OWTU won bargaining power for electricity workers.

66. Kambon, *For Bread, Justice, and Freedom*, 173; *Vanguard*, October 29, 1965, 4–5; Vanguard, June 8, 1968, 1; *Vanguard*, August 24, 1968, 7.

67. On pledges of support, see *Vanguard*, May 14, 1965, 8; *Vanguard*, October 29, 1965, 4; *Vanguard*, November 26, 1965, 4; *Vanguard*, December 23, 1965, 5; *Vanguard*, May 3, 1969, 4. On financial assistance and solidarity strikes, see *Vanguard*, May 3, 1969, 7; *Vanguard*, May 17, 1969, 2; see also the open letter to the prime minister from the executive committee of the OWTU supporting the bus workers' strike, *Vanguard*, May 17, 1969, 4-5; *Vanguard*, September 15, 1978, 1. On joint actions, see *Vanguard*, February 10, 1968, 5; *Vanguard*, June 8, 1968, 1, 8; see also *Vanguard*, May 3, 1969, 2, for a march on April 26, 1969, involving oil, electricity, transport, and dock workers and NJAC members from south, central, and north Trinidad as well as Tobago; *Vanguard*, December 8, 1978, 1, 3.

68. *TG*, March 16, 1965, 1. These unions were the Amalgamated Workers Union, ATSEFWTU, Communication Workers Union, and Federated Workers Union. The National Federation of Labour supported the ISA.

69. *Vanguard*, November 26, 1965, 4.

70. *Vanguard*, January 27, 1968, 8.

71. *Vanguard*, May 28, 1965, 3.

72. *Vanguard*, January 27, 1968, 8.

73. *Vanguard Supplement*, July 23, 1965, 1.

74. Andreas, *Disenfranchised*; Trotz, *Point*.

75. *Vanguard*, October 1, 1965, 3. See also *Vanguard*, March 21, 1970, 2; C. L. R. James, "West Indian Middle Classes," reprinted in *Vanguard*, January 17, 1970, 3, 6, and February 7, 1970, 3, 7.

76. *Vanguard*, October 1, 1965, 3; see also *Vanguard*, August 6, 1965, 4; *Vanguard*, January 17, 1970, 1.

77. *Vanguard*, August 27, 1965, 6.

78. *Vanguard*, August 6, 1965, 8; OWTU President General George Weekes, in *Vanguard*, March 22, 1969, 2.

79. *Vanguard*, May 3, 1969, 2.

80. *Vanguard*, May 17, 1969, 3; *Vanguard*, June 28, 1969, 5.

81. *Vanguard*, August 13, 1965, 5.

82. OWTU President General Weekes, speech delivered March 19, 1970, printed in *Vanguard*, April 4, 1970, 4; see also *Vanguard*, July 30, 1965, 4.

83. *Vanguard*, April 5, 1969, 1, 8.

84. Weekes, speech at March of Resistance, June 3, 1968, printed in *Vanguard*, June 8, 1968, 2.

85. *Vanguard*, November 16, 1968, 2.

86. Swan, "I & I Shot the Sheriff," 197.

87. Rodney, *Groundings with My Brothers*, 9–31.

88. Quinn, *Black Power*, 25.

89. Samaroo, "February Revolution (1970)."

90. *Vanguard*, July 23, 1965, 6; *Vanguard*, March 22, 1969, 2; *Vanguard*, January 3, 1970, 2; see also OWTU President General Weekes, speech to OWTU General Council, July 29, 1967, excerpt in *Vanguard*, October 19, 1968, 7.

91. *Vanguard*, September 27, 1969, 3.

92. *Vanguard*, July 30, 1965, 4.

93. *Vanguard*, December 6, 1969, 8; *Vanguard*, January 9, 1971, 7.

94. *Vanguard*, July 9, 1965, 4; see also OWTU President General Weekes, speech, Industrial Relations Seminar, September 20, 1969, printed in *Vanguard*, September 27, 1969, 3.

95. Quinn, *Black Power*, 26.

96. "OWTU Statement on the February Revolution," *Vanguard*, April 18, 1970, 5. The unions used the portmanteau Trinago for Trinidad and Tobago.

97. *Vanguard*, October 25, 1969, 1; *Vanguard*, January 9, 1971, 7; see also Matthews, *Multinational Corporations*.

98. *Vanguard*, March 22, 1969, 2, 5, 7; *Vanguard*, May 17, 1969, 2.

99. *Vanguard*, March 22, 1969, 5.

100. *Express*, April 11, 1970, 11.

101. *Express*, April 6, 1970, 3.

102. "OWTU Statement on the February Revolution," *Vanguard*, April 18, 1970, 4.

103. *Vanguard*, August 6, 1965, 7.

104. *Vanguard*, February 7, 1970, 2; *Vanguard*, March 21, 1970, 4.

105. For example, see *Vanguard*, April 4, 1970, 3; and the activities of the Indian Revival and Reform Association, in *Vanguard*, November 3, 1978, 4.

106. *Vanguard*, February 7, 1970, 1.

107. Rodney, "Black Power and the West Indies," 3, excerpt from *Groundings with My Brothers*, reprinted in *Vanguard*, January 3, 1970, 3, 6.

108. "Tributes Flow for 'Brinz,'" *Daily Express*, July 15, 2023.

109. *Vanguard*, February 7, 1970, 2.

110. *Vanguard*, March 22, 1969, 1.

111. *Vanguard*, July 25, 1970, 5. The Women's Section was formerly called the Women's Auxiliary. For discussion of the name change, see *Vanguard*, August 25, 1978, 3.

112. *Vanguard*, May 22, 1971, 8.

113. OWTU President General Weekes, speech at meeting co-organized with Student Guild, March 3, 1969, printed in *Vanguard*, March 22, 1969, 2.

114. Amin, *Delinking*.

115. OWTU President General Weekes, excerpt of speech at OWTU General Council meeting, July 29, 1967, printed in *Vanguard*, October 19, 1968, 7; see also Weekes's call to workers to join the March of Confrontation (October 5, 1968) organized by the OWTU, the National Union of Government and Federated Workers, the Seamen and Waterfront Workers Trade Union, the Progressive Workers Union, and the Young Power Movement, printed in *Vanguard*, October 5, 1968, 1; and Weekes, speech at March of Resistance, June 3, 1968, printed in *Vanguard*, June 8, 1968, 2.

116. Pilgrim, *Power*; Brinsley Samaroo, "Afro-Indian Solidarity," *Vanguard*, March 21, 1970, 4–5; Teelucksingh, "Black Power Movement."

117. Winston Leonard, "OWTU Strikes Blow for Black Struggle," *Vanguard*, January 9, 1971, 4–5.

118. *Vanguard*, December 23, 1965; *Vanguard*, December 10, 1965, 2; *Vanguard*, July 23, 1965, 8; *Vanguard*, August 6, 1965, 4; see also *Vanguard*, August 13, 1965, 3; *Vanguard*, April 18, 1970, 7; *Vanguard*, October 29, 1965, 4; *Vanguard*, October 22, 1965.

119. On Diwali, see *Vanguard*, October 22, 1965, 5; *Vanguard*, October 19, 1968, 3, 7; *Vanguard*, October 24, 1970, 1. On Eid, see *Vanguard*, December 14, 1968, 7. On Christmas, see *Vanguard*, December 23, 1965, 4-6.

120. *Vanguard*, October 22, 1965, 1.

121. A. Desai, "Indian South Africans"; Hall, "New Ethnicities"; Hall, "Frontlines and Backyards"; Shilliam, *Black Pacific*.

122. B. Knight, "Altheia Jones-Lecointe"; Narayan, "British Black Power."

123. Bunce and Field, *Darcus Howe*, 72; Henry and Buhle, *C. L. R. James's Caribbean*.

124. *Vanguard*, August 27, 1965, 6; *Vanguard*, October 1, 1965, 7; *Vanguard*, November 26, 1965, 1; *Vanguard*, January 27, 1968, 5; *Vanguard*, March 2, 1968, 2; *Vanguard*, March 30, 1968, 5; *Vanguard*, August 24, 1968, 7, 8; *Vanguard*, November 2, 1968, 5; *Vanguard*, January 9, 1971, 7; *Vanguard*, March 11, 1972, 5.

125. On the Congo, see *Vanguard*, July 9, 1965, 2. On the Vietnam War, see *Vanguard*, May 1, 1968, 8. On labor struggles around the world, see *Vanguard*, August 24, 1968, 8; *Vanguard*, December 14, 1968, 6; *Vanguard*, May 3, 1969, 5.

126. *Vanguard*, March 2, 1968, 4; *Vanguard*, March 30, 1968, 5; Syl Lowhar, "From Non-violence to Violence," University of the West Indies Students' Guild, press release, *Vanguard*, April 20, 1968, 10; *Vanguard*, May 1, 1968, 3; *Vanguard*, September 21, 1968, 5; *Vanguard*, February 22, 1969, 8; *Vanguard*, August 9, 1969, 4–5; *Vanguard*, August 23, 1969, 5; *Vanguard*, December 20, 1969, 3.

127. *Vanguard*, July 6, 1968, 7.

128. *Vanguard*, August 6, 1965, 6.

129. *Vanguard*, July 30, 1965, 3; *Vanguard*, August 8, 1970, 5.

130. *Vanguard*, July 30, 1965, 8; *Vanguard*, August 20, 1965; *Vanguard*, September 17, 1965, 1; *Vanguard*, October 15, 1965, 5; *Vanguard*, November 12, 1965, 6; *Vanguard*, October 11, 1969, 2.

131. In 1976 radical unions made a second attempt to win state power through the formation of a labor party, the United Labor Front. The union secured ten of thirty-six seats, which was better than the WFP's results but not enough to take over the state.

132. Kiely, *Politics of Labour*, 110–11; Vincent, "Oilfields Workers' Trade Union."

133. Look Lai, "C. L. R. James," 199; Vincent, "Oilfields Workers' Trade Union."

134. Vincent, "Oilfields Workers' Trade Union."

135. Sara Abraham has shown that there is at least one instance of a multiracial party that saw electoral victory, but this was a party of professional middle-class and business elites. See Abraham, "Exceptional Victories."

136. *Vanguard*, February 10, 1968, 5; *Vanguard*, June 8, 1968, 1, 8.

137. *Vanguard*, October 5, 1968, 1; *Vanguard*, October 12, 1968, 1.

138. *Vanguard*, August 13, 1965, 6.

139. *Vanguard*, June 22, 1968, 3.

140. Ronald Hoolasie, "Whither Sugar and Sugar Workers," letter to the editor, *Vanguard*, August 13, 1965, 6. See also NTUC May Day Resolutions, *Vanguard*, May 14, 1965, 7; *Vanguard*, April 30, 1965, 5; *Vanguard*, May 28, 1965, 3, 8; TIWU Resolutions, *Vanguard*, June 25, 1965, 3; *Vanguard*, July 30, 1965; *Vanguard*, December 10, 1965, 2; *Vanguard*, August 10, 1968, 2; *Vanguard*, November 16, 1968, 2; *Vanguard*, December 19, 1970, 5.

141. OWTU President General George Weekes, speech at the opening session of negotiations between Texaco and the OWTU, September 3, 1968, printed in *Vanguard*, September 7, 1968, 2; see also OWTU resolution, *Vanguard*, October 12, 1968, 1; OWTU, 40th anniversary booklet, 33.

142. On acquisition of BP, see excerpts from *Oil in Turmoil and OWTU Memorandum on the Formation of a National Oil Co.*, 1967, proposal to Trinidad and Tobago government, reprinted *Vanguard*, October 5, 1968, 2. On acquisition of Texaco, which was negotiated after the 1970 uprising, see OWTU, "OWTU Intensifies Struggle Against Imperialism," in OWTU Department of Education and Research, Information Bulletin, No. 3, January 13, 1979, OWTU library. Also see "Texaco Must Go" campaign in the 1970s in OWTU, *General Council's Report by the General Secretary: Annual Conference of Delegates 1937–1979*, October 27, 1979, 21–25, OWTU library.

143. OWTU, "OWTU Intensifies Struggle Against Imperialism," January 13, 1979.

144. *Vanguard*, November 17, 1978, 3.

145. *Vanguard*, October 24, 1970, 5. See also *Vanguard*, June 8, 1968, 1; *Vanguard*, June 27, 1970, 1.

146. *Vanguard*, August 6, 1965, 5.

147. NTUC May Day Resolutions, *Vanguard*, May 14, 1965, 7; *Vanguard*, May 28, 1965, 3, 8; TIWU Resolutions, *Vanguard*, June 25, 1965, 3; *Vanguard*, November 16, 1968, 2.

148. NTUC May Day Resolutions, *Vanguard*, May 14, 1965, 7; *Vanguard*, May 28, 1965, 3, 8; TIWU Resolutions, *Vanguard*, June 25, 1965, 3; *Vanguard*, November 16, 1968, 2; *Vanguard*, January 25, 1969, 7; *Vanguard*, May 22, 1971, 3; *Vanguard*, May 22, 1971, 3.

149. "Women's Section," *Vanguard*, May 28, 1965, 7; *Vanguard*, July 23, 1965, 7; *Vanguard*, July 30, 1965, 7; *Vanguard*, December 8, 1978, 3.

150. *Vanguard*, August 25, 1978, 3; see also *Vanguard*, June 30, 1978, 3; *Vanguard*, October 20, 1978, 3; *Vanguard*, November 17, 1978, 3.

151. *Vanguard*, May 14, 1965, 5; see also *Vanguard*, December 23, 1965.

152. *Vanguard*, November 16, 1968, 2. See also OWTU, *General Council's Report 1937–1976*, December 4, 1976, 26–35.

153. The OWTU previously had ties to the Cipriani Labor College (established in 1966) but withdrew its support to protest the unilateral dismissal of the college director, Earl Augustus, by the minister of education. *Vanguard*, January 13, 1968, 2. The OWTU then established the College of Labor and Industrial Relations. This college accepted students sixteen years and older (OWTU members and nonmembers alike) and had an Institute for the Training of Women in Creative Domestic Arts, which provided "training and education in the lore, techniques, and marketing of indigenous products, e.g., local confectionery, marmalades, fruit mixtures, beverages." Some of the products were successfully marketed in Jamaica, Puerto Rico, and a few other Caribbean islands. *Vanguard*, March 30, 1968, 6. See also *Vanguard*, January 13, 1968, 2; *Vanguard*, January 11, 1969, 6; *Vanguard*, January 25, 1969, 3. The college also had all-day seminars for women. *Vanguard*, April 20, 1968, 2. For other education initiatives by the OWTU, see *Vanguard*, November 12, 1965, 1; *Vanguard*, December 10, 1965, 1; *Vanguard*, January 27, 1968, 8; *Vanguard*, February 8, 1969, 10.

154. *Express*, April 2, 1970, 1.

155. OWTU President General Weekes, speech in Fyzabad, June 19, 1965, printed in *Vanguard*, June 11, 1965, 3; *Vanguard*, July 30, 1965, 4; *Vanguard*, December 6, 1969, 1, 8; *Vanguard*, August 8, 1970, 1; see OWTU, letter to Eric Williams advocating for this change, February 25, 1970, printed in *Vanguard*, March 7, 1970, 7.

156. *Vanguard*, October 25, 1969, 2.

157. C. Thomas, *Rise of the Authoritarian State*.

158. OWTU, *General Council's Report 1937–1979*, 13–14; *Vanguard*, July 30, 1965, 1; *Vanguard*, March 30, 1968, 6.

159. Leader of Trinidad and Tobago Labour Congress Clive Spencer, speech at Tripartite Conference on Unemployment and Retrenchment, June 10, 1968, printed in *Vanguard*, June 22, 1968, 3–4; *Vanguard*, December 20, 1969, 1.

160. *Vanguard*, March 8, 1969, 1; *Vanguard*, February 22, 1969, 1, 10.

161. *Express*, April 22, 1970, 3; *Express*, April 24, 1970, 8; *TG*, March 5, 1965, 1; *TG*, March 6, 1965, 1; *TG*, March 17, 1965, 2; *Vanguard*, July 6, 1968, 2, 7; *Vanguard*, August 6, 1965; *Vanguard*, March 8, 1969, 6; *Vanguard*, March 21, 1970, 3; *Vanguard*, April 18, 1970, 1; *Vanguard*, May 17, 1969, 1; *Vanguard*, May 31, 1969, 1; *Vanguard*, July 25, 1970, 1; *Vanguard*, March 20, 1971, 6.

162. On police intimidation, see *Vanguard*, July 6, 1968, 7. On police raids, see *Vanguard*, June 12, 1970, 1, 4–8. On private companies' actions, see *Vanguard*, September 7, 1968, 7; *Vanguard*, December 5, 1970, 1.

163. *Vanguard*, December 23, 1965; *Vanguard*, July 30, 1965.

164. Quoted in *TG*, January 24, 1970, 1.

165. *TG*, March 11, 1965, 1–2.

166. Williams, *Inward Hunger*, 311.

167. *TG*, March 14, 1965, 1.

168. *TG*, March 17, 1965, 1; *Vanguard*, April 30, 1965, 3; *Vanguard*, June 25, 1965, 1, 4, 8; *Vanguard*, December 10, 1965, 1-2; *Vanguard*, January 27, 1968, 4; *Vanguard*, March 30, 1968, 7; *Vanguard*, June 8, 1968, 7.

169. *Vanguard*, August 27, 1965, 6; OWTU resolution, passed by General Council on March 16, 1965, printed in *Vanguard*, August 13, 1965, 2; see also *Vanguard*, May 14, 1965, 1; *Vanguard*, June 25, 1965, 5. On the ISA as a form of McCarthyism, see *Vanguard*, April 30, 1965, 2.

170. Quoted in Kambon, *For Bread, Justice, and Freedom*, 176.

171. *TG*, March 19, 1965, 1. Only Arthur Robinson, deputy prime minister and deputy leader of the PNM, criticized and then stepped down from the PNM, which served as an important vindication for labor, but the vast majority of the ruling party stood firm. See *Express*, April 14, 1970, 1, 10–11; *Vanguard*, August 22, 1970, 6.

172. Steinberg, *Statesman's Year-Book 1967–68*, 514.

173. Paxton, *Statesman's Year-Book 1973–74*, 499.

174. Bernard, *Against the Odds*; *Express*, April 24, 1970, 1.

175. Bernard, *Against the Odds*.

176. Smart, "Strategic Development," 70–75.

177. *Vanguard*, April 4, 1970, 1, 8.

178. *Vanguard*, August 5, 1972.

179. Quoted in Palmer, *Eric Williams*, 300.

180. Quoted in Palmer, *Eric Williams*, 299.

181. Quoted in Palmer, *Eric Williams*, 298.

182. *Express*, April 23, 1970.

183. Quoted in Palmer, *Eric Williams*, 301.

184. Palmer, *Eric Williams*, 300–301.

185. *Express*, April 25, 1970, 2.

186. C. Singh, *Multinationals*, 95.

187. Chalmin, *Making of a Sugar Giant*, 511–16; *Express*, April 6, 1970, 1.

188. For discussion about the OWTU and CIA, see *Vanguard*, June 14, 1969, 5; OWTU, 40th anniversary booklet, 31; Weekes, *Why I Resigned*.

189. Prime Minister Eric Williams, nationwide broadcast, speech, May 3, 1970, 5, accessed November 25, 2024, https://ericwilliams.gov.tt/wp-content/uploads/2023/09 /EW126.pdf.

190. Vitalis, *Oilcraft*, 67.

191. Trinidad and Tobago was initially an associate member of OPEC, but Iraq vetoed its full membership in 1973 on the grounds that it had low oil exports. Trinidad and Tobago was denied a second time when officials offended one of the OPEC member country representatives.

192. GOTT, *Accounting for the Petrodollar 1973–1983*, table 2, 2.

193. GOTT, *Third Five-Year Plan*, 3–7, 14.

194. GOTT, *Third Five-Year Plan*, 7–8.

195. GOTT, *Third Five-Year Plan*, 8; see also Matthews, *Multinational Corporations*, 89–108.

196. Prime Minister Eric Williams, 1972 Budget Statement, 11, Trinidad and Tobago Ministry of Finance library; GOTT, *White Paper on Public Participation in Industrial and Commercial Activities*, 1972, 1975.

197. GOTT, *Third Five-Year Plan*, 19.

198. Sebastien, "State-Sector Development," 118.

199. GOTT, *Accounting for the Petrodollar*, 22–23.

200. GOTT, *White Paper on Public Participation*, 1972, 7.

201. OWTU, *Oil in Turmoil and OWTU Memorandum on the Formation of a National Oil Co.*, 1967, 1–10, OWTU library.

202. GOTT, *Third Five-Year Plan*, 171–72.

203. GOTT, *Ministry of Petroleum and Mines Annual Administrative Report for the Year 1968*, 2, accessed March 10, 2023, https://www.energy.gov.tt/wp-content/uploads/2013 /11/Annual_Administrative_Report_1968.pdf.

204. OWTU, 40th anniversary booklet, 33.

205. Cabinet Secretary to OWTU President General Weekes, January 2, 1979; Appendix XIV in OWTU, *General Council's Report 1937–1979*, October 27, 1979, 106–11; OWTU to Williams, May 1, 1978, Appendix XII, in OWTU, *General Council's Report 1937–1979*, October 27, 1979, 92–99, OWTU library; OWTU, opening statement to the Commission of Enquiry into Texaco Trinidad, Inc., in OWTU, *General Council's Report 1937–1979*, October 27, 1979, 92–99, 112–17. The OWTU maintained that beyond a commission of

inquiry into Texaco, only pressure from the working class would drive them out. See "OWTU Intensifies Struggle Against Imperialism," January 13, 1979.

206. Minister of Finance George Chambers, *Budget Speech of the Honourable G. M. Chambers, Minister of Finance, to the House of Representatives of Trinidad and Tobago,* December 20, 1974, 48, Ministry of Finance library.

207. Minister of Finance George Chambers, *Budget Speech,* December 20, 1974, 37–41.

208. Farrell, *Underachieving Society,* 128; Thorburn, "Nationalism, Identity."

209. Farrell, *Underachieving Society,* 128.

210. Auty and Gelb, "Oil Windfalls," 1165; GOTT, *White Paper on Natural Gas,* 2; GOTT, *Accounting for the Petrodollar 1973–1983,* table VIIIA, table VIIIB.

211. GOTT, *Ministry of Petroleum and Mines Annual Report for the Year 1979,* 1, https://www.energy.gov.tt/wp-content/uploads/2013/11/Annual_Administrative_Report_1979.pdf.

212. WTO, Trade Policy Review Trinidad and Tobago: Report by the Secretariat, August 17, 2005, https://www.wto.org/english/tratop_e/tpr_e/s151-4_e.doc.

213. Boopsingh and McGuire, *From Oil to Gas,* xv.

214. *Vanguard,* March 11, 1972, 1; OWTU, *Progress, Struggle, Leadership, Dedication, 1937–1969,* 32nd anniversary celebration of the Union, booklet, OWTU library.

215. OWTU, 32nd anniversary booklet; *Vanguard,* May 1, 1968, 8; *Vanguard,* January 17, 1970, 4–5; *Vanguard,* February 7, 1970, 6; *Vanguard,* August 22, 1970, 3; *Vanguard,* January 9, 1971, 7; *Vanguard,* February 6, 1971, 4–5; *Vanguard,* September 29, 1978, 3.

216. OWTU, 40th anniversary booklet, 72.

217. Pollard, "Erosion of Agriculture," 829.

218. *Express,* April 21, 1970, 10; *Vanguard,* June 27, 1970, 1, 8; OWTU, 40th anniversary booklet, 68–72.

219. *Vanguard,* July 12, 1969, 1; *Vanguard,* August 9, 1969, 1.

220. Minister of Finance George Chambers, *Budget Speech,* December 20, 1974, 9.

221. Farrell, *Underachieving Society,* 142.

222. GOTT, *Ministry of Petroleum and Mines Annual Report for the Year 1970,* 23–25; GOTT, *Ministry of Petroleum and Mines Annual Report for the Year 1971,* 17–19; GOTT, *Ministry of Petroleum and Mines Annual Report for the Year 1974,* vii; GOTT, *Ministry of Petroleum and Mines Annual Report for the Year 1976,* 21–22.

223. GOTT, *Ministry of Petroleum and Mines Annual Report for the Year 1975,* 21.

224. GOTT, *Ministry of Petroleum and Mines Annual Report for the Year 1979,* 26.

225. GOTT, *Third Five-Year Plan 1969–1973,* 171.

226. GOTT, *Third Five-Year Plan 1969–1973,* 171.

227. GOTT, *Third Five-Year Plan 1969–1973,* 171; GOTT, *Ministry of Petroleum and Mines Annual Report for the Year 1970,* 25–26; GOTT, *Ministry of Petroleum and Mines Annual Report for the Year 1971,* 22–23; GOTT, *Ministry of Petroleum and Mines Annual Report for the Year 1973,* 19–20; GOTT, *Ministry of Petroleum and Mines Annual Report for the Year 1974,* 18–20; GOTT, *Ministry of Petroleum and Mines Annual Report for the Year 1976,* 1, 23; GOTT, *Ministry of Petroleum and Mines Annual Report for the Year 1977,* 20–23.

228. GOTT, *Third Five-Year Plan 1969–1973,* 171.

229. Prime Minister Eric Williams to OWTU President General George Weekes, October 9, 1968, reprinted in *Vanguard*, October 12, 1968, 3.

230. *Vanguard*, December 14, 1968, 2, 4–5; see also *Vanguard*, November 16, 1968, 5; *Vanguard*, October 12, 1968; *Vanguard*, June 14, 1969, 4. Williams wanted only one OWTU representative on the oil company board, not two as he had granted for the Canefarmers Association in sugar.

231. GOTT, *Third Five-Year Plan 1969–1973*, 18.

232. GOTT, *Review of the Economy 1975*, 58, report, Ministry of Finance library.

233. C. Harvey, "Educational Change," 347. Moreover, declining birth rates and earlier entrance into secondary schools meant there were fewer primary school students in 1985.

234. C. Campbell, *Endless Education*.

235. GOTT, *Review of the Economy 1975*, 56–57.

236. World Bank, World Development Indicators, "Mortality Rate, Infant (per 1,000 live births)—Trinidad and Tobago," accessed January 20, 2023, https://data.worldbank .org/indicator/SP.DYN.IMRT.IN?locations=TT.

237. OWTU, *General Council's Report to the 39th Annual Conference of Delegates*, November 4, 1978, 12.

238. Minister of Finance George Chambers, *Budget Speech*, December 20, 1974, 61–62; Prime Minister and Minister of Finance Eric Williams, *Budget Speech of 1980 of Dr. The Honourable E. E. Williams*, November 30, 1979, 48, Ministry of Finance library.

239. Minister of Finance George Chambers, *Budget Speech*, December 20, 1974, 61–62; Prime Minister and Minister of Finance Eric Williams, *Budget Speech of 1980*, November 30, 1979, 48.

240. Minister of Finance George Chambers, *Budget Speech*, December 20, 1974, 68–74; Prime Minister and Minister of Finance Eric Williams, *Budget Speech of 1980*, November 30, 1979, 44–50; GOTT, *Accounting for the Petrodollar 1973–1983*, table XIX.

241. GOTT, *Accounting for the Petrodollar*, 52–54; GOTT *Accounting for the Petrodollar 1973–1983*, table XXXII.

242. *Vanguard*, May 22, 1971, 3. Oil workers and some others had already won private union-negotiated pension plans from their employers. *Vanguard* January 9, 1971, 2. They did not trust the government's scheme and pushed for an opt-out system so that they could keep their security and benefits from their employers and contribute to the national insurance scheme independently. *Vanguard*, May 22, 1971, 3; *Vanguard*, March 25, 1972, 1.

243. Prime Minister and Minister of Finance Eric Williams, *Budget Speech of 1980*, November 30, 1979, 26–38.

244. GOTT *Accounting for the Petrodollar*; GOTT *Accounting for the Petrodollar 1973–1983*; Pantin, *Black Power Day*, 47.

245. *Vanguard*, April 3, 1971, 4–5.

246. *Vanguard*, January 9, 1971, 1, 5, 7; *Vanguard*, May 22, 1971, 6, 7; *Vanguard*, September 15, 1978, 1; *Vanguard*, September 29, 1978, 1.

247. OWTU, 40th anniversary booklet, 38, 41; OWTU, *General Council's Report 1937–1974*, 7–8; R. Thomas, *Development of Labour Law*, 53–54; see also *Vanguard*, September 5, 1970, 2–7.

248. Freedom House, Freedom in the World, Comparative and Historical Data Files: Country and Territory Rankings and Statuses, 1973–2024, accessed January 12, 2023, https://freedomhouse.org/report/freedom-world.

249. *Vanguard*, July 30, 1965, 1.

250. Reddock, "Industrialisation."

251. Hintzen, *Costs of Regime Survival*.

252. Hintzen, *Costs of Regime Survival*, 73; Hosein and Gookool, "Export Mineral Rents."

253. Hintzen, *Costs of Regime Survival*, 75–77.

254. On time-to-build lags, see Pacheco-De-Almeida et al., "Commitment Versus Flexibility Trade-Off"; M. Lieberman, "Excess Capacity."

255. Edwards, "No Colonial Working Class, No Post-Colonial Development"; Ross, *Oil Curse*, 20, 197–200.

256. UNDP, Trends in the Human Development Index 1990–2022, dataset, accessed January 20, 2023, https://hdr.undp.org/data-center/human-development-index#/indicies/HDI.

CHAPTER 6. COMPARING WORKER MOVEMENTS

1. Itzigsohn and Brown, *Sociology of W. E. B. Du Bois*, 199; Rodney, "Race and Class"; see also Go, *Postcolonial Thought*.

2. Bolland, *Politics of Labour*; Burrowes, *Seeds of Solidarity*; Ewing, "Caribbean Labour Politics"; A. Fraser, *1935 Riots in St Vincent*; Palmer, *Freedom's Children*; Post, *Arise Ye Starvelings*; Putnam, *Radical Moves*.

3. Abraham, *Labour*; Bissessar, *Ethnic Conflict*; Bissessar and La Guerre, *Trinidad and Tobago and Guyana*; D. Brown, "Ethnic Politics and Public Sector Management"; Hintzen, "Ethnicity, Class, and International Capitalist Penetration"; Ramsaran and Lewis, *Caribbean Masala*; S. Wilson, *Politics of Identity*.

4. Beckford, *Persistent Poverty*; Girvan et al., "Debt Problem"; Mandle, *Patterns*; Payne and Sutton, *Dependency Under Challenge*.

5. Hintzen, *Costs of Regime Survival*.

6. Gafar, "Poverty, Income Growth, and Inequality," 476–77.

7. Bolland, *Politics of Labour*, 336.

8. International Development Association and International Monetary Fund, "Guyana Poverty Reduction Strategy Paper Joint Staff Assessment," August 28, 2002, 2, 7, accessed December 11, 2023, https://documents1.worldbank.org/curated/ru/605091468771559168/pdf/multiopage.pdf#page=30.99.

9. Bissessar and La Guerre, *Trinidad and Tobago and Guyana*, 36.

10. Great Britain, *Report of the British Guiana Commission*, 40. Note that the Portuguese were not considered white in Guyana for much of the colonial period.

11. Mohamed, "African Labor in Guyana," 107; Rodney, *History*, 25–26.

12. Girvan and Vale, "Guyana-Alcan Conflict," 90; Carmichael, "Rise and Fall," 16–17.

13. Hintzen, *Costs of Regime Survival*, 155.

14. Carmichael, "Rise and Fall," 1–3.

15. Baptiste, "Exploitation of Caribbean Bauxite," 111–12, 114, 116.

16. Quinn, "Colonial Legacies," 12.

17. Rodney, *History*, 121.

18. Rodney, *History*, 15.

19. Rodney, *History*, 139–45.

20. Quinn, "Colonial Legacies," 12–13.

21. Bolland, *Politics of Labour*, 174, 181–82.

22. Sallahuddin, *Guyana*, 27.

23. C. Singh, *Guyana*, 15.

24. Bolland, *Politics of Labour*, 350. See also Chase, *History of Trade Unionism*, 85–87.

25. Abraham, *Labour*, 45–48; Burrowes, *Seeds of Solidarity*; Chase, *History of Trade Unionism*; Premdas, "Political Parties," 34–35.

26. Abraham, *Labour*, 45; Chase, *History of Trade Unionism*, 78.

27. Bolland, *Politics of Labour*, 213, 348; Ewing, "Caribbean Labour Politics," 43; Rodney, *Decolonial Marxism*, 15.

28. Rodney, *Decolonial Marxism*, 15.

29. Chase, *History of Trade Unionism*, 77.

30. Colony of British Guiana, *Blue Book 1917*, M55; Colony of Trinidad and Tobago, *Blue Book 1917*, N63; Great Britain Colonial Office, *Annual Report on the Social and Economic Progress of the People of British Guiana 1937*, 33; Great Britain Colonial Office, *Annual Report on the Social and Economic Progress of the People of Trinidad and Tobago 1937*, 44.

31. Rodney, *History*, 120–27.

32. Mandle, "Decline in Mortality."

33. Colony of Trinidad and Tobago, *Annual Report Trinidad and Tobago, 1951*, 20, 38–39, 68–79; Great Britain Colonial Office, *Report on British Guiana for the Year 1952*, 41, 90–100. The colonial government in Trinidad and Tobago directly ran and controlled far more schools than the colonial government in Guyana (sixty-three versus twelve).

34. Abraham, *Labour*, 47.

35. Abraham, *Labour*, 55; Alexander, *History of Organized Labor*, 356; Chase, *History of Trade Unionism*, 90, 141–49.

36. Bissessar and La Guerre, *Trinidad and Tobago and Guyana*, 67; Bolland, *Politics of Labour*, 602.

37. Seecharan, "Cheddi Jagan, Communism and the African-Guyanese."

38. Bolland, *Politics of Labour*, 602.

39. Bolland, *Politics of Labour*, 604–10; Chase, *History of Trade Unionism*, 141.

40. G. Lewis, *Growth*, 285.

41. Bissessar and La Guerre, *Trinidad and Tobago and Guyana*, 70.

42. Bolland, *Politics of Labour*, 616–17; Spinner, *Political and Social History*, 83.

43. Bolland, *Politics of Labour*, 614.

44. Hintzen, *Costs of Regime Survival*, 36–37.

45. Seecharan, "Cheddi Jagan, Communism and the African-Guyanese." On Kwayana's concept of "racial insecurity," see Westmaas, "Organic Activist," 171; and Hinds, *Ethno-Politics*, 67.

46. Hintzen, *Costs of Regime Survival*, 49–50; Spinner, *Political and Social History*, 74, 80–81.

47. Kwayana, "Burnhamism, Jaganism," 40.

48. Bolland, *Politics of Labour*, 614, 625; Palmer, *Cheddi Jagan*, 57–58.

49. Bolland, *Politics of Labour*, 625; Hintzen, *Costs of Regime Survival*, 50.

50. Rabe, *U.S. Intervention*, 101.

51. Rabe, *U.S. Intervention*, 93.

52. Bissessar and La Guerre, *Trinidad and Tobago and Guyana*, 85.

53. Bissessar and La Guerre, *Trinidad and Tobago and Guyana*, 85–86; Rabe, *U.S. Intervention*; Andaiye, "1964."

54. Bissessar and La Guerre, *Trinidad and Tobago and Guyana*, 86.

55. International Labour Organization, "ILOSTAT Indicators and Data Tools," Country Catalogue, accessed June 25, 2024, https://ilostat.ilo.org/data/.

56. Rodney, *Groundings with My Brothers*; Westmaas, "Organic Activist"; Trotz, *Point*.

57. Rodney, *Groundings with My Brothers*, 19–31.

58. Abraham, *Labour*, 115–25; Kwayana, *Bauxite Strike*.

59. Quinn, "Sitting on a Volcano," 136–37, 142–43.

60. Kwayana, "Burnhamism, Jaganism," 43.

61. Rose, *Dependency and Socialism*, 355.

62. Hintzen, *Costs of Regime Survival*, 158–62.

63. Lange, *Lineages of Despotism*, 134.

64. Quinn, "Colonial Legacies," 20–21; Rose, *Dependency and Socialism*, 194–95.

65. Rose, *Dependency and Socialism*, 356, 358.

66. Rose, *Dependency and Socialism*, 358–59. In response, the Guyanese state borrowed extensively from its Caribbean neighbors, especially Trinidad and Tobago and Barbados.

67. Gafar, *Guyana*, 9.

68. Rabe, *U.S. Intervention*, 165.

69. Bissessar and La Guerre, *Trinidad and Tobago and Guyana*, 88.

70. Danns, "Militarization and Development," 30.

71. C. Thomas, "State Capitalism in Guyana."

72. Canterbury, *Neoextractivism*, 174–78.

73. Bulkan and Trotz, "Oil Fuels"; Canterbury, *Neoextractivism*, 211–30; Hinds, "Problems of Democratic Transition in Guyana."

74. Bolland, *Politics of Labour*, 366.

75. Hart, *Rise and Organize*; Post, *Arise Ye Starvelings*.

76. Bolland, *Politics of Labour*, 582–83; Hart, *Towards Decolonisation*, 301.

77. Girvan and Girvan, "Making the Rules."

78. Ambursley, "Jamaica," 84; Bolland, *Politics of Labour*, 402–5, 454–56; H. Campbell, "Jamaica," 22; Stone, "Clientelism, Power and Democracy."

79. R. Lewis, "Jamaican Black Power," 65–66.

80. Patterson, *Confounding Island*; Riley, *Poverty and Life Expectancy*.

81. Ambursley, "Jamaica," 83–87; Hintzen, *Reproducing Domination*, 58, 62.

82. Ambursley, "Jamaica," 84–86; Stephens and Stephens, "Democratic Socialism."

83. Ambursley, "Jamaica," 80.

84. Patterson, *Confounding Island*.

85. Butler, *Copper Empire*, 4, 61.

86. Cooper, *Decolonization and African Society*, 336; Mwendapole, *Trade Union Movement*; Perrings, *Black Mineworkers*; Perrings, "Consciousness, Conflict and Proletarianization."

87. Butler, *Copper Empire*, 56; Cooper, *Decolonization and African Society*, 220, 338.

88. Meebelo, *African Proletarians*, 62; Parpart, "Household and the Mine Shaft," 41; Perrings, *Black Mineworkers*, 218; Cooper, *Decolonization and African Society*, 3.

89. Henderson, "Wage-Earners and Political Protest," 293.

90. Burawoy, *Color of Class*; Cooper, *Decolonization and African Society*, 60–61, 130, 367–68; Parpart, *Labor and Capital*.

91. Phiri, "Capricorn Africa Society Revisited," 72–73.

92. Bates, *Unions, Parties*, 6; Larmer, *Mineworkers in Zambia*; Larmer, "Unrealistic Expectations?," 321–22; LeBas, *From Protest to Parties*, 83; Meebelo, *African Proletarians*, 418–20, 433–37.

93. Larmer, *Mineworkers in Zambia*, 38–39.

94. LeBas, *From Protest to Parties*, 84; Larmer, "Unrealistic Expectations?," 327–46.

95. Larmer, *Mineworkers in Zambia*, 64.

96. M. Kelly, *Education in Zambia*; Turshen, *Privatizing Health Services*.

97. "World Development Indicators," databank, accessed October 16, 2024, https://databank.worldbank.org/source/world-development-indicators/preview/on.

98. Edwards, "No Colonial Working Class."

CONCLUSION

1. Rodney, "Contemporary Political Trends," 8.

2. Amin et al., *Dynamics of Global Crisis*; D. Harvey, *Brief History of Neoliberalism*; Silver and Arrighi, "Polanyi's 'Double Movement'"; Watson, "Liberalism."

3. Holton, "State Petroleum Enterprises"; Keston Perry, "Continuity, Change and Contradictions."

4. GOTT, *Ministry of Petroleum and Mines Annual Report for the Year 1979*, 1.

5. P. Lewis, "Bringing Small States Back In"; Watson, "Caribbean Basin Initiative."

6. Byron, "Strategic Repositioning"; T. John, "Canadian Imperialism."

7. Watson, "Liberalism."

8. Cited in Meeks and Girvan, *Thought of New World*, xiii.

9. Byron, "Strategic Repositioning," 228–29; Meighoo, *Politics in a "Half-Made Society"*; Ramsaran, "'Myth' of Development."

10. Thomas-Hope, "Migration in Trinidad and Tobago," 4.

11. Agozino et al., "Guns, Crime."

12. International Labour Organization. "ILOSTAT Indicators and Data Tools," Country Catalogue, accessed June 5, 2023, https://ilostat.ilo.org/data/.

13. "Trade Union Membership Declining," *TG*, February 7, 2021.

14. F. Knight, "Struggle"; Warwick and O'Connell, "How Oil Workers Fought."

15. Lake, "Better Strategy?"

16. "5 Years After Petrotrin's Closure," *TG*, October 9, 2023.

17. Antoine, "Embracing Collective Rights."

18. Farrell, *Underachieving Society*, 226–29; Jobson, "Road Work."

19. Bergquist, *Labor in Latin America*; Heller, *Labor of Development*; Selwyn, *Struggle for Development*; Rueschemeyer et al., *Capitalist Development and Democracy*.

20. James, "Revolutionary Solution."

21. Padmore, *Pan-Africanism or Communism?*, 17.

22. James, "Revolution and the Negro."

23. Agarwala, *Informal Labor*; Bradlow, *Urban Power*; Doner, *Politics of Uneven Development*; Esping-Andersen, "Power and Distributional Regimes"; Gibson, *Movement-Driven Development*; Heller, *Labor of Development*; Huber and Stephens, *Democracy and the Left*; Kuhonta, *Institutional Imperative*; Paschel, *Becoming Black Political Subjects*; Plys, *Brewing Resistance*; Sandbrook et al., *Social Democracy*; Seidman, *Manufacturing Militance*; Selwyn, *Struggle for Development*; Slater, *Ordering Power*; Vu, *Paths to Development*; Yashar, *Contesting Citizenship in Latin America*.

24. Larson, "Black Lives Matter"; Gilmore, *Golden Gulag*.

25. Acemoglu et al., "African Success Story"; Kohli, *State-Directed Development*; Lange, *Lineages of Despotism*; Mahoney, *Colonialism and Postcolonial Development*.

26. Mahoney, *Colonialism and Postcolonial Development*, 254.

27. Acemoglu et al., "African Success Story"; D. Scott, "Colonial Governmentality"; Steinmetz, "Colonial State," 608.

28. For other examples of multiracial worker unity, see Goldfield, *Southern Key*; Jung, *Reworking Race*; Letwin, *Challenge of Interracial Unionism*; Virdee, *Racism, Class*; see also Kelley, *Hammer and Hoe*.

29. Fallon and Viterna, "Women, Democracy, and the State"; Hill Collins, *Intersectionality as Critical Social Theory*; Jones, *End to the Neglect*.

30. Esnard, *Entrepreneurial Women*, 165–89; Mohammed, "Women's Responses"; Reddock, *Reflections on Gender*.

31. Michaels and Reed, *No Politics*; Cedric Johnson, *Panthers Can't Save Us*; Usmani and Zachariah, "Class Path"; W. Wilson, *Bridge*.

32. On the de-emphasis of racial identity, see Boswell et al., *Racial Competition*; Foner and Lewis, *Black Worker*; Gerteis, *Class and the Color Line*; Zeitlin and Weyher, "Black and White." On race not needing to be de-emphasized, see Kelley, *Hammer and Hoe*; Jung, *Reworking Race*; Pulido, *Black, Brown, Yellow, and Left*.

33. For works that focus on elites' role, see Kurtz, "Social Foundations"; Orihuela, "How Do 'Mineral States' Learn?" For works that attribute success to capitalist forces, see Acemoglu et al., "African Success Story"; Jones Luong and Weinthal, *Oil Is Not a Curse*; Rosser, "Escaping the Resource Curse."

34. Esping-Andersen, "Three Political Economies."

35. Okruhlik, "Rentier Wealth," 309.

36. Bair, "Global Capitalism"; Gereffi, "Global Value Chains."

37. Alimahomed-Wilson and Ness, *Choke Points*; Silver, *Forces of Labor*.

38. Keston Perry and Sealey-Huggins, "Racial Capitalism"; Riofrancos, *Resource Radicals*.

39. Evans, *Embedded Autonomy*; Sandbrook et al., *Social Democracy*.

40. On China, see Andreas, *Disenfranchised*. On Cuba, see Cushion, *Hidden History*. On Venezuela, see Ellner, "Trade Union Autonomy and the Emergence of a New Labor Movement in Venezuela"; and Gill, *Encountering US Empire in Socialist Venezuela*. On

Mauritius as a "classic" social democracy, see Sandbrook et al., *Social Democracy*. On labor-party-state relations in Mauritius, see Seegobin and Collen, "Mauritius."

41. Althusser, "Ideology and Ideological State Apparatuses." See also Gramsci, *Selections from the Prison Notebooks*; Hall, "Rediscovery of 'Ideology'"; Jobson, "Road Work."

APPENDIX

1. Emigh, "Power of Negative Thinking"; Barrett and Whyte, "Dependency Theory and Taiwan."

2. Adams et al., *Remaking Modernity*; Aminzade, "Historical Sociology and Time"; Mahoney and Rueschemeyer, *Comparative Historical Analysis*.

3. Bhambra, *Connected Sociologies*; Boatcă, *Global Inequalities Beyond Occidentalism*; Go, *Postcolonial Thought*; Clergé, "New Black Sociology"; Go and Lawson, *Global Historical Sociology*; Hammer and White, "Sociology of Colonial Subjectivity"; Itzigsohn and Brown, *Sociology of W. E. B. Du Bois*; Magubane, "Overlapping Territories and Intertwined Histories"; Meghji, *Decolonizing Sociology*; Silver, *Forces of Labor*.

4. Rodney, *How Europe Underdeveloped Africa*, 17; see also Du Bois, *Dusk of Dawn*, 155.

5. Rodney, *How Europe Underdeveloped Africa*, 15–21.

6. Many scholars have pointed to the epistemological and methodological problems of conducting research using colonial archives. See Derrida, *Archive Fever*; Guha and Spivak, *Selected Subaltern Studies*; Spivak, *Critique of Postcolonial Reason*; Stoler, *Along the Archival Grain*. Thus, this book deploys the methodological craft of Black radical scholars and postcolonial historians who read colonial archives "against the grain," attending to gaps and silences in the record.

7. Paige, "Conjuncture, Comparison."

Bibliography

Abraham, Sara. "Exceptional Victories: Multiracialism in Trinidad and Tobago and Guyana." *Ethnopolitics* 4, no. 4 (2005): 465–80.

Abraham, Sara. *Labour and the Multiracial Project in the Caribbean*. Lanham, MD: Lexington Books, 2007.

Acemoglu, Daron, Simon Johnson, and James A. Robinson. "An African Success Story: Botswana." In *In Search of Prosperity: Analytic Narratives on Economic Growth*, edited by Dani Rodrik, 80–119. Princeton, NJ: Princeton University Press, 2003.

Acemoglu, Daron, Simon Johnson, and James Robinson. "The Colonial Origins of Comparative Development: An Empirical Investigation." *American Economic Review* 91, no. 5 (2001): 1369–401.

Adams, Julia, Elisabeth Clemens, and Ann Shola Orloff, eds. *Remaking Modernity: Politics, History, and Sociology*. Durham, NC: Duke University Press, 2005.

Adi, Hakim. *Pan-Africanism: A History*. London: Bloomsbury, 2018.

Agarwala, Rina. *Informal Labor, Formal Politics, and Dignified Discontent in India*. Cambridge: Cambridge University Press, 2013.

Agozino, Biko, Ben Bowling, Elizabeth Ward, and Godfrey St Bernard. "Guns, Crime and Social Order in the West Indies." *Criminology and Criminal Justice* 9, no. 3 (2009): 287–305.

Ahlman, Jeffrey. *Living with Nkrumahism: Nation, State, and Pan-Africanism in Ghana*. Athens: Ohio University Press, 2017.

Alesina, Alberto, Arnaud Devleeschauwer, William Easterly, Sergio Kurlat, and Romain Wacziarg. "Fractionalization." *Journal of Economic Growth* 8, no. 2 (2003): 155–94.

Alexander, Robert. *A History of Organized Labor in the English-Speaking West Indies*. Westport, CT: Praeger, 2004.

Alimahomed-Wilson, Jake, and Immanuel Ness, eds. *Choke Points: Logistics Workers Disrupting the Global Supply Chain*. London: Pluto, 2018.

Allahar, Anton. "False Consciousness, Class Consciousness and Nationalism." *Social and Economic Studies* 53, no. 1 (2004): 95–123.

Allen, Theodore. *The Invention of the White Race*. London: Verso, 1994.

Althusser Louis. "Ideology and Ideological State Apparatuses." In *Lenin and Philosophy, and Other Essays*, translated by Ben Brewster, 170–86. New York: Monthly Review Press, 1971.

Ambedkar, Babasaheb. "Castes in India: Their Mechanism, Genesis and Development." In *Class, Caste, Gender*, edited by Manoranjan Mohanty, 131–53. New Delhi: Sage Publications, 2004.

Ambursley, Fitzroy. "Jamaica: The Demise of 'Democratic Socialism.'" *New Left Review*, no. 128 (1981): 76–87.

Amenta, Edwin, Neal Caren, Sheera Joy Olasky, and James E. Stobaugh. "All the Movements Fit to Print: Who, What, When, Where, and Why SMO Families Appeared in the *New York Times* in the Twentieth Century." *American Sociological Review* 74, no. 4 (2009): 636–56.

Amin, Samir. *Delinking: Towards a Polycentric World*. London: Zed Books, 1990.

Amin, Samir. "Imperialism and Globalization." *Monthly Review*, June 1, 2001.

Amin, Samir. *Imperialism and Unequal Development*. New York: Monthly Review Press, 1977.

Amin, Samir, Giovanni Arrighi, Andre Gunder Frank, and Immanuel Wallerstein. *Dynamics of Global Crisis*. New York: Monthly Review Press, 1982.

Aminzade, Ronald. "Historical Sociology and Time." *Sociological Methods and Research* 20, no. 4 (1992): 456–80.

Amsden, Alice. *Asia's Next Giant: South Korea and Late Industrialization*. New York: Oxford University Press, 1989.

Amuzegar, Jahangir. *Managing the Oil Wealth: OPEC's Windfalls and Pitfalls*. New York: I. B. Tauris, 2001.

Andaiye. "1964: The Rupture of Neighborliness and Its Legacy for Indian/African Relations With D. Alissa Trotz [2008; 2018]." In *The Point Is to Change the World: Selected Writings of Andaiye*, edited by Alissa Trotz, 58–76. London: Pluto, 2020.

Andreas, Joel. *Disenfranchised: The Rise and Fall of Industrial Citizenship in China*. New York: Oxford University Press, 2019.

Antoine, Rose-Marie Belle. "Embracing Collective Rights: Unions and the New Struggle for Relevance and Autonomy—a View from the Commonwealth Caribbean." In *Autonomie collective et droit du travail: Mélanges en l'honneur du professeur Pierre Verge*, edited by Dominic Roux, 277–325. Quebec: Les Presses de l'Université Laval, 2014.

Antunes de Oliveira, Felipe. "Who Are the Super-Exploited? Gender, Race, and the Intersectional Potentialities of Dependency Theory." In *Dependent Capitalisms in Contemporary Latin America and Europe*, edited by Aldo Madariaga and Stefano Palestini, 101–28. Cham, Switzerland: Palgrave Macmillan, 2021.

Arrighi, Giovanni. "The Development Illusion: A Reconceptualization of the Semiperiphery." In *Semiperipheral States in the World-Economy*, edited by William Martin, 11–42. Westport, CT: Greenwood Press, 1990.

Arrighi, Giovanni. *The Long Twentieth Century: Money, Power, and the Origins of Our Times*. London: Verso, 1994.

Arrighi, Giovanni, Terence Hopkins, and Immanuel Wallerstein. *Anti-Systemic Movements*. 1989. London: Verso Books, 2011.

Arrighi, Giovanni, and Beverly Silver. "Labor Movements and Capital Migration: The United States and Western Europe in World-Historical Perspective." In *Labor in the Capitalist World-Economy*, edited by Charles Bergquist, 183–216. Beverly Hills, CA: Sage Publications, 1984.

Austin, David. "All Roads Lead to Montreal: Black Power, the Caribbean, and the Black Radical Tradition in Canada." *Journal of African American History* 92, no. 4 (2007): 516–39.

Auty, Richard. *Sustaining Development in Mineral Economies: The Resource Curse Thesis*. London: Routledge, 1993.

Auty, Richard, and Alan Gelb. "Oil Windfalls in a Small Parliamentary Democracy: Their Impact on Trinidad and Tobago." *World Development* 14, no. 9 (1986): 1161–75.

Auty, Richard, and Alan Gelb. "Political Economy of Resource-Abundant States." In *Resource Abundance and Economic Development*, edited by Richard Auty, 126–46. Oxford: Oxford University Press, 2001.

Bair, Jennifer. "Global Capitalism and Commodity Chains: Looking Back, Going Forward." *Competition and Change* 9, no. 2 (2005): 153–80.

Baldwin, Kate, and John Huber. "Economic Versus Cultural Differences: Forms of Ethnic Diversity and Public Goods Provision." *American Political Science Review* 104, no. 4 (2010): 644–62.

Banerjee, Abhijit, Lakshmi Iyer, and Rohini Somanathan. "History, Social Divisions, and Public Goods in Rural India." *Journal of the European Economic Association* 3, no. 2–3 (2005): 639–47.

Baptiste, Fitzroy André. "The Exploitation of Caribbean Bauxite and Petroleum, 1914–1945." *Social and Economic Studies* 37, no. 1/2 (1988): 107–42.

Baran, Paul. *The Political Economy of Growth*. New York: Monthly Review Press, 1957.

Barrett, Richard, and Martin King Whyte. "Dependency Theory and Taiwan: Analysis of a Deviant Case." *American Journal of Sociology* 87, no. 5 (1982): 1064–89.

Basdeo, Sahadeo. "Indian Participation in Labour Politics in Trinidad 1919–1939." *Caribbean Quarterly* 32, no. 3–4 (1986): 50–65.

Bashi, Vilna. *The Ethnic Project: Transforming Racial Fiction into Ethnic Factions*. Stanford, CA: Stanford University Press, 2013.

Basualdo, Victoria. "Labor and Structural Change: Shop-Floor Organization and Militancy in Argentine Industrial Factories (1943–1983)." PhD diss., Columbia University, 2010.

Bates, Robert. *Unions, Parties, and Political Development, a Study of Mineworkers in Zambia*. New Haven, CT: Yale University Press, 1971.

Bayart, Jean-François. *The State in Africa: The Politics of the Belly, Second Edition*. 1993. Cambridge, MA: Polity, 2009.

Beblawi, Hazem, and Giacomo Luciani, eds. *The Rentier State*. London: Croom Helm, 1987.

Beckford George. *Persistent Poverty: Underdevelopment in Plantation Economies of the Third World*. 1972. Kingston, Jamaica: University of the West Indies Press, 1999.

Beckford, George. "The Plantation System and the Penetration of International Capitalism." In *George Beckford Papers*, edited by Kari Levitt, 239–41. Kingston, Jamaica: Canoe Press, 2000.

Bedasse, Monique. *Jah Kingdom: Rastafarians, Tanzania, and Pan-Africanism in the Age of Decolonization*. Chapel Hill: University of North Carolina Press, 2017.

Bedasse, Monique, Kim Butler, Carlos Fernandes, Dennis Laumann, Tejasvi Nagaraja, Benjamin Talton, and Kira Thurman. "*AHR* Conversation: Black Internationalism." *American Historical Review* 125, no. 5 (2020): 1699–739.

Bellin, Eva. "The Robustness of Authoritarianism in the Middle East: Exceptionalism in Comparative Perspective." *Comparative Politics* 36, no. 2 (2004): 139–57.

Bellin, Eva. *Stalled Democracy: Capital, Labor, and the Paradox of State-Sponsored Development*. Ithaca, NY: Cornell University Press, 2002.

Bender, Daniel, and Jana Lipman, eds. *Making the Empire Work: Labor and United States Imperialism*. New York: New York University Press, 2015.

Bendix, Reinhard. *Nation-Building and Citizenship: Studies of Our Changing Social Order*. 1964. New York, Routledge, 2017.

Bergquist, Charles. *Labor in Latin America: Comparative Essays on Chile, Argentina, Venezuela, and Colombia*. Stanford, CA: Stanford University Press, 1986.

Bernard, Eustace. *Against the Odds*. Port of Spain, Trinidad and Tobago: Inprint Caribbean, 1991.

Besson, Gérard. "Black Gold, the Real El Dorado." *First Magazine*. Port of Spain, Trinidad and Tobago: Paria Publishing, 2012. Accessed January 20, 2023. https://issuu.com/pariapub/docs/black_gold_1.

Besson, Gérard. "Black Gold, Part 2: War and Peace." *First Magazine*. Port of Spain, Trinidad and Tobago: Paria Publishing, 2012. Accessed January 20, 2023. https://issuu.com/pariapub/docs/black_gold_2.

Best, Lloyd. "Outlines of a Model of Pure Plantation Economy." *Social and Economic Studies* 17, no. 3 (1968): 283–326.

Best, Lloyd, and Kari Levitt. *Essays on the Theory of Plantation Economy: A Historical and Institutional Approach to Caribbean Economic Development*. Kingston, Jamaica: University of the West Indies Press, 2009.

Bhambra, Gurminder. *Connected Sociologies*. London: Bloomsbury Academic, 2014.

Bissessar, Ann Marie. "Determinants of Gender Mobility in the Public Service of Trinidad and Tobago." *Public Personnel Management* 28, no. 3 (1999): 409–22.

Bissessar, Ann Marie. "The Difficulty of Protecting Merit in a Plural Society: The Case of Trinidad and Tobago." *Review of Public Personnel Administration* 26, no. 1 (2006): 74–90.

Bissessar, Ann Marie. *Ethnic Conflict in Developing Societies: Trinidad and Tobago, Guyana, Fiji, and Suriname*. Cham, Switzerland: Palgrave Macmillan, 2017.

Bissessar, Ann Marie. "Local Governance Structures in Trinidad and Tobago: Muddling Through." *Social and Economic Studies* 59, no. 4 (2010): 127–44.

Bissessar, Ann Marie, and John Gaffar La Guerre. *Trinidad and Tobago and Guyana: Race and Politics in Two Plural Societies*. Lanham, MD: Lexington Books, 2013.

Bissessar, Ann, and Roger Hosein. "Role of the State in the Economic Development of Trinidad and Tobago with Special Reference to the Petrochemical Sector." Paper presented at the Caribbean Centre for Money and Finance 33rd Annual Monetary Studies Conference, Belize City, November 19–23, 2001.

Boatcă, Manuela. *Global Inequalities Beyond Occidentalism*. London: Routledge, 2016.

Bogues, Anthony. *Black Heretics, Black Prophets: Radical Political Intellectuals*. New York: Routledge, 2003.

Bolland, O. Nigel. *The Politics of Labour in the British Caribbean: The Social Origins of Authoritarianism and Democracy in the Labour Movement*. Kingston, Jamaica: Ian Randle Publishers, 2001.

Bond, David. "Oil in the Caribbean: Refineries, Mangroves, and the Negative Ecologies of Crude Oil." *Comparative Studies in Society and History* 59, no. 3 (2017): 600–28.

Bonilla, Yarimar. *Non-Sovereign Futures: French Caribbean Politics in the Wake of Disenchantment*. Chicago: University of Chicago Press, 2015.

Bonilla-Silva, Eduardo. "The Essential Social Fact of Race." *American Sociological Review* 64, no. 6 (1999): 899–906.

Bonini, Astra. "Complementary and Competitive Regimes of Accumulation: Natural Resources and Development in the World-System." *Journal of World-Systems Research* 18, no. 1 (2012): 50–68.

Boomert, Arie. *The Indigenous Peoples of Trinidad and Tobago from the First Settlers Until Today*. Leiden, the Netherlands: Sidestone Press, 2016.

Boone, Catherine. "States and Ruling Classes in Postcolonial Africa: The Enduring Contradictions of Power." In *State Power and Social Forces: Domination and Transformation in the Third World*, edited by Joel Migdal, Atul Kohli, and Vivienne Shue, 108–40. Cambridge: Cambridge University Press, 1994.

Boopsingh, Trevor, and Gregory McGuire, eds. *From Oil to Gas and Beyond: A Review of the Trinidad and Tobago Model and Analysis of Future Challenges*. Lanham, MD: University Press of America, 2014.

Bornschier, Volker, and Christopher Chase-Dunn. *Transnational Corporations and Underdevelopment*. New York: Praeger, 1985.

Boswell, Terry, Cliff Brown, John Brueggemann, and T. Ralph Peters. *Racial Competition and Class Solidarity*. Albany: State University of New York Press, 2006.

Bradlow, Benjamin H. *Urban Power: Democracy and Inequality in São Paulo and Johannesburg*. Princeton, NJ: Princeton University Press, 2024.

Braithwaite, Lloyd. "Social Stratification in Trinidad: A Preliminary Analysis." *Social and Economic Studies* 2, no. 2/3 (1953): 5–175.

Branch, Daniel. "Loyalists, Mau Mau, and Elections in Kenya: The First Triumph of the System, 1957–1958." *Africa Today* 53, no. 2 (2006): 27–50.

Brereton, Bridget. "The Historical Background to the Culture of Violence in Trinidad and Tobago." *Caribbean Review of Gender Studies* no. 4 (2010): 1–16.

Brereton, Bridget. *A History of Modern Trinidad: 1783–1962*. Kingston, Jamaica: Heinemann, 1981.

Brereton, Bridget. *Race Relations in Colonial Trinidad, 1870–1900*. 1979. Cambridge: Cambridge University Press, 2002.

Brereton, Bridget. "Resistance to Enslavement and Oppression in Trinidad, 1802–1849." *Journal of Caribbean History* 43, no. 2 (2009): 157–76.

Brown, Deryck. "Ethnic Politics and Public Sector Management in Trinidad and Guyana." *Public Administration and Development* 19, no. 4 (1999): 367–79.

Brown, Warwick. "The Royal Navy's Fuel Supplies, 1898–1939: The Transition from Coal to Oil." PhD diss., King's College London, University of London, 2003.

Bulkan, Arif, and Alissa Trotz. "Oil Fuels Guyana's Internecine Conflict." *Current History* 120, no. 823 (2021): 71–77.

Bunce, Robin, and Paul Field. *Darcus Howe: A Political Biography*. London: Bloomsbury Academic, 2014.

Bunker, Stephen, and Paul Ciccantell. *Globalization and the Race for Resources*. Baltimore, MD: Johns Hopkins University Press, 2005.

Burawoy, Michael. *The Color of Class*. Manchester, UK: Manchester University Press, 1972.

Burden-Stelly, Charisse. "The Absence of Political Economy Is African Diaspora Studies." *Black Perspectives*, March 20, 2018. https://www.aaihs.org/the-absence-of -political-economy-in-african-diaspora-studies/.

Burden-Stelly, Charisse. *Black Scare/Red Scare: Theorizing Capitalist Racism in the United States*. Chicago: University of Chicago Press, 2023.

Burden-Stelly, Charisse, and Jodi Dean. *Organize, Fight, WIN: Black Communist Women's Political Writing*. London: Verso, 2022.

Burden-Stelly, Charisse, and Gerald Horne. "From Pan-Africanism to Black Internationalism." In *Routledge Handbook of Pan-Africanism*, edited by Reiland Rabaka, 69–86. London: Routledge, 2020.

Burnett, Carla. "'Unity Is Strength': Labor, Race, Garveyism, and the 1920 Panama Canal Strike." *Global South* 6, no. 2 (2012): 39–64.

Burrowes, Nicole. *Seeds of Solidarity: African-Indian Relations and the 1935 Labor Rebellions in British Guiana*. Cambridge: Cambridge University Press, forthcoming.

Butler, Larry. *Copper Empire: Mining and the Colonial State in Northern Rhodesia, c. 1930–64*. New York: Palgrave Macmillan, 2007.

Byron, Jessica. "Strategic Repositioning: Foreign Policy Shifts in Barbados and Trinidad and Tobago, 1990–2000." *Social and Economic Studies* 56, no. 1/2 (2007): 209–39.

Cabral, Amílcar. "The Weapon of Theory." Address delivered to the First Tricontinental Conference of the Peoples of Asia, Africa and Latin America, Havana, 1966. Accessed December 2, 2022. https://www.marxists.org/subject/africa/cabral/1966/weapon -theory.htm.

Calhoun, Craig. "'New Social Movements' of the Early Nineteenth Century." *Social Science History* 17, no. 3 (1993): 385–427.

Campbell, Carl. "The Rise of a Free Coloured Plantocracy in Trinidad 1783–1813." *Boletin de Estudios Latinoamericanos y del Caribe*, no. 29 (1980): 33–53.

Campbell, Carl. *Endless Education: Main Currents in the Education System of Modern Trinidad and Tobago, 1939–1986*. Kingston, Jamaica: Press University of the West Indies, 1997.

Campbell, Carl. *The Young Colonials: A Social History of Education in Trinidad and Tobago, 1834–1939*. Kingston, Jamaica: Press University of the West Indies, 1996.

Campbell, Horace. "Jamaica: The Myth of Economic Development and Racial Tranquility." *Black Scholar* 4, no. 5 (1973): 16–23.

Campbell, Horace. *Rasta and Resistance: From Marcus Garvey to Walter Rodney*. Trenton, NJ: Africa World Press, 1987.

Campbell, Horace, and Rodney Worrell. *Pan-Africanism, Pan-Africanists, and African Liberation in the 21st Century: Two Lectures.* Washington, DC: New Academia, 2006.

Canterbury, Dennis. *Neoextractivism and Capitalist Development.* London: Routledge, 2018.

Cardoso, Fernando, and Enzo Faletto. *Dependency and Development in Latin America.* Berkeley: University of California Press, 1979.

Carmichael, Sylvester. "The Rise and Fall of Guyana Bauxite." Master's thesis, Colorado School of Mines, 2002.

Carrington, Edwin. "Industrialization in Trinidad and Tobago since 1950." *New World Quarterly* 4, no. 2 (1968): 37–43.

Carter, Marina, and Khal Torabully. *Coolitude: An Anthology of the Indian Labour Diaspora.* London: Anthem, 2002.

Casey, Matthew. *Empire's Guestworkers: Haitian Migrants in Cuba During the Age of US Occupation.* Cambridge: Cambridge University Press, 2017.

Cederman, Lars-Erik, Andreas Wimmer, and Brian Min. "Why Do Ethnic Groups Rebel? New Data and Analysis." *World Politics* 62, no. 1 (2010): 87–119.

Chalmin, Philippe. *The Making of a Sugar Giant: Tate and Lyle, 1859–1989.* Chur, Switzerland: Harwood Academic, 1990.

Chandra, Kanchan. *Why Ethnic Parties Succeed: Patronage and Ethnic Head Counts in India.* New York: Cambridge University Press, 2004.

Chang, Dae-Oup. "Labour and 'Developmental State': A Critique of the Developmental State Theory of Labour." In *Beyond the Development State: Industrial Policy into the Twenty-First Century,* edited by Ben Fine, Daniela Tavasci, and Jyoti Saraswati, 85–109. London: Pluto, 2013.

Chase, Ashton. *A History of Trade Unionism in Guyana, 1900–1961.* Ruimveldt, Guyana: New Guyana, 1964.

Chatterjee, Partha. *Nationalist Thought and the Colonial World: A Derivative Discourse?* London: Zed Books, 1986.

Chatterjee, Partha. *The Nation and Its Fragments: Colonial and Postcolonial Histories.* Princeton, NJ: Princeton University Press, 1993.

Chaudhry, Kiren. "Economic Liberalization and the Lineages of the Rentier State." *Comparative Politics* 27, no. 1 (1994): 1–25.

Chibber, Vivek. *Locked in Place: State-Building and Late Industrialization in India.* Princeton, NJ: Princeton University Press, 2003.

Churchill, Sefa Awaworyi, and Russell Smyth. "Ethnic Diversity and Poverty." *World Development* 95 (2017): 285–302.

Clarke, Sabine. "An Industrialisation Programme for Trinidad." In *Science at the End of Empire,* 129–53. Manchester, UK: Manchester University Press, 2018.

Clawson, Dan. *The Next Upsurge: Labor and the New Social Movements.* Ithaca, NY: Cornell University Press, 2003.

Clemens, Elisabeth. *The People's Lobby: Organizational Innovation and the Rise of Interest Group Politics in the United States, 1890–1925.* Chicago: University of Chicago Press, 1997.

Clergé, Orly. "The New Black Sociology: Bringing Diasporic and Internationalist Perspectives." In *The New Black Sociologists: Historical and Contemporary Perspectives,* edited by Marcus A. Hunter, 219–36. New York: Routledge, 2018.

Collier, Ruth Berins, and David Collier. *Shaping the Political Arena: Critical Junctures, the Labor Movement, and Regime Dynamics in Latin America.* Princeton, NJ: Princeton University Press, 1991.

Colony of British Guiana. *British Guiana Blue Book 1917.* Georgetown, British Guiana: The Argosy Co. Ltd., 1918.

Colony of Trinidad and Tobago. *Administration Report of the Mines Department, 1947.* Accessed February 3, 2023. https://www.energy.gov.tt/wp-content/uploads/2013/11/Annual_Administration_Report_1947_(Mines_Dept.).pdf.

Colony of Trinidad and Tobago. *Administration Report of the Petroleum Department, 1948.* Accessed February 3, 2023. https://www.energy.gov.tt/wp-content/uploads/2013/11/Annual_Administration_Report_1948_(Petroleum_Dept.).pdf.

Colony of Trinidad and Tobago. *Administration Report of the Petroleum Department for the Year 1950.* Accessed February 6, 2023. https://www.energy.gov.tt/wp-content/uploads/2013/11/Annual_Administration_Report_1950_(Petroleum_Dept.).pdf.

Colony of Trinidad and Tobago. *Annual Report Trinidad and Tobago, 1951.* Port of Spain, Trinidad and Tobago: Government Printing Office, 1951.

Colony of Trinidad and Tobago. *Mines: Administration Report of the Inspector of Mines and Petroleum Technologist for the Year 1936.* Port of Spain, Trinidad and Tobago: Government Printer, 1937. Accessed March 15, 2023. https://www.energy.gov.tt/wp-content/uploads/2013/11/Annual_Administration_Report_1936_(Mines_Dept.).pdf.

Colony of Trinidad and Tobago, *Mines Department Administrative Report of the Inspector of Mines for the Year 1913–1914.* Port of Spain, Trinidad and Tobago: Government Printing Office, 1914. Accessed February 20, 2023. https://www.energy.gov.tt/wp-content/uploads/2013/11/Annual_Administration_Report_1913-14_(Mines_Dept.).pdf.

Colony of Trinidad and Tobago. *Mines Department: Report of the Inspector of the Mines for the Year 1914–1915.* Port of Spain, Trinidad and Tobago: Government Printing Office, 1915. Accessed March 15, 2023. https://www.energy.gov.tt/wp-content/uploads/2013/11/Annual_Administration_Report_1914-15_(Mines_Dept.).pdf.

Colony of Trinidad and Tobago. *Mines Department: Report of the Inspector of the Mines for the Year 1930.* Port of Spain, Trinidad and Tobago: Government Printing Office, 1931. Accessed March 15, 2023. https://www.energy.gov.tt/wp-content/uploads/2013/11/Annual_Administration_Report_1930_(Mines_Dept.).pdf.

Colony of Trinidad and Tobago. *Mines: Report of the Inspector Mines and Petroleum Technologist for 1938.* Port of Spain, Trinidad and Tobago: Government Printer, 1938. Accessed April 12, 2023. https://www.energy.gov.tt/wp-content/uploads/2013/11/Annual_Administration_Report_1938_(Mines_Dept.).pdf.

Colony of Trinidad and Tobago. *Mines: Report of the Inspector Mines and Petroleum Technologist for the Year 1945.* Accessed February 2, 2023. https://www.energy.gov.tt/wp-content/uploads/2013/11/Annual_Administration_Report_1945_(Mines_Dept.).pdf.

Colony of Trinidad and Tobago. *Report of the Inspector Mines and Petroleum Technologist for the Year 1943.* Accessed February 2, 2023. https://www.energy.gov.tt/wp-content/uploads/2013/11/Annual_Administration_Report_1943_(Mines_Dept.).pdf.

Colony of Trinidad and Tobago. *Trinidad and Tobago Blue Book 1917.* Port of Spain, Trinidad and Tobago: Government Printing Office, 1918.

Combahee River Collective. "A Black Feminist Statement." 1978. *Women's Studies Quarterly* 42, no. 3/4 (2014): 271–80.

Cooper, Frederick. *Decolonization and African Society: The Labor Question in French and British Africa.* Cambridge: Cambridge University Press, 1996.

Cox, Oliver Cromwell. *Capitalism as a System.* 1964. New Smyrna Beach, FL: Oliver Cromwell Cox Online Institute, 2004.

Cox, Oliver Cromwell. *Caste, Class, and Race: A Study in Social Dynamics.* New York: Monthly Review Press, 1948.

Craig, Susan. *Community Development in Trinidad and Tobago, 1943–1973: From Welfare to Patronage.* Jamaica: University of the West Indies, 1974.

Craig, Susan. "Political Patronage and Community Resistance: Village Councils in Trinidad and Tobago." In *Rural Development in the Caribbean,* edited by P. I. Gomes, 173–93. London: C. Hurst, 1985.

Craig-James, Susan. "Smiles and Blood: The Ruling Class Response to the Workers' Rebellion of 1937 in Trinidad and Tobago." In *The Trinidad Labor Riots of 1937: Perspectives 50 Years Later,* edited by Roy Thomas, 81–140. St. Augustine, Trinidad and Tobago: Extra-Mural Studies Unit, University of the West Indies, 1987.

Crenshaw, Kimberlé. "Demarginalizing the Intersection of Race and Sex: A Black Feminist Critique of Antidiscrimination Doctrine." *University of Chicago Legal Forum* (1989): 139–68.

Crenshaw, Kimberlé. "Mapping the Margins: Intersectionality, Identity, and Violence Against Women of Color." *Stanford Law Review* 43, no. 6 (1991): 1241–99.

Cudjoe, Selwyn. *The Slave Master of Trinidad: William Hardin Burnley and the Nineteenth-Century Atlantic World.* Amherst: University of Massachusetts Press, 2018.

Curless, Gareth. "The Triumph of the State: Singapore's Dockworkers and the Limits of Global History, c. 1920–1965." *Historical Journal* 60, no. 4 (2017): 1097–123.

Cushion, Steve. *A Hidden History of the Cuban Revolution: How the Working Class Shaped the Guerillas' Victory.* New York: Monthly Review Press, 2016.

Dalley, Fred. *General Industrial Conditions and Labour Relations in Trinidad: Report.* Port of Spain, Trinidad and Tobago: Government Printing Office, 1954.

Dalley, Fred. *Trade Union Organization and Industrial Relations in Trinidad.* London: H.M.S.O., 1947.

Danns, George. "Militarization and Development: An Experiment in Nation Building." *Transition* 1, no. 1 (1978): 23–44.

Davenport, Christian. "State Repression and Political Order." *Annual Review of Political Science* 10 (2007): 1–23.

Davies, Carole Boyce. *Left of Karl Marx: The Political Life of Black Communist Claudia Jones.* Durham, NC: Duke University Press, 2007.

Davies, Carole Boyce. "Sisters Outside: Tracing the Caribbean/Black Radical Intellectual Tradition." *Small Axe* 13, no. 1 (2009): 217–29.

Davies, Carole Boyce, and Charisse Burden-Stelly. "Claudia Jones Research and Collections: Questions of Process and Knowledge Construction." *Journal of Intersectionality* 3, no. 1 (2019): 4–9.

Davies, Colin. "British Oil Policy in the Middle East, 1919–1932." PhD diss., University of Edinburgh, 1974.

Davis, Angela. "Reflections on the Black Woman's Role in the Community of Slaves." *Black Scholar* 12, no. 6 (1981): 2–15.

Davis, Charles, and Kenneth Coleman. "Labor and the State: Union Incorporation and Working-Class Politicization in Latin America." *Comparative Political Studies* 18, no. 4 (1986): 395–417.

Davis, Diane. *Discipline and Development: Middle Classes and Prosperity in East Asia and Latin America*. Cambridge: Cambridge University Press, 2004.

Dawson, Michael. *Black Visions: The Roots of Contemporary African-American Political Ideologies*. Chicago: University of Chicago Press, 2001.

Dawson, Michael. "Hidden in Plain Sight: A Note on Legitimation Crises and the Racial Order." *Critical Historical Studies* 3, no. 1 (2016): 143–61.

De Barros, Juanita, Steven Palmer, and David Wright. *Health and Medicine in the Circum-Caribbean, 1800–1968*. New York: Routledge, 2009.

De Leon, Cedric, Manali Desai, and Cihan Tuğal. "Political Articulation: Parties and the Constitution of Cleavages in the United States, India, and Turkey." *Sociological Theory* 27, no. 3 (2009): 193–219.

Derrida, Jacques. *Archive Fever: A Freudian Impression*. Chicago: University of Chicago Press, 1996.

Desai, Ashwin. "Indian South Africans and the Black Consciousness Movement Under Apartheid." *Diaspora Studies* 8, no. 1 (2015): 37–50.

Desai, Manali. "The Relative Autonomy of Party Practices: A Counterfactual Analysis of Left Party Ascendancy in Kerala, India, 1934–1940." *American Journal of Sociology* 108, no. 3 (2002): 616–57.

Deyo, Frederic. *Beneath the Miracle: Labor Subordination in the New Asian Industrialism*. Berkeley: University of California Press, 1989.

Doner, Richard. *The Politics of Uneven Development*. Cambridge: Cambridge University Press, 2009.

Doner, Richard, Bryan Ritchie, and Dan Slater. "Systemic Vulnerability and the Origins of Developmental States: Northeast and Southeast Asia in Comparative Perspective." *International Organization* 59, no. 2 (2005): 327–61.

Dos Santos, Theotonio. "The Structure of Dependence." *American Economic Review* 60, no. 2 (1970): 231–36.

Du Bois, W. E. B. *Black Reconstruction in America*. 1935. New York: Free Press, 1992.

Du Bois, W. E. B. "The Class Struggle." *Crisis* 22, no. 4 (1921): 151–52.

Du Bois, W. E. B. *Color and Democracy*. New York: Harcourt, Brace, 1945.

Du Bois, W. E. B. *Dusk of Dawn: An Essay Toward an Autobiography of a Race Concept*. 1940. New Brunswick, NJ: Transaction, 1997.

Du Bois, W. E. B. "Marxism and the Negro Problem." *Crisis* 40, no. 5 (1933): 103–18.

Du Bois, W. E. B. *The World and Africa: An Inquiry into the Part Which Africa Has Played in World History*. New York: Viking, 1947.

Dülffer, Jost, and Marc Frey, eds. *Elites and Decolonization in the Twentieth Century*. Hampshire, UK: Palgrave Macmillan, 2011.

Easterly, William, and Ross Levine. "Africa's Growth Tragedy: Policies and Ethnic Divisions." *Quarterly Journal of Economics* 112, no. 4 (1997): 1203–50.

Edgerton, David. *Britain's War Machine: Weapons, Resources, and Experts in the Second World War*. Oxford: Oxford University Press, 2011.

Edwards, Zophia. "Applying the Black Radical Tradition: Class, Race, and a New Foundation for Studies of Development." *Political Power and Social Theory* 37 (2020): 155–83.

Edwards, Zophia. "Beyond Intersectionality: A Political Economy Approach to the Intersections of Race, Class, Gender, and Nation." *Sociology of Race and Ethnicity* 9, no. 2 (2023): 248–51.

Edwards, Zophia. "No Colonial Working Class, No Post-Colonial Development: A Comparative-Historical Analysis of Two Oil-Rich Countries." *Studies in Comparative International Development* 53, no. 4 (2018): 477–99.

Edwards, Zophia. "Postcolonial Sociology as a Remedy for Global Diffusion Theory." *Sociological Review* 68, no. 6 (2020): 1179–95.

Eidlin, Barry. "Why Is There No Labor Party in the United States? Political Articulation and the Canadian Comparison, 1932 to 1948." *American Sociological Review* 81, no. 3 (2016): 488–516.

Elkins, William. "Black Power in the British West Indies: The Trinidad Longshoremen's Strike of 1919." *Science and Society* 33, no. 1 (1969): 71–75.

Elkins, William. "Hercules and the Society of Peoples of African Origin." *Caribbean Studies* 11, no. 4 (1972): 47–59.

Elkins, William. "Marcus Garvey, the 'Negro World,' and the British West Indies: 1919–1920." *Science and Society* 36, no. 1 (1972): 63–77.

Ellner, Steve. "Trade Union Autonomy and the Emergence of a New Labor Movement in Venezuela." In *Venezuela: Hugo Chávez and the Decline of an "Exceptional Democracy,"* edited by Steve Ellner and Miguel Tinker Salas, 77–98. Lanham, MD: Rowman and Littlefield, 2007.

Emigh, Rebecca. "The Power of Negative Thinking: The Use of Negative Case Methodology in the Development of Sociological Theory." *Theory and Society* 26, no. 5 (1997): 649–84.

Esnard, Talia. *Entrepreneurial Women in the Caribbean: Critical Insights and Policy Implications*. Cham, Switzerland: Palgrave Macmillan, 2023.

Esping-Andersen, Gosta. "Power and Distributional Regimes." *Politics and Society* 14, no. 2 (1985): 223–56.

Esping-Andersen, Gosta. "The Three Political Economies of the Welfare State." *Canadian Review of Sociology/Revue Canadienne de Sociologie* 26, no. 1 (1989): 10–36.

Evans, Peter. "Constructing the 21st Century Developmental State: Potentialities and Pitfalls." In *Constructing a Democratic Developmental State in South Africa*, edited by Omano Edigheji, 37–58. Cape Town, South Africa: Human Sciences Research Council Press, 2011.

Evans, Peter. *Dependent Development*. Princeton, NJ: Princeton University Press, 1979.

Evans, Peter. *Embedded Autonomy: States and Industrial Transformation*. Princeton, NJ: Princeton University Press, 1995.

Evans, Peter, and Patrick Heller. "Human Development, State Transformation, and the Politics of the Developmental State." In *The Oxford Handbook of Transformations of the State*, edited by Stephan Leibfried, Evelyne Huber, Matthew Lange, Jonah Levy, Frank Nullmeier, and John Stephens, 691–713. Oxford: Oxford University Press, 2015.

Ewing, Adam. *The Age of Garvey: How a Jamaican Activist Created a Mass Movement and Changed Global Black Politics*. Princeton, NJ: Princeton University Press, 2014.

Ewing, Adam. "Caribbean Labour Politics in the Age of Garvey, 1918–1938." *Race and Class* 55, no. 1 (2013): 23–45.

Fallon, Kathleen, and Jocelyn Viterna. "Women, Democracy, and the State." In *The Sociology of Development Handbook*, edited by Gregory Hooks, 414–39. Berkeley: University of California Press, 2016.

Fanon, Frantz. *Wretched of the Earth*. 1961. New York: Grove, 2004.

Farrell, Terrence. *The Underachieving Society: Development Strategy and Policy in Trinidad and Tobago, 1958–2008*. Kingston, Jamaica: University of the West Indies Press, 2012.

Ferreira, Jo-Anne. "Madeiran Portuguese Migration to Guyana, St. Vincent, Antigua and Trinidad: A Comparative Overview." *Portuguese Studies Review* 14, no. 2 (2006/7): 63–85.

Fick, Carolyn. *The Making of Haiti: The Saint Domingue Revolution from Below*. Knoxville: University of Tennessee Press, 1990.

Fields, Barbara. "Slavery, Race and Ideology in the United States of America." *New Left Review*, no. 181 (1990): 95–118.

Figueira, Daurius. *Simbhoonath Capildeo: Lion of the Legislative Council, Father of the Hindu Nationalism in Trinidad and Tobago*. New York: iUniverse, 2003.

Figueira, Daurius. *Tubal Uriah Butler of Trinidad and Tobago Kwame Nkrumah of Ghana: The Road to Independence*. New York: iUniverse, 2007.

Fink, Leon, and Julie Greene. "Builders of Empire: Rewriting the Labor and Working-Class History of Anglo-American Global Power." *Labor* 13, no. 3–4 (2016): 1–10.

Fishwick, Adam. "Labour Control and Developmental State Theory: A New Perspective on Import-Substitution Industrialization in Latin America." *Development and Change* 50, no. 3 (2019): 655–78.

Fletcher, Bill, and Fernando Gapasin. *Solidarity Divided: The Crisis in Organized Labor and a New Path Toward Social Justice*. Berkeley: University of California Press, 2008.

Fletcher, Leonard. "The Decline of Friendly Societies in Trinidad and Tobago." *Caribbean Studies* 24, no. 3/4 (1991): 59–78.

Fletcher, Leonard. "Politics, Public Policy and Friendly Societies in Trinidad and Tobago." *Social and Economic Studies* 39, no. 3 (1990): 95–126.

Foner, Philip. "The IWW and the Black Worker." *Journal of Negro History* 55, no. 1 (1970): 45–64.

Foner, Philip, and Ronald Lewis, eds. *The Black Worker*. Vol. 3, *The Black Worker During the Era of the Knights of Labor*. Philadelphia: Temple University Press, 1978.

Forte, Maximilian. "Carib Identity, Racial Politics and the Problem of Indigenous Recognition in Trinidad and Tobago." In *Who Is an Indian? Race, Place, and the Politics of Indigeneity in the Americas*, edited by Maximilian Forte, 172–93. Toronto: University of Toronto Press, 2013.

Forte, Maximilian. "Writing the Caribs Out: The Construction and Demystification of the 'Deserted Island' Thesis for Trinidad." Paper presented at the International Seminar on the History of the Atlantic World, 1500–1825, Harvard University, Cambridge, MA, 2004. Accessed June 22, 2023. https://indigenouscaribbean.wordpress.com/wp-content/uploads/2008/05/forteatlantic2004.pdf.

Franck, Raphael, and Ilia Rainer. "Does the Leader's Ethnicity Matter? Ethnic Favoritism, Education, and Health in Sub-Saharan Africa." *American Political Science Review* 106, no. 2 (2012): 294–325.

Frank, Andre Gunder. *Dependent Accumulation and Underdevelopment*. New York: Monthly Review Press, 1979.

Fraser, Adrian. *The 1935 Riots in St Vincent: From Riots to Adult Suffrage*. Kingston, Jamaica: University of the West Indies Press, 2016.

Fraser, Nancy. "Expropriation and Exploitation in Racialized Capitalism: A Reply to Michael Dawson." *Critical Historical Studies* 3, no. 1 (2016): 163–78.

Fredrickson, George. *Black Liberation: A Comparative History of Black Ideologies in the United States and South Africa*. New York: Oxford University Press, 1995.

Freedom House. *Freedom in the World 2024*. Country and Territory Ratings and Statuses, 1973–2024. Washington, DC: Freedom House, 2024. Accessed December 5, 2024. https://freedomhouse.org/report/freedom-world.

Gafar, John. *Guyana: From State Control to Free Markets*. New York: Nova Science, 2003.

Gafar, John. "Poverty, Income Growth, and Inequality in some Caribbean Countries." *Journal of Developing Areas* 32, no. 4 (1998): 467–90.

Gamson, William. *The Strategy of Social Protest*. 2nd ed. Belmont, CA: Wadsworth Publishing, 1990.

Garvey, Marcus. "The Negro, Communism, Trade Unionism and His (?) Friend." In *The Philosophies and Opinions of Marcus Garvey, Or, Africa for the Africans*, edited by Amy Jacques Garvey, 69–71. Dover, MA: Majority Press, 1986.

Gereffi, Gary. "Global Value Chains in a Post-Washington Consensus World." *Review of International Political Economy* 21, no. 1 (2014): 9–37.

Gerring, John, Daniel Ziblatt, Johan Van Gorp, and Julián Arévalo. "An Institutional Theory of Direct and Indirect Rule." *World Politics* 63, no. 3 (2011): 377–433.

Gerteis, Joseph. *Class and the Color Line: Interracial Class Coalition in the Knights of Labor and the Populist Movement*. Durham, NC: Duke University Press, 2007.

Geschwender, James. *Class, Race, and Worker Insurgency: The League of Revolutionary Black Workers*. Cambridge: Cambridge University Press, 1977.

Getachew, Adom. *Worldmaking After Empire*. Princeton, NJ: Princeton University Press, 2019.

Gibson, Christopher. *Movement-Driven Development: The Politics of Health and Democracy in Brazil*. Stanford, CA: Stanford University Press, 2019.

Gill, Timothy. *Encountering US Empire in Socialist Venezuela: The Legacy of Race, Neocolonialism, and Democracy Promotion*. Pittsburgh, PA: University of Pittsburgh Press, 2022.

Gilmore, Ruth Wilson. *Golden Gulag: Prisons, Surplus, Crisis, and Opposition in Global-izing California*. Berkeley: University of California Press, 2007.

Girvan, Norman. *Aspects of the Political Economy of Race in the Caribbean and the Amer-icas: A Preliminary Interpretation*. Mona, Jamaica: Institute of Social and Economic Research, University of the West Indies, 1975.

Girvan, Norman. "The Development of Dependency Economics in the Caribbean and Latin America: Review and Comparison." *Social and Economic Studies* 22, no. 1 (1973): 1–33.

Girvan, Norman, and Cherita Girvan. "Making the Rules of the Game: Company-Country Agreements in the Bauxite Industry." *Social and Economic Studies* 20, no. 4 (1971): 378–419.

Girvan, Norman, Mario Arana Sevilla, Miguel Ceara Hatton, and Ennio Rodríguez. "The Debt Problem of Small Peripheral Economies: Case Studies from the Caribbean and Central America." *Caribbean Studies* 24, no. 1 (1991): 45–115.

Girvan, Norman, and Michel Vale. "The Guyana-Alcan Conflict and the Nationalization of Demba." *International Journal of Politics* 3, no. 3 (1973): 87–111.

Go, Julian. *Postcolonial Thought and Social Theory*. New York: Oxford University Press, 2016.

Go, Julian. "Three Tensions in the Theory of Racial Capitalism." *Sociological Theory* 39, no. 1 (2021): 38–47.

Go, Julian, and George Lawson, eds. *Global Historical Sociology*. Cambridge: Cambridge University Press, 2017.

Göçek, Fatma Müge. *Rise of the Bourgeoisie, Demise of Empire: Ottoman Westernization and Social Change*. New York: Oxford University Press, 1996.

Goldfield, Michael. *The Decline of Organized Labor in the United States*. Chicago: University of Chicago Press, 1987.

Goldfield, Michael. *The Southern Key: Class, Race, and Radicalism in the 1930s and 1940s*. New York: Oxford University Press, 2020.

Goldthree, Reena. "'A Greater Enterprise Than the Panama Canal': Migrant Labor and Military Recruitment in the World War I–Era Circum-Caribbean." *Labor* 13, no. 3–4 (2016): 57–82.

Gomes, Albert. *Through a Maze of Colour*. Port of Spain, Trinidad and Tobago: Key Caribbean, 1974.

Government of Kerala. *Economic Review 2019*. Vol. 1. Kerala, India: Government Press, 2020.

Government of Trinidad and Tobago. *Accounting for the Petrodollar*. Port of Spain, Trinidad and Tobago: Government Printery, 1980.

Government of Trinidad and Tobago. *Accounting for the Petrodollar 1973–1983*. Port of Spain, Trinidad and Tobago: Government Printery, 1984.

Government of Trinidad and Tobago. *Five-Year Development Programme 1958–1962*. Port of Spain, Trinidad and Tobago: Government Printing Office, 1960.

Government of Trinidad and Tobago. *Ministry of Petroleum and Mines Annual Report for the Year 1970*. Port of Spain, Trinidad and Tobago: Central Statistical Office Printing Unit, 1970. Accessed May 20, 2023. https://www.energy.gov.tt/publications/annual-administrative-reports/.

Government of Trinidad and Tobago. *Ministry of Petroleum and Mines Annual Report for the Year 1971*. Port of Spain, Trinidad and Tobago: Government Printery, 1972. Accessed May 20, 2023. https://www.energy.gov.tt/publications/annual-administrative-reports/.

Government of Trinidad and Tobago. *Ministry of Petroleum and Mines Annual Report for the Year 1973*. Port of Spain, Trinidad and Tobago: Government Printery, 1973. Accessed May 20, 2023. https://www.energy.gov.tt/publications/annual-administrative-reports/.

Government of Trinidad and Tobago. *Ministry of Petroleum and Mines Annual Report for the Year 1974*. Port of Spain, Trinidad and Tobago: Government Printery, 1980. Accessed May 18, 2023. https://www.energy.gov.tt/publications/annual-administrative-reports/.

Government of Trinidad and Tobago. *Ministry of Petroleum and Mines Annual Report for the Year 1975*. Port of Spain, Trinidad and Tobago: Government Printery, 1980. Accessed May 18, 2023. https://www.energy.gov.tt/publications/annual-administrative-reports/.

Government of Trinidad and Tobago. *Ministry of Petroleum and Mines Annual Report for the Year 1976*. Port of Spain, Trinidad and Tobago: Government Printery, 1980. Accessed May 19, 2023. https://www.energy.gov.tt/publications/annual-administrative-reports/.

Government of Trinidad and Tobago. *Ministry of Petroleum and Mines Annual Report for the Year 1977*. Port of Spain, Trinidad and Tobago: Government Printery, 1982. Accessed May 18, 2023. https://www.energy.gov.tt/publications/annual-administrative-reports/.

Government of Trinidad and Tobago. *Ministry of Petroleum and Mines Annual Report for the Year 1979*. Port of Spain, Trinidad and Tobago: Trinidad and Tobago Printing and Packaging Limited. Accessed May 20, 2023. https://www.energy.gov.tt/publications/annual-administrative-reports/.

Government of Trinidad and Tobago. *Third Five-Year Plan 1969–1973*. Port of Spain, Trinidad and Tobago: Government Printery, 1969.

Government of Trinidad and Tobago. *White Paper on Natural Gas*. Port of Spain, Trinidad and Tobago: Government Printery, 1981.

Government of Trinidad and Tobago. *White Paper on Public Participation in Industrial and Commercial Activities*. Port of Spain, Trinidad and Tobago: Government Printery, 1972, 1975.

Gramsci Antonio. *Selections from the Prison Notebooks*. Edited by Quintin Hoare and Geoffrey Nowell-Smith. 1971. New York: International Publishers, 1992.

Gray, Kevin. *Labour and Development in East Asia: Social Forces and Passive Revolution*. London: Routledge, 2015.

Great Britain. *Report of the British Guiana Commission: Presented by the Secretary of State for the Colonies to Parliament by Command of His Majesty*. London: H.M.S.O., 1927.

Great Britain. *Report of the Sugar Industry of the West Indies and British Guiana (West Indian Sugar Commission, 1929–30)*. London: H.M.S.O., 1930.

Great Britain Colonial Office. *Annual Report on the Colony of Trinidad and Tobago for the Year 1948*. London: H.M.S.O., 1950.

Great Britain Colonial Office. *Annual Report on the Social and Economic Progress of the People of British Guiana 1937*. London: H.M.S.O., 1938.

Great Britain Colonial Office. *Annual Report on the Social and Economic Progress of the People of Trinidad and Tobago 1936*. London: H.M.S.O., 1937.

Great Britain Colonial Office. *Annual Report on the Social and Economic Progress of the People of Trinidad and Tobago 1937*. London: H.M.S.O., 1939.

Great Britain Colonial Office. *Annual Report of the Social and Economic Progress of the People of Trinidad and Tobago 1938*. London: H.M.S.O., 1939.

Great Britain Colonial Office. *Annual Report on Trinidad and Tobago, B.W.I., for the Year 1947*. London: H.M.S.O., 1949.

Great Britain Colonial Office. *Annual Report on Trinidad and Tobago for the Year 1946*. London: H.M.S.O., 1948.

Great Britain Colonial Office. *Annual Report on Trinidad and Tobago for the Year 1949*. London: H.M.S.O., 1951.

Great Britain Colonial Office. *The Colonial Office List 1946*. London: H.M.S.O., 1946.

Great Britain Colonial Office. *The Colonial Office List 1950*. London: H.M.S.O., 1950.

Great Britain Colonial Office. *The Colonial Office List 1955*. London: H.M.S.O., 1955.

Great Britain Colonial Office. *The Colonial Office List 1960*. London: H.M.S.O., 1960.

Great Britain Colonial Office. *The Colonial Office List 1962*. London: H.M.S.O., 1962.

Great Britain Colonial Office. *Report on British Guiana for the Year 1952*. London: H.M.S.O., 1954.

Great Britain Colonial Office. *West India Royal Commission Report 1938–1939* (Moyne Report). Cmd. 6607. London: H.M.S.O., 1945.

Guha, Ranajit, and Gayatri Chakravorty Spivak, eds. *Selected Subaltern Studies*. New York: Oxford University Press, 1988.

Hall, Stuart. "Frontlines and Backyards: The Terms of Change." In *Black British Culture and Society*, edited by Kwesi Owusu, 135–40. London: Routledge, 2000.

Hall, Stuart. "New Ethnicities." In *Selected Writings on Race and Difference*, edited by Ruth Wilson Gilmore and Paul Gilroy, 246–56. Durham, NC: Duke University Press, 2021.

Hall, Stuart. "Race, Articulation, and Societies Structured in Dominance." In *Selected Writings on Race and Difference*, edited by Ruth Wilson Gilmore and Paul Gilroy, 195–245. Durham, NC: Duke University Press, 2021.

Hall, Stuart. "The Rediscovery of 'Ideology': Return of the Repressed in Media Studies." In *Culture, Society and the Media*, edited by Michael Gurevitch, Tony Bennett, James Curran, and Janet Wollacott, 56–90. New York: Methuen, 1982.

Hammer, Ricarda, and Alexandre White. "Toward a Sociology of Colonial Subjectivity: Political Agency in Haiti and Liberia." *Sociology of Race and Ethnicity* 5, no. 2 (2019): 215–28.

Haraksingh, Kusha. "Control and Resistance Among Overseas Indian Workers: A Study of Labour on the Sugar Plantations of Trinidad, 1875–1917." *Journal of Caribbean History* 14 (1981): 1–17.

Harding, John, and G. E. J. Gent. *The Dominions Office and Colonial Office List for 1935.* London: Waterlow and Sons Limited, 1935.

Harding, John, and G. E. J. Gent. *The Dominions Office and Colonial Office List for 1937.* London: Waterlow and Sons Limited, 1937.

Harding, John, and G. E. J. Gent. *The Dominions Office and Colonial Office List for 1938.* London: Waterlow and Sons Limited, 1938.

Harding, John, and G. E. J. Gent. *The Dominions Office and Colonial Office List for 1939.* London: Waterlow and Sons Limited, 1939.

Harding, John, and G. E. J. Gent. *The Dominions Office and Colonial Office List for 1940.* London: Waterlow and Sons Limited, 1940.

Harpelle, Ronald. "Cross Currents in the Western Caribbean: Marcus Garvey and the UNIA in Central America." *Caribbean Studies* 31, no. 1 (2003): 35–73.

Hart, Richard. *From Occupation to Independence: A Short History of the Peoples of the English-Speaking Caribbean Region.* London: Pluto, 1998.

Hart, Richard. *Rise and Organize: The Birth of the Workers and National Movements in Jamaica, 1936–1939.* London: Karia Press, 1989.

Hart, Richard. *Towards Decolonisation: Political, Labour and Economic Developments in Jamaica 1938–1945.* Kingston, Jamaica: Canoe Press, University of the West Indies, 1999.

Harvey, Claudia. "Educational Change and Its Social Impact on National Development in Trinidad and Tobago, 1962–1987." In *Trinidad and Tobago: The Independence Experience, 1962–1987,* edited by Selwyn Ryan, 345–80. St. Augustine, Trinidad and Tobago: Institute of Social and Economic Research, University of the West Indies, 1988.

Harvey, David. *A Brief History of Neoliberalism.* Oxford: Oxford University Press, 2005.

Hattam, Victoria. *Labor Visions and State Power: The Origins of Business Unionism in the United States.* Princeton, NJ: Princeton University Press, 1993.

Heller, Patrick. *The Labor of Development: Workers and the Transformation of Capitalism in Kerala, India.* Ithaca, NY: Cornell University Press, 1999.

Henderson, Ian. "Wage-Earners and Political Protest in Colonial Africa: The Case of the Copperbelt." *African Affairs* 72, no. 288 (1973): 288–99.

Henry, Paget. *Caliban's Reason: Introducing Afro-Caribbean Philosophy.* New York: Routledge, 2000.

Henry, Paget, and Paul Buhle, eds. *C. L. R. James's Caribbean.* Durham, NC: Duke University Press, 1992.

Higgins, George. *A History of Trinidad Oil.* Port of Spain, Trinidad and Tobago: Trinidad Express Newspapers, 1996.

Higman, B. W. *Slave Populations of the British Caribbean, 1807–1834.* Baltimore, MD: Johns Hopkins University Press, 1984.

Hill, Robert, ed. *The Marcus Garvey and Universal Negro Improvement Association Papers.* Vol. 11, *The Caribbean Diaspora, 1910–1920.* 1983. Durham, NC: Duke University Press, 2011.

Hill Collins, Patricia. *Intersectionality as Critical Social Theory.* Durham, NC: Duke University Press, 2019.

Hinds, David. *Ethno-Politics and Power Sharing in Guyana: History and Discourse.* Washington, DC: New Academia Publishing, 2011.

Hinds, David. "Problems of Democratic Transition in Guyana: Mistakes and Miscalculations in 1992." *Social and Economic Studies* 54, no. 1 (2005): 67–82.

Hintzen, Percy. *The Costs of Regime Survival: Racial Mobilization, Elite Domination and Control of the State in Guyana and Trinidad.* Cambridge: Cambridge University Press, 1989.

Hintzen, Percy. "Ethnicity, Class, and International Capitalist Penetration in Guyana and Trinidad." *Social and Economic Studies* 34, no. 3 (1985): 107–63.

Hintzen, Percy. *Reproducing Domination: On the Caribbean Postcolonial State.* With Aaron Kamugisha and Charisse Burden-Stelly. Jackson: University Press of Mississippi, 2022.

Hipsher, Patricia L. "Democratization and the Decline of Urban Social Movements in Chile and Spain." *Comparative Politics* 28, no. 3 (1996): 227, 273–97.

Hobsbawm, Eric J. *Labouring Men: Studies in the History of Labour.* New York: Basic, 1964.

Hobson, Rolf. *Imperialism at Sea: Naval Strategic Thought, the Ideology of Sea Power, and the Tirpitz Plan, 1875–1914.* Boston: Brill Academic, 2002.

Holton, Graham. "State Petroleum Enterprises and the International Oil Industry: The Case of Trinidad and Tobago." PhD diss., La Trobe University, 1994.

Home, Robert. *Of Planting and Planning: The Making of British Colonial Cities.* New York: Routledge, 2013.

Horne, Gerald. *The Apocalypse of Settler Colonialism: The Roots of Slavery, White Supremacy, and Capitalism in Seventeenth-Century North America and the Caribbean.* New York: Monthly Review Press, 2017.

Horne, Gerald. *Black Liberation/Red Scare: Ben Davis and the Communist Party.* Cranbury, NJ: Associated University Press, 1994.

Hosein, Roger, and Rebecca Gookool. "Export Mineral Rents, Rentierism and Make Work Programmes: An Assessment of the Welfare Consequences for a Small Gas Exporting Economy." *Social and Economic Studies* 67, no. 4 (2018): 205–34.

Huber, Evelyne, and John Stephens. *Democracy and the Left: Social Policy and Inequality in Latin America.* Chicago: University of Chicago Press, 2012.

Huber, Evelyne, and John Stephens. *Development and Crisis of the Welfare State: Parties and Policies in Global Markets.* Chicago: University of Chicago Press, 2001.

Humphreys, Macartan, Jeffrey Sachs, and Joseph Stiglitz. *Escaping the Resource Curse.* New York: Columbia University Press, 2007.

Hung, Ho-fung. "Labor Politics Under Three Stages of Chinese Capitalism." *South Atlantic Quarterly* 112, no. 1 (2013): 203–12.

Hunter, Herbert, and Sameer Abraham. *Race, Class, and the World System: The Sociology of Oliver C. Cox.* New York: Monthly Review Press, 1987.

International Labour Organization. "ILOSTAT Indicators and Data Tools." Country Catalogue. Accessed June 5, 2023. https://ilostat.ilo.org/data/.

International Labour Organization. *Year Book of Labour Statistics 1970.* Geneva: International Labour Organization, 1970.

International Labour Organization. *Year Book of Labour Statistics 1973.* Geneva: International Labour Organization, 1973.

Isaac, Larry, and Lars Christiansen. "How the Civil Rights Movement Revitalized Labor Militancy." *American Sociological Review* 67, no. 5 (2002): 722–46.

Isham, Jonathan, Michael Woolcock, Lant Pritchett, and Gwen Busby. "The Varieties of Resource Experience: Natural Resource Export Structures and the Political Economy of Economic Growth." *World Bank Economic Review* 19, no. 2 (2005): 141–74.

Itzigsohn, José, and Karida Brown. *The Sociology of W. E. B. Du Bois: Racialized Modernity and the Global Color Line*. New York: New York University Press, 2020.

Jacklin, Laurie. "British Colonial Healthcare in a Post-Emancipation Plantation Society: Creolizing Public Health and Medicine in Trinidad, to 1916." PhD diss., McMaster University, 2009.

Jacobs, Richard, ed. *Butler Versus the King: Riots and Sedition in 1937*. Port of Spain, Trinidad and Tobago: Key Caribbean, 1976.

Jacobs, Richard. "The Politics of Protest in Trinidad: The Strikes and Disturbances of 1937." *Caribbean Studies* 17, no. 1/2 (1977): 5–54.

James, C. L. R. *The Black Jacobins: Toussaint L'Ouverture and the San Domingo Revolution*. 1938. New York: Vintage Books, 1989.

James, C. L. R. *Every Cook Can Govern*. 1956. Detroit, MI: Bewick, 1992.

James, C. L. R. *A History of Pan-African Revolt*. 1938. Oakland, CA: PM Press, 2012.

James, C. L. R. *The Life of Captain Cipriani: An Account of the British Government in the West Indies*. 1932. Durham, NC: Duke University Press, 2014.

James, C. L. R. "Revolution and the Negro." 1939. Accessed December 7, 2024. https://www.marxists.org/archive/james-clr/works/1939/12/negro-revolution.htm.

James, C. L. R. "The Revolutionary Solution to the Negro Problem in the United States." *Radical America* 4, no. 4 (1970): 12–18.

James, C. L. R. "The West Indian Middle Classes." In *Caribbean Political Thought: The Colonial State to Caribbean Internationalisms*, edited by Aaron Kamugisha, 249–56. 1961. Kingston, Jamaica: Ian Randle, 2013.

Jayaram, Narayana. "The Dynamics of Language in Indian Diaspora: The Case of Bhojpuri/Hindi in Trinidad." *Sociological Bulletin* 49, no. 1 (2000): 41–62.

Jayaram, Narayana. "The Metamorphosis of Caste Among Trinidad Hindus." *Contributions to Indian Sociology* 40, no. 2 (2006): 143–73.

Jenkins, J. Craig, and Charles Perrow. "Insurgency of the Powerless: Farm Worker Movements (1946–1972)." *American Sociological Review* 42, no. 2 (1977): 249–68.

Jensen, Nathan, and Leonard Wantchekon. "Resource Wealth and Political Regimes in Africa." *Comparative Political Studies* 37, no. 7 (2004): 816–41.

Jha, J. C. "Indian Heritage in Trinidad, West Indies." *Caribbean Quarterly* 19, no. 2 (1973): 28–50.

Jobson, Ryan. "Road Work: Highways and Hegemony in Trinidad and Tobago." *Journal of Latin American and Caribbean Anthropology* 23, no. 3 (2018): 457–77.

John, Meredith. *The Plantation Slaves of Trinidad, 1783–1816: A Mathematical and Demographic Enquiry*. Cambridge: Cambridge University Press, 1988.

John, Tamanisha. "Canadian Imperialism in Caribbean Structural Adjustment, 1980–2000." In *Capitalism and Class Power*, edited by Ronald Cox, 133–76. Boston: Brill, 2023.

Johnson, Caswell. "Emergence of Political Unionism in Economies of British Colonial Origin: The Cases of Jamaica and Trinidad." *American Journal of Economics and Sociology* 39, no. 2 (1980): 151–64.

Johnson, Cedric. *The Panthers Can't Save Us Now: Debating Left Politics and Black Lives Matter.* London: Verso Books, 2022.

Johnson, Chalmers. MITI *and the Japanese Miracle: The Growth of Industrial Policy, 1925–1975.* Stanford, CA: Stanford University Press, 1982.

Johnson, Gaye Theresa, and Alex Lubin, eds. *Futures of Black Radicalism.* London: Verso Books, 2017.

Johnson, Howard. "Oil, Imperial Policy and the Trinidad Disturbances, 1937." *Journal of Imperial and Commonwealth History* 4, no. 1 (1975): 29–54.

Jones, Claudia. *An End to the Neglect of the Problems of the Negro Woman!* New York: National Women's Commission CPUSA, 1949.

Jones Luong, Pauline, and Erika Weinthal. *Oil Is Not a Curse: Ownership Structure and Institutions in Soviet Successor States.* New York: Cambridge University Press, 2010.

Jordan-Zachery, Julia. "Let Men Be Men: A Gendered Analysis of Black Ideological Response to Familial Policies." *National Political Science Review* 11 (2007): 177–92.

Joseph-Gabriel, Annette. *Reimagining Liberation: How Black Women Transformed Citizenship in the French Empire.* Champaign: University of Illinois Press, 2020.

Jung, Moon-Kie. *Reworking Race: The Making of Hawaii's Interracial Labor Movement.* New York: Columbia University Press, 2006.

Kale, Madhavi. *Fragments of Empire: Capital, Slavery, and Indian Indentured Labor Migration in the British Caribbean.* Philadelphia: University of Pennsylvania Press, 1998.

Kale, Sunila, and Nimah Mazaheri. "Natural Resources, Development Strategies, and Lower Caste Empowerment in India's Mineral Belt: Bihar and Odisha During the 1990s." *Studies in Comparative International Development* 49 (2014): 343–69.

Kambon, Khafra. *For Bread, Justice, and Freedom: A Political Biography of George Weekes.* London: New Beacon Books, 1988.

Karl, Terry. *The Paradox of Plenty: Oil Booms and Petro-States.* Berkeley: University of California Press, 1997.

Katznelson, Ira. "Working-Class Formation: Constructing Cases and Comparisons." In *Working-Class Formation: Nineteenth-Century Patterns in Western Europe and the United States,* edited by Ira Katznelson and Aristide R. Zolberg, 3–42. Princeton, NJ: Princeton University Press, 1986.

Kelley, Robin. "Building Bridges: The Challenge of Organized Labor in Communities of Color." *New Labor Forum,* no. 5 (1999): 42–58.

Kelley, Robin. *Freedom Dreams: The Black Radical Imagination.* Boston: Beacon, 2002.

Kelley, Robin. *Hammer and Hoe: Alabama Communists During the Great Depression.* 1990. Chapel Hill: University of North Carolina Press, 2015.

Kelly, Michael. *The Origins and Developments of Education in Zambia from Pre-Colonial Time to 1996: A Book of Notes and Readings.* Lusaka, Zambia: Image, 1999.

Kelshall, Gaylord. *The U-Boat War in the Caribbean.* Annapolis, MD: Naval Institute Press, 1994.

Kennedy, Randall. "Who Can Say 'Nigger'? And Other Considerations." *Journal of Blacks in Higher Education* 26 (1999/2000): 86–96.

Khan, Aisha. "What Is 'a Spanish'? Ambiguity and 'Mixed' Ethnicity in Trinidad." In *Trinidad Ethnicity*, edited by Kevin Yelvington, 180–207. Knoxville: University of Tennessee Press, 1993.

Kiely, Ray. *The Politics of Labour and Development in Trinidad*. Kingston, Jamaica: Press University of the West Indies, 1996.

Kimeldorf, Howard. *Reds or Rackets? The Making of Radical and Conservative Unions on the Waterfront*. Berkeley: University of California Press, 1988.

Kissoon, Feriel Nissa. "The 'Creole Indian': The Emergence of East Indian Civil Society in Trinidad and Tobago c. 1897–1945." PhD diss., King's College, University of London, 2014.

Knight, Bryan. "Altheia Jones-Lecointe: The Black Panther Who Became a Mangrove Nine Hero." *Guardian* (UK), September 9, 2021. https://www.theguardian.com/society/2021/sep/09/altheia-jones-lecointe-the-black-panther-who-became-a-mangrove-nine-hero.

Knight, Franklin, ed. *General History of the Caribbean, Volume 3: The Slave Societies of the Caribbean*. London: UNESCO Publishing, 1997.

Knight, Franklin. "The Struggle of the British Caribbean Sugar Industry, 1900–2013." *Journal of Caribbean History* 48, no. 1/2 (2014): 149–66.

Kohli, Atul. *State-Directed Development: Political Power and Industrialization in the Global Periphery*. Cambridge: Cambridge University Press, 2004.

Korpi, Walter. *The Democratic Class Struggle*. 1983. New York: Routledge, 2019.

Kuhonta, Erik. *The Institutional Imperative: The Politics of Equitable Development in Southeast Asia*. Stanford, CA: Stanford University Press, 2011.

Kurtz, Marcus. "The Social Foundations of Institutional Order: Reconsidering War and the 'Resource Curse' in Third World State Building." *Politics and Society* 37, no. 4 (2009): 479–520.

Kwayana, Eusi. *The Bauxite Strike and the Old Politics*. 1972. Atlanta: On Our Own Authority! Publishing, 2012.

Kwayana, Eusi. "Burnhamism, Jaganism and the People of Guyana." *Black Scholar* 4, no. 8/9 (1973): 40–46.

La Guerre, John Gaffar. "The Race Factor and the Election of 1950 in Trinidad and Tobago." *Social and Economic Studies* 29, no. 2/3 (1980): 321–35.

La Guerre, John Gaffar, and Cherita Girvan. "The General Elections of 1946 in Trinidad and Tobago." *Social and Economic Studies* 21, no. 2 (1972): 184–204.

Lake, Véron. "A Better Strategy? The Evolving Livelihood Strategies of Caribbean Banana and Sugar Workers in a Globalised Economy." Master's thesis, Saint Mary's University, 2010.

Lal, Priya. *African Socialism in Postcolonial Tanzania*. New York: Cambridge University Press, 2015.

Lambert, Rob. "Political Unionism and Working Class Hegemony: Perspectives on the South African Congress of Trade Unions, 1955–1965." *Labour, Capital and Society/ Travail, capital et société* 18, no. 2 (1985): 244–77.

Lambert, Rob, and Eddie Webster. "The Re-Emergence of Political Unionism in Contemporary South Africa?" In *Popular Struggles in South Africa*, edited by Williams Cobbett and Robin Cohen, 20–41. London: James Currey, 1988.

Lange, Matthew. *Comparative-Historical Methods*. London: Sage Publications, 2013.

Lange, Matthew. *Lineages of Despotism and Development: British Colonialism and State Power*. Chicago: University of Chicago Press, 2009.

Lans, Cheryl. "A Review of the Plant-Based Traditions of the Cocoa Panyols of Trinidad." *GeoJournal* 83, no. 6 (2018): 1425–54.

La Porta, Rafael, Florencio Lopez-de-Silanes, Andrei Shleifer, and Robert Vishny. "The Quality of Government." *Journal of Law, Economics, and Organization* 15, no. 1 (1999): 222–79.

Larmer, Miles. *Mineworkers in Zambia: Labour and Political Change in Post-Colonial Africa*. London: I. B. Tauris, 2007.

Larmer, Miles. "Unrealistic Expectations? Zambia's Mineworkers from Independence to the One-Party State, 1964–1972." *Journal of Historical Sociology* 18, no. 4 (2005): 318–52.

Larson, Eric. "Black Lives Matter and Bridge Building: Labor Education for a 'New Jim Crow' Era." *Labor Studies Journal* 41, no. 1 (2016): 36-66.

Lawrence, Adria. *Imperial Rule and the Politics of Nationalism: Anti-Colonial Protest in the French Empire*. New York: Cambridge University Press, 2013.

LeBas, Adrienne. *From Protest to Parties: Party-Building and Democratization in Africa*. Oxford: Oxford University Press, 2011.

Lederman, Daniel, and William Maloney, eds. *Natural Resources, Neither Curse nor Destiny*. Washington, DC: International Bank for Reconstruction and Development/ World Bank, 2007.

Ledgister, F. S. J. *Class Alliances and the Liberal Authoritarian State: The Roots of Post-Colonial Democracy in Jamaica, Trinidad and Tobago, and Surinam*. Trenton, NJ: Africa World Press, 1998.

Lee, Cheol-Sung. "Labor Unions and Good Governance: A Cross-National, Comparative Analysis." *American Sociological Review* 72 (2007): 585–609.

Legassick, Martin, and David Hemson. *Foreign Investment and the Reproduction of Racial Capitalism in South Africa*. London: Anti-Apartheid Movement, 1976.

Letwin, Daniel. *The Challenge of Interracial Unionism: Alabama Coal Miners, 1878–1921*. Chapel Hill: University of North Carolina Press, 1998.

Lewis, Gordon. *The Growth of the Modern West Indies*. Kingston, Jamaica: Ian Randle, 2004.

Lewis, Gordon. "The Trinidad and Tobago General Election of 1961." *Caribbean Studies* 2, no. 2 (1962): 2–30.

Lewis, Patsy. "Bringing Small States Back In: The Caribbean and Pacific in a New World Order." *Social and Economic Studies* 56, no. 1/2 (2007): 1–31.

Lewis, Rupert. "Jamaican Black Power in the 1960s." In *Black Power in the Caribbean*, edited by Kate Quinn, 53–75. Gainesville: University Press of Florida, 2014.

Lieberman, Evan, and Gwyneth McClendon. "The Ethnicity–Policy Preference Link in Sub-Saharan Africa." *Comparative Political Studies* 46, no. 5 (2013): 574–602.

Lieberman, Marvin. "Excess Capacity as a Barrier to Entry: An Empirical Appraisal." *Journal of Industrial Economics* 35, no. 4 (1987): 607–27.

Lonsdale, John. "The Emergence of African Nations: A Historiographical Analysis." *African Affairs* 67, no. 266 (1968): 11–28.

Look Lai, Walton. *The Chinese in the West Indies, 1806–1995: A Documentary History.* Kingston, Jamaica: Press University of West Indies, 1998.

Look Lai, Walton. "C. L. R. James and Trinidadian Nationalism." In *C. L. R. James's Caribbean*, edited by Paget Henry and Paul Buhle, 174–209. Durham, NC: Duke University Press, 1992.

Loveman, Mara. "Is 'Race' Essential?" *American Sociological Review* 64, no. 6 (1999): 891–98.

Loveman, Mara. *National Colors: Racial Classification and the State in Latin America.* Oxford: Oxford University Press, 2014.

Lowe, Lisa. *The Intimacies of Four Continents.* Durham, NC: Duke University Press, 2015.

MacDonald, Scott. *Trinidad and Tobago: Democracy and Development in the Caribbean.* New York: Praeger, 1986.

Magubane, Zine. "Overlapping Territories and Intertwined Histories: Historical Sociology's Global Imagination." In *Remaking Modernity*, edited by Julia Adams, Elizabeth Clemens, and Ann Orloff, 92–108. Durham, NC: Duke University Press, 2005.

Mahase, Radica. "'Plenty a Dem Run Away'—Resistance by Indian Indentured Labourers in Trinidad, 1870–1920." *Labor History* 49, no. 4 (2008): 465–80.

Mahdavy, Hossein. "The Patterns and Problems of Economic Development in Rentier States: The Case of Iran." In *Studies in the Economic History of the Middle East*, edited by M. A. Cook, 428–67. London: Oxford University Press, 1970.

Mahoney, James. *Colonialism and Postcolonial Development: Spanish America in Comparative Perspective.* New York: Cambridge University Press, 2010.

Mahoney, James. "Comparative-Historical Analysis and Development Studies: Methods, Findings, Future." *Sociology of Development* 1, no. 1 (2015): 77–90.

Mahoney, James, and Dietrich Rueschemeyer, eds. *Comparative Historical Analysis in the Social Sciences.* Cambridge: Cambridge University Press, 2003.

Maingot, Anthony. *The United States and the Caribbean: Challenges of an Asymmetrical Relationship.* 1994. New York: Routledge, 2018.

Makalani, Minkah. *In the Cause of Freedom: Radical Black Internationalism from Harlem to London, 1917–1939.* Chapel Hill: University of North Carolina Press, 2011.

Mamdani, Mahmood. *Citizen and Subject: Contemporary Africa and the Legacy of Late Colonialism.* Princeton, NJ: Princeton University Press, 1996.

Mandle, Jay R. "The Decline in Mortality in British Guiana, 1911–1960." *Demography* 7, no. 3 (1970): 301–15.

Mandle, Jay R. *Patterns of Caribbean Development: An Interpretive Essay on Economic Change.* London: Routledge, 2010.

Mann, Michael. *The Sources of Social Power: The Rise of Classes and Nation-States, 1760–1914.* Cambridge: Cambridge University Press, 1986.

Marable, Manning. *Black Liberation in Conservative America.* Boston: South End, 1997.

Marable, Manning. *How Capitalism Underdeveloped Black America.* 1983. Chicago: Haymarket Books, 2015.

Maraj, Bhadase Sagan. *Hostile and Recalcitrant*. Edited by Devant Maharaj, Ranjanie Ramlakhan, and Bhadase Seetahal Maharaj. San Juan, Trinidad and Tobago: Prudential Printers, 2001.

Marini, Ruy Mauro. *The Dialectics of Dependency*. 1972. New York: Monthly Review Press, 2022.

Martin, Tony. *Marcus Garvey, Hero: A First Biography*. Dover, MA: Majority Press, 1983.

Martin, Tony. *The Pan-African Connection: From Slavery to Garvey and Beyond*. 1983. Dover, MA: Majority Press, 1984.

Martin, Tony. "Revolutionary Upheaval in Trinidad, 1919: Views from British and American Sources." *Journal of Negro History* 58, no. 3 (1973): 313–26.

Marx, Karl. *Capital Volume I*. 1867. London: Penguin, 1982.

Matlon, Jordanna. *A Man Among Other Men: The Crisis of Black Masculinity in Racial Capitalism*. Ithaca, NY: Cornell University Press, 2022.

Matthews, Harry. *Multinational Corporations and Black Power*. Cambridge, MA: Schenkman, 1976.

Mawby, Spencer. "Workers in the Vanguard: The 1960 Industrial Relations Ordinance and the Struggle for Independence in Aden." *Labor History* 57, no. 1 (2016): 35–52.

McAdam, Doug, John McCarthy, and Meyer Zald, eds. *Comparative Perspectives on Social Movements: Political Opportunity Structures, Mobilizing Structures, and Cultural Framings*. Cambridge: Cambridge University Press, 1996.

McCann, Gerard. "Possibility and Peril: Trade Unionism, African Cold War, and the Global Strands of Kenyan Decolonization." *Journal of Social History* 53, no. 2 (2019): 348–77.

Meebelo, Henry. *African Proletarians and Colonial Capitalism: The Origins, Growth, and Struggles of the Zambian Labour Movement to 1964*. Lusaka, Zambia: Kenneth Kaunda Foundation, 1986.

Meeks, Brian. "The 1970 Revolution: Chronology and Documentation." In *The Black Power Revolution of 1970*, edited by Selwyn Ryan and Taimoon Stewart, 135–77. St. Augustine, Trinidad and Tobago: Institute of Social and Economic Research, University of the West Indies, 1995.

Meeks, Brian. "The Rise and Fall of Caribbean Black Power." In *From Toussaint to Tupac: The Black International Since the Age of Revolution*, edited by Michael O. West, William G. Martin, and Fanon Che Wilkins, 197–214. Chapel Hill: University of North Carolina Press, 2009.

Meeks, Brian, and Norman Girvan, eds. *The Thought of New World: The Quest for Decolonisation*. Caribbean Reasonings. Kingston, Jamaica: Ian Randle, 2010.

Meghji, Ali. *Decolonizing Sociology: An Introduction*. Cambridge: Polity Press, 2021.

Meighoo, Kirk Peter. *Politics in a "Half-Made Society": Trinidad and Tobago, 1925–2001*. Kingston, Jamaica: Ian Randle, 2003.

Mercer, William, and A. E. Collins. *The Colonial Office List for 1919*. London: Waterlow and Sons Limited, 1919.

Mercer, William, A. E. Collins, and A. J. Harding. *The Colonial Office List for 1920*. London: Waterlow and Sons Limited, 1920.

Mercer, William, A. E. Collins, and J. R. W. Robinson. *The Colonial Office List for 1915*. London: Waterlow and Sons Limited, 1915.

Mercer, William, A. J. Harding, and G. E. J. Gent. *The Dominions Office and Colonial Office List for 1930*. London: Waterlow and Sons Limited, 1930.

Meyer, David. "Protest and Political Opportunities." *Annual Review of Sociology* 30 (2004): 125–45.

Michaels, Walter Benn, and Adolph Reed Jr. *No Politics but Class Politics*. London: Eris, 2022.

Michels, Robert. *Political Parties: A Sociological Study of the Oligarchical Tendencies of Modern Democracy*. New York: Hearst's International Library Co., 1915.

Migdal, Joel S. *Strong Societies and Weak States: State-Society Relations and State Capabilities in the Third World*. Princeton, NJ: Princeton University Press, 1988.

Migdal, Joel S., Atul Kohli, and Vivienne Shue, eds. *State Power and Social Forces: Domination and Transformation in the Third World*. Cambridge: Cambridge University Press, 1994.

Miles, William. *Hausaland Divided: Colonialism and Independence in Nigeria and Niger*. Ithaca, NY: Cornell University Press, 1994.

Milkman, Ruth, and Kim Voss, eds. *Rebuilding Labor: Organizing and Organizers in the New Union Movement*. Ithaca, NY: Cornell University Press, 2004.

Millette, James. "The Civil Commission of 1802: An Account and an Explanation of an Issue in the Early Constitutional and Political History of Trinidad." *Jamaican Historical Review* 6, no. 1 (1966): 29–111.

Millette, James. *The Genesis of Crown Colony Government: Trinidad 1783–1810*. Curepe, Trinidad and Tobago: Moko Enterprises, 1970.

Mintz, Sidney. *Three Ancient Colonies*. Cambridge, MA: Harvard University Press, 2012.

Mitchell, Brian. *International Historical Statistics: The Americas, 1750–1988*. 1983. New York: Stockton Press, 1993.

Mitchell, Timothy. *Carbon Democracy: Political Power in the Age of Oil*. London: Verso, 2011.

Mkandawire, Thandika. "Thinking About Developmental States in Africa." *Cambridge Journal of Economics* 25, no. 3 (2001): 289–314.

Modelski, George, and William Thompson. *Seapower in Global Politics, 1494–1993*. London: Macmillan Press, 1988.

Mohamed, Wazir. "African Labor in Guyana and the Expansion of the Second Slavery." In *New Frontiers of Slavery*, edited by Dale Tomich, 101–25. Albany: State University of New York Press, 2016.

Mohammed, Patricia. *Gender Negotiations Among Indians in Trinidad 1917–1947*. Basingstoke, UK: Palgrave in Association with Institute of Social Studies, 2002.

Mohammed, Patricia. "Women's Responses in the 70s and 80s in Trinidad: A Country Report." *Caribbean Quarterly* 35, no. 1–2 (1989): 36–45.

Montalvo, Jose, and Marta Reynal-Querol. "Ethnic Diversity and Economic Development." *Journal of Development Economics* 76, no. 2 (2005): 293–323.

Moody, Kim. *An Injury to All: The Decline of American Unionism*. London: Verso, 1988.

Morris, Aldon. *The Origins of the Civil Rights Movement*. New York: Free Press, 1984.

Munasinghe, Viranjini. *Callaloo or Tossed Salad? East Indians and the Cultural Politics of Identity in Trinidad*. Ithaca, NY: Cornell University Press, 2001.

Mwendapole, M. R. *A History of the Trade Union Movement in Zambia up to 1968*. Lusaka, Zambia: University of Zambia Institute for African Studies, 1977.

Narayan, John. "British Black Power: The Anti-Imperialism of Political Blackness and the Problem of Nativist Socialism." *Sociological Review* 67, no. 5 (2019): 945–67.

Nkrumah, Kwame. *Neo-Colonialism: The Last Stage of Imperialism*. London: Thomas Nelson and Sons, 1965.

Nobles, Melissa. *Shades of Citizenship: Race and the Census in Modern Politics*. Stanford, CA: Stanford University Press, 2000.

O'Connor, P. E. T. *Some Trinidad Yesteryears*. Port of Spain, Trinidad and Tobago: Inprint Caribbean, 1978.

Okruhlik, Gwenn. "Rentier Wealth, Unruly Law, and the Rise of Opposition: The Political Economy of Oil States." *Comparative Politics* 31, no. 3 (1999): 295–315.

Olivier, Sydney Haldane. *Report of the West India Sugar Commission 1929–30*. London: H. M. Stationery Office, 1930.

Orihuela, José Carlos. "How Do 'Mineral-States' Learn? Path-Dependence, Networks, and Policy Change in the Development of Economic Institutions." *World Development* 43 (2013): 138–48.

Owen, Edgar Wesley. *Trek of the Oil Finders: A History of Exploration for Petroleum*. Tulsa, OK: American Association of Petroleum Geologists, 1975.

Owolabi, Olukunle. *Ruling Emancipated Slaves and Indigenous Subjects: The Divergent Legacies of Forced Settlement and Colonial Occupation in the Global South*. Oxford: Oxford University Press, 2023.

Oxaal, Ivar. *Race and Revolutionary Consciousness: A Documentary Interpretation of the 1970 Black Power Revolt in Trinidad*. Cambridge, MA: Schenkman, 1971.

Pacheco-De-Almeida, Gonçalo, James Henderson, and Karel Cool. "Resolving the Commitment Versus Flexibility Trade-Off: The Role of Resource Accumulation Lags." *Academy of Management Journal* 51, no. 3 (2008): 517–36.

Padmore, George. *The Life and Struggles of Negro Toilers*. 1931. Los Angeles: Sun Dance Press, 1971.

Padmore, George. *Pan-Africanism or Communism?* 1956. London: Dennis Dobson, 1971.

Padmore, George. *The Voice of Coloured Labour*. Manchester, UK: Panaf, 1945.

Paige, Jeffery. "Conjuncture, Comparison, and Conditional Theory in Macrosocial Inquiry." *American Journal of Sociology* 105, no. 3 (1999): 781–800.

Palmer, Colin. *Cheddi Jagan and the Politics of Power: British Guiana's Struggle for Independence*. Chapel Hill: University of North Carolina Press, 2010.

Palmer, Colin. *Eric Williams and the Making of the Modern Caribbean*. Chapel Hill: University of North Carolina Press, 2006.

Palmer, Colin. *Freedom's Children: The 1938 Labor Rebellion and the Birth of Modern Jamaica*. Chapel Hill: University of North Carolina Press, 2014.

Pan American Health Organization. *Register of Malaria Eradication of Trinidad and Tobago*. 1965. Accessed November 21, 2021. https://iris.paho.org/bitstream/handle/10665.2/6086/trt%20report%201965.pdf?sequence=1&isAllowed=y.

Pan American Health Organization. "Trinidad and Tobago." Accessed June 15, 2021. https://www.paho.org/en/trinidad-and-tobago.

Panitch, Leo. "Trade Unions and the Capitalist State." *New Left Review* 125, no. 1 (1981): 21-43.

Pantin, Raoul. *Black Power Day: The 1970 February Revolution, a Reporter's Story*. Santa Cruz, Trinidad and Tobago: Hatuey Productions, 1990.

Paone, Rocco. "Strategic Raw Materials and US Security." *American Intelligence Journal* 4, no. 2 (1982): 9–18.

Paret, Marcel. *Fractured Militancy: Precarious Resistance in South Africa After Racial Inclusion*. Ithaca, NY: Cornell University Press, 2022.

Parpart, Jane. "The Household and the Mine Shaft: Gender and Class Struggles on the Zambian Copperbelt, 1926–64." *Journal of Southern African Studies* 13, no. 1 (1986): 36–56.

Parpart, Jane. *Labor and Capital on the African Copperbelt*. 1983. Philadelphia: Temple University Press, 2018.

Parris, Carl. "Joint Venture I: The Trinidad-Tobago Telephone Company 1968–1972." *Social and Economic Studies* 30, no. 1 (1981): 108–26.

Paschel, Tianna. *Becoming Black Political Subjects: Movements and Ethno-Racial Rights in Colombia and Brazil*. Princeton, NJ: Princeton University Press, 2016.

Pasley, Victoria. "The Black Power Movement in Trinidad: An Exploration of Gender and Cultural Changes and the Development of a Feminist Consciousness." *Journal of International Women's Studies* 3, no. 1 (2001): 24–40.

Patterson, Orlando. *The Confounding Island: Jamaica and the Postcolonial Predicament*. Cambridge, MA: Belknap Press of Harvard University Press, 2019.

Paxton, John, ed. *The Statesman's Year-Book: Statistical and Historical Annual of the States of the World for the Year 1973–1974*. London: Macmillan, 1973.

Payne, Anthony, and Paul K. Sutton, eds. *Dependency Under Challenge: The Political Economy of the Commonwealth Caribbean*. Manchester, UK: Manchester University Press, 1984.

Perrings, Charles. *Black Mineworkers in Central Africa: Industrial Strategies and the Evolution of an African Proletariat in the Copperbelt, 1911–41*. London: Heinemann, 1979.

Perrings, Charles. "Consciousness, Conflict and Proletarianization: An Assessment of the 1935 Mineworkers' Strike on the Northern Rhodesian Copperbelt." *Journal of Southern African Studies* 4, no. 1 (1977): 31–51.

Perry, Keisha-Khan. *Black Women Against the Land Grab: The Fight for Racial Justice in Brazil*. Minneapolis: University of Minnesota Press, 2013.

Perry, Keston K. "Continuity, Change and Contradictions in Late Steel-Based Industrialization: The 'Global Color Line' in Trinidad and Tobago's Postcolonial Economy." *Sociology Compass* 16, no. 12 (2022): 1–17.

Perry, Keston, and Leon Sealey-Huggins. "Racial Capitalism and Climate Justice: White Redemptive Power and the Uneven Geographies of Eco-Imperial Crisis." *Geoforum* 145 (2023): 103772.

Phillips, Lisa. *A Renegade Union: Interracial Organizing and Labor Radicalism*. Urbana: University of Illinois Press, 2013.

Phiri, Bizeck Jube. "The Capricorn Africa Society Revisited: The Impact of Liberalism in Zambia's Colonial History, 1949–1963." *International Journal of African Historical Studies* 24, no. 1 (1991): 65–83.

Pilgrim, Chike, ed. *Power*. Port of Spain, Trinidad and Tobago: Chike Pilgrim, 2020.

Piven, Frances Fox, and Richard Cloward. *Poor People's Movements: Why They Succeed, How They Fail*. New York: Vintage Books, 1977.

Plys, Kristin. *Brewing Resistance: Indian Coffee House and the Emergency in Postcolonial India*. Cambridge: Cambridge University Press, 2020.

Podobnik, Bruce. *Global Energy Shifts: Fostering Sustainability in a Turbulent Age*. Philadephia: Temple University Press, 2006.

Pollard, H. J. "The Erosion of Agriculture in an Oil Economy: The Case of Export Crop Production in Trinidad." *World Development* 13, no. 7 (1985): 819–35.

Posner, Daniel. *Institutions and Ethnic Politics in Africa*. New York: Cambridge University Press, 2005.

Post, Ken. *Arise Ye Starvelings: The Jamaican Labor Rebellion of 1938 and Its Aftermath*. The Hague: Martinus Nijhoff, 1978.

Premdas, Ralph. "Political Parties in a Bifurcated State: The Case of Guyana." PhD diss., University of Illinois at Urbana-Champaign, 1970.

Pribble, Jennifer. "Worlds Apart: Social Policy Regimes in Latin America." *Studies in Comparative International Development* 46, no. 2 (2011): 191–216.

Proctor, Jesse Harris, Jr. "East Indians and the Federation of the British West Indies." *India Quarterly* 17, no. 4 (1961): 370–95.

Pulido, Laura. *Black, Brown, Yellow, and Left: Radical Activism in Los Angeles*. Berkeley: University of California Press, 2006.

Putnam, Lara. "Nothing Matters but Color: Transnational Circuits, the Interwar Caribbean, and the Black International." In *From Toussaint to Tupac: The Black International Since the Age of Revolution*, edited by Michael O. West, William G. Martin, and Fanon Che Wilkins, 107–30. Chapel Hill: University of North Carolina Press, 2009.

Putnam, Lara. *Radical Moves: Caribbean Migrants and the Politics of Race in the Jazz Age*. Chapel Hill: University of North Carolina Press, 2013.

Quadagno, Jill. "Social Movements and State Transformation: Labor Unions and Racial Conflict in the War on Poverty." *American Sociological Review* 57, no. 5 (1992): 616–34.

Quest, Matthew. "'Every Cook Can Govern': Direct Democracy, Workers' Self Management and the Creative Foundations of C. L. R. James' Political Thought." *CLR James Journal* 19, no. 1/2 (2013): 374–91.

Quinn, Kate. *Black Power in the Caribbean*. Gainesville: University Press of Florida, 2014.

Quinn, Kate. "Colonial Legacies and Post-Colonial Conflicts in Guyana." In *Post-Colonial Trajectories in the Caribbean*, edited by Rosemarijn Hoefte, Matthew Bishop, and Peter Clegg, 10–29. New York: Routledge, 2017.

Quinn, Kate. "'Sitting on a Volcano': Black Power in Burnham's Guyana." In *Black Power in the Caribbean*, edited by Kate Quinn, 136–58. Gainesville: University Press of Florida, 2014.

Rabaka, Reiland. *Africana Critical Theory: Reconstructing the Black Radical Tradition, from W. E. B. Du Bois and C. L. R. James to Frantz Fanon and Amilcar Cabral*. Lanham, MD: Lexington Books, 2009.

Rabaka, Reiland. "Revolutionary Fanonism: On Frantz Fanon's Modification of Marxism and Decolonization of Democratic Socialism." *Socialism and Democracy* 25, no. 1 (2011): 126–45.

Rabe, Stephen. *U.S. Intervention in British Guiana: A Cold War Story*. Chapel Hill: University of North Carolina Press, 2005.

Ragoonath, Bishnu. "Shifting Nature of Decentralisation: A Review of the Evolution of Local Government in Trinidad and Tobago." *Indian Journal of Public Administration* 39, no. 4 (1993): 685–700.

Ramdin, Ron. *From Chattel Slave to Wage Earner: A History of Trade Unionism in Trinidad and Tobago*. London: Martin, Brian and O'Keefe, 1982.

Ramesar, Marianne. "The Impact of the Indian Immigrants on Colonial Trinidad Society." *Caribbean Quarterly* 22, no. 1 (1976): 5–18.

Ramsaran, Dave. "The 'Myth' of Development: The Case of Trinidad and Tobago." In *Caribbean Sovereignty, Development and Democracy in an Age of Globalization*, edited by Linden Lewis, 115–37. New York: Routledge, 2013.

Ramsaran, Dave, and Linden Lewis. *Caribbean Masala: Indian Identity in Guyana and Trinidad*. Jackson: University Press of Mississippi, 2018.

Reddock, Rhoda. "Competing Victimhoods: A Framework for the Analysis of Post-Colonial Multi-Ethnic Societies." *Social Identities* 25, no. 6 (2019): 809–27.

Reddock, Rhoda. "The Early Women's Movement in Trinidad and Tobago, 1900–1937." In *Subversive Women: Women's Movements in Africa, Asia, Latin America and the Caribbean*, edited by Saskia Wieringa, 101–20. New York: Zed Books, 1995.

Reddock, Rhoda. *Elma François, the NWCSA, and the Worker's Struggle for Change in the Caribbean*. London: New Beacon Books, 1988.

Reddock, Rhoda. "Freedom Denied: Indian Women and Indentureship in Trinidad and Tobago, 1845–1917." *Economic and Political Weekly* 20, no. 43 (1985): WS79–87.

Reddock, Rhoda. "Industrialisation and the Rise of the Petty Bourgeoisie in Trinidad and Tobago." Master's thesis, Institute of Social Studies, 1980.

Reddock, Rhoda. "Radical Caribbean Social Thought: Race, Class Identity and the Postcolonial Nation." *Current Sociology* 62, no. 4 (2014): 493–511.

Reddock, Rhoda. *Reflections on Gender and Democracy in the Anglophone Caribbean: Historical and Contemporary Considerations*. Amsterdam, the Netherlands: South-South Exchange Programme for Research on the History of Development and the Council for the Development of Social Science Research in Africa, 2004.

Reddock, Rhoda. *Women, Labour and Politics in Trinidad and Tobago: A History*. London: Zed Books, 1994.

Reddock, Rhoda. "Women and Slavery in the Caribbean: A Feminist Perspective." *Latin American Perspectives* 12, no. 1 (1985): 63–80.

Reed, Michael. "Gabon: A Neo-Colonial Enclave of Enduring French Interest." *Journal of Modern African Studies* 25, no. 2 (1987): 283–320.

Rennie, Bukka. *The History of the Working-Class in the 20th Century (1919–1956): The Trinidad and Tobago Experience*. 1974. Port of Spain, Trinidad and Tobago: Majority Press, 2011.

Rice, AJ. "Political Economy and the Tradition of Radical Black Study." *Souls* 22, no. 1 (2020): 44–55.

Richardson, Bonham. "Caribbean Migrations, 1838–1985." In *The Modern Caribbean*, edited by Franklin Knight and Colin Palmer, 203–28. Chapel Hill: University of North Carolina Press, 1989.

Riley, James. *Poverty and Life Expectancy: The Jamaica Paradox*. New York: Cambridge University Press, 2005.

Riofrancos, Thea. *Resource Radicals: From Petro-Nationalism to Post-Extractivism in Ecuador*. Durham, NC: Duke University Press, 2020.

Robertson, Graeme. "Leading Labor: Unions, Politics, and Protest in New Democracies." *Comparative Politics* 36, no. 3 (2004): 253–72.

Robinson, Arthur. *The Mechanics of Independence: Patterns of Political and Economic Transformation in Trinidad and Tobago*. Kingston, Jamaica: University of West Indies Press, 2001.

Robinson, Cedric. *Black Marxism: The Making of the Black Radical Tradition*. 1983. Chapel Hill: University of North Carolina Press, 2000.

Rocklin, Alexander. "Making the Chief Servant Mad: Disability, the Regulation of Afro-Caribbean Religions, and the Political Prophesy of Tubal Uriah Butler." *Journal of Africana Religions* 9, no. 2 (2021): 203–26.

Rodney, Walter. "Aspects of the International Class Struggle in Africa, the Caribbean and America." In *Pan-Africanism: Struggle Against Neo-Colonialism and Imperialism—Documents of the Sixth Pan-African Congress*, edited by Horace Campbell, 18–41. Toronto: Afro-Carib Publications, 1975.

Rodney, Walter. "Class Contradictions in Tanzania." Lecture at North-Western University, April 1975. In *The State in Tanzania: A Selection of Articles*, edited by Haroub Othman, 18–41. Dar es Salaam, Tanzania: Dar es Salaam University Press, 1980.

Rodney, Walter. "Contemporary Political Trends in the English-Speaking Caribbean." 1975. In *Caribbean Political Thought: The Colonial State to Caribbean Internationalisms*, edited by Aaron Kamugisha, 1–8. Kingston, Jamaica: Ian Randle, 2013.

Rodney, Walter. *Decolonial Marxism: Essays from the Pan-African Revolution*. Edited by Asha Rodney, Patricia Rodney, Ben Mabie, and Jessie Benjamin. London: Verso Books, 2022.

Rodney, Walter. *The Groundings with My Brothers*. 1969. Edited by Asha Rodney and Jessie Benjamin. London: Verso, 2019.

Rodney, Walter. *A History of the Guyanese Working People, 1881–1905*. Baltimore, MD: Johns Hopkins University Press, 1981.

Rodney, Walter. *How Europe Underdeveloped Africa*. 1972. New York: Verso, 2018.

Rodney, Walter. "Race and Class in Guyanese Politics." Speech at Columbia University, 1978. Posted October 14, 2015, by Kilombo Uk. YouTube, 1 hr. 30min. https://www.youtube.com/watch?v=9szjOu-yIPs.

Rose, Euclid. *Dependency and Socialism in the Modern Caribbean: Superpower Intervention in Guyana, Jamaica, and Grenada, 1970–1985*. Lanham, MD: Lexington Books, 2002.

Ross, Michael. *The Oil Curse: How Petroleum Wealth Shapes the Development of Nations*. Princeton, NJ: Princeton University Press, 2012.

Rosser, Andrew. "Escaping the Resource Curse: The Case of Indonesia." *Journal of Contemporary Asia* 37, no. 1 (2007): 38–58.

Roush, G. A. "Strategic Mineral Supplies 15: Strategic and Critical Minerals." *Military Engineer* 30, no. 173 (1938): 370–74.

Rueschemeyer, Dietrich, and Peter Evans. "The State and Economic Transformation: Towards an Analysis of the Conditions Underlying Effective Intervention." In *Bringing the State Back In*, edited by Peter Evans, Dietrich Rueschemeyer, and Theda Skocpol, 44–77. New York: Cambridge University Press, 1985.

Rueschemeyer, Dietrich, Evelyne Huber Stephens, and John Stephens. *Capitalist Development and Democracy*. Chicago: University of Chicago Press, 1992.

Ryan, Selwyn. *Race and Nationalism in Trinidad and Tobago*. Toronto: University of Toronto Press, 1972.

Sachs, Jeffrey, and Andrew Warner. "Natural Resource Abundance and Economic Growth." National Bureau of Economic Research (NBER) Working Paper 5398. National Bureau of Economic Research, Cambridge, MA, December 1995.

Salandy, Tyehimba. "Contestations of Memory and Erasure: Rastafarians, Modernity and Coloniality in Trinidad and Tobago." In *Decolonial Perspectives on Entangled Inequalities: Europe and the Caribbean*, edited by Encarnación Gutiérrez Rodríguez and Rhoda Reddock, 239–58. London: Anthem, 2021.

Sallahuddin. *Guyana: The Struggle for Liberation*. Georgetown, Guyana: Guyana National Printers, 1994.

Samaroo, Brinsley. "The February Revolution (1970) as a Catalyst for Change in Trinidad and Tobago." In *Black Power in the Caribbean*, edited by Kate Quinn, 97–116. Gainesville: University Press of Florida, 2014.

Samaroo, Brinsley. *Adrian Cola Rienzi: The Life and Times of an Indo-Caribbean Progressive*. Macoya, Trinidad and Tobago: Royards Publishing Company, 2021.

Samaroo, Brinsley. "The Making of the 1946 Trinidad Constitution." *Caribbean Studies* 15, no. 4 (1976): 5–28.

Samaroo, Brinsley, and Cherita Girvan. "The Trinidad Workingmen's Association and the Origins of Popular Protest in a Crown Colony." *Social and Economic Studies* 21, no. 2 (1972): 205–22.

Sandbrook, Richard, Marc Edelman, Patrick Heller, and Judith Teichman. *Social Democracy in the Global Periphery: Origins, Challenges, Prospects*. Cambridge: Cambridge University Press, 2007.

Schmidt, Elizabeth. *Cold War and Decolonization in Guinea, 1946–1958*. Athens: Ohio University Press, 2007.

Scipes, Kim. "Social Movement Unionism or Social Justice Unionism? Disentangling Theoretical Confusion Within the Global Labor Movement." *Class, Race and Corporate Power* 2, no. 3 (2014): article 9. https://digitalcommons.fiu.edu/classracecorporatepower/vol2/iss3/9.

Scipes, Kim. "Understanding the New Labor Movements in the 'Third World': The Emergence of Social Movement Unionism." *Critical Sociology* 19, no. 2 (1992): 81–101.

Scott, David. "Colonial Governmentality." *Social Text*, no. 43 (1995): 191–220.

Scott, David. "On the Very Idea of a Black Radical Tradition." *Small Axe: A Caribbean Journal of Criticism* 17, no. 1 (2013): 1–6.

Scott, James. *Weapons of the Weak: Everyday Forms of Peasant Resistance*. New Haven, CT: Yale University Press, 1985.

Sebastien, Raphael. "State-Sector Development in Trinidad and Tobago, 1956–1982." *Contemporary Marxism*, no. 10 (1985): 110–27.

Seecharan, Clem. "Cheddi Jagan, Communism and the African Guyanese." India Diaspora Council. Accessed May 3, 2024. https://indiandiasporacouncil.org/pdf/Cheddi-Jagan-Communism-and-the-African-Guyanese.pdf#page=6.00.

Seegobin, Ram, and Lindsay Collen. "Mauritius: Class Forces and Political Power." *Review of African Political Economy* 4, no. 8 (1977): 109–18.

Segal, Daniel. "'Race' and 'Colour' in Pre-Independence Trinidad and Tobago." In *Trinidad Ethnicity*, edited by Kevin Yelvington, 81–115. Knoxville: University of Tennessee Press, 1993.

Seidman, Gay. *Manufacturing Militance: Workers' Movements in Brazil and South Africa, 1970–1985*. Berkeley: University of California Press, 1994.

Selwyn, Benjamin. *The Struggle for Development*. Cambridge: Polity Press, 2017.

Sen, Amartya. *Development as Freedom*. Oxford: Oxford University Press, 1999.

Shilliam, Robbie. *The Black Pacific: Anti-Colonial Struggles and Oceanic Connections*. London: Bloomsbury Academic, 2015.

Shivji, Issa. "The Concept of 'Working People.'" *Agrarian South: Journal of Political Economy* 6, no. 1 (2017): 1–13.

Silver, Beverly. "The Contradictions of Semiperipheral Success." In *Semiperipheral States in the World-Economy*, edited by William Martin, 161–81. New York: Greenwood, 1990.

Silver, Beverly. *Forces of Labor: Workers' Movements and Globalization Since 1870*. Cambridge: Cambridge University Press, 2003.

Silver, Beverly, and Giovanni Arrighi. "Polanyi's 'Double Movement': The Belle Époques of British and US Hegemony Compared." *Politics and Society* 31, no. 2 (2003): 325–55.

Singh, Chaitram. *Guyana: Politics in a Plantation Society*. New York: Praeger, 1988.

Singh, Chaitram. *Multinationals, the State, and the Management of Economic Nationalism: The Case of Trinidad*. New York: Praeger, 1989.

Singh, Kelvin. "Adrian Cola Rienzi and the Labour Movement in Trinidad (1925–44)." *Journal of Caribbean History* 16 (1982): 10–35.

Singh, Kelvin. "Conflict and Collaboration: Tradition and Modernizing Indo-Trinidadian Elites (1917–56)." *NWIG: New West Indian Guide* 70, no. 3/4 (1996): 229–53.

Singh, Kelvin. *Race and Class Struggles in a Colonial State: Trinidad 1917–1945*. Kingston, Jamaica: Press University of the West Indies, 1994.

Slater, Dan. *Ordering Power*. Cambridge: Cambridge University Press, 2010.

Slater, Dan, and Nicholas Rush Smith. "The Power of Counterrevolution: Elitist Origins of Political Order in Postcolonial Asia and Africa." *American Journal of Sociology* 121, no. 5 (2016): 1472–516.

Smart, Rodney. "The Strategic Development of the Trinidad and Tobago Defence Force." Master's thesis. U.S. Army Command and General Staff College, 2009.

Smith, Adrian. "Enduring Unfreedom: Law and the State in Trinidadian Sugar Production." PhD diss., McGill University, 2011.

Somers, Margaret. "Narrativity, Narrative Identity, and Social Action: Rethinking English Working-class Formation." *Social Science History* 16, no. 4 (1992): 591-630.

Spence, Daniel. *Colonial Naval Culture and British Imperialism, 1922–67*. Manchester, UK: Manchester University Press, 2015.

Spence, Lester, Todd Shaw, and Robert Brown. "'True to Our Native Land': Distinguishing Attitudinal Support for Pan-Africanism from Black Separatism." *Du Bois Review* 2, no. 1 (2005): 91–111.

Spinner, Thomas. *A Political and Social History of Guyana, 1945–1983*. Boulder, CO: Westview, 1984.

Spivak, Gayatri. *A Critique of Postcolonial Reason: Toward a History of the Vanishing Present*. Cambridge, MA: Harvard University Press, 1999.

Steinberg, S. H., ed. *The Statesman's Year-Book: Statistical and Historical Annual of the States of the World for the Year 1967–1968*. New York: St. Martin's Press, 1967.

Steinmetz, George. "The Colonial State as a Social Field: Ethnographic Capital and Native Policy in the German Overseas Empire Before 1914." *American Sociological Review* 73 (2008): 589–612.

Stephens, Evelyne Huber, and John Stephens. "Democratic Socialism in Dependent Capitalism: An Analysis of the Manley Government in Jamaica." *Politics and Society* 12, no. 3 (1983): 373–411.

Stephenson, Jacqueline, Natalie Persadie, Ann Marie Bissessar, and Talia Esnard. "Race Relations in the Caribbean: The Myth of Representative Bureaucracy." In *Diversity, Equality, and Inclusion in Caribbean Organisations and Society*, 15–42. Cham, Switzerland: Palgrave Macmillan, 2020.

Stevens, Margaret. *Red International and Black Caribbean: Communists in New York City, Mexico and the West Indies, 1919–1939*. London: Pluto, 2017.

Stoler, Ann Laura. *Along the Archival Grain*. Princeton, NJ: Princeton University Press, 2009.

Stone, Carl. "Clientelism, Power and Democracy." In *Caribbean Political Thought: The Colonial State to Caribbean Internationalisms*, edited by Aaron Kamugisha, 67–82. 1980. Kingston, Jamaica: Ian Randle, 2013.

St. Pierre, Maurice. *Eric Williams and the Anticolonial Tradition: The Making of a Diasporan Intellectual*. Charlottesville: University of Virginia Press, 2015.

Sudama, Trevor. "Class, Race, and the State in Trinidad and Tobago." *Latin American Perspectives* 10, no. 4 (1983): 75–96.

Suh, Doowon. "What Happens to Social Movements After Policy Success? Framing the Unintended Consequences and Changing Dynamics of the Korean Women's Movement." *Social Science Information* 53, no. 1 (2014): 3–34.

Swan, Quito. "I & I Shot the Sheriff: Black Power and Decolonization in Bermuda, 1968–1977." In *Black Power in the Caribbean*, edited by Kate Quinn, 197–218. Gainesville: University Press of Florida, 2014.

Tarrow, Sidney. *Power in Movement: Social Movements and Contentious Politics*. 1994. Cambridge: Cambridge University Press, 2011.

Teelucksingh, Jerome. "The Black Power Movement in Trinidad and Tobago." *Black Diaspora Review* 4, no. 1 (2014): 157–86.

Teelucksingh, Jerome. *Ideology, Politics, and Radicalism of the Afro-Caribbean*. New York: Palgrave Macmillan, 2016.

Teelucksingh, Jerome. *Labour and the Decolonization Struggle in Trinidad and Tobago*. New York: Palgrave Macmillan, 2015.

Telles, Edward. *Pigmentocracies: Ethnicity, Race, and Color in Latin America*. Chapel Hill: University of North Carolina Press, 2014.

Telles, Edward. *Race in Another America*. Princeton, NJ: Princeton University Press, 2004.

Thomas, Clive. *Dependence and Transformation: The Economics of the Transition to Socialism*. New York: Monthly Review Press, 1974.

Thomas, Clive. *The Rise of the Authoritarian State in Peripheral Societies*. New York: Monthly Review Press, 1984.

Thomas, Clive. "State Capitalism in Guyana: An Assessment of Burnham's Cooperative Republic." In *Crisis in the Caribbean*, edited by Fitzroy Ambursley and Robin Cohen, 27–48. New York: Monthly Review Press, 1983.

Thomas, Martin. *Violence and Colonial Order: Police, Workers and Protest in the European Colonial Empires, 1918–1940*. Cambridge: Cambridge University Press, 2012.

Thomas, Roy. *The Development of Labour Law in Trinidad and Tobago*. Wellesley, MA: Calaloux, 1989.

Thomas-Hope, Elizabeth. "Migration in Trinidad and Tobago." Policy brief. UNDP LAC PDS No. 37, October 11, 2022. https://www.undp.org/latin-america/publications/migration-trinidad-and-tobago-current-trends-and-policies.

Thompson, E. P. *The Making of the English Working Class*. 1963. New York: Open Road Integrated Media, 2016.

Thompson Patterson, Louise. "Toward a Brighter Dawn." 1936. *Viewpoint Magazine*, October 31, 2015. https://viewpointmag.com/2015/10/31/toward-a-brighter-dawn-1936/.

Thorburn, Diana. "Nationalism, Identity, and the Banking Sector: The English-Speaking Caribbean in the Era of Financial Globalization." In *Ethnicity, Class, and Nationalism: Caribbean and Extra-Caribbean Dimensions*, edited by Anton Allahar, 57–84. Lanham, MD: Lexington Books, 2005.

Tilly, Charles. *From Mobilization to Revolution*. Reading, MA: Addison-Wesley, 1978.

Tilly, Charles, and Louise Tilly, eds. *Class Conflict and Collective Action*. Beverly Hills, CA: Sage Publications, 1981.

Tilly, Charles, and Louise Tilly, eds. *Big Structures, Large Processes, Huge Comparisons*. New York: Russell Sage, 1984.

Titus, Noel. *The Amelioration and Abolition of Slavery in Trinidad, 1812–1834*. Bloomington, IN: AuthorHouse, 2009.

Toprani, Anand. "Oil and Grand Strategy: Great Britain and Germany, 1918–1941." PhD diss., Georgetown University, 2012.

Trotman, David. *Crime in Trinidad: Conflict and Control in a Plantation Society, 1838–1900*. Knoxville: University of Tennessee Press, 1986.

Trotman, David. "Women and Crime in Late Nineteenth Century Trinidad." *Caribbean Quarterly* 30, no. 3/4 (1984): 60–72.

Trotter, Joe William, Jr. *Workers on Arrival: Black Labor in the Making of America*. Berkeley: University of California Press, 2019.

Trotz, Alissa, ed. *The Point Is to Change the World: Selected Writings of Andaiye*. London: Pluto, 2020.

Ture, Kwame, and Charles Hamilton. *Black Power: Politics of Liberation in America*. 1967. New York: Vintage Books, 1992.

Turshen, Meredeth. *Privatizing Health Services in Africa*. Piscataway, NJ: Rutgers University Press, 1999.

United Nations Development Program (UNDP). Gender Inequality Index Dataset. Accessed December 3, 2024. https://hdr.undp.org/data-center/thematic-composite -indices/gender-inequality-index#/indicies/GII.

United Nations Development Program (UNDP). Human Development Index Dataset. Accessed December 3, 2024. https://hdr.undp.org/data-center/human-development -index#/indicies/HDI.

United Nations Economic Commission for Latin America and the Caribbean, CEPAL-STAT: Statistical Databases and Publications. "Life expectancy at birth." Accessed December 3, 2024. https://statistics.cepal.org/portal/cepalstat/dashboard.html ?theme=1&lang=en.

Usmani, Adaner, and David Zachariah. "The Class Path to Racial Liberation." *Catalyst* 5, no. 3 (2021): 51–88.

Valdez, Inés. "Capitalism, Imperialism, and the Paradox of Dependent Democratic Founding." Working Paper, Johns Hopkins University, 2024.

Vertovec, Steven. *The Hindu Diaspora: Comparative Patterns*. New York: Routledge, 2000.

Vertovec, Steven. "'Official' and 'Popular' Hinduism in Diaspora: Historical and Contemporary Trends in Surinam, Trinidad and Guyana." *Contributions to Indian Sociology* 28, no. 1 (1994): 123–47.

Vicente, Pedro. "Does Oil Corrupt? Evidence from a Natural Experiment in West Africa." *Journal of Development Economics* 92, no. 1 (2010): 28–38.

Vincent, Godfrey. "The Oilfields Workers' Trade Union and the Challenge of Working Class Political Party Formation and Electoral Politics, 1965–1977." *WorkingUSA* 19, no. 4 (2016): 487–502.

Virdee, Satnam. "Racialized Capitalism: An Account of Its Contested Origins and Consolidation." *Sociological Review* 67, no. 1 (2019): 3–27.

Virdee, Satnam. *Racism, Class and the Racialized Outsider*. Basingstoke, UK: Palgrave Macmillan, 2014.

Vitalis, Robert. *Oilcraft: The Myths of Scarcity and Security That Haunt U.S. Energy Policy*. Stanford, CA: Stanford University Press, 2020.

Vithayathil, Trina. *Counting Caste*. Cambridge: Cambridge University Press, 2025.

Voss, Kim, and Rachel Sherman. "Breaking the Iron Law of Oligarchy: Union Revitalization in the American Labor Movement." *American Journal of Sociology* 106, no. 2 (2000): 303–49.

Vu, Tuong. *Paths to Development in Asia: South Korea, Vietnam, China, and Indonesia*. Cambridge: Cambridge University Press, 2010.

Wade, Robert. *Governing the Market: Economic Theory and the Role of Government in East Asian Industrialization*. 1990. Princeton, NJ: Princeton University Press, 2004.

Wallerstein, Immanuel. *The Capitalist World-Economy*. Vol. 2. Cambridge: Cambridge University Press, 1979.

Wallerstein, Immanuel. *The Modern World-System III: The Second Era of Great Expansion of the Capitalist World-Economy, 1730s–1840s*. 1989. Berkeley: University of California Press, 2011.

Waring, Gerald. *The Geology of the Island of Trinidad, B. W. I*. Baltimore, MD: Johns Hopkins University Press, 1926.

Warwick, Ozzi, and David O'Connell. "How Oil Workers in Trinidad and Tobago Fought to Revolutionize Fossil Fuels." *Jacobin*, November 13, 2022. https://jacobin .com/2022/11/oil-workers-trinidad-tobago-ownership-fossil-fuels-trade-union -organizing.

Waterman, Peter. "A Trade Union Internationalism for the 21st Century: Meeting the Challenges from Above, Below and Beyond." In *Labour and the Challenges of Globalization: What Prospects for Transnational Solidarity?*, edited by Andreas Bieler, Ingemar Lindberg, and Devan Pillay, 248–63. London: Pluto, 2008.

Watson, Hilbourne. "The Caribbean Basin Initiative and Caribbean Development: A Critical Analysis." *Contemporary Marxism* 10 (1985): 1–37.

Watson, Hilbourne. "Liberalism and Neo-Liberal Capitalist Globalization: Contradictions of the Liberal Democratic State." *GeoJournal* 60, no. 1 (2004): 43–59.

Webster, Eddie. "The Rise of Social-Movement Unionism: The Two Faces of the Black Trade Union Movement in South Africa." 1988. In *State, Resistance and Change in South Africa*, edited by Philip Frankel, Noam Pines, and Mark Swilling, 174–96. New York: Routledge, 2023.

Weir, Margaret, and Theda Skocpol. "State Structures and the Possibilities for 'Keynesian' Responses to the Great Depression in Sweden, Britain, and the United States." In *Bringing the State Back In*, edited by Peter Evans, Dietrich Rueschemeyer, and Theda Skocpol, 107–63. New York: Cambridge University Press, 1985.

West, Michael. "The Seeds Are Sown: The Impact of Garveyism in Zimbabwe in the Interwar Years." *International Journal of African Historical Studies* 35, no. 2/3 (2002): 335–62.

West, Michael O., and William G. Martin. "Contours of the Black International." In *From Toussaint to Tupac: The Black International Since the Age of Revolution*, edited by Michael O. West, William G. Martin, and Fanon Che Wilkins, 1–44. Chapel Hill: University of North Carolina Press, 2009.

Westmaas, Nigel. "An Organic Activist: Eusi Kwayana, Guyana, and Global Pan-Africanism." In *Black Power in the Caribbean*, edited by Kate Quinn, 159–80. Gainesville: University Press of Florida, 2014.

Williams, Eric. *Capitalism and Slavery*. 1944. Chapel Hill: University of North Carolina Press, 1994.

Williams, Eric. *History of the People of Trinidad and Tobago*. 1962. Buffalo, New York: EWorld, 2002.

Williams, Eric. *Inward Hunger: The Making of a Prime Minister*. 1969. London: Ebenezer Baylis and Son, 1971.

Wilson, Stacey-Ann. *Politics of Identity in Small Plural Societies: Guyana, the Fiji Islands, and Trinidad and Tobago*. New York: Palgrave Macmillan, 2012.

Wilson, William Julius. *The Bridge over the Racial Divide: Rising Inequality and Coalition Politics*. Berkeley: University of California Press, 1999.

Wimmer, Andreas. "Race-Centrism: A Critique and a Research Agenda." *Ethnic and Racial Studies* 38, no. 13 (2015): 2186–205.

Winant, Howard. "Race, Ethnicity and Social Science." *Ethnic and Racial Studies* 38, no. 13 (2015): 2176–85.

Wood, Donald. *Trinidad in Transition: The Years After Slavery*. Oxford: Oxford University Press, 1968.

Woodberry, Robert. "The Missionary Roots of Liberal Democracy." *American Political Science Review* 106, no. 2 (2012): 244–74.

Worcester, Kent. *C. L. R. James: A Political Biography*. Albany: State University of New York Press, 1996.

World Bank. "World Development Indicators." Databank. Accessed December 5, 2024. https://databank.worldbank.org/source/world-development-indicators/preview/on.

Wright, Erik Olin. "Working-Class Power, Capitalist-Class Interests, and Class Compromise." *American Journal of Sociology* 105, no. 4 (2000): 957–1002.

Wynter, Sylvia. "1492: A New World View." In *Race, Discourse, and the Origin of the Americas: A New World View*, edited by Vera Lawrence Hyatt and Rex Nettleford, 1–57. Washington, DC: Smithsonian Institution Press, 1995.

Yashar, Deborah. *Contesting Citizenship in Latin America: The Rise of Indigenous Movements and the Postliberal Challenge*. Cambridge: Cambridge University Press, 2005.

Yates, Douglas. *The Rentier State in Africa: Oil Rent Dependency and Neocolonialism in the Republic of Gabon*. Trenton, NJ: Africa World Press, 1996.

Young, Crawford. *The African Colonial State in Comparative Perspective*. New Haven, CT: Yale University Press, 1994.

Young, Crawford. *The Post-Colonial State in Africa: Fifty Years of Independence, 1960–2010*. Madison: University of Wisconsin Press, 2012.

Zeilig, Leo, ed. *Class Struggle and Resistance in Africa*. 2002. Chicago: Haymarket Books, 2009.

Zeitlin, Maurice, and L. Frank Weyher. "'Black and White, Unite and Fight': Interracial Working-Class Solidarity and Racial Employment Equality." *American Journal of Sociology* 107, no. 2 (2001): 430–67.

Index

Note: page numbers followed by *f* refer to figures.

British Caribbean, 141, 182, 236n187; colonies, 26–28, 36, 63, 70, 181, 195, 237n216;
federation, 127; slave emancipation in, 25;
territories, 66, 118
British Empire, 14, 40–41, 49, 69–70, 73, 102,
156; bauxite and, 182; companies, 236n187;
decline of, 115; housing development and,
109; oil and, 75, 101, 103; Trade Disputes
Ordinance and, 104–5
British Guiana, 90, 185, 189, 236n187. *See also*
Guyana
British Guiana Labour Union (BGLU), 64, 187
British imperial system, 49, 75, 116
British Petroleum (BP), 121, 149, 161, 165, 170,
173, 256n142
British Trades Union Congress (TUC), 128,
134
British West Indies Regiment, 51, 64, 229n28
bureaucracy, 7, 140; racially exclusive, 37; state,
4, 82, 106, 114, 176
bureaucratization, 16, 49, 140, 197
Burma, 40–41
Burnham, Forbes, 136, 189–93
Burnley, William Hardin, 24–25, 28–29, 37
Bustamante, Alexander, 195
Butler, Tubal Uriah "Buzz," 85–86, 89–94,
99–100, 102, 120, 124, 132–36, 238n4; DLP
and, 168; Indian elites and, 127; Maraj and,
137; mental state of, 241n102; Oilfield Workers' Trade Union (OWTU) and, 119–20, 150,
251n38; West Indian National Party and,
129; Weekes and, 149; Williams and, 137
Butler Day, 150, 251n38
Butlerites, 123, 136, 149
Butler Party, 90–91, 123, 127, 129, 132, 136–37

cabildo, 35–37
Cabral, Amílcar, 33, 55, 125, 226n104
cacao, 21–23, 31–32, 40, 50, 93; estates, 39, 42,
53, 71; plantation slavery and, 6; production, 20, 25, 228n51
Canefarmers Association, 176, 260n230
capital, 11, 24, 26, 28, 33, 43, 75, 80, 100, 102;
accumulation, 8–9, 12, 23, 25, 35, 39, 44, 68,
70, 81–82, 116, 138, 158, 178, 186, 211; British,
39–40, 236n187; bureaucratization and,
197; concentration, 185; development and,
208; foreign, 13, 41, 76, 115, 126–28, 140–42,

144, 146, 156, 159, 170–72, 179, 192, 200,
202, 244n7; international, 226n104; labor
and, 15, 103, 116, 211; liberation unionism
and, 108, 184; local, 73, 76, 156, 200; MPCA
leaders and, 188; North American, 185;
owners of, 7; postwar social compacts and,
201; private, 15, 50, 76, 83, 105, 175, 195;
racism and, 68; representatives of, 110; state
and, 17, 50, 63, 65, 81, 99, 101, 103, 130, 135,
138, 146, 155, 171–72, 178–79, 200, 206, 211;
white, 6, 10, 12, 20, 63, 76, 84, 86–87, 96,
104, 137; white supremacy and, 44
capital accumulation, 9, 35, 44, 68, 70, 81–82,
178, 186; ideological state apparatus and,
211; petty bourgeoisie and, 138; private, 195;
racial order of, 8; regimes of, 12, 116; slavery
and, 23, 25, 39; worker strikes and, 84
capitalism, 4, 7–10, 47, 204; contradictions of,
49; human well-being and, 3; race and, 7–9,
81, 199, 220n36; racism and, 159; restructuring of, 209; socialism and, 48. *See also* white
capitalist system
capitalist class, 4, 7–8, 49, 101, 134, 141, 200,
220n43
capitalist development, 7, 10, 46
Caroni Limited, 173, 203
caste, 29, 130; passing, 225n71
Cédula de Población, 23, 32
Central Intelligence Agency (CIA), 170, 190,
258n188
Chamber of Commerce, 69, 72, 77, 101, 133, 167
children, 32–33, 69, 78, 96, 109, 120, 177;
compulsory education for, 66; enslaved, 24;
essay competitions for, 151; Indian, 31, 38;
liberation unionism and, 57–58, 95, 207;
police killing of, 98; in poverty, 110
China, 2, 28, 43, 46, 62, 191, 265n40; postrevolutionary, 210
chocolate, 22, 40
Churchill, Winston, 40
Cipriani, Arthur A., 56, 64, 78, 88–89, 120,
124, 142, 150, 238n19; bureaucratic conservatism of, 154; Garvey and, 61; Legislative
Council and, 80–81. *See also* Trinidad
Workingmen's Association (TWA)
Citrine, Walter, 121, 134
civil liberties, 2–3, 5, 16, 178, 184, 196; extension of, 201; suspension of, 134

civil servants, 33, 38, 51, 53, 98, 126, 139

class, 6–12, 20, 61; against class, 99; compromise, 76, 200, 211; discourse of, 83; diversity, 130; empire and, 161; in Guyana, 185; interests, 7, 61–62, 92, 130; oppression, 221n52; politics, 157; practices, 44; race and, 61, 68, 81, 115, 123, 158–59, 161, 199; structure, 7, 185; struggle, 7, 153, 205; suicide, 56; superexploitation and, 58; tensions, 104; women and, 166. *See also* capitalist class; middle class; petty bourgeoisie; working class

class consciousness, 7, 43–44, 92, 130, 146, 187; Garvey's Pan-African project and, 82; race/racial consciousness and, 12, 60–61, 91, 93; racial concerns and, 158; racial identity and, 62, 207. *See also* working-class consciousness

coconuts, 31, 50, 98

coffee, 87; estates, 32, 39; plantations, 23; slavery and, 6

collective action, 7–8, 20–21, 51, 63, 70; Garvey and, 61; institutionalized forms of, 119; multiracial, 137; radical, 11; repression and, 69; workers', 3, 15, 47, 49, 205, 211

College of Labor and Industrial Relations, 166, 256n153

colonial administrators, 34, 36–37, 48, 81, 105, 141, 197; Black race consciousness and, 67; Butler and, 135, 137; imperial government and, 73–74; plantation slavery and, 6; white economic elite and, 70. *See also* petty bourgeoisie

Colonial Development and Welfare Act, 79, 107

colonial era, 2, 15, 164, 178–79

colonialism, 6, 8–10, 21, 47, 58, 104, 156, 167; anticolonialism, 60, 62; developmental legacies of, 217n9

Colonial Office, 36, 80, 97, 101, 109, 138

colonial rule, 6, 96, 126, 156, 209; British, 2, 34; French, 223n22; Spanish, 185

colonization, British, 23, 32; European, 91

coloreds, 32, 36, 225n93, 226n120

Combined Court, 186

Communication Workers Union, 121, 253n68

communism, 59, 121, 127, 137, 189, 205

Communist International (Comintern), 59, 205

Communist Party, 207–8, 211; social movement unionism and, 14; US, 58, 83

community development, 176, 207

conservatism, 32, 89; bureaucratic, 120, 144, 148, 154, 178

constitutional independence, 16, 112, 115, 125, 218n11

copra, 50, 87

corruption, 5, 37, 99, 164–65; state, 177, 192

Cox, Oliver Cromwell, 8–9, 73

Crick, Daisy, 95, 150–51

Crown Colony, 36, 38, 73–74, 99, 103, 186; government, 189; rule, 32, 186

Crown lands, 22, 25, 32, 41–42, 50, 236n187

Cuba, 27, 137, 191–92, 210

Daaga, Makandal, 144, 158

Dalley, Fred, 128, 134–35

De Bourg, John Sydney, 42, 52, 63, 70

decolonization, 7, 16, 133, 172, 178, 197, 202; formal, 15, 17, 116, 138, 194–95; labor and, 146, 219n21; liberation unionism and, 115, 121, 145, 204; period, 145–46, 184; studies of, 114

democracy, 11, 196, 200, 205–6, 209, 211; community-level, 110; direct, 12, 221n56; economic, 168; imperialism and, 189; labor and, 219n21; liberation unionism and, 16, 43, 178–80; multiparty, 193; organized labor and, 7; origins of, 116; OWTU and, 150, 154; parliamentary, 2; political, 199; representative, 123; resource dependence and, 5; social, 12, 266n40; workplace, 155

Democratic Labour Party (DLP), 125, 129, 131–33, 138, 156, 164, 168

democratization, 14, 109, 115, 119, 165

dependency, 9, 20–21, 201, 220n35, 244n7; neocolonial, 116; scholars, 41; structural, 13, 182

development outcomes, 7, 16, 182, 184, 200, 208–10

development policies, 3, 16, 190

Development Program, 171, 180

disease, 24, 31, 140; crop, 21, 228n151; deficiency, 2; Dutch, 6, 118; European, 21; gastrointestinal, 192. *See also* hookworms; leprosy; malaria

dispossession, 9, 19, 21–22, 27, 147

diversity, 48, 130; development and, 6; ethnic, 207, 218n9, 237n216; racial, 3–4, 207, 209, 237n216; religious, 131

dockworkers, 45–46, 51–54, 230n48. *See also* stevedores

domestic work, 31, 46, 58. *See also* workers: domestic

domination, 35, 115; British, 21, 23, 32; British colonial, 13, 34, 93; colonial, 3, 8–10, 12, 36, 47, 76, 90, 92, 162, 218n11; Crown Colony, 36, 38; economic, 158; imperialist, 165; plans for East-Indian, 136–37; racial, 11–12, 27, 162, 208

Dominica, 23

drainage, 37, 107, 140, 176, 193

Du Bois, W. E. B., 3, 8–9, 12, 181; *Black Reconstruction in America*, 19; Pan-African Congresses, 60, 231n89; on whiteness, 11

East Indian National Association (EINA), 42, 55–56

East Indian National Congress (EINC), 42, 55–56, 237n216

economic development, 4–5, 12, 16, 138–39, 182–83, 190–91, 198–99; broad-based, 171, 200, 206; general strike of 1919 and, 75; improvements in, 2, 82; institution building and, 171; liberation unionism and, 111, 145; redistributive, 184

economic interdependence, 29, 172

education, 4, 79, 140, 166, 176–77, 179, 204; access to, 2, 14, 79, 176; colonial, 11, 33; compulsory, 66–67; English-language, 34; formal, 31; Hindi, 131; mass, 122; political, 127, 150, 166; postprimary, 66; public, 38, 82, 108, 187–88, 194–95, 197, 201, 210; system, 131, 140; women and, 256n153

elites, 205, 265n33; Black, 10; business, 36, 67–69, 73, 255n135; economic, 4, 10, 16, 30, 49, 67, 88, 110; independence and, 114; Indian, 127, 130; Indigenous, 5; local, 72–73, 189, 200; political, 10, 115, 126, 182; white, 11, 16–17, 22, 36, 49, 67–69, 73, 88, 99, 110, 233n140

emancipation, 25–27, 47, 60, 157–58; enslaver compensation and, 223n24; Friendly Societies before, 42; health services after, 38; middle class and, 32–33; plantation

economy and, 9; plantation labor after, 185; racial, 83; West Indian, 75; women and, 24

Emancipation Day, 58, 66–67, 166

empire, 20–21, 118, 161, 207. *See also* British Empire

employer class, 166–67

enslaved people, 23–24, 32, 36, 48, 205, 223n24, 226n120

enslavement, 22, 24, 28, 157, 207

equity, 4; gender, 67, 207

equity-enhancing development, 4, 184–85, 196, 200, 206

estates: agricultural, 26, 30, 46; amalgamation of, 32, 39–40; British, 39–40; cacao, 39, 53, 71, 75; colonial administrators and, 37; Creoles and, 30; emancipation and, 25; free coloreds and, 32–33; Indian population and, 31–32; industrial, 141; overseers at, 33; slavery and, 24, 29; strikes on, 69; sugar, 25, 27, 29–30, 43, 53, 56, 71, 89, 95, 97

Ethiopia, 91–93

ethnicity, 20, 22

Executive Council, 36, 71, 110–11, 123–24, 135–36, 227n124

expropriation, 9, 35, 114

extraction, 141, 208; gas, 3; labor, 15; oil, 1, 3, 41; resource, 15, 17, 30, 49

Fanon, Frantz, 33, 125, 130, 133–34, 137, 155, 248n113; labor aristocracy and, 114, 206; Marxism and, 8, 10

farmers, 174, 203, 209; cane, 27, 32–33, 39, 65, 224n42; peasant, 22; small, 65–66. *See also* Canefarmers Association; Workers and Farmers Party (WFP)

fascism, 58, 114, 168

February Revolution, 144, 178, 250n4

Federated Workers' Trade Union (FWTU), 94, 111, 253n68, 254n115

Federation of Trade Unions, 121, 247n86

feminism: Black, 48; Marxist, 8

Fletcher, Arthur George Murchison, 98–101, 104, 109, 241n101

flogging, 24–25, 31

François, Elma, 63–64, 89, 93–94, 134, 248n117

freedom, 12, 22, 161, 205, 207; Black, 47–48, 61; Black struggles for, 14; civic,

political economy, 6, 8, 145, 201; of colonialism, 8; of race, 8; of race-class-gender, 221n52; of racism, 8, 158

Port of Spain, 42, 46, 50–52, 54–56, 64, 93, 120, 123; Black Caribbean immigrants in, 27; Borough Council, 37, 42, 51; City Council, 80–81; housing in, 109; slavery and, 24; UNIA in, 63; welfare services in, 38

postindependence period, 3, 15, 142, 144, 154, 160, 197, 204

poverty, 6, 8, 22, 27, 35, 43, 93, 195; children in, 110

proletarianization, 21, 46

public goods, 3, 6, 16, 76, 82, 195, 207

public utilities, 2, 117

public works, 1, 21, 27, 37, 46, 75

Puerto Rico, 141, 256n153

race, 10–12, 20–22, 29, 83, 93, 133, 160–61, 163, 190, 200, 207–8, 220n35, 221n52, 265n32; capitalism and, 7–9, 81, 199, 200n36; class and, 61, 68, 81, 115, 123, 158–59, 161, 199; feudalism and, 220n31; Marx and, 220n43; Pan-Africanism and, 82; party politics and, 123, 142, 192; politicization of, 144, 159; women and, 166

race consciousness, 73, 130, 132, 146, 161, 205, 207–8; Black, 61, 67, 92; Garveyism and, 60–61

racial divisions, 44, 53, 57, 97, 146, 184

racialization, 10, 20–22, 28, 30, 46, 68, 160

racial political articulation, 130, 132–33, 164, 190, 193–94, 203

racial pride, 33, 208; Black, 60, 62, 157, 191

racial uplift: Black, 61, 158; Pan-African, 200

racism, 8–10, 63, 105, 130, 158–60, 164; African soldiers and, 169; anti-Indian, 148; Black workers and, 35; British, 38, 50; British West Indies Regiment soldiers and, 64; critique of, 221n52; states and, 68, 139; TWA and, 65; in the workplace, 88

radicalism, 15, 63, 116, 135, 149–50, 155; Black working-class, 145

Ramdin, Ron, 63, 229n28

rank and file, 52, 88–89, 129, 150, 153, 197

rationalization, 4; state, 140

redistribution, 43, 65–66, 116, 150, 165, 192, 196, 209

redistributive development, 16–17, 142, 193–94, 200, 205, 208–9

representation, 197; communal system of, 237n216; Indian, 62, 81–82, 190; labor, 88, 110; militant, 153; multiracial, 162; political, 38; proportional, 190; symbolic, 157

repression, 36, 49, 51, 72, 88, 136, 193–94, 210, 248n113; anticommunist, 121; British colonial, 98; labor, 7, 39, 44, 134; of liberation unionism, 76; police, 68; political, 12; racialized, 50; state, 20–21, 69, 84, 115, 133, 141, 164, 167–69, 184, 197, 201, 204, 211, 222n9; violent, 219n26

resource dependence, 5, 180, 208, 218n19

Rhodesia. *See* Zambia

rice, 50, 185; mill, 51

Richardson, Bonham, 25, 224n53

Rienzi, Adrian Cola, 56, 64, 86, 92, 94, 124, 135, 242n131; English literacy and, 111; OWTU and, 97, 119–20; Trinidad Citizens League (TCL) and, 89; TTTUC and, 121. *See also* All Trinidad Sugar Estates and Factory Workers' Trade Union (ATSEFWTU); Trinidad Workingmen's Association (TWA)

rights, 10, 32; abortion, 166; British, 90; civil, 42, 162, 165; democratic, 3; human, 14, 129, 168, 192; political, 5, 16, 65, 178, 183–84, 196, 207; workers', 158

roads, 4, 26, 66–67, 107, 138–39, 176, 186; blocking, 98

Robinson, Cedric, 145, 220n31

Rodney, Walter, 8–10, 12, 75, 134, 136, 141, 160, 193; on Combined Court, 186; on formal decolonization, 116; on flag independence, 138; on generalizability, 181; *History of the Guyanese Working People*, 19, 187, 217n1; Jamaican government's banning of, 162; on petty bourgeoisie, 33, 125, 226n104; political Blackness and, 191; on racial identity, 44, 130; on working-class power, 199

Rojas, John, 89, 119–20, 129, 149

Roodal, Timothy, 80, 136

rum, 26, 50

San Fernando, 27, 55–56, 85, 93, 108–9, 123; Borough Council, 37, 81; cost of living in, 50

sanitation, 2, 4, 37–38, 66–67, 82, 139, 186–87, 197; services, 201; works, 107

23, 29, 39–40; prices, 39, 203, 224n42; production, 27–28; sector, 119; slavery and, 6;
unions, 94, 101, 119, 130–31, 142, 168; unity
of oil and, 154
sugar workers, 94–95, 119–20, 122–23, 134,
144, 153–54, 160, 164, 174; Indian, 55, 95,
128, 130, 150, 187–88, 203; Maraj and, 142;
strikes, 53

Tanzania, 169, 191
Tate and Lyle, 128, 170, 173
Texaco, 121, 149, 157, 165, 170, 173–74; acquisition of Trinidad Leaseholds, 137, 256n142;
commission of inquiry into, 258–59n205;
racism and, 160
tourism, 148, 176
Trade Disputes (Arbitration and Inquiry)
Ordinance, 104, 148
trade unions, 65, 94, 105, 119, 126, 168, 210;
CIA infiltration of, 170; farmers and, 209;
marginalization of, 114; militant, 7; in party
politics, 163; weakening of, 115; World Fed-
eration of Trade Unions (WFTU), 121
Transport and Industrial Workers' Union
(TIWU), 151, 153, 159, 161, 164
Trinidad and Tobago Trades Union Congress
(TTTUC), 120–21, 134, 247n86
Trinidad Citizens League (TCL), 89–90
Trinidad Labour Party (TLP), 86, 89–90, 94.
See also Trinidad Workingmen's Association
(TWA)
Trinidad Leaseholds Limited, 41, 87, 137
Trinidad Light Horse troops, 71, 97
Trinidad Light Infantry Volunteers, 71, 97
Trinidad Workingmen's Association (TWA),
42–43, 45–46, 52–65, 67–70, 76–81,
88–90, 94, 122, 159, 230n48, 238n19; BGLU
and, 187; bureaucratic conservatism of, 120,
154; *Labour Leader*, 62–63, 75; liberation
unionism and, 84; OWTU and, 149–50;
Wages Committee, 76–77, 81. See also
Cipriani, Arthur A.; Crick, Daisy
Tull, Carl, 121, 148
Ture, Kwame, 88, 157, 166

underdevelopment, 4, 9, 41
unemployment, 50, 65, 89, 164–65, 172, 193,
238n21; African workers and, 43; foreign

direct investment and, 147; levy on oil
companies, 179; relief, 166, 180
unionism, 58, 195; Black liberation and, 205;
Black radical trade, 167; business, 14, 47,
206; Garveyism and, 61, 63, 82; Hawaiian,
62; labor, 47, 52; political, 14, 47, 142, 195,
206; postrebellion, 195; radical trade, 189;
social justice, 14, 47, 207; social movement, 14, 47, 54, 65; trade, 52, 61, 134, 207;
working-class, 3, 14. See also liberation
unionism
United British Oilfields of Trinidad, 41, 97
United Kingdom, 27, 39, 64, 141, 169–70;
Afro-Trinbagonian activists in, 162; decline
of power, 118–19; Guyana and, 189, 192;
Labour Party, 59, 89, 128; migration to, 203;
neocolonial dependency on, 116; oil and,
117; Royal Air Force, 101, 103; Royal Navy,
40, 50, 103
United States, 11, 115–19, 141, 205; bauxite and,
186; Black laborers from, 28; Caribbean
Regiment in, 149; Guyana and, 192; Jamaica
and, 196; oil and, 40, 74, 117–18, 202; oil
drilling crews from, 35; Organization of
American States and, 169; out-migration
to, 203; socialism and, 16; social movement
unionism in, 14; strikes in, 46, 54; Williams
and, 169–70
unity, 3, 12, 64, 92, 207, 239n40; African and
Asian, 62; African-Indian, 90, 132, 160,
162, 189; diasporic, 96; interracial, 131,
146; labor's, 122; lack of, 70; liberation
unionism and, 63, 82, 95, 151, 179, 197, 200;
multiracial, 62, 130, 154, 161, 208, 265n28;
multisectoral, 58; of oil and sugar, 154; oil
worker, 119; Pan-African, 91, 157; racial,
55, 60, 132, 189; regional, 136; of the ruling
class, 49; trade union, 121, 155; TWA and, 59;
worker, 27, 120, 146, 155, 159–60, 195, 204,
208, 265n28; working-class, 68, 90, 133
Universal Negro Improvement Association
(UNIA), 60, 62–63, 91, 157, 159, 182
universal suffrage, 7, 109–10, 114, 119, 122,
187–89, 195, 197; labor and, 219n21

Venezuela, 35, 43, 60, 265n40; cacao and, 40;
cocoa payoles and, 22; Hugo Chávez–era,
210; oil and, 117–18; Williams and, 170

Vertovec, Steven, 130–31

violence, 30, 69, 133, 153, 195, 239n60; against Black people, 72; ethnic, 6; imperial, 92; interracial, 6; physical, 24; political, 196; racial, 60, 190; racist, 31; sexual, 12, 31, 95; state, 2; vigilante, 71; white, 97; against women, 29

war, 6, 40, 92, 162; British and American capabilities, 117; on communism, 189; oil and, 102–3. *See also* World War I; World War II

water, 37, 176–77, 197; distribution, 139; supplies, 2, 107, 138, 187, 192

Weekes, George, 144, 149–50, 153, 155–56, 158, 160–62, 176, 254n115. *See also* Oilfield Workers' Trade Union (OWTU)

welfare, 3, 11–13, 38, 42–43, 76, 110, 162, 189, 200, 205–7, 210; benefits, 7; Caribbean Labor Congress (CLC) and, 121; expansion, 180; provision of, 4, 177; social, 2, 44, 79, 109, 115, 138, 197, 201, 204, 209; state, 7, 14, 35, 116, 219n21; state building and, 16

West Indies, 72, 128, 141; Black Power in, 160; British, 43, 65; exportable produce of, 25; West Indies Federation, 121, 131

West Indies Federation, 121, 131

white capitalist system, 9, 11–13, 15, 17–19, 65, 83, 180–82, 210–11; dependent economies in, 210; deprivation and, 86; liberation unionism and, 185, 198; race-class dynamics of, 81; racialized subjects of, 92; state and, 199; Trinidad and Tobago and, 115, 161, 179; white workers and, 209

white creoles, 34, 72, 73, 99

white supremacy, 3, 10, 24, 44, 58, 71, 193

Williams, Eric, 28, 118, 125, 127–28, 131–32, 137–38, 141, 169–71, 247n99; Black Power and, 168, 191; British Petroleum (BP) and, 173; *Capitalism and Slavery*, 125, 156; on

Castro, 128, 247n76; radical trade union movement and, 155–56; state repression and, 169; Weekes and, 176. *See also* People's National Movement (PNM)

Wilson, Harold, 169

worker movements, 14–15, 18; Black, 48

Workers and Farmers Party (WFP), 163–64, 255n131

working class, 21, 47, 49, 156, 162, 217n1; alliances and, 55; Black, 10, 24, 26, 47, 145; capital and, 86; Cipriani and, 124; divisions among, 123; employer class and, 166; housing for, 107–8; industrial, 11; petty bourgeoisie and, 56; racialized, 33–34, 43, 46, 68; racially united, 137; racism and, 68; state and, 86, 178; Texaco and, 259n205; TWA and, 88, 90; unions and, 129; white, 11; Workingmen's Association and, 77

working-class consciousness, 56, 191

working-class unionism, 3, 14

Workingmen's Association (WMA), 42. *See also* Trinidad Workingmen's Association (TWA)

World Bank, 2, 180, 193, 202

World Federation of Trade Unions (WFTU), 121

World War I, 31, 40–41, 46, 50, 52–53, 67, 69, 73–74; colonial period before, 30, 43; workers before, 20; working class and, 49

World War II, 106, 116–17; buildup to, 196; colonial period before, 191; communism after, 189; Guyana and, 186, 188; liberation unionism after, 18, 114, 117–18, 144; middle class and, 32; oil workers after, 149; Trinidadian oil before, 101; union solidarity after, 120; workers after, 204

Zambia, 169, 173, 194, 196–98, 205

www.ingramcontent.com/pod-product-compliance
Lightning Source LLC
Chambersburg PA
CBHW020823270326
41928CB00006B/422